FUNDAMENTALS OF
English
Grammar

FOURTH EDITION

with ANSWER KEY

PEARSON
Longman

Betty S. Azar
Stacy A. Hagen

Fundamentals of English Grammar, Fourth Edition
with Answer Key

Copyright © 2011, 2003, 1992, 1985 by Betty Schrampfer Azar

Azar Associates: Shelley Hartle, Editor, and Sue Van Etten, Manager

Pearson Education, 10 Bank Street, White Plains, NY 10606

Staff credits: The people who made up the *Fundamentals of English Grammar, Fourth Edition* team, representing editorial, production, design, and manufacturing, are, Dave Dickey, Christine Edmonds, Ann France, Amy McCormick, Robert Ruvo, and Ruth Voetmann.

Text composition: S4Carlisle Publishing Services
Text font: 10.5/12 Plantin

Illustrations: Don Martinetti—pages 13, 15, 25, 27, 40, 59, 64, 68, 70, 76, 92, 106, 115, 129, 131, 144, 155, 169, 171, 172, 173, 174, 181, 183, 196, 203, 216, 217, 219, 224, 230, 232, 234, 242, 244, 245, 250, 253, 254, 258, 263, 266, 277, 278, 292, 299, 300, 304, 305, 308, 309, 313, 327, 344, 347, 349, 356, 364, 373, 374, 385, 386; Chris Pavely—pages 4, 7, 8, 19, 33, 38, 41, 43, 44, 47, 53, 75, 76, 90, 98, 101, 108, 111, 112, 125, 126, 165, 166, 186, 202, 213, 227, 229, 231, 233, 260, 268, 275, 276, 281, 319, 322, 331, 337, 338, 360, 363, 377, 386, 389, 391, 392

Library of Congress Cataloging-in-Publication Data

Azar, Betty Schrampfer, 1941-
  Fundamentals of English grammar / Betty S. Azar, Stacy A. Hagen.—4th ed.
    p. cm.
  ISBN-13: 978-0-13-707169-2 (with answer key)
  ISBN-10: 0-13-707169-8 (with answer key) 1. English language—Textbooks for foreign speakers.
    2. English language--Grammar--Problems, exercises, etc. I. Hagen, Stacy A., 1956- II. Title.

PE1128.A965 2011
428.2'4—dc22

                                                                        2010050069

Printed in the United States of America

ISBN 10: 0-13-707169-8
ISBN 13: 978-0-13-707169-2

1 2 3 4 5 6 7 8 9 10—V011—16 15 14 13 12 11

ISBN 10: 0-13-231513-0 (International Edition)
ISBN 13: 978-0-13-231513-5 (International Edition)

1 2 3 4 5 6 7 8 9 10—V011—16 15 14 13 12 11

To my sister, Jo

B.S.A.

For D. P. and H. B.
with appreciation

S.H.

Contents

Preface to the Fourth Edition

Fundamentals of English Grammar is a developmental skills text for lower-intermediate and intermediate English language learners. It uses a grammar-based approach integrated with communicative methodologies to promote the development of all language skills in a variety of ways. Starting from a foundation of understanding form and meaning, students engage in meaningful communication about real actions, real things, and their real lives in the classroom context. *Fundamentals of English Grammar* functions principally as a classroom teaching text but also serves as a comprehensive reference text for students and teachers.

The eclectic approach and abundant variety of exercise material remain the same as in the earlier editions, but this fourth edition incorporates new ways and means. In particular:

- **WARM-UP EXERCISES FOR THE GRAMMAR CHARTS**
  Newly created for the fourth edition, these innovative exercises precede the grammar charts and introduce the point(s) to be taught. They have been carefully crafted to help students *discover* the target grammar as they progress through each warm-up exercise.

- **LISTENING PRACTICE**
  Numerous listening exercises help students interact with the spoken language in a variety of settings that range from the relaxed, casual speech of everyday conversation to more academic content. An audio CD accompanies the student text, and a full listening script can be found in the back of the book.

- **READINGS**
  Students can read and respond to a wide selection of readings that focus on the target grammar structure(s).

- **WRITING TASKS**
  New writing activities that practice target structures have been created for every chapter. A writing sample precedes each task so students have a model to follow.

- **EXPANDED SPEAKING ACTIVITIES**
  Students have even more opportunities to share their experiences, express their opinions, and relate the target grammar to their personal lives. The text often uses the students' own life experiences as context and regularly introduces topics of interest to stimulate the free expression of ideas in structured as well as open discussions.

- **CORPUS-INFORMED CONTENT**
  Based on our corpus research, grammar content has been added, deleted, or modified to reflect the discourse patterns of spoken and written English.

TIPS FOR USING THE NEW FEATURES IN THIS TEXT

- **WARM-UPS**

The Warm-Up exercises are a brief pre-teaching tool for the charts. They highlight the key point(s) that will be introduced in the chart that follows the Warm-Up exercise. Before beginning the task, teachers will want to familiarize themselves with the material in the chart. Then, with the teacher's guidance, students can discover many or sometimes all of the new patterns as they complete the Warm-Up activity. After students finish the exercise, teachers may find that no further explanation is necessary, and the charts can serve as a useful reference.

- **LISTENING**

The Listening exercises have been designed to help students understand American English as it is actually spoken. As such, it includes reductions and other phenomena that are part of the natural, relaxed speech of everyday English. Because the audio uses English that may be spoken at a rate faster than what students are used to, they may need to hear sentences two or three times while completing a task.

The Listening exercises do not encourage immediate pronunciation (unless they are linked to a specific pronunciation task). Receptive skills precede productive ones, and it is essential that students be able to hear the speech patterns before they begin using them in their own speech.

Students are encouraged to listen to longer passages the first time through without looking at their text. Teachers can then explain any vocabulary that has not already been clarified. During the second listening, students complete the assigned task. Teachers will want to pause the audio appropriately. Depending on the level of the class, pauses may be needed after every sentence, or even within a sentence.

It is inevitable that sound representations in the text will at times differ from the instructor's speech, whether it be due to register or regional variation. As a general rule, if the instructor expects that students will hear a variation, or if students themselves raise the questions, alternate representations can be presented.

A listening script with all the listening exercises can be found at the back of the book.

- **READINGS**

The Readings give students an opportunity to work with the grammar structures in extended contexts. One approach is to have students read the passage alone the first time through. Then they work in small groups or as a class to clarify vocabulary questions. A second reading may be necessary. Varied reading tasks then allow students to check their comprehension, to use the target structures, and to expand upon the topic in speaking or writing.

- **WRITING TASKS**

As students gain confidence in using the target structures, they are encouraged to express their ideas in complete paragraphs. A model paragraph accompanies each assignment and question-prompts help students develop their ideas.

Peer editing can be used for correction. A useful technique is to pair students, have them exchange papers, and then have the *partner* read the paragraph aloud. The writer can *hear* if the content is what he or she intended. This also keeps the writer from automatically self-correcting while reading aloud. (Self-correcting can be a problem if writers are unaware that they are making corrections as they read.)

For classes that have not had much experience with writing, the teacher may want to assign students to small groups. Each group composes a paragraph together. The teacher collects the paragraph and adds comments, and then makes a copy for each group member. Students correct the paragraph *individually*.

When correcting student writing, teachers may want to focus primarily on the structures taught in the chapter.

* **LET'S TALK**

Each Let's Talk activity is set up as one of the following: **pairwork, small group, class activity, interview,** or **game**. Successful language learning requires social interaction, and these tasks encourage students to speak with others about their ideas, their everyday lives, and the world around them. Students tend to speak more easily and freely when they can connect language to their own knowledge and experiences.

* **CHECK YOUR KNOWLEDGE**

Toward the end of the chapter, students can practice sentence-level editing skills by correcting errors common to this level. The sentences can be done as homework or in small groups.

This task can easily be set up as a game. The teacher calls out an item number at random. Students work in teams to correct the sentence, and the first team to edit it correctly wins a point.

See the *Fundamentals of English Grammar Teacher's Guide* for detailed information about teaching from this book, including expansion activities and step-by-step instructions.

Fundamentals of English Grammar is accompanied by

* A comprehensive *Workbook*, consisting of self-study exercises for independent work.
* An all-new *Teacher's Guide*, with step-by-step teaching suggestions for each chart, notes to the teacher on key grammar structures, vocabulary lists, and expansion activities and *PowerPoint* presentations for key chapters.
* An expanded *Test Bank*, with additional quizzes, chapter tests, and mid-term and final exams.
* *Test-Generator* software that allows teachers to customize their own tests using quizzes and tests from the *Test Bank*.
* *Azar Interactive*, a computer-based program keyed to the text, provides easily understood content, all-new exercises, readings, listening and speaking activities, and comprehensive tests.
* *PowerPoint* presentations for key chapters. Based on real-world readings, these lessons are designed for use in the classroom as "beyond-the-book" activities. They can be found in the new *Teacher's Guide* or downloaded from *AzarGrammar.com*.
* A *Chartbook*, a reference book consisting only of the grammar charts.
* *AzarGrammar.com*, a website that provides a variety of supplementary classroom materials and a place where teachers can support each other by sharing their knowledge and experience.
* *Fun with Grammar*, a teacher resource text by Suzanne Woodward with communicative activities correlated with the Azar-Hagen Grammar Series. It is available as a text or as a download on *AzarGrammar.com*.

The Azar-Hagen Grammar Series consists of

* *Understanding and Using English Grammar* (blue cover), for upper-level students.
* *Fundamentals of English Grammar* (black), for mid-level students.
* *Basic English Grammar* (red), for lower or beginning levels.

Acknowledgments

We couldn't have done this fourth edition without the many talented professionals who assisted us. We began our revision with the insights and suggestions from these reviewers: Michael Berman, Montgomery College; Jeff Bette, Westchester Community College; Mary Goodman, Everest University; Linda Gossard, DPT Business School, Denver; Roberta Hodges, Sonoma State American Language Institute; Suzanne Kelso, Boise State University; Steven Lasswell, Santa Barbara City College; Diane Mahin, University of Miami; Maria Mitchell, DPT Business School, Philadelphia; Monica Oliva, Miami Sunset Adult Center; Amy Parker, University of Michigan; Casey Peltier, Northern Virginia Community College.

We are fortunate to have an outstanding editorial staff who oversaw this book from planning to production. We'd like to thank Shelley Hartle, managing editor extraordinaire, whose meticulous and perceptive editing shaped every page; Amy McCormick, editorial director, whose vision, attentiveness, and care for the series guided our writing; Ruth Voetmann, development editor, for her keen eye, valuable advice, and unfailing patience; Janice Baillie, our outstanding copy-editor who scrutinized and honed every page; Sue Van Etten, our accomplished and very talented business and web-site manager; Robert Ruvo, our skilled and responsive production manager at Pearson Education.

We'd also like to express our appreciation to the writers of the supplementary texts: Rachel Spack Koch, *Workbook;* Kelly Roberts Weibel, *Test Bank;* and Martha Hall, *Teacher's Guide.* They have greatly enriched the series with their innovative ideas and creativity.

Finally, we'd like to thank the dedicated leadership team at Pearson Education that guided this project: Pietro Alongi, Rhea Banker, and Paula Van Ells.

The colorful artwork is due to the inspired talents of Don Martinetti and Chris Pavely.

Finally, we would like to thank our families, who supported and encouraged us every step of the way. They are a continual source of inspiration.

Betty S. Azar
Stacy A. Hagen

Chapter 1
Present Time

□ **Exercise 1. Listening and reading.**

Part I. Listen to the conversation between Sam and Lisa. They are college students in California. They are beginning a weeklong training to be resident assistants* for their dorm. They are interviewing each other. Later they will introduce each other to the group.

CD 1
Track 2

SAM: Hi. My name is Sam.

LISA: Hi. I'm Lisa. It's nice to meet you.

SAM: Nice to meet you too. Where are you from?

LISA: I'm from Boston. How about you?

SAM: I'm from Quebec. So, how long have you been here?

LISA: Just one day. I still have a little jet lag.

SAM: Me too. I got in yesterday morning. So — we need to ask each other about a hobby. What do you like to do in your free time?

LISA: I spend a lot of time outdoors. I love to hike. When I'm indoors, I like to surf the Internet.

SAM: Me too. I'm studying Italian right now. There are a lot of good websites for learning languages on the Internet.

LISA: I know. I found a good one for Japanese. I'm trying to learn a little.
Now, when I introduce you to the group, I have to write your full name on the board. What's your last name, and how do you spell it?

SAM: It's Sanchez. S-A-N-C-H-E-Z.

LISA: My last name is Paterson — with one "t": P-A-T-E-R-S-O-N.

SAM: It looks like our time is up. Thanks. It's been nice talking to you.

LISA: I enjoyed it too.

---

resident assistant = a student who lives in a dormitory and helps other students with everyday life in the dorm; also called an "R.A."

Part II. Read the conversation in Part I. Use the information in the conversation to complete Sam's introduction of Lisa to the class.

SAM: I would like to introduce Lisa Paterson. Lisa is from ___*Boston*___ . She has been here

_____. In her free time, she _____

_____ .

Part III. Now it is Lisa's turn to introduce Sam to the class. What is she going to say? Create an introduction. Begin with ***I would like to introduce Sam.***

□   **Exercise 2. Let's talk: interview.**
Interview a partner. Then introduce your partner to the class. As your classmates are introduced to the class, write their names on a sheet of paper.

Find out your partner's:
    name
    native country or hometown
    free-time activities or hobbies
    favorite food
    reason for being here
    length of time here

□   **Exercise 3. Let's write.**
Write answers to the questions. Then, with your teacher, decide what to do with your writing. See the list of suggestions at the end of the exercise.

1. What is your name?
2. Where are you from?
3. Where are you living?
4. Why are you here (in this city)?
    a. Are you a student? If so, what are you studying?
    b. Do you work? If so, what is your job?
    c. Do you have another reason for being here?
5. What do you like to do in your free time?
6. What is your favorite season of the year? Why?
7. What are your three favorite TV programs or movies? Why do you like them?
8. Describe your first day in this class.

Suggestions for your writing:
    a. Give it to a classmate to read. Your classmate can then summarize the information in a spoken report to a small group.
    b. Work with a partner and correct errors in each other's writing.
    c. Read your composition aloud in a small group and answer any questions about it.
    d. Hand it in to your teacher, who will correct the errors and return it to you.
    e. Hand it in to your teacher, who will return it at the end of the term when your English has progressed, so you can correct your own errors.

❏ **Exercise 4. Warm-up.** (Charts 1-1 and 1-2)

Read the statements and circle *yes* or *no*. Choose responses that are true for you. Share your answers with a partner (e.g., *I use a computer every day.* OR *I don't use a computer every day.*). Your partner will report your information to the class (e.g., *Eric doesn't use a computer every day.*).

1. I use a computer every day.	yes	no
2. I am sitting in front of a computer right now.	yes	no
3. I check emails every day.	yes	no
4. I send text messages several times a day.	yes	no
5. I am sending a text message now.	yes	no

1-1 Simple Present and Present Progressive

Simple Present		
past — now — future XXXXXXXXXXX	(a) Ann *takes* a shower *every day*. (b) I *usually* **read** the newspaper in the morning. (c) Babies *cry*. Birds *fly*. (d) NEGATIVE: It ***doesn't snow*** in Bangkok. (e) QUESTION: ***Does*** the teacher **speak** slowly?	The SIMPLE PRESENT expresses *daily habits* or *usual activities,* as in (a) and (b). The simple present expresses *general statements of fact,* as in (c). In general, the simple present is used for events or situations that exist always, usually, or habitually in the past, present, and future.
Present Progressive		
start — now — finish? in progress	(f) Ann can't come to the phone *right now* because she **is taking** a shower. (g) I **am reading** my grammar book *right now*. (h) Jimmy and Susie are babies. They **are crying**. I can hear them *right now*. Maybe they are hungry. (i) NEGATIVE: It **isn't snowing** *right now*. (j) QUESTION: **Is** the teacher **speaking** *right now*?	The PRESENT PROGRESSIVE expresses *an activity that is in progress (is occurring, is happening) right now.* The event is in progress at the time the speaker is saying the sentence. The event began in the past, is in progress now, and will probably continue into the future. FORM: *am, is, are* + *-ing*

1-2 Forms of the Simple Present and the Present Progressive

	Simple Present				Present Progressive			
STATEMENT	I	work.			I	am		working.
	You	work.			You	are		working.
	He, She, It	works.			He, She, It	is		working.
	We	work.			We	are		working.
	They	work.			They	are		working.
NEGATIVE	I	do	not	work.	I	am	not	working.
	You	do	not	work.	You	are	not	working.
	He, She, It	does	not	work.	He, She, It	is	not	working.
	We	do	not	work.	We	are	not	working.
	They	do	not	work.	They	are	not	working.
QUESTION	Do	I		work?	Am	I		working?
	Do	you		work?	Are	you		working?
	Does	he, she, it		work?	Is	he, she, it		working?
	Do	we		work?	Are	we		working?
	Do	they		work?	Are	they		working?

Contractions

pronoun + *be*	I + am = **I'm** working.
	you, we, they + are = **You're, We're, They're** working.
	he, she, it + is = **He's, She's, It's** working.
do + *not*	does + not = **doesn't** She **doesn't** work.
	do + not = **don't** I **don't** work.
be + *not*	is + not = **isn't** He **isn't** working.
	are + not = **aren't** They **aren't** working.
	(am + not = am not* I am not working.)

*NOTE: *am* and *not* are not contracted.

□ **Exercise 5. Listening and grammar.** (Charts 1-1 and 1-2)

CD 1
Track 3

Listen to the passage on the next page. Discuss the verbs in *italics*. Is the activity of the verb a usual activity or happening right now (an activity in progress)?

Lunch at the Fire Station

It's 12:30, and the firefighters *are waiting* for their next call. They *are taking* their lunch
                                                         1   2
break. Ben, Rita, and Jada *are sitting* at a table in the fire station. Their co-worker Bruno
                                       3
is making lunch for them. He is an excellent cook. He often *makes* lunch. He *is fixing* spicy
    4   5   6
chicken and rice. Their captain *isn't eating*. He *is doing* paperwork. He *skips* lunch on busy
                                               7   8   9
days. He *works* in his office and *finishes* his paperwork.
           10   11

□ **Exercise 6. Listening.** (Charts 1-1 and 1-2)

CD 1
Track 4

Listen to the statements about Irene and her job. Decide if the activity of each verb is a usual
activity or happening right now. Choose the correct answer.

Example: You will hear: Irene works for a video game company.

   You will choose: (usual activity)   happening right now

1. usual activity   happening right now

2. usual activity   happening right now

3. usual activity   happening right now

4. usual activity   happening right now

5. usual activity   happening right now

□ **Exercise 7. Looking at grammar.** (Charts 1-1 and 1-2)

Complete the sentences. Use the simple present or the present progressive form of the verbs
in parentheses.

1. Shhh. The baby (*sleep*) __is sleeping__ . The baby (*sleep*) __sleeps__ for ten
   hours every night.

2. Right now I'm in class. I (*sit*) _____ at my desk. I usually (*sit*)
   _____ at the same desk in class every day.

3. Ali (*speak*) _____ Arabic. Arabic is his native language, but right
   now he (*speak*) _____ English.

4. A: (*it, rain*) _____ a lot in southern Spain?
   B: No. The weather (*be*) _____ usually warm and sunny.

5. A: Look out the window. (*it, rain*) _____?
   B: It (*start*) _____ to sprinkle.

6. A: Look. It's Yumiko.

   B: Where?

   A: Over there. She (*walk*) _____ out of the café.

7. A: Oscar usually (*walk*) _____ to work.

   (*you, walk*) _____ to work every day too?

   B: Yes.

   A: (*Oscar, walk*) _____ with you?

   B: Sometimes.

❏ **Exercise 8. Let's talk.** (Charts 1-1 and 1-2)
Your teacher will ask one student to perform an action and another student to describe it using the present progressive.

Example: stand next to your desk
To STUDENT A: Would you please stand next to your desk? (*Student A stands up.*)
To STUDENT B: Who is standing next to his/her desk? OR What is (Student A) doing?
STUDENT B: (Student A) is standing next to his/her desk.

1. stand up	7. erase the board
2. smile	8. hold your pen in your left hand
3. whistle	9. knock on the door
4. open or close the door	10. scratch your head
5. read your grammar book	11. count aloud the number of people in the classroom
6. shake your head "no"	12. look at the ceiling

❏ **Exercise 9. Listening.** (Charts 1-1 and 1-2)
Listen to the questions. Write the words you hear.

CD 1
Track 5
A problem with the printer

Example: You will hear: Is the printer working?
            You will write: ___*Is*___ the printer working?

1. _____ need more paper?

2. _____ have enough ink?

3. _____ fixing it yourself?

4. _____ know how to fix it?

5. _____ have another printer in the office?

6. Hmmm. Is it my imagination or _____ making a strange noise?

❑ **Exercise 10. Game: trivia.** (Charts 1-1 and 1-2)
Work in small groups. Complete each sentence with the correct form of the verb in parentheses. Then circle "T" for true or "F" for false. The group with the most correct answers wins.*

1. In one soccer game, a player (*run*) _____ seven miles on average.   T   F

2. In one soccer game, players (*run*) _____ seven miles on average.   T   F

3. Right-handed people (*live*) _____ 10 years longer than left-handed people.   T   F

4. Mountains (*cover*) _____ 3% of Africa and 25% of Europe.   T   F

5. The Eiffel Tower (*have*) _____ 3,000 steps.   T   F

6. Honey (*spoil*) _____ after one year.   T   F

7. The letter "e" (*be*) _____ the most common letter in English.   T   F

8. It (*take*) _____ about seven seconds for food to get from our mouths to our stomachs.   T   F

9. A man's heart (*beat*) _____ faster than a woman's heart.   T   F

10. About 145,000 people in the world (*die*) _____ every 24 hours.   T   F

❑ **Exercise 11. Let's talk.** (Charts 1-1 and 1-2)
Work with a partner. Take turns describing your pictures to each other and finding the differences. Use the present progressive. Partner A: Cover Partner B's pictures in your book. Partner B: Cover Partner A's pictures in your book.

Example:

Partner A   **Partner B**

PARTNER A: In my picture, the airplane is taking off.
PARTNER B: In my picture, the airplane is landing.

---

*See *Trivia Answers*, p. 421.

Partner A

Partner B

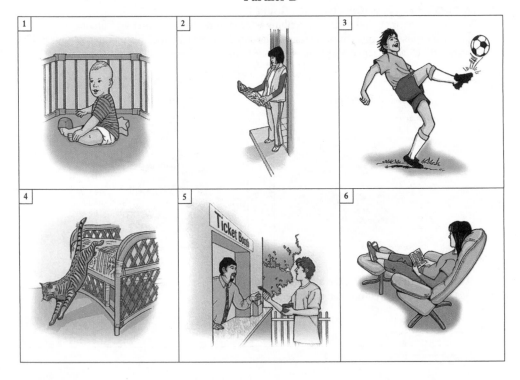

❑ **Exercise 12. Let's read and write.** (Charts 1-1 and 1-2)
Part I. Read the paragraph and answer the questions.

Hair Facts

Here are some interesting facts about our hair. Human hair grows about one-half inch per month or 15 centimeters a year. The hair on our scalp is dead. That's why it doesn't hurt when we get a haircut. The average person has about 100,000 strands of hair.* Every day we lose 75 to 150 strands of hair. One strand of hair grows for two to seven years. After it stops growing, it rests for a while and then falls out. Hair grows faster in warmer weather, and women's hair grows faster than men's hair.

Questions:
1. How fast does hair grow?
2. Why don't haircuts hurt?
3. About how many strands of hair are on your head right now?
4. Where is a good place to live if you want your hair to grow faster?

Part II. Choose one part of the body, for example: fingernails, skin, eyebrows, eyes, heart, lungs, etc. Make a list of interesting facts about this part of the body. Organize the facts into a paragraph. Begin with the given topic sentence. *Note:* If you are researching information on the Internet, search this topic: "interesting _____ facts" (e.g., interesting hair facts).

Topic sentence: Here are some interesting facts about our _____ .

❑ **Exercise 13. Warm-up.** (Chart 1-3)
How often do you do each activity? Give the percentage (0% → 100%). Your teacher will ask which ones you always do, sometimes do, or never do.

1. _____ I take the bus to school.

2. _____ I go to bed late.

3. _____ I skip breakfast.

4. _____ I eat vegetables at lunch time.

5. _____ I cook my own dinner.

6. _____ I am an early riser.**

---

strands of hair = pieces of hair

**early riser* = a person who gets up early in the morning

1-3 Frequency Adverbs

100%
↑
 	
50%
 	
0%
	positive {
	always
	almost always
	usually
	often
	frequently
	generally
	sometimes
	occasionally
	
	negative {
	seldom
	rarely
	hardly ever
	almost never
	not ever, never
		Frequency adverbs usually occur in the middle of a sentence and have special positions, as shown in examples (a) through (e) below.
		
		The adverbs in **boldface** may also occur at the beginning or the end of a sentence.
		
		I sometimes get up at 6:30.
		Sometimes I get up at 6:30.
		I get up at 6:30 sometimes.
		
		The other adverbs in the list (not in boldface) rarely occur at the beginning or the end of a sentence. Their usual position is in the middle of a sentence.

s + FREQ ADV + v (a) Karen ***always*** ***tells*** the truth.	Frequency adverbs usually come between the subject and the simple present verb except main verb *be*. *INCORRECT: Always Karen tells the truth.*
s + BE + FREQ ADV (b) Karen ***is*** ***always*** on time.	Frequency adverbs follow *be* in the simple present (*am, is, are*) and simple past (*was, were*).
(c) Do *you always* eat breakfast?	In a question, frequency adverbs come directly after the subject.
(d) Ann ***usually doesn't** eat* breakfast.	In a negative sentence, most frequency adverbs come in front of a negative verb (except *always* and *ever*).
(e) Sue ***doesn't always** eat* breakfast.	***Always*** follows a negative helping verb, as in (e), or a negative form of *be*.
(f) CORRECT: Anna ***never eats*** meat. *INCORRECT: Anna doesn't never eat meat.*	Negative adverbs (*seldom, rarely, hardly ever, never*) are NOT used with a negative verb.
(g) — Do you ***ever take*** the bus to work? — Yes, I do. I often take the bus.	***Ever*** is used in questions about frequency, as in (g). It means "at any time."
(h) I ***don't ever*** walk to work. *INCORRECT: I ever walk to work.*	***Ever*** is also used with ***not***, as in (h). ***Ever*** is NOT used in statements.

❏ **Exercise 14. Grammar and speaking.** (Chart 1-3)

Part I. Look at your answers in Exercise 13. Make complete sentences using the appropriate frequency word from Chart 1-3.

Example: 1. 0% = *I **never** take the bus to school.* OR
              50% = *I **sometimes** take the bus to school.*

Part II. Walk around the room and find people who do the activities with the same frequency as you.

Example:
SPEAKER A: I **always** take the bus to school. Do you **always** take the bus to school?
SPEAKER B: No, I don't. I **sometimes** take the bus to school. Do you **usually** go to bed late?
SPEAKER A: Yes, I do. I **usually** go to bed late.

❑ **Exercise 15. Let's talk.** (Chart 1-3)
Answer the questions. Discuss the meaning of the frequency adverbs.

What is something that . . .
1. you seldom do?
2. a polite person often does?
3. a polite person never does?
4. our teacher frequently does in class?
5. you never do in class?
6. you rarely eat?
7. you occasionally do after class?
8. drivers generally do?
9. people in your country always or usually do to celebrate the New Year?

❑ **Exercise 16. Looking at grammar.** (Chart 1-3)
Add the given adverbs to each sentence. Put the adverbs in their usual midsentence position. Make any necessary changes to the sentence.

Example: Emily doesn't get to work on time.
  a. usually → Emily **usually** doesn't get to work on time.
  b. often → Emily **often** doesn't get to work on time.

1. Kazu doesn't shave in the morning.
   a. frequently
   b. occasionally
   c. sometimes
   d. always
   e. ever
   f. never
   g. hardly ever
   h. rarely
   i. seldom

2. I don't eat breakfast.
   a. usually
   b. always
   c. seldom
   d. ever

3. My roommate isn't home in the evening.
   a. generally
   b. sometimes
   c. always
   d. hardly ever

☐ **Exercise 17. Looking at grammar.** (Chart 1-3)

Complete the sentences using the information in the chart. Use a frequency adverb in each sentence to describe Mia's weekly activities.

Mia's Week	S	M	Tu	W	Th	F	S
1. wake up early				x			
2. make breakfast		x	x		x		
3. go to the gym	x	x		x		x	x
4. be late for the bus		x	x	x	x		
5. cook dinner	x	x	x	x	x	x	x
6. read a book	x	x	x	x		x	x
7. do homework		x				x	
8. go to bed early				'			

1. Mia _____seldom / rarely wakes_____ up early.

2. She _____sometimes makes_____ breakfast.

3. She _____frequently goes_____ to the gym.

4. She _____is often_____ late for the bus.

5. She _____always cooks_____ dinner.

6. She _____frequently reads_____ a book.

7. She _____hardly ever does_____ her homework.

8. She _____never goes_____ to bed early.

☐ **Exercise 18. Let's talk: pairwork.** (Charts 1-1 → 1-3)

Work with a partner. Use frequency adverbs to talk about yourself and to ask your partner questions.

Example: walk to school

PARTNER A (*book open*): I usually walk to school. How about you? Do you usually walk to school?

PARTNER B (*book closed*): I usually walk to school too. OR
I seldom walk to school. I usually take the bus.

Change roles.

1. wear a suit to class
2. go to sleep before 11:00 P.M.
3. get at least one email a day
4. read in bed before I go to sleep
5. speak to people who sit next to me on an airplane

6. wear a hat to class
7. believe the things I hear in the news
8. get up before nine o'clock in the morning
9. call my family or a friend if I feel homesick or lonely
10. have chocolate ice cream for dessert

□ **Exercise 19. Warm-up.** (Chart 1-4)
Combine the given words into sentences. Add **-s** where necessary. Do not add any other words.

1. A dolphin \ swim s *in the ocean*

2. Dolphins\ swim *in the Ocean*

1-4 Singular/Plural	
(a) SINGULAR: *one bird*	SINGULAR = one, not two or more
(b) PLURAL: *two birds, three birds, many birds, all birds, etc.*	PLURAL = two, three, or more
(c) Bird**s** sing.	**A plural noun** ends in **-s**, as in (c).
(d) A bird sing**s**.	**A singular verb** ends in **-s**, as in (d).
(e) A *bird* *sings* outside my window. *It* *sings* loudly. *Ann* *sings* beautifully. *She* *sings* songs to her children. *Tom* *sings* very well. *He* *sings* professionally.	A singular verb follows a singular subject. Add **-s** to the simple present verb if the subject is (1) a singular noun (e.g., *a bird, Ann, Tom*) or (2) *he, she,* or *it.**

*He, she, and *it* are third person singular personal pronouns. See Chart 6-10, p. 164, for more information about personal pronouns.

□ **Exercise 20. Looking at grammar.** (Chart 1-4)
Look at each word that ends in **-s**. Is it a noun or verb? Is it singular or plural?

subject

Sentence	Noun	Verb	Sing.	Plural
1. Plants grow quickly in warm weather.	x			x
2. Ali lives in an apartment.		x	x	
3. Bettina listens to the radio every morning.		x	x	
4. The students at this school work hard.	x			x
5. An ambulance takes sick people to the hospital.		x	x	
6. Ambulances take sick people to the hospital.	x			x
7. Cell phones offer text-messaging.	x			x
8. The earth revolves around the sun.		x	x	

□ **Exercise 21. Listening.** (Chart 1-4)

Listen to the statements. Add -s where necessary. Write Ø if no -s is needed.

CD 1
Track 6

Natural disasters: a flood

1. The weather __Ø__ cause _s_ some natural disaster _s_ .

2. Heavy rains sometimes create __/__ flood _s_ .

3. A big flood __/__ cause _s_ a lot of damage.

4. In town _s_ , flood _s_ can damage building _s_ , home _s_ , and road _s_ .

5. After a flood __/__ , a town __/__ need _s_ a lot of financial help for repair _s_ .

□ **Exercise 22. Warm-up.** (Chart 1-5)

Write the third person form for each verb under the correct heading. Can you figure out the rules for when to add -s, -es, and -ies?

mix	speak	stay	study	take	try	wish

Add -s only.	Add -es.	Add -ies.
speaks	mixes	studies
stays	wishes	tries
takes		

1-5 Spelling of Final -s/-es

(a) visit	→	visits	Final -s, not -es, is added to most verbs.
speak	→	speaks	INCORRECT: visites, speakes
(b) ride	→	rides	Many verbs end in -e. Final -s is simply added.
write	→	writes	
(c) catch	→	catches	Final -es is added to words that end in -ch, -sh, -s, -x, and -z.
wash	→	washes	
miss	→	misses	PRONUNCIATION NOTE:
fix	→	fixes	Final -es is pronounced /əz/ and adds a syllable.*
buzz	→	buzzes	
(d) fly	→	flies	If a word ends in a consonant + -y, change the -y to -i and add -es, as in (d).
			INCORRECT: flys
(e) pay	→	pays	If a word ends in a vowel + -y, simply add -s,** as in (e).
			INCORRECT: paies or payes
(f) go	→	goes	The singular forms of the verbs go, do, and have are irregular.
do	→	does	
have	→	has	

*See Chart 6-1, p. 147, for more information about the pronunciation of final -s/-es.

**Vowels = a, e, i, o, u. Consonants = all other letters in the alphabet.

❑ **Exercise 23. Looking at grammar.** (Charts 1-4 and 1-5)
Underline the verb(s) in each sentence. Add final *-s/-es* if necessary. Do not change any other words.

1. A frog jump^s^.
2. Frogs jump. → (*no change*)
3. A boat float~s~ on water.
4. Rivers flow toward the sea.
5. My mother worry about me. *worries*
6. A student buy~s~ a lot of books at the beginning of each term.
7. Airplanes fly all around the world.
8. The teacher ask~s~ us a lot of questions in class every day.
9. Mr. Cook watch^es^ game shows on TV every evening.
10. Water freeze~s~ at 32°F (0°C) and boil~s~ at 212°F (100°C).
11. Mrs. Taylor never cross~es~ the street in the middle of a block. She always walk~s~ to the corner and use~s~ the crosswalk.

❑ **Exercise 24. Grammar and listening.** (Chart 1-5)

CD 1
Track 7

Add *-s/-es/-ies* to the verbs. Check your answers with a partner. Listen to the pronunciation of the verbs.

1. talk _s_
2. fish _es_
3. hope _s_
4. teach _es_
5. move _s_
6. kiss _es_
7. push _es_
8. wait _s_
9. mix _es_
10. bow _s_
11. study _ies_
12. buy _s_
13. enjoy _s_
14. try _ies_
15. carry _ies_

❑ **Exercise 25. Let's talk: pairwork.** (Chart 1-5)
Work with a partner. Look at the pictures and make conversations. Take turns being Partner A and Partner B. Follow this model. Use *he, she,* or *they* as appropriate.

PARTNER A: What is he doing?
PARTNER B: He _____.
PARTNER A: Does he _____ often?
PARTNER B: No, he doesn't. He rarely _____.

□ **Exercise 26. Game.** (Charts 1-4 and 1-5)
Your teacher will assign each student an item number. (If there are fewer than 24 students, some students will have two numbers. If there are more than 24 students, some students will have the same number.) Find your number in the list and write the words that appear beside it on a slip of paper. Then close your book.

Walk around the classroom and say your words to other classmates. You are looking for the other half of your sentence. When you find the person with the other half, combine the information on both of your slips of paper into a sentence.

Write the sentence on the board or on a piece of paper. Make changes to the verb if necessary.

Example: 1. A star
2. shine in the sky at night
→ *A star shines in the sky at night.*

1. A car
2. causes air pollution.
3. stretch when you pull on it.
4. A hotel
5. support a huge variety of marine life.
6. A bee
7. Does exercise
8. cause great destruction when it reaches land.
9. A river
10. improves your health?

11. An elephant
12. A hurricane
13. produce one-fourth of the world's coffee.
14. Oceans
15. use its long trunk like a hand to pick things up.
16. Brazil
17. supply its guests with clean towels.
18. A rubber band
19. collects nectar* from flowers.
20. flows downhill.

□ **Exercise 27. Warm-up.** (Chart 1-6)
Circle the correct completions.

CHARLIE: Shhh! I _____ something on our roof.
 a. hear   b. am hearing

I _____ there is a person up there.
 a. think   b. am thinking

DAD: I _____ .
 a. don't know   b. am not knowing

It _____ more like a small animal, maybe a cat or squirrel.
 a. sounds   b. is sounding

---

*nectar = a sugary liquid inside flowers

1-6 Non-Action Verbs

(a) I *know* Ms. Chen.
    INCORRECT: *I am knowing Ms. Chen.*
 	
(b) I'm hungry. I *want* a sandwich.
    INCORRECT: *I am wanting a sandwich.*
 	
(c) This book *belongs* to Mikhail.
    INORRECT: *This book is belonging to Mikhail.*
	Some verbs are generally not used in progressive tenses. These verbs are called "non-action verbs."* They express a situation that exists, not an action in progress.

Non-action Verbs

hear	believe	be	own	need	like	forget
see	think	exist	have	want	love	remember
sound	understand		possess	prefer	hate	
	know	seem	belong			agree
	mean	look like				disagree

COMPARE: (d) I *think* that grammar is easy. (e) I *am thinking* about grammar right now. (f) Tom *has* a car. (g) I'm *having* a good time.	***Think*** and ***have*** can be used in the progressive. In (d): When ***think*** means "believe," it is non-progressive. In (e): When ***think*** expresses thoughts that are going through a person's mind, it can be progressive. In (f): When ***have*** means "own" or expresses possession, it is not used in the progressive. In (g): In expressions where ***have*** does not mean "own" (e.g., *have a good time, have a bad time, have trouble, have a problem, have lunch, have a snack, have company, have an operation*), ***have*** can be used in the progressive.

*Non-action verbs are also called "non-progressive" or "stative" verbs.

□ **Exercise 28. Looking at grammar.** (Chart 1-6)
Choose the correct responses.

1. A: What do you like better: coffee or tea?
   B: I _____ tea.
       a. am preferring   (b.) prefer

2. A: Can you help me set the table for dinner?
   B: In a minute. I _____ my report.
       a. am finishing   b. finish
       action verb.

3. A: Are you busy?
   B: I _____ a few minutes.
       a. have   b. am having

4. A: _____ a good time?
       a. Are you having   b. Do you have
   B: Yes, I _____ myself.
       a. am enjoying   b. I enjoy

5. A: There's goes Salma on her new racing bike.
   B: Yeah, she really _____ bikes.
       a. is loving   b. loves
   A: That's for sure! She _____ several.
       a. is owning   b. owns

☐ **Exercise 29. Looking at grammar.** (Chart 1-6)
Complete the sentences with the simple present or present progressive form of **think** and **have**.

1. A: How is your new job going?
   B: Pretty good. I (*think*) _____think_____ I am doing okay.

2. A: You look upset. What's on your mind?
   B: I'm worried about my daughter. I (*think*) _____think_____ she's in trouble.

3. A: You look far away.* What's on your mind?
   B: I (*think*) _am thinking_ about my vacation next week. I can't wait!

4. A: Hey, there! How's the party going?
   B: Great! We (*have*) _are having_ a lot of fun.

5. A: Could I borrow some money?
   B: Sorry, I only (*have*) _have_ a little change** on me.

☐ **Exercise 30. Looking at grammar.** (Chart 1-6)
Complete the sentences. Use the simple present or present progressive form of the verbs in parentheses.

1. Right now I (*look*) _am looking_ out the window. I (*see*) _see_ a window washer on a ladder.

2. A: (*you, need*) _Do you need_ some help, Mrs. Bernini?
      (*you, want*) _Do you want_ me to carry that box for you?
   B: Yes, thank you. That's very nice of you.

3. A: Who is that man? I (*think*) _think_ that I (*know*) _know_ him, but I (*forget*) _forget / forgot_ his name.
   B: That's Mr. Martinez.
   A: That's right! I (*remember*) _remember_ him now.

---

look far away = look like you are thinking about other things; daydream

**change* = coins

4. A: (*you, believe*) _Do you believe_ in ghosts?

   B: No. In my opinion, ghosts (*exist*) _exist_ only in people's imaginations.

5. Right now the children (*be*) _are_ at the beach. They (*have*) _are having_ a good time. They (*have*) _have_ shovels, and they (*build*) _are building_ a sandcastle. They (*like*) _like_ to build big sandcastles. Their parents (*lie*) _are lying_ on the beach and (*listen*) _listening_ to music. They (*listen, not*) _are not listening_ to their children's conversations, but they (*hear*) _hear_ them anyway.

☐ **Exercise 31. Warm-up.** (Chart 1-7)
Choose the correct response for each question.

1. Does Janet eat fish?
   a. Yes, she does.   b. Yes, she is.   c. Yes, she eats.

2. Do you eat fish?
   a. No, I don't.   b. No, I am not.   c. No, I don't eat.

3. Are you vegetarian?
   a. Yes, I do.   b. Yes, I am.   c. Yes, I like.

1-7 Present Verbs: Short Answers to Yes/No Questions

	Question	Short Answer	Long Answer
QUESTIONS WITH *DO/DOES*	*Does* Bob *like* tea?	Yes, he *does*. No, he *doesn't*.	Yes, he likes tea. No, he doesn't like tea.
	Do you *like* tea?	Yes, I *do*. No, I *don't*.	Yes, I like tea. No, I don't like tea.
QUESTIONS WITH *BE*	*Are* you *studying*?	Yes, I *am*.* No, I *'m not*.	Yes, I am (I'm) studying. No, I'm not studying.
	Is Yoko a student?	Yes, she *is*.* No, she *'s not*. OR No, she *isn't*.	Yes, she is (she's) a student. No, she's not a student. OR No, she isn't a student.
	Are they *studying*?	Yes, they *are*.* No, they *'re not*. OR No, they *aren't*.	Yes, they are (they're) studying. No, they're not studying. OR No, they aren't studying.

**Am, is,* and *are* are NOT contracted with pronouns in short answers.

INCORRECT SHORT ANSWERS: Yes, I'm. Yes, she's. Yes, they're.

❑ **Exercise 32. Looking at grammar.** (Chart 1-7)
Complete the conversations. Use the simple present or present progressive form of the verbs in parentheses. Give short answers to the questions as necessary.

1. A: (*Tanya, have*) __Does Tanya__ have a bike?

   B: Yes, __she does__. She (*have*) __has__ a racing bike.

2. A: (*it, rain*) _____ right now?

   B: No, _____. At least, I (*think, not*) _____ so.

3. A: (*your friends, write*) _____ a lot of emails?

   B: Yes, _____. I (*get*) _____ lots of emails all the time.

4. A: (*the weather, affect**) _____ your mood?

   B: Yes, _____. I (*get*) _____ grumpy when it's rainy.

---

*The word *affect* is a verb: *The weather **affects** my mood.*
The word *effect* is a noun: *Warm, sunny weather has a good **effect** on my mood.*

5. A: (*Jean, study*) _____ at the library this evening?

   B: No, _____. She (*be*) _____ at the gym. She

      (*play*) _____ table tennis with her friend.

   A: (*Jean, play*) _____ table tennis every evening?

   B: No, _____. She usually (*study*) _____ at the library.

   A: (*she, be*) _____ a good player?

   B: Yes, _____. She (*play*) _____ table tennis a lot.

   A: (*you, play*) _____ table tennis?

   B: Yes, _____. But I (*be, not*) _____ very good.

□ **Exercise 33. Listening.** (Chart 1-7)

Part I. Listen to these examples. Notice the reduced pronunciation of the phrases in *italics*.

CD 1
Track 8

At the doctor's office

1.	Do you	→ *Dyou*	*Do you* have an appointment?
2.	Does he	→ *Dze*	*Does he* have an appointment?
3.	Does she	→ *Duh-she*	*Does she* have an appointment?
4.	Do we	→ *Duh-we*	*Do we* have an appointment?
5.	Do they	→ *Duh-they*	*Do they* have an appointment?
6.	Am I	→ *Mi*	*Am I* late for my appointment?
7.	Is it	→ *Zit*	*Is it* time for my appointment?*
8.	Does it	→ *Zit*	*Does it* hurt?

Part II. Complete each question with the unreduced form of the words you hear.

Example: You will hear: Do you want to tell me what the problem is?

   You will write: _____*Do you*_____ want to tell me what the problem is?

1. _____ have pain anywhere?

2. _____ hurt anywhere else?

3. _____ have a cough or sore throat?

4. _____ have a fever?

5. _____ need lab tests?

6. _____ very sick?

7. _____ serious?

8. _____ need to make another appointment?

9. _____ want to wait in the waiting room?

10. _____ pay now or later?

---

*See Chapter 5 for more examples of questions with *be* in spoken English.

□ **Exercise 34. Let's talk: interview.** (Chart 1-7)
Make questions with the given words. Then walk around the room and ask and answer questions. Your answers should have both a short and a long response.

Example: be \ Texas \ in South America?
SPEAKER A: Is Texas in South America?
SPEAKER B: No, it isn't. Texas is in North America.

1. the earth \ revolve \ around the sun \ right now?

2. the moon \ revolve \ around the earth \ every 28 days?

3. be \ the sun and moon planets?

4. be \ Toronto in western Canada?

5. whales \ lay \ eggs?

6. your country \ have \ gorillas in the wild?

7. be \ gorillas \ intelligent?

8. mosquitoes \ carry \ malaria?

9. you \ like \ vegetarian food?

10. be \ our teacher \ from Australia?

11. it \ rain \ outside \ right now?

12. be \ you \ tired of this interview?

□ **Exercise 35. Listening.** (Chart 1-7)
Choose the correct responses.

CD 1
Track 9
Example: You will hear: You look hot and tired. Are you thirsty?
You will choose: a. Yes, I am.
b. Yes, I do.

1. a. Yes, I want.
   b. Yes, I do.

2. a. Yes, I am.
   b. Yes, I do.

3. a. Yes, it is.
   b. Yes, it does.

4. a. Yes, we do.
   b. Yes, we need.

5. a. Yes, he does.
   b. Yes, he is.

6. a. Yes, they are.
   b. Yes, they do.

□ **Exercise 36. Looking at grammar.** (Chapter 1)
Complete the sentences. Use the simple present or the present progressive form of the verbs in parentheses.

1. A: My sister (*have*) __*has*__ a new car. She bought it last month.

   B: (*you, have*) __*Do you have*__ a car?

   A: No, I __*don't*__. Do you?

   B: No, but I have a motorcycle.

2. A: What are the children doing? (*they, watch*) _____ TV?

   B: No, they _____. They (*play*) _____ outside.

3. A: Jacob, (*you, listen*) _____ to me?

   B: Of course I am, Mom. You (*want*) _____ me to take out the garbage. Right?

   A: Yes, and I mean now!

4. A: Hey, Becky, where (*be*) _____ you?

   B: I (*be*) _____ in the bedroom.

   A: What (*you, do*) _____?

   B: I (*try*) _____ to sleep!

5. A: What (*you, think*) _____ about at night before you fall asleep?

   B: I (*think*) _____ about my day. But I (*think, not*) _____ about anything negative. What (*think*) _____ about?

   A: I (*think, not*) _____ about anything. I (*count*) _____ sheep.★

6. A: A penny for your thoughts.

   B: Huh?

   A: That means: What (*you, think*) _____ about right now?

   B: I (*think*) _____ about my homework. I (*think, not*) _____ _____ about anything else right now.

   A: I (*believe, not*) _____ you. You (*think*) _____ about your wedding plans!

7. A: (*you, know*) _____ any tongue-twisters?

   B: Yes, I _____. Here's one: She sells seashells down by the seashore.

   A: That (*be*) _____ hard to say! Can you say this: Sharon wears Sue's shoes to zoos to look at cheap sheep?

   B: That (*make, not*) _____ any sense.

   A: I (*know*) _____, but it's fun to say.

★*count sheep* = fall asleep naturally by closing your eyes and counting imaginary sheep

☐ **Exercise 37. Reading, grammar, and listening.** (Chapter 1)

Part I. Read the passage and choose the correct completions.

Aerobic Exercise

Jeremy and Nancy believe exercise is important. They go to an exercise class three times a week. They like aerobic exercise.

Aerobic exercise is a special type of exercise. It increases a person's heart rate. Fast walking, running, and dancing are examples of aerobic exercise. During aerobic exercise, a person's heart beats fast. This brings more oxygen to the muscles. Muscles work longer when they have more oxygen.

Right now Jeremy and Nancy are listening to some lively music. They are doing special dance steps. They are exercising different parts of their body.

How about you? Do you like to exercise? Do your muscles get exercise every week? Do you do some type of aerobic exercise?

1. Jeremy and Nancy (*think,*) *are thinking* exercise is good for them.

2. They *prefer, are preferring* aerobic exercise.

3. Aerobic exercise *makes, is making* a person's heart beat fast.

4. Muscles *need, are needing* oxygen.

5. With more oxygen, muscles *work, are working* longer.

6. Right now Jeremy and Nancy *do, are doing* a special kind of dance.

7. *Do you exercise, Are you exercising* every week?

8. *Do you exercise, Are you exercising* right now?

Part II. Listen to the passage and complete the sentences with the words you hear. Cover Part I with a piece of paper.

CD 1
Track 10

Aerobic Exercise

Jeremy and Nancy _____ exercise is important. They _____ to
          1   2

an exercise class three times a week. They _____ aerobic exercise.
                                                        3

Aerobic exercise _____ a special type of exercise. It _____ a
                              4   5

person's heart rate. Fast walking, running, and dancing _____ examples of aerobic
                                                                    6

exercise. During aerobic exercise, a person's heart _____ fast. This
                                                                7

_____ more oxygen to the muscles. Muscles _____ longer when they
          8   9

_____ more oxygen.
     10

Right now Jeremy and Nancy _____ to some lively music. They
                                            11

_____ special dance steps. They _____ different
          12   13

parts of their body.

How about you? _____ you _____ to exercise? _____ your

                 14   15   16

muscles _____ exercise every week? _____ you _____ some type

       17   18   19

of aerobic exercise?

❑ **Exercise 38. Check your knowledge.** (Chapter 1)

Edit the passage to correct errors in verb tense usage.

Omar's Visit

                              owns

    (1) My friend Omar ~~is owning~~ his own car now. It's brand new.* Today he driving to a

small town north of the city to visit his aunt. He love to listen to music, so the CD player is

play one of his favorite CDs — loudly. Omar is very happy: he is drive his own car and listen

to loud music. He's look forward to his visit with his aunt.

    (2) Omar is visiting his aunt once a week. She's elderly and live alone. She is thinking

Omar a wonderful nephew. She love his visits. He try to be helpful and considerate in every

way. His aunt don't hearing well, so Omar is speaks loudly and clearly when he's with her.

    (3) When he's there, he fix things for her around her apartment and help her with her

shopping. He isn't staying with her overnight. He usually is staying for a few hours and then is

heading back to the city. He kiss his aunt good-bye and give her a hug before he is leaving.

Omar is a very good nephew.

---

*brand new = completely new

Chapter 2
Past Time

❑ **Exercise 1. Warm-up.** (Chart 2-1)

Check (✓) the statements that are true for you. Share your answers with a partner.

1. _____ I stayed up late last night.

2. _____ I slept well last night.

3. _____ I was tired this morning.

2-1 Expressing Past Time: The Simple Past

(a) Mary *walked* downtown *yesterday*. (b) I *slept* for eight hours *last night*.	The simple past is used to talk about activities or situations that began and ended in the past (e.g., *yesterday, last night, two days ago, in 2010*).
(c) Bob *stayed* home yesterday morning. (d) Our plane *landed* on time last night.	Most simple past verbs are formed by adding *-ed* to a verb, as in (a), (c), and (d).
(e) I *ate* breakfast this morning. (f) Sue *took* a taxi to the airport yesterday.	Some verbs have irregular past forms, as in (b), (e), and (f). See Chart 2-4.
(g) I *was* busy yesterday. (h) They *were* at home last night.	The simple past forms of *be* are *was* and *were*.

Forms of the Simple Past: Regular Verbs

STATEMENT	I, You, She, He, It, We, They *worked* yesterday.
NEGATIVE	I, You, She, He, It, We, They *did not* (*didn't*) *work* yesterday.
QUESTION	*Did* I, you, she, he, it, we, they *work* yesterday?
SHORT ANSWER	Yes, I, you, she, he, it, we, they *did*. OR No, I, you, she, he, it, we, they *didn't*.

Forms of the Simple Past: *Be*

STATEMENT	I, She, He, It *was* in class yesterday. We, You, They *were* in class yesterday.
NEGATIVE	I, She, He, It *was not* (*wasn't*) in class yesterday. We, You, They *were not* (*weren't*) in class yesterday.
QUESTION	*Was* I, she, he, it in class yesterday? *Were* we, you, they in class yesterday?
SHORT ANSWER	Yes, I, she, he, it *was*. Yes, we, you, they *were*. No, I, she, he, it *wasn't*. No, we, you, they *weren't*.

□ **Exercise 2. Looking at grammar.** (Chart 2-1)
Create your own chart by writing the negative and question forms of the words in *italics*. Omit the rest of each sentence.

	Negative	Question
1. *He needed* water.	*He didn't need*	*Did he need*
2. *She drank* tea.		
3. *They played* baseball.	*They didn't play*	*Did they play*
4. *I left* early.	*I didn't feel*	*Did I feel*
5. *They wore* boots.	*They didn't wear*	*Did they wear*
6. *We had* time.	*We didn't have*	*Did we have*
7. *It was* fun.	*It wasn't fun*	*Was it fun*
8. *You were* late.	*You weren't late*	*Were you late*

□ **Exercise 3. Let's talk.** (Chart 2-1)
All of the sentences contain inaccurate information. Make true statements by
    (1) making a negative statement and
    (2) making an affirmative statement using accurate information.
                   positive
1. Thomas Edison invented the telephone.
    → *Thomas Edison didn't invent the telephone.*
    → *Alexander Graham Bell invented the telephone.*
2. I came to school by hot-air balloon today. *I didn't come*
              didn't swim   *She came to.*
3. The students in this class swam into the classroom today.
      that   *swam*
4. (*Teacher's name*) is a movie director. *Tom isn't a movie director*
  didn't sleep   *Lisa is a movie director*
5. I slept in a tree last night.
  kid slept
6. The Internet became popular in the 1970s.

□ **Exercise 4. Listening.** (Chapter 1 and Chart 2-1)
Listen to each sentence. Choose the correct completion(s). More than one completion may be possible.

CD 1
Track 11

Example: You will hear: It snows . . .
         You will choose: (in the winter.)   every day.   now.

1.	French.	together.	last week.
2.	right now.	yesterday.	last summer.
3.	in the evening.	last night.	behind the mountains.
4.	at this moment.	our class.	yesterday.
5.	two weeks ago.	right now.	at this moment.

Exercise 5. Listening. (Chart 2-1)

The differences between **was/wasn't** and **were/weren't** can be hard to hear in spoken
English. The "t" in the negative contraction is often dropped, and you may only hear an /n/
sound.

CD 1
Track 12

Part I. Listen to these examples.

1. I was in a hurry. I wasn't in a hurry.
2. They were on time. They weren't on time.
3. He was at the doctor's. He wasn't at the doctor's.
4. We were early. We weren't early.

Part II. Circle the words you hear. Before you begin, you may want to check your
understanding of these words: *wedding, nervous, excited, ceremony, reception.*

At a wedding

1.	was	wasn't	6.	was	wasn't
2.	was	wasn't	7.	was	wasn't
3.	were	weren't	8.	was	wasn't
4.	were	weren't	9.	were	weren't
5.	was	wasn't	10.	were	weren't

❑ **Exercise 6. Warm-up.** (Chart 2-2)

Do you know the spelling rules for these verbs?

Part I. Write the **-ing** form of each verb under the correct heading.

die	give	hit	try

Drop final **-e**. Add **-ing**.	Double final consonant. Add **-ing**.	Change **-ie** to **-y**. Add **-ing**.	Just add **-ing**.
_____	*hitting*	*dying*	*trying*.

Part II. Write the **-ed** form of each verb under the correct heading.

enjoy	tie	stop	study

Double final consonant. Add **-ed**.	Change **-y** to **-i**. Add **-ed**.	Just add **-ed**.	Just add **-d**.
stopped	*studied*	*enjoyed*	*tied*

2-2 Spelling of -ing and -ed Forms

End of Verb	Double the Consonant?	Simple Form	-ing	-ed	
-e	NO	(a) smile hope	smiling hoping	smiled hoped	-ing form: Drop the -e, add -ing. -ed form: Just add -d.
Two Consonants	NO	(b) help learn	helping learning	helped learned	If the verb ends in two consonants, just add -ing or -ed.
Two Vowels + One Consonant	NO	(c) rain heat	raining heating	rained heated	If the verb ends in two vowels + a consonant, just add -ing or -ed.
One Vowel + One Consonant	YES	ONE-SYLLABLE VERBS			If the verb has one syllable and ends in one vowel + one consonant, double the consonant to make the -ing or -ed form.*
		(d) stop plan	stopping planning	stopped planned	
	NO	TWO-SYLLABLE VERBS			If the first syllable of a two-syllable verb is stressed, do not double the consonant.
		(e) vísit óffer	visiting offering	visited offered	
	YES	(f) prefér admít	preferring admitting	preferred admitted	If the second syllable of a two-syllable verb is stressed, double the consonant.
-y	NO	(g) play enjoy	playing enjoying	played enjoyed	If the verb ends in a vowel + -y, keep the -y. Do not change the -y to -i.
		(h) worry study	worrying studying	worried studied	If the verb ends in a consonant + -y, keep the -y for the -ing form, but change the -y to -i to make the -ed form.
-ie		(i) die tie	dying tying	died tied	-ing form: Change the -ie to -y and add -ing. -ed form: Just add -d.

*EXCEPTIONS: Do not double "w" or "x": *snow, snowing, snowed, fix, fixing, fixed.*

□ **Exercise 7. Looking at spelling.** (Chart 2-2)
Write the **-ing** and **-ed** forms of these verbs.

		-ing	-ed
1.	wait	_____	_____
2.	clean	*cleaning*	*cleaned*
3.	plant	*planting*	*planted*
4.	plan	*planning*	*planned*
5.	hope	*hoping*	*hoped*
6.	hop	*hopping*	*hopped*

7.	play	_playing_	_played_
8.	study	_studying_	_studied_
9.	try	_trying_	_tried_
10.	die	_dying_	_died_
11.	sleep	_sleeping_	slept (no -ed)
12.	run	_running_	ran (no -ed)

□ **Exercise 8. Listening.** (Chart 2-2)

CD 1
Track 13

Complete the sentences with the verbs you hear. Pay special attention to spelling.

1. Shhh. The movie is _____ .

2. Oh, no. The elevator door is stuck. It isn't _____ .

3. Here's a letter for you. I _____ it accidentally.

4. I'm _____ to the phone message that you already _____ to.

5. Are you _____ to me or telling me the truth?

6. We _____ the party.

7. I'm _____ the nice weather today.

8. You look upset. What _____?

□ **Exercise 9. Warm-up.** (Charts 2-3 and 2-4)

There are four main parts to a verb. Can you complete the chart?

	Simple Form	Simple Past	Past Participle	Present Participle
1.	help	_helped_	_helped_	_helping_
2.	stay	_stayed_	_stayed_	_staying_
3.	take	_took_	_taken_	_taking_
4.	give	_gave_	_given_	_giving_
5.	be	_was were_	_been_	_being_

2-3 The Principal Parts of a Verb

Regular Verbs

SIMPLE FORM	SIMPLE PAST	PAST PARTICIPLE	PRESENT PARTICIPLE
finish	finished	finished	finishing
stop	stopped	stopped	stopping
hope	hoped	hoped	hoping
wait	waited	waited	waiting
play	played	played	playing
try	tried	tried	trying

Irregular Verbs

see	saw	seen	seeing
make	made	made	making
sing	sang	sung	singing
eat	ate	eaten	eating
put	put	put	putting
go	went	gone	going

Principal Parts of a Verb

(1) THE SIMPLE FORM	English verbs have four principal forms, or "parts." **The simple form** is the form that is found in a dictionary. It is the base form with no endings on it (no final *-s*, *-ed*, or *-ing*).
(2) THE SIMPLE PAST	**The simple past** ends in *-ed* for regular verbs. Most verbs are regular, but many common verbs have irregular past forms. See the reference list of irregular verbs that follows in Chart 2-4.
(3) THE PAST PARTICIPLE	**The past participle** also ends in *-ed* for regular verbs. Some verbs are irregular. It is used in perfect tenses (Chapter 4) and the passive (Chapter 10).
(4) THE PRESENT PARTICIPLE	**The present participle** ends in *-ing* (for both regular and irregular verbs). It is used in progressive tenses (e.g., the present progressive and the past progressive).

2-4 Common Irregular Verbs: A Reference List

SIMPLE FORM	SIMPLE PAST	PAST PARTICIPLE	SIMPLE FORM	SIMPLE PAST	PAST PARTICIPLE
be	was, were	been	lend	lent	lent
beat	beat	beaten	let	let	let
become	became	become	lie	lay	lain
begin	began	begun	light	lit/lighted	lit/lighted
bend	bent	bent	lose	lost	lost
bite	bit	bitten	make	made	made
blow	blew	blown	mean	meant	meant
break	broke	broken	meet	met	met
bring	brought	brought	pay	paid	paid
build	built	built	put	put	put
burn	burned/burnt	burned/burnt	quit	quit	quit
buy	bought	bought	read	read	read
catch	caught	caught	ride	rode	ridden
choose	chose	chosen	ring	rang	rung
come	came	come	rise	rose	risen
cost	cost	cost	run	ran	run
cut	cut	cut	say	said	said
dig	dug	dug	see	saw	seen
do	did	done	sell	sold	sold
draw	drew	drawn	send	sent	sent
dream	dreamed/dreamt	dreamed/dreamt	set	set	set
drink	drank	drunk	shake	shook	shaken
drive	drove	driven	shoot	shot	shot
eat	ate	eaten	shut	shut	shut
fall	fell	fallen	sing	sang	sung
feed	fed	fed	sink	sank	sunk
feel	felt	felt	sit	sat	sat
fight	fought	fought	sleep	slept	slept
find	found	found	slide	slid	slid
fit	fit	fit	speak	spoke	spoken
fly	flew	flown	spend	spent	spent
forget	forgot	forgotten	spread	spread	spread
forgive	forgave	forgiven	stand	stood	stood
freeze	froze	frozen	steal	stole	stolen
get	got	got/gotten	stick	stuck	stuck
give	gave	given	swim	swam	swum
go	went	gone	take	took	taken
grow	grew	grown	teach	taught	taught
hang	hung	hung	tear	tore	torn
have	had	had	tell	told	told
hear	heard	heard	think	thought	thought
hide	hid	hidden	throw	threw	thrown
hit	hit	hit	understand	understood	understood
hold	held	held	upset	upset	upset
hurt	hurt	hurt	wake	woke/waked	woken/waked
keep	kept	kept	wear	wore	worn
know	knew	known	win	won	won
leave	left	left	write	wrote	written

❑ **Exercise 10. Looking at grammar.** (Chart 2-4)
Complete the sentences. Use the simple past of any irregular verb that makes sense.
More than one answer may be possible.

1. Alima walked to the office today. Rebecca ___drove___ her car. Olga
   ___rode___ her bike. Yoko ___took___ the bus.

2. It got so cold last night that the water in the pond ___froze___.

3. Katya had a choice between a blue raincoat and a brown one. She finally
   ___wore___ the blue one.

4. My husband gave me a painting for my birthday. I ___put___ it on a wall in
   my office.

5. Last night around midnight, when I was sound asleep, the telephone ___rang___.
   It ___waked / woke___ me up.

6. The sun ___rose___ at 6:04 this morning and ___set___ at 6:59 last
   night.

7. I ___sent___ an email to my cousin after I finished studying last night.

8. Ms. Morita ___made___ chemistry at the local high school last year.

9. Oh, my gosh! Call the police! Someone ___stole___ my car!

10. The police ___caught___ the car thieves quickly and ___sent___ them
    to jail.

11. The earthquake was strong, and the ground ___shook___ for two minutes.

12. A bird ___sang___ into the grocery store through an open door.

13. My dog ___dug___ a hole in the yard and buried his bone.

14. I don't have any money in my wallet. I ___lost___ it all
    yesterday. I'm flat broke.*

15. Ann does funny things. She ___wore___ a tuxedo to her
    brother's wedding last week.

---

flat broke = completely out of money

□ **Exercise 11. Looking at grammar.** (Charts 2-1 → 2-4)
Create your own chart by writing the simple past, negative, and question forms of the words in *italics*. Omit the rest of each sentence.

	Simple Past	**Negative**	**Question**
1. *He skips* lunch.	He skipped	He didn't skip	Did he skip
2. *They leave* early.			
3. *She does* a lot.	She did	She didn't do	Did she do
4. *He is* sick.	He was sick	He wasn't sick	Was he sick
5. *We drive* to work.	We drove	We didn't drive	Did we drive
6. *You are* right.	You were	You weren't	Were you right
7. *I plan* my day.	I planned	I didn't plan	Did I plan

□ **Exercise 12. Let's talk: pairwork.** (Charts 2-1 → 2-4)
Work with a partner. Answer the questions with *Yes* and a complete sentence.

A broken arm

Imagine that you came to class today with a big cast on your arm. You slipped on some ice yesterday and fell down.

1. Did you have a bad day yesterday? → *Yes, I had a bad day yesterday.*
2. Did you fall down?
3. Did you hurt yourself when you fell down?
4. Did you break your arm?
5. Did you go to the emergency room?

Change roles.
6. Did you see a doctor?
7. Did you sit in the waiting room for a long time?
8. Did the doctor put a cast on your arm?
9. Did you pay a lot of money?
10. Did you come home exhausted?

□ **Exercise 13. Looking at grammar.** (Charts 2-1 → 2-4)
Complete the conversations with the correct form of the words in parentheses.

1. A: (*you, sleep*) __Did you sleep__ well last night?

   B: Yes, __I did__. I (*sleep*) __slept__ very well.

2. A: (*Ella's plane, arrive*) __Did Ella's p__ on time yesterday?

   B: Yes, __it did__. It (*get*) __got__ in at exactly 6:05.

   No. it didn't

3. A: (you, go) _____ away last weekend?

   B: No, _____. I (stay) _____ home because I (feel, not)

   _____ good.

4. A: (you, eat) _____ breakfast this morning?

   B: No, _____. I (have, not) _____ enough time. I

   was late for class because my alarm clock (ring, not) _____.

5. A: (Da Vinci, paint) _____ the *Mona Lisa*?

   B: Yes, _____. He also (paint) _____ other famous

   pictures.

☐ **Exercise 14. Looking at grammar.** (Charts 2-1 → 2-4)
Read the facts about each person. Complete the sentences with the correct form of the given verbs.

SITUATION 1: Whirlwind Wendy is energetic and does everything very quickly. Here is her typical morning.

Activities:
   wake up at 4:00 A.M.
   clean her apartment
   ride her bike five miles
   get vegetables from her garden
   watch a cooking show on TV
   make soup for dinner
   bring her elderly mother a meal
   read the day's paper
   fix herself lunch

Yesterday, Wendy . . .

1. _____woke_____ up at 4:00 A.M.

2. ___didn't clean___ her car.

3. ___didn't ride___ her bike ten miles.

4. _____got_____ vegetables from her garden.

5. ___didn't watch___ a comedy show on TV.

6. _____made_____ soup for dinner.

7. ___brought___ her elderly mother a meal.

8. ___didn't read___ a book.

9. ___didn't fix___ herself a snack.

SITUATION 2: Sluggish Sam is lazy and slow. He doesn't get much done in a day. Here is his typical day.

Activities:

sleep for 12 hours	come home
wake up at noon	lie on the couch
take two hours to eat breakfast	think about his busy life
go fishing	begin dinner at 8:00
fall asleep on his boat	finish dinner at 11:00

Yesterday, Sam . . .

1. ___slept___ for 12 hours.

2. ___didn't wake___ up at 5:00 A.M.

3. ___took___ two hours to eat breakfast.

4. ___didn't go___ hiking.

5. ___fell___ asleep on his boat.

6. ___came___ home.

7. ___didn't lie___ on his bed.

8. ___thought___ about his busy life.

9. ___didn't begin___ dinner at 5:00.

10. ___finished___ dinner at 11:00.

☐ **Exercise 15. Let's talk: pairwork.** (Charts 2-1 → 2-4)
Work with a partner. Partner A tells Partner B to perform an action. After Partner B does this, A will ask B a question in the past tense.

Example: Open your book.
PARTNER A: Open your book.
PARTNER B: (*opens his/her book*)
PARTNER A: What did you do?
PARTNER B: I opened my book.

1. Shut your book.
2. Stand up.
3. Hide your pen.
4. Turn to page 10 in your book.
5. Put your book in your lap.
6. Nod your head "yes."
7. Tear a piece of paper. *Tore*
8. Spell the past tense of "speak."
   spelled

Change roles.
9. Write your name on the board.
10. Draw a triangle under your name.
11. Shake your head "no."
12. Invite our teacher to have lunch with us.
13. Read a sentence from your grammar book.
14. Wave "good-bye."
15. Ask me for a pencil.
16. Repeat this question: "Which came first: the chicken or the egg?"

❏ **Exercise 16. Listening.** (Charts 2-1 → 2-4)

Part I. ***Did*** is often reduced at the beginning of questions. The pronoun that follows ***did*** may also change. Listen to the reduced pronunciations with ***did***.

CD 1
Track 14

1.	Did you	→	*Did-ja*	Did you forget something?
			Did-ya	Did you forget something?
2.	Did I	→	*Dih-di*	Did I forget something?
			Di	Did I forget something?
3.	Did he	→	*Dih-de*	Did he forget something?
			De	Did he forget something?
4.	Did she	→	*Dih-she*	Did she forget something?
5.	Did we	→	*Dih-we*	Did we forget something?
6.	Did they	→	*Dih-they*	Did they forget something?

Part II. You will hear questions. Complete each answer with the non-reduced form of the verb you hear.

1. Yes, he __did__. He __cut__ it with a knife.

2. Yes, she _____. She _____ it all yesterday.

3. Yes, I _____. I _____ them yesterday.

4. Yes, they _____. They _____ it.

5. Yes, you _____. You _____ it.

6. Yes, she _____. She _____ them.

7. Yes, he _____. He _____ it to him.

8. Yes, I _____. I _____ them yesterday.

9. Yes, he _____. He _____ it.

10. Yes, you _____. You _____ her.

❏ **Exercise 17. Listening.** (Charts 2-1 → 2-4)

Listen to the questions. Complete each answer with the correct form of the verb you hear.

CD 1
Track 15

Luka wasn't home last night.

1. Yes, he __went__ to a party last night.

2. Yes, he _____ a good time.

3. Yes, he _____ a lot of food.

4. Yes, he _____ a lot of soda.

5. Yes, he _____ some new people.

6. Yes, he _____ hands with them when he met them.

7. Yes, he _____ with friends.

8. Yes, he _____ with his friends and _____.

□ **Exercise 18. Looking at grammar.** (Charts 2-1 → 2-4)
Rewrite the paragraph. Use the past tense. Begin your new paragraph with *Yesterday morning*.

The Daily News

Every morning, Jake reads the newspaper online. He wants to know the latest news. He enjoys the business section most. His wife, Eva, doesn't read any newspapers on her computer. She downloads them on her ebook* reader. She looks at the front pages first. She doesn't have a lot of time. She finishes the articles later in the day. Both Jake and Eva are very knowledgeable about the day's events.

□ **Exercise 19. Listening.** (Charts 2-1 → 2-4)

Part I. Answer the questions. Then listen to the passage with your book closed.

CD 1
Track 16

Did you get the flu** last year?
Were you very sick?
What symptoms did you have?

Part II. Open your book and read the statements. Circle "T" for true and "F" for false.

1. The flu kills a lot of people worldwide every year.   T   F

2. The flu virus from 1918 to 1920 was a usual flu virus.   T   F

3. Most of the people who died were very young or very old.   T   F

Part III. Listen to the passage again. Complete the sentences with the words you hear.

A Deadly Flu

Every year, the flu _____ 200,000 to 300,000 people around the world. But in
                        1
1918, a very strong flu virus _____ millions of people. This flu _____ in
                               2   3
1918 and _____ until 1920. It _____ around the world, and between
           4   5
20 million and 100 million people _____. Unlike other flu viruses that usually
                                   6
_____ the very young and the very old, many of the victims _____ healthy
  7   8
young adults. This _____ unusual and _____ people especially afraid.
                     9   10

---

*ebook = electronic book

**the flu = the influenza virus; symptoms usually include fever, aches, tiredness, cough, and runny nose.

Exercise 20. Warm-up: listening. (Chart 2-5)

🎧 *Part I.* Listen to each pair of verbs. Decide if the verb endings have the same sound or a
CD 1 different sound.
Track 17

Example: You will hear: plays   played
             You will choose: same   (different)

1. same   different   3. same   different

2. same   different   4. same   different

Part II. Listen to the sentences. They contain past tense verbs. What sound does the **-ed**
ending have: /t/, /d/, or /əd/?

Example: You will hear: Jack played a game of tennis.
             You will choose: /t/   (/d/)   /əd/

1. /t/   /d/   /əd/   3. /t/   /d/   /əd/

2. /t/   /d/   /əd/   4. /t/   /d/   /əd/

2-5 Regular Verbs: Pronunciation of -ed Endings

(a) talked	=	talk/t/	Final **-ed** is pronounced /t/ after voiceless sounds.
stopped	=	stop/t/	You make a voiceless sound by pushing air through your mouth.
hissed	=	hiss/t/	No sound comes from your throat.
watched	=	watch/t/	Examples of voiceless sounds: /k/, /p/, /s/, /ch/, /sh/.
washed	=	wash/t/	
(b) called	=	call/d/	Final **-ed** is pronounced /d/ after voiced sounds.
rained	=	rain/d/	You make a voiced sound from your throat. Your voice box vibrates.
lived	=	live/d/	Examples of voiced sounds: /l/, /n/, /v/, /b/, and all vowel sounds.
robbed	=	rob/d/	
stayed	=	stay/d/	
(c) waited	=	wait/əd/	Final **-ed** is pronounced /əd/ after "t" and "d" sounds.
needed	=	need/əd/	Adding /əd/ adds a syllable to a word.

☐ **Exercise 21. Listening.** (Chapter 1 and Chart 2-5)

🎧 Listen to each sentence and choose the verb form you hear.
CD 1 *Example:* You will hear: I needed more help.
Track 18   You will choose: need   needs   (needed)

1. agree   agrees   agreed   5. end   ends   ended

2. agree   agrees   agreed   6. stop   stops   stopped

3. arrive   arrives   arrived   7. touch   touches   touched

4. explain   explains   explained

□ **Exercise 22. Listening.** (Chapter 1 and Chart 2-5)

Listen to each sentence and choose the correct completion.

CD 1
Track 19

Example: You will hear: We worked in small groups . . .

　　　　　You will choose: right now. (yesterday.)

1. every day.　　　　　yesterday.

2. right now.　　　　　last week.

3. six days a week.　　yesterday.

4. now.　　　　　　　last weekend.

5. every day.　　　　　yesterday.

6. every day.　　　　　yesterday.

□ **Exercise 23. Listening and pronunciation.** (Chart 2-5)

Listen to the past tense pronunciation of each word. Write the **-ed** ending you hear: /t/, /d/, or /əd/. Practice pronouncing the verbs.

CD 1
Track 20

1. cooked /t /　　　5. started /　/　　　9. added /　/

2. served /　/　　　6. dropped /　/　　10. passed /　/

3. wanted /　/　　　7. pulled /　/　　　11. returned /　/

4. asked /　/　　　8. pushed /　/　　　12. pointed /　/

□ **Exercise 24. Let's listen and talk.** (Charts 2-1 → 2-5)

Part I. Listen to the conversation between two friends about their weekends and answer the questions.

CD 1
Track 21

1. One person had a good weekend. Why?
2. His friend didn't have a good weekend. Why not?

Part II. Complete the conversation with your partner. Use past tense verbs. Practice saying it until you can do it without looking at your book. Then change roles and create a new conversation. Perform one of the conversations for the class.

A: Did you have a good weekend?

B: Yeah, I _____.

A: Really? That sounds like fun!

B: It _____ great! I _____.

How about you? How was your weekend?

A: I _____.

B: Did you have a good time?

A: Yes. / No. / Not really. _____

_____.

☐ **Exercise 25. Warm-up.** (Chart 2-6)
Match the sentences in Column A with the descriptions in Column B.

Column A

1. I looked at the limousine.
   The movie star was waving
   out the window. _____

2. I looked at the limousine.
   The movie star waved at me. _____

Column B

a. First I looked at the limousine.
   Then the movie star waved.

b. First the movie star began waving.
   Then I looked at the limousine.

2-6 Simple Past and Past Progressive

Simple Past	(a) Mary *walked* downtown yesterday. (b) I *slept* for eight hours last night.	The SIMPLE PAST is used to talk about *an activity or situation that began and ended at a particular time in the past* (e.g., *yesterday, last night, two days ago, in 2007*), as in (a) and (b).
Past Progressive	(c) I sat down at the dinner table at 6:00 P.M. yesterday. Tom came to my house at 6:10 P.M. I *was eating* dinner *when Tom came*. (d) I went to bed at 10:00. The phone rang at 11:00. I *was sleeping* when the phone rang.	The PAST PROGRESSIVE expresses *an activity that was in progress (was occurring, was happening) at a point of time in the past* (e.g., *at 6:10*) or at the time of another action (e.g., *when Tom came*). In (c): eating was in progress at 6:10; eating was in progress *when Tom came*. FORM: *was/were* + *-ing*
(e) *When the phone rang,* I was sleeping. (f) The phone rang *while* I was sleeping.	*when* = at that time *while* = during that time Examples (e) and (f) have the same meaning.	

Forms of the Past Progressive

STATEMENT		I, She, He, It	*was working.*			
		You, We, They	*were working.*			
NEGATIVE		I, She, He, It	*was not* (*wasn't*) *working.*			
		You, We, They	*were not* (*weren't*) *working.*			
QUESTION	*Was*	I, she, he, it	*working?*			
	Were	you, we, they	*working?*			
SHORT ANSWER	Yes,	I, she, he, it *was.*		Yes,	you, we, they	*were.*
	No,	I, she, he, it *wasn't.*		No,	you, we, they	*weren't.*

□ **Exercise 26. Looking at grammar.** (Chart 2-6)
Complete each sentence with the simple past or past progressive form of the verb(s) in parentheses.

1. At 6:00 P.M. Robert sat down at the table and began to eat. At 6:05, Robert (*eat*)
    _____was eating_____ dinner.

2. While Robert (*eat*) _____ dinner, Ann (*come*) _____
    through the door.

3. In other words, when Ann (*come*) _____ through the door, Robert (*eat*)
    _____ dinner.

4. Robert went to bed at 10:30. At 11:00, Robert (*sleep*) _____.

5. While Robert (*sleep*) _____, his cell phone (*ring*) _____.

6. In other words, when his cell phone (*ring*) _____, Robert (*sleep*)
    _____.

7. Robert left his house at 8:00 A.M. and (*begin*) _____ to walk to class.

8. While he (*walk*) _____ to class, he (*see*) _____
    Mr. Ito.

9. When Robert (*see*) _____ Mr. Ito, he (*stand*) _____ in his
    driveway. He (*hold*) _____ a broom.

10. Mr. Ito (*wave*) _____ to Robert when he (*see*) _____ him.

□ **Exercise 27. Looking at grammar.** (Chart 2-6)
Complete the sentences, orally or in writing, using the information in the chart. Use the
simple past for one clause and the past progressive for the other.

Activity in Progress	Beth	David	Lily
sit in a café	order a salad	pay a few bills	spill coffee on her lap
stand in an elevator	send a text message	run into an old friend	drop her glasses
swim in the ocean	avoid a shark	saw a dolphin	find a shipwreck

1. While Beth ___was sitting___ in a café, she ___ordered___ a salad.

2. David ___paid___ a few bills while he ___was sitting___ in a café.

3. Lily _____ coffee on her lap while she _____ in a café.

4. While Beth _____ in an elevator, she _____ a text
   message on her cell phone.

5. David _____ an old friend while he _____ in an
   elevator.

6. Lily _____ her glasses while she _____ in an
   elevator.

7. Beth _____ a shark while she _____ in the ocean.

8. While David _____ in the ocean, he _____ a dolphin.

9. While Lily _____ in the ocean, she _____ a shipwreck.

❏ **Exercise 28. Let's talk.** (Chart 2-6)

Your teacher will tell two students to perform a task. After they do, two other students will describe it. Only the teacher's book is open.

Example: To A: Write on the board.   To B: Open the door.

To STUDENT A: Please write your name on the board. (*Student A writes on the board.*)
                What are you doing?
    STUDENT A: I'm writing on the board.
      TEACHER: Good. Keep writing.

To STUDENT B: Open the door. (*Student B opens the door.*) What did you just do?
    STUDENT B: I opened the door.
To STUDENT A: Please stop writing.

To STUDENT C: Describe the two actions that just occurred, using *when*.
    STUDENT C: When (_____) opened the door, (_____) was writing on the board.

To STUDENT D: Now describe the actions, using *while*.
    STUDENT D: While (_____) was writing on the board, (_____) opened the door.

1. To A: Write a note to (_____).   To B: Knock on the door.

2. To A: Read your book.   To B: Take (_____)'s grammar book.

3. To A: Look at me.   To B: Leave the room.

4. To A: Put your head on your desk.   To B: Drop your pencil.

5. To A: Look under your desk.   To B: Begin doing your homework.

❏ **Exercise 29. Looking at grammar.** (Chart 2-6)

Read each pair of sentences and answer the question.

1. a. Julia was eating breakfast. She heard the breaking news* report.
   b. Sara heard the breaking news report. She ate breakfast.

   QUESTION: Who heard the news report during breakfast?

2. a. Carlo was fishing at the lake. A fish was jumping out of the water.
   b. James was fishing at the lake. A fish jumped out of the water.

   QUESTION: Who saw a fish jump just one time?

3. a. When the sun came out, Paul walked home.
   b. When the sun came out, Vicky was walking home.

   QUESTION: Who walked home after the sun came out?

---

breaking news = a special news report on the TV or radio

□ **Exercise 30. Reading.** (Chart 2-6)

Read the passage and then read the statements. Circle "T" for true and "F" for false.

The First Cell Phone

The first cell phone call took place* in 1973. A man named Martin Cooper made the first call. He was working for the Motorola communications company. When Cooper placed the call, he was walking down a street in New York. People stared at him and wondered about his behavior. This was before cordless phones,** so it looked very strange.

It took another ten years before Motorola had a phone to sell to the public. That phone weighed about a pound (.45 kilogram), and it was very expensive. Now, as you know, cell phones are small enough to put in a pocket, and millions of people around the world have them.

1. A customer for Motorola made the first cell phone call.	T	F
2. Many people looked at Cooper when he was talking on the phone.	T	F
3. In the 1970s, cordless phones were very popular.	T	F
4. A few years after the first call, Motorola sold phones to the public.	T	F
5. The first cell phone was very small.	T	F

□ **Exercise 31. Listening.** (Chart 2-6)

Listen to each conversation. Then listen again and complete the sentences with the words you hear.

CD 1
Track 22

At a checkout stand in a grocery store

1. A: Hi. _____ what you needed?

   B: Almost everything. I _____ for sticky rice, but I

   _____ it.

   A: _____ on aisle 10, in the Asian food section.

2. A: This is the express lane. Ten items only. It _____ like you have more than

   ten. _____ count them?

   B: I _____ I _____ ten. Oh, I _____ I have more.

   Sorry.

   A: The checkout stand next to me is open.

3. A: _____ any coupons you wanted to use?

   B: I _____ a couple in my purse, but I can't find them now.

   A: What _____ they for? I might have some extras here.

   B: One _____ for eggs, and the other _____ for ice cream.

   A: I think I have those.

---

*take place = occur, happen

**cordless phones = phones without cords to the receiver

Exercise 32. Looking at grammar. (Charts 1-1 and 2-6)
Underline the present progressive and past progressive verbs in the following conversations.
Discuss the way they are used. What are the similarities between the two tenses?

1. A: Where are Jan and Mark? Are they on vacation?
   B: Yes, they're traveling in Kenya for a few weeks.

2. A: I invited Jan and Mark to my birthday party, but they didn't come.
   B: Why not?
   A: They were on vacation. They were traveling in Kenya.

3. A: What was I talking about when the phone interrupted me? I forget!
   B: You were describing the Web site you found on the Internet yesterday.

4. A: I missed the beginning of the news report. What's the announcer talking about?
   B: She's describing damage from the earthquake in Pakistan.

❑ **Exercise 33. Looking at grammar.** (Chapter 1 and Charts 2-1 → 2-6)
Complete the sentences. Use the simple present, present progressive, simple past, or past
progressive form of the verbs in parentheses.

Part I.

Right now Toshi and Oscar (*sit*) ___are sitting___ in the library. Toshi (*do*)
                                        1

_____ his homework, but Oscar (*study, not*) _____. He
        2   3

(*stare*) _____ out the window. Toshi (*want*) _____ to know
              4   5

what Oscar (*look*) _____ at.
                          6

TOSHI: Oscar, what (*you, look*) _____ at?
                                          7

OSCAR: I (*watch*) _____ the skateboarder. Look at that
                          8

guy in the orange shirt. He (*turn*) _____ around
                                            9

in circles on his back wheels. He's amazing!

TOSHI: It (*be*) _____ easier than it (*look*) _____.
                      10   11

I can teach you some skateboarding basics if you'd like.
OSCAR: Great! Thanks!

Part II.

Yesterday Toshi and Oscar (*sit*) ___were sitting___ in the library. Toshi (*do*)
                                          12

_____ his homework, but Oscar (*study, not*) _____. He
        13   14

(*stare*) _____ out the window. Toshi (*want*) _____ to know
              15   16

what Oscar (*look*) _____ at. Oscar (*point*) _____ to the
                          17   18

skateboarder. He (*say*) _____ that he was amazing. Toshi (*offer*)
                              19

_____ to teach him some skateboarding basics.
        20

Exercise 34. Warm-up. (Chart 2-7)

Check (✓) the sentences that have this meaning:

    First action: We gathered our bags.

    Second action: The train arrived at the station.

1. ____ We gathered our bags before the train arrived at the station.

2. ____ Before the train arrived at the station, we gathered our bags.

3. ____ After we gathered our bags, the train arrived at the station.

4. ____ As soon as the train arrived at the station, we gathered our bags.

5. ____ We didn't gather our bags until the train arrived at the station.

2-7 Expressing Past Time: Using Time Clauses

(a) <u>After I finished my work,</u> <u>I went to bed.</u>
     time clause   main clause
 	
(b) <u>I went to bed</u> <u>after I finished my work.</u>
     main clause   time clause
	After I finished my work = a time clause*
	I went to bed = a main clause
	
	Examples (a) and (b) have the same meaning.
	
	A time clause can
	    (1) come in front of a main clause, as in (a).
	    (2) follow a main clause, as in (b).

(c) I went to bed ***after*** *I finished my work.*
 	
(d) ***Before*** *I went to bed,* I finished my work.
 	
(e) I stayed up ***until*** *I finished my work.*
 	
(f) ***As soon as*** *I finished my work,* I went to bed.
 	
(g) The phone rang ***while*** *I was watching* TV.
 	
(h) ***When*** *the phone rang,* I was watching TV.
	These words introduce time clauses:
	
	   after
	   before
	   until + *subject and verb* = a time clause
	   as soon as
	   while
	   when

	In (e): *until* = to that time and then no longer** In (f): *as soon as* = immediately after

	PUNCTUATION: Put a comma at the end of a time clause when the time clause comes first in a sentence (comes in front of the main clause):
	    time clause + *comma* + *main clause*
	    main clause + ***no*** *comma* + *time clause*

(i) When the phone ***rang,*** I ***answered*** it.	In a sentence with a time clause introduced by *when*, both the time clause verb and the main verb can be simple past. In this case, the action in the *when*-clause happened first. In (i): First: *The phone rang.* Then: *I answered it.*
(j) While I ***was doing*** my homework, my roommate ***was watching*** TV.	In (j): When two actions are in progress at the same time, the past progressive can be used in both parts of the sentence.

*A *clause* is a structure that has a subject and a verb.

****Until** can also be used to say that something does NOT happen before a particular time: *I didn't go to bed **until** I finished my work.*

❑ **Exercise 35. Looking at grammar.** (Chart 2-7)
Check (✓) all the clauses. Remember: a clause must have a subject and a complete verb.

1. _____ applying for a visa
2. _____ while the woman was applying for a visa
3. _____ the man took passport photos
4. _____ when the man took passport photos
5. _____ as soon as he finished
6. _____ he needed to finish
7. _____ after she sent her application
8. _____ sending her application

❑ **Exercise 36. Looking at grammar.** (Chart 2-7)
<u>Underline</u> the clauses. Then decide what happened first (1) and what happened second (2).

                            1   *2*

1. a. <u>After the taxi dropped me off</u>, <u>I remembered my coat in the backseat</u>.
   b. I remembered my coat in the backseat after the taxi dropped me off.

2. a. Before I got out of the taxi, I double-checked the address.
   b. Before I double-checked the address, I got out of the taxi.

3. a. As soon as I tipped the driver, he helped me with my luggage.
   b. As soon as the driver helped me with my luggage, I tipped him.

❑ **Exercise 37. Looking at grammar.** (Chart 2-7)
Combine each set of sentences into one sentence by using a time clause. Discuss correct punctuation.

1. *First:* I got home.

   Then: I ate dinner.

   After   *I got home, I ate dinner.*

     I ate dinner   after   *I got home.*

2. *First:* I unplugged the coffee pot.

   Then: I left my apartment this morning.

   Before _____

   _____ before _____

3. *First:* I lived on a farm.

   Then: I was seven years old.

   Until _____

   _____ until _____

4. *First:* I heard the doorbell.

   Then: I opened the door.

   As soon as _____

   _____ as soon as _____

5. *First:* It began to rain.

   Then: I stood under my umbrella.

   When _____

   _____ when _____

6. *At the same time:* I was lying in bed with the flu.

   My friends were swimming at the beach.

   While _____

   _____ while _____

□ **Exercise 38. Looking at grammar.** (Charts 2-1 → 2-7)
Complete the sentences. Use the simple past or the past progressive form of the verbs in parentheses. Use brackets to identify the time clauses.

1. My mom called me around 5:00. My husband came home a little after that. [When he

   (*get*) __got__ home,] I (*talk*) __was talking__ to my mom on the phone.

2. I (*buy*) _____ a small gift before I (*go*) _____ to the hospital

   yesterday to visit my friend.

3. Yesterday afternoon I (*go*) _____ to visit the Lopez family. When I (*get*)

   _____ there, Mrs. Lopez (*be*) _____ in the yard. She (*plant*)

   _____ flowers. Mr. Lopez (*be*) _____ in the garage.

   He (*change*) _____ the oil on his car. The kids (*play*)

   _____ in the front yard. In other words, while Mr. Lopez (*change*)

   _____ the oil in the car, the kids (*throw*) _____

   a ball in the yard.

4. I (*hit*) _____ my thumb while I (*use*) _____ the hammer.
   Ouch! That (*hurt*) _____.

5. As soon as we (*hear*) _____ about the hurricane, we (*begin*)

   _____ to get ready for the storm.

6. It was a long walk home. Mr. Chu (*get*) _____ tired and (*stop*)

   _____ after an hour. He (*rest*) _____ until he (*feel*)

   _____ strong enough to continue.

Exercise 39. Listening. (Chapter 1 and Charts 2-1 → 2-7)

Listen to the passage with your book closed. Then listen again and complete the sentences with the words you hear.

CD 1
Track 23

Jennifer's Problem

Jennifer _____ for an insurance company. When people _____ help
            1   2

with their car insurance, they _____ her. Right now it is 9:05 A.M., and Jennifer
                             3

_____ at her desk.
     4

She _____ to work on time this morning. Yesterday Jennifer _____ late
        5   6

to work because she _____ a minor auto accident. While she _____
               7   8

to work, her cell phone _____. She _____ for it.
                     9   10

While she _____ for her phone, Jennifer _____ control of the
              11   12

car. Her car _____ into a row of mailboxes beside the road and _____.
        13   14

Fortunately no one was hurt in the accident.

Jennifer _____ okay, but her car _____. It _____ repairs.
         15   16   17

Jennifer _____ very embarrassed now. She _____ a bad decision, especially
       18   19

since it is illegal to talk on a cell phone and drive at the same time where she lives.

☐ **Exercise 40. Warm-up.** (Chart 2-8)

Part I. Think about your experiences when you were a beginning learner of English. Check (✓) the statements that are true for you.

When I was a beginning learner of English, . . .

1. _____ I remained quiet when someone asked me a question.

2. _____ I checked my dictionary frequently.

3. _____ I asked people to speak very, very slowly.

4. _____ I translated sentences into my language a lot.

Part II. Look at the sentences you checked. Are these statements no longer true? If the answer is "yes," another way to express your idea is with *used to*. Which of these sentence(s) are true for you?

1. I used to remain quiet when someone asked me a question.

2. I used to check my dictionary frequently.

3. I used to ask people to speak very, very slowly.

4. I used to translate sentences into my language a lot.

2-8 Expressing Past Habit: *Used To*

(a) I *used to live* with my parents. Now I live in my own apartment.	*Used to* expresses a past situation or habit that no longer exists at present.
(b) Ann *used to be* afraid of dogs, but now she likes dogs.	FORM: ***used to*** + *the simple form of a verb*
(c) Al *used to smoke*, but he doesn't anymore.	
(d) *Did* you *used to live* in Paris? (OR *Did* you *use to live* in Paris?)	QUESTION FORM: ***did*** + *subject* + ***used to*** (OR ***did*** + *subject* + ***use to***)*
(e) I *didn't used to drink* coffee at breakfast, but now I always have coffee in the morning. (OR I *didn't use to drink* coffee.)	NEGATIVE FORM: ***didn't used to*** (OR ***didn't use to***)* *Didn't use(d) to* occurs infrequently. More commonly, people use *never* to express a negative idea with *used to*, as in (f).
(f) I *never used to drink* coffee at breakfast, but now I always have coffee in the morning.	

*Both forms (***used to*** and ***use to***) are possible in questions and negatives. English language authorities do not agree on which is preferable. This book uses both forms.

☐ **Exercise 41. Looking at grammar.** (Chart 2-8)
Make sentences with a similar meaning by using ***used to***. Some of the sentences are negative, and some of them are questions.

1. *When I was a child, I was shy. Now I'm not shy.*

   I ___used to be___ shy, but now I'm not.

2. *When I was young, I thought that people over 40 were old.*

   I _____ that people over 40 were old.

3. *Now you live in this city. Where did you live before you came here?*

   Where _____ ?

4. *Did you work for the phone company at some time in the past?*

   _____ for the phone company?

5. *When I was younger, I slept through the night. I never woke up in the middle of the night.*

   I _____ in the middle of the night, but now I do.

   I _____ through the night, but now I don't.

6. *When I was a child, I watched cartoons on TV. I don't watch cartoons anymore. Now I watch news programs.*

   I _____ cartoons on TV, but I don't anymore.

   I _____ news programs, but now I do.

7. *How about you?*

   What _____ on TV when you were little?

Exercise 42. Interview: find someone who . . . . (Chart 2-8)
Walk around the classroom. Make a question with **used to** for each item. When you find a person who says *"yes,"* write down his/her name and go on to the next question. Share a few of your answers with the class.

Find someone who used to . . .

1. play in the mud. → *Did you use to play in the mud?*
2. play with dolls or toy soldiers.
3. roller skate.
4. swing on a rope swing.
5. catch frogs or snakes.
6. get into trouble at school.
7. dress up in your mother's or father's clothes.

❑ **Exercise 43. Listening.** (Chart 2-8)

CD 1
Track 24

Used to is often pronounced "usta." Listen to the examples. Then complete the sentences with the non-reduced words you hear.

Examples: I used to (*usta*) ride my bike to work, but now I take the bus.
I didn't used to (*usta*) be late when I rode my bike to work.
Did you use to (*usta*) ride your bike to work?

1. I ___used to stay___ up past midnight, but now I often go to bed at 10:00 because I have an 8:00 class.

2. What time _____ to bed when you were a child?

3. Tom _____ tennis after work every day, but now he doesn't.

4. I _____ breakfast, but now I always have something to eat in the morning because I read that students who eat breakfast do better in school.

5. I _____ grammar, but now I do.

❑ **Exercise 44. Check your knowledge.** (Chart 2-8)
Edit the sentences. Correct the errors in verb tense usage.

1. Alex used to ~~living~~ *live* in Cairo.

2. Junko used to worked for an investment company.

3. Margo was used to teach English, but now she works at a publishing company.

4. Where you used to live?

5. I didn't was used to get up early, but now I do.

6. Were you used to live in Singapore?

7. My family used to going to the beach every weekend, but now we don't.

Exercise 45. Let's read and write. (Chapter 2)

Part I. Read the passage about a famous author. Then read the statements. Circle "T" for true and "F" for false.

J. K. Rowling

Did you know that J. K. Rowling used to be an English language teacher before she became successful as the author of the *Harry Potter* series? She taught English to students in Portugal. She lived there from 1991 to 1994. During that time, she also worked on her first *Harry Potter* book.

After she taught in Portugal, she went back to Scotland. By then she was a single mother with a young daughter. She didn't have much money, but she didn't want to return to teaching until she completed her book. Rowling enjoyed drinking coffee, so she did much of her writing in a café while her daughter took naps. She wrote quickly, and when her daughter was three, Rowling finished *Harry Potter and the Philosopher's Stone.**

Many publishers were not interested in her book. She doesn't remember how many rejection letters she got, maybe twelve. Finally a small publishing company, Bloomsbury, accepted it. Shortly after its publication, the book began to sell quickly, and Rowling soon became famous. Now there are seven *Harry Potter* books, and Rowling is one of the wealthiest and most successful women in the world.

1. Rowling finished the first *Harry Potter* book in 1993.	T	F
2. Rowling did a lot of writing in a café.	T	F
3. At first, publishers loved her work.	T	F
4. Soon after her book came out, many people bought it.	T	F
5. Rowling still works as a teacher.	T	F

Part II. Choose a writer or a singer you are interested in. Find information about this person's life. Make a list of important or interesting events. Put the information into a paragraph. Edit your verbs carefully.

---

*In the United States and India, this title was changed to *Harry Potter and the Sorcerer's Stone*.

Chapter 3
Future Time

❑ **Exercise 1. Warm-up.** (Chart 3-1)
Which sentences express future meaning? Do the future sentences have the same meaning or a different meaning?

1. The train is going to leave a few minutes late today.
2. The train left a few minutes late today.
3. The train will leave a few minutes late today.

3-1 Expressing Future Time: *Be Going To* and *Will*

Future		
	(a) I *am going to leave* at nine tomorrow morning.	***Be going to*** and ***will*** are used to express future time.
	(b) I *will leave* at nine tomorrow morning.	Examples (a) and (b) have the same meaning.
		Sometimes ***will*** and ***be going to*** express different meanings. The differences are discussed in Chart 3-5.
(c) Sam *is* in his office *this morning*.		***Today***, ***tonight***, and ***this +*** ***morning***, ***afternoon***, ***evening***, ***week***, *etc.*, can express present, past, or future time, as in (c) through (e).
(d) Ann *was* in her office *this morning* at eight, but now she's at a meeting.		
(e) Bob *is going to be* in his office *this morning* after his dentist appointment.		

NOTE: The use of *shall* (with *I* or *we*) to express future time is possible but is infrequent and quite formal; for example: ***I shall*** *leave at nine tomorrow morning.* ***We shall*** *leave at ten tomorrow morning.*

□ **Exercise 2. Listening.** (Chart 3-1)

Listen to each sentence. If it expresses future time, circle *yes*. If it does not, circle *no*.

Example: You will hear: The airport will be busy.
You will choose: (yes) no

At the airport

1. yes no   5. yes no

2. yes no   6. yes no

3. yes no   7. yes no

4. yes no   8. yes no

□ **Exercise 3. Warm-up.** (Chart 3-2)

Complete these future sentences (*be going to*) with the correct form of *be* (+ *not*). Make true statements.

1. I _am not_ going to sleep in* tomorrow morning.

2. Our teacher _is not_ going to retire next month.

3. We _are not_ going to have a class party next week.

4. *To a student next to you:* You _are not_ going to speak English tomorrow.

3-2 Forms with *Be Going To*	
(a) We *are going to be* late. (b) She*'s going to come* tomorrow. INCORRECT: *She's going to comes tomorrow.*	*Be going to* is followed by the simple form of the verb, as in (a) and (b).
(c) **Am** I **Is** he, she, it } *going to be* late? **Are** they, we, you	QUESTION FORM: *be* + subject + *going to*
(d) I *am not* He, She, It *is not* } *going to be* late. They, We, You *are not*	NEGATIVE FORM: *be* + *not* + *going to*
(e) "Hurry up! We're *gonna* be late!"	*Be going to* is more common in speaking and informal writing than in formal writing. In informal speaking, it is sometimes pronounced "gonna" /gənə/. "Gonna" is not usually a written form.

---

*sleep in = sleep late; not wake up early in the morning

□ **Exercise 4. Looking at grammar.** (Charts 3-1 and 3-2)
Complete the sentences with a form of *be going to* and the words in parentheses.

1. A: What (*you, do*) _are you going to do_ next?
   B: I (*pick*) _am going to pick_ up a prescription at the pharmacy.

2. A: Where (*Alex, go*) _is Alex going_ after work?
   B: He (*stop*) _is going to stop_ at the post office and run some other errands.*

3. A: (*you, finish*) _Are you going to finish_ the project soon?
   B: Yes, (*finish*) _I am going to finish_ it by noon today.

4. A: What (*Dr. Ahmad, talk*) _is Dr Ahmad going to talk_ about in her lecture tonight?
   B: She (*discuss*) _is going to discuss_ how to reduce health-care costs.

5. A: When (*you, call*) _are you going to call_ your sister?
   B: I (*call, not*) _am not going to call_ her. I (*text*) _am going to text_ her.

□ **Exercise 5. Let's talk: pairwork.** (Charts 3-1 and 3-2)
Work with a partner. Take turns asking and answering questions with *be going to*.

Example: what \ you \ do \ after class?
SPEAKER A: What are you going to do after class?
SPEAKER B: I'm going to get a bite to eat** after class.

Example: you \ watch TV \ tonight?
SPEAKER A: Are you going to watch TV tonight?
SPEAKER B: Yes, I'm going to watch TV tonight. OR No, I'm not going to watch TV tonight.

1. where \ you \ go \ after your last class \ today? _I'm going home_
2. what time \ you \ wake up \ tomorrow?
3. what \ you \ have \ for breakfast \ tomorrow?
4. you \ be \ home \ this evening? _Are you going to be home this evening_
5. where \ you \ be \ next year?
6. you \ become \ famous \ some day?
7. you \ take \ a trip \ sometime next year?
8. you \ do \ something unusual \ in the near future?

---

run errands = go somewhere to pick up or deliver something

**get a bite to eat* = get something to eat

□ **Exercise 6. Listening.** (Charts 3-1 and 3-2)

Part I. Listen to the pronunciation of the reduced forms of **going to** in the conversation.

CD 1
Track 26

Looking for an apartment

A: We're going to look for an apartment to rent this weekend.
B: Are you going to look in this area?
A: No, we're going to search in an area closer to our jobs.
B: Is the rent going to be cheaper in that area?
A: Yes, apartment rents are definitely going to be cheaper.
B: Are you going to need to pay a deposit?
A: I'm sure we're going to need to pay the first and last month's rent.

Part II. Listen to the conversation and write the non-reduced form of the words you hear.

A: Where ___*are you going to*___ move to?
 ¹

B: We _____ look for something outside the city. We
 ²

 _____ spend the weekend apartment-hunting.*
 ³

A: What fees _____ need to pay?
 ⁴

B: I think we _____ need to pay the first and last month's rent.
 ⁵

A: _____ there _____ be other fees?
 ⁶   ⁷

B: There _____ probably _____ be an application fee and a
 ⁸   ⁹

 cleaning fee. Also, the landlord _____ probably _____ run a
 ¹⁰   ¹¹

 credit check,** so we _____ need to pay for that.
 ¹²

□ **Exercise 7. Let's talk: interview.** (Chapters 1 and 2; Charts 3-1 and 3-2)
Walk around the room. Ask and answer questions using **what** + **do** + the given time expression. Share some of your classmates' answers with the class.

Example: this evening
SPEAKER A: What are you going to do this evening?
SPEAKER B: I'm going to get on the Internet for a while.

1. yesterday
2. tomorrow
3. right now
4. every day
5. a week from now

6. the day before yesterday
7. the day after tomorrow
8. last week
9. every week
10. this weekend

---

apartment-hunting = looking for an apartment

**run a credit check* = get information about a person's financial history including the employer's name, one's income, the
  amount of money in the bank, and a history of late or unpaid bills

58 CHAPTER 3

☐ **Exercise 8. Let's talk: pairwork.** (Chapters 1 and 2; Charts 3-1 and 3-2)
Work with a partner. Complete the conversation with your own words. Be creative! The conversation reviews the forms (statement, negative, question, short answer) of the simple present, simple past, and *be going to*.

Example:
SPEAKER A: I rode a skateboard to school yesterday.
SPEAKER B: Really? Wow! Do you ride a skateboard to school often?
SPEAKER A: Yes, I do. I ride a skateboard to school almost every day.
 Did you ride a skateboard to school yesterday?
SPEAKER B: No, I didn't. I came by helicopter.
SPEAKER A: Are you going to come to school by helicopter tomorrow?
SPEAKER B: No, I'm not. I'm going to ride a motorcycle to school tomorrow.

A: I _____ yesterday.

B: Really? Wow! _____ you _____ often?

A: Yes, I _____. I _____ almost every day.

 _____ you _____ yesterday?

B: No, I _____. I _____ .

A: Are you _____ tomorrow?

B: No, I _____. I _____ tomorrow.

☐ **Exercise 9. Warm-up.** (Chart 3-3)
Complete the sentences with *will* or *won't*.

1. It __won't__ rain tomorrow.

2. We __will__ study Chart 3-3 next.

3. I __won't__ teach the class next week.

4. *To your teacher:* You __wont__ need to assign homework for tonight.

3-3 Forms with *Will*

STATEMENT	I, You, She, He, It, We, They *will come* tomorrow.	
NEGATIVE	I, You, She, He, It, We, They *will not* (*won't*) *come* tomorrow.	
QUESTION	*Will* I, you, she, he, it, we, they *come* tomorrow?	
SHORT ANSWER	Yes, } I, you, she, he, it, we, they { *will.** No, } { *won't.*	
CONTRACTIONS	I'*ll* she'*ll* we'*ll* you'*ll* he'*ll* they'*ll* it'*ll* texting ,note FB Twitter	*Will* is usually contracted with pronouns in both speech and informal writing.
	Bob + *will* = "Bob'*ll*" the teacher + *will* = "the teacher'*ll*"	*Will* is often contracted with nouns in speech, but usually not in writing.

*Pronouns are NOT contracted with helping verbs in short answers.
    CORRECT: *Yes, I will.*
  INCORRECT: *Yes, I'll.*

❏ **Exercise 10. Listening.** (Chart 3-3)

Part I. Listen to the pronunciation of contractions with *will* in these sentences.

CD 1
Track 27

1. I'll be ready to leave soon.
2. You'll need to come.
3. He'll drive us.
4. She'll come later.
5. We'll get there a little late.
6. They'll wait for us.

Part II. Listen to the sentences and write the contractions you hear.

1. Don't wait up for me tonight. ___I'll___ be home late.

2. I paid the bill this morning. ___I will pay___ get my check in the next day or two.

3. We have the better team. ___We will___ probably win the game.

4. Henry twisted his ankle while running down a hill. ___He will___ probably take a break from running this week.

5. We can go to the beach tomorrow, but ___it will___ probably be too cold to go swimming.

6. I invited some guests for dinner. ___they will___ probably get here around seven.

7. Karen is doing volunteer work for a community health-care clinic this week. ___She will___ be gone a lot in the evenings.

❏ **Exercise 11. Listening.** (Chart 3-3)

Part I. Listen to the sentences. Notice the pronunciation of contractions with nouns + **will**.

CD 1
Track 28

At the doctor's office

1. The doctor'll be with you in a few minutes.
2. Your appointment'll take about an hour.
3. Your fever'll be gone in a few days.
4. Your stitches'll disappear over the next two weeks.
5. The nurse'll schedule your tests.
6. The lab'll have the results next week.
7. The receptionist at the front desk'll set up* your next appointment.

Part II. Listen to the sentences and write the words you hear. Write the full form of the contractions.

At the pharmacy

1. Your prescription ___will be___ ready in ten minutes.

2. The medicine ___will make___ you feel a little tired.

3. The pharmacist ___will   take___ your doctor's office.

4. This cough syrup ___will   help___ your cough.   *suppress stop coughing*.

5. Two aspirin ___will   be___ enough.

6. The generic** drug ___will costs___ less.

7. This information ___will   benefit___ all the side effects*** for this medicine.

❏ **Exercise 12. Warm-up.** (Chart 3-4)

How certain is the speaker in each sentence? Write the percentage next to each sentence: 100%, 90%, or 50%.

What is going to happen to gasoline prices?

1. ___50%___ Gas prices may rise.
2. ___50%___ Maybe gas prices will rise.
3. ___100%___ Gas prices will rise.
4. ___90%___ Gas prices will probably rise.
5. ___100%___ Gas prices are going to rise.
6. ___100%___ Gas prices won't rise.

---

set up = schedule

**generic* = medicine with no brand name

***side effects* = reactions, often negative, that a patient can have from a medicine

3-4 Certainty About the Future

100% sure	(a) I *will be* in class tomorrow. OR I *am going to be* in class tomorrow.	In (a): The speaker uses *will* or *be going to* because he feels sure about his future activity. He is stating a fact about the future.
90% sure	(b) Po *will probably be* in class tomorrow. OR Po *is probably going to be* in class tomorrow.	In (b): The speaker uses *probably* to say that he expects Po to be in class tomorrow, but he is not 100% sure. He's almost sure, but not completely sure.

	(c) Anna *probably won't be* in class tomorrow.
	OR
	Anna *probably isn't going to be* in class tomorrow.
		Word order with *probably:**
		  (1) in a statement, as in (b):
		    helping verb + *probably*
		  (2) with a negative verb, as in (c):
		    probably + *helping verb*

50% sure	(d) Ali *may come* to class tomorrow. OR Ali *may not come* to class tomorrow. I don't know what he's going to do.	*May* expresses a future possibility: maybe something will happen, and maybe it won't happen.** In (d): The speaker is saying that maybe Ali will come to class, or maybe he won't come to class. The speaker is guessing.
	(e) *Maybe* Ali *will come* to class, and *maybe* he *won't*. OR *Maybe* Ali *is going to come* to class, and *maybe* he *isn't*.	*Maybe* + *will/be going to* gives the same meaning as *may*. Examples (d) and (e) have the same meaning. *Maybe* comes at the beginning of a sentence.

*Probably is a midsentence adverb. See Chart 1-3, p. 10, for more information about the placement of midsentence adverbs.
**See Chart 7-3, p. 182, for more information about *may*.

☐ **Exercise 13. Listening.** (Chart 3-4)

Listen to the sentences. Decide how certain the speaker is in each one: 100%, 90%, or 50%.

CD 1
Track 29

Example: You will hear: The bank will be open tomorrow.

             You will write: *100%*

My day tomorrow

1. _____

2. _____

3. _____

4. _____

5. _____

6. _____

❑ **Exercise 14. Looking at grammar.** (Chart 3-4)
For each situation, predict what probably will happen and what probably won't happen. Use either **will** or **be going to**. Include **probably** in your prediction.

1. Antonio is late to class almost every day.
   (be on time tomorrow? be late again?)
   → *Antonio probably won't be on time tomorrow. He'll probably be late again.* *going ...* *She's going* *probably*

2. Rosa has a terrible cold. She feels miserable. *Rosa is probably not going.*
   (go to work tomorrow? stay home and rest?) *Rosa probably won't go to work tomorrow*
   She'll probably stay home and rest

3. Sami didn't sleep at all last night. *She probably will* *go to bed early tonight.*
   (go to bed early tonight? stay up all night again tonight?) *will*
   She probably won't stay up all night again tonight.

4. Gina loves to run, but right now she has sore knees and a sore ankle.
   (run in the marathon race this week? skip the race?) *She probably won't run in marathon*
   race this week. She'll skip the race *probably*

❑ **Exercise 15. Looking at grammar.** (Chart 3-4)
Rewrite the sentences using the words in parentheses.

1. I may be late. (*maybe*)

   Maybe I will be late.

2. Lisa may not get here. (*maybe*)

   Maybe Lisa will not get here

3. Maybe you will win the contest. (*may*)

   You may win the contest .

4. The plane may land early. (*maybe*)

   Maybe the plane will land early

5. Maybe Sergio won't pass the class. (*may*)

   Sergio may not pass the class

❑ **Exercise 16. Let's talk: interview.** (Chart 3-4)
Walk around the room. Ask and answer questions. Ask two classmates each question. Answer the questions using **will, be going to,** or **may.** Include **probably** or **maybe** as appropriate. Share some of your classmates' answers with the class.

Example: What will you do after class tomorrow?
   → *I'll probably go back to my apartment.* OR *I'm not sure. I may go to the bookstore.*

1. What will the weather be like tomorrow?
2. Where will you be tomorrow afternoon?
3. What are you going to do on your next vacation?
4. Who will be the most famous celebrity next year?
5. What will a phone look like ten years from now?
6. Think about forms of communication (like email, social websites, phone, texting, etc.).
   What do you think will be the most common form ten years from now?
7. When do you think scientists will discover a cure for cancer?

□ **Exercise 17. Listening.** (Chart 3-4)

Think about life 100 years from now. What will it be like? Listen to each sentence. Do you agree or disagree? Circle *yes* or *no*. Discuss your answers.

CD 1
Track 30

Predictions about the future

1.	yes	no	6.	yes	no
2.	yes	no	7.	yes	no
3.	yes	no	8.	yes	no
4.	yes	no	9.	yes	no
5.	yes	no	10.	yes	no

□ **Exercise 18. Reading, grammar, and speaking.** (Chart 3-4)

Part I. Read the passage.

An Old Apartment

Ted and Amy live in an old, run-down apartment and want to move. The building is old and has a lot of problems. The ceiling leaks when it rains. The faucets drip. The toilet doesn't always flush properly. The windows don't close tightly, and heat escapes from the rooms in the winter. In the summer, it is very hot because there is no air conditioner.

Their apartment is in a dangerous part of town. Ted and Amy both take the bus to work and have to walk a long distance to the bus stop. Their apartment building doesn't have laundry facilities, so they also have to walk to a laundromat to wash their clothes. They are planning to have children in the near future, so they want a park or play area nearby for their children. A safe neighborhood is very important.

Part II. Ted and Amy are thinking about their next apartment and are making a list of what they want and don't want. Complete the sentences with *will* or *won't*.

Our next apartment

1. It ___won't___ have leaky faucets.

2. The toilet _____ flush properly.

64 CHAPTER 3

3. It _____ have windows that close tightly.

4. There _____ be air-conditioning for hot days.

5. It _____ be in a dangerous part of town.

6. It _____ be near a bus stop.

7. There _____ be laundry facilities in the building.

8. We _____ need to walk to a laundromat.

9. A play area _____ be nearby.

Part III. Imagine you are moving to a new home. Decide the six most important things you want your home to have (*It will have . . .*). You can brainstorm ideas in small groups and then discuss your ideas with the class.

□ **Exercise 19. Warm-up.** (Chart 3-5) *before*
In which conversation does Speaker B have a prior plan (a plan made before the moment of speaking)?

1. A: Oh, are you leaving? *plan*
   B: Yes. I'm going to pick up my children at school. They have dentist appointments. *yes*

2. A: Excuse me, Mrs. Jones. The nurse from your son's school is on the phone. He's got a fever and needs to go home.
   B: Okay. Please let them know I'll be there in 20 minutes. *No*

3-5 *Be Going To* vs. *Will*	
(a) She *is going to succeed* because she works hard.	*Be going to* and *will* mean the same when they are used to make <u>predictions</u> about the future.
(b) She *will succeed* because she works hard.	Examples (a) and (b) have the same meaning.
(c) I bought some wood because I *am going to build* a bookcase for my apartment.	*Be going to* (but not *will*) is used to express a prior plan (i.e., a plan made before the moment of speaking).
	In (c): The speaker plans to build a bookcase.
(d) This chair is too heavy for you to carry alone. I *'ll help* you.	*Will* (but not *be going to*) is used to express a decision the speaker makes at the moment of speaking.
	In (d): The speaker decides or volunteers to help at the immediate present moment; he did not have a prior plan or intention to help.

□ **Exercise 20. Looking at grammar.** (Charts 3-1 → 3-5)
Discuss the *italicized* verb(s). Is the speaker expressing plans made before the moment of speaking (prior plans)? If so, circle *yes*. If not, circle *no*.

PRIOR PLAN?

Desition in the moment

1. A: Did you return Carmen's phone call?
   B: No, I forgot. Thanks for reminding me. I'*ll call* her right away.   yes   no

2. A: I'*m going to call* Martha later this evening. Do you want to talk to
      her too?   yes   no
   B: No, I don't think so.

3. A: Jakob is in town for a few days.
   B: Really? Great! I'*ll give* him a call. Is he staying at his Aunt Lara's?   yes   no

4. A: Alex is in town for a few days.
   B: I know. He called me yesterday. We'*re going to get* together for dinner
      after I get off work tonight.   yes   no

5. A: I need some fresh air. I'm going for a short walk.
   B: I'*ll come* with you.   yes   no

6. A: I'*m going to take* Hamid to the airport tomorrow morning.
      Do you want to come along?   yes   no
   B: Sure.

7. A: We'*re going to go* to Uncle Scott's over the break.   yes   no
      Are you interested in coming with us?
   B: Gee, I don't know. I'*ll think* about it. When do you need to know?   yes   no

□ **Exercise 21. Looking at grammar.** (Charts 3-1 → 3-5)
Restate the sentences orally or in writing. Use **be going to**.

My trip to Thailand

1. I'm planning to be away for three weeks.
2. My husband and I are planning to stay in small towns and camp on the beach.
3. We're planning to bring a tent.
4. We're planning to celebrate our wedding anniversary there.
5. My father, who was born in Thailand, is planning to join us, but he's planning to stay in a hotel.

□ **Exercise 22. Looking at grammar.** (Charts 3-1 → 3-5)
Complete the sentences with **be going to** or **will**. Use **be going to** to express a prior plan.

1. A: Are you going by the post office today? I need to mail this letter.
   B: Yeah, I _'ll_____ mail it for you.
   A: Thanks.

2. A: Why are you carrying that package?

   B: It's for my sister. I _'m going to_ mail it to her.

3. A: Why did you buy so many eggs?

   B: I _am going to_ make a special dessert.

4. A: I have a book for Joe from Rachel. I'm not going to see him today.

   B: Let me have it. I ____will____ give it to him. He's in my algebra class.

5. A: Did you apply for the job you told me about?

   B: No, I _am going to_ take a few more classes and get more experience.

6. A: Did you know that I found an apartment on 45th Street? I'm planning to move soon.

   B: That's a nice area. I _am going to_ help you move if you like.

   A: Great! I'd really appreciate that.

7. A: Why can't you come to the party?

   B: We _are going to_ be with my husband's family that weekend.

8. A: I have to leave. I don't have time to finish the dishes.

   B: No problem. I ____will____ do them for you.

9. A: Do you want to go to the meeting together?

   B: Sure. I ____will____ meet you by the elevator in ten minutes.

□ **Exercise 23. Listening.** (Chart 3-1 → 3-5)
Listen to each question and circle the <u>expected</u> response (a. or b.).

CD 1
Track 31

1. a. Sure, I'll do it.
   b. Sure, I'm going to do it.

2. a. Yes. I'll look at laptop computers.
   b. Yes. I'm going to look at laptop computers.

3. a. Yeah, but I'll sell it. I don't need it now that I live in the city.
   b. Yeah, but I'm going to sell it. I don't need it now that I live in the city.

4. a. Uh, I'll get your coat and we can go.
   b. Uh, I'm going to get your coat and we can go.

□ **Exercise 24. Warm-up.** (Chart 3-6)
Complete the sentences with your own words. What do you notice about the verb tenses and the words in **boldface**?

1. **After** I leave school today, I'm going to _____.

2. **Before** I come to school tomorrow, I will _____.

3. **If** I have time this weekend, I will _____.

3-6 Expressing the Future in Time Clauses and *If*-Clauses

time clause
(a) ⌐*Before I go to class tomorrow,*¬ I'm going to eat breakfast.
 	
                 time clause
(b) I'm going to eat breakfast ⌐*before I go to class*
tomorrow.¬
	In (a) and (b): *before I go to class tomorrow* is a future time clause.
	
	   before
	   after
	   when } + subject and verb = a time clause
	   as soon as
	   until
	   while

(c) *Before I go home tonight,* I'm going to stop at the market. (d) I'm going to eat dinner at 6:00 tonight. *After I eat dinner,* I'm going to study in my room. (e) I'll give Rita your message *when I see her.* (f) It's raining right now. *As soon as the rain **stops**,* I'm going to walk downtown. (g) I'll stay home *until the rain **stops**.* (h) *While you're at school tomorrow,* I'll be at work.	The simple present is used in a future time clause. ***Will*** and ***be going to*** are NOT used in a future time clause. INCORRECT: *Before I will go to class, I'm going to eat breakfast.* INCORRECT: *Before I am going to go to class tomorrow, I'm going to eat breakfast.* All of the example sentences (c) through (h) contain future time clauses.
(i) Maybe it will rain tomorrow. *If it **rains** tomorrow,* I'm going to stay home.	In (i): *If it rains tomorrow* is an ***if***-clause. ***if*** + subject and verb = an ***if***-clause When the meaning is future, the simple present (not ***will*** or ***be going to***) is used in an ***if***-clause.

☐ **Exercise 25. Looking at grammar.** (Chart 3-6)
Choose the correct verbs.

1. Before *I'm going to return,* (*I return*) to my country next year, I'm going to finish my graduate degree in computer science.

2. The boss will review your work after she *will return, returns* from vacation next week.

3. I'll give you a call on my cell phone as soon as my plane *will land, lands.*

4. I don't especially like my current job, but I'm going to stay with this company until I *find, will find* something better.

5. When you *will be, are* in Australia next month, are you going to go snorkeling at the Great Barrier Reef?

6. I need to know what time the meeting starts. Please be sure to call me as soon as you *find out, will find out* anything about it.

7. If it *won't be, isn't* cold tomorrow, we'll go to the beach.
   If it *is, will be* cold tomorrow, we'll go to a movie.

□ **Exercise 26. Looking at grammar.** (Chart 3-6)

Use the given verbs to complete the sentences. Use *be going to* for the future.

1. *take, read*

   I _*'m going to read*_ the textbook **before** I _*take*_ the final exam next month.

2. *return, call*

   Mr. Lee _____ his wife **as soon as** he _____

   to the hotel tonight.

3. *make, go*

   Before I _____ to my job interview tomorrow, I _____

   a list of questions I want to ask about the company.

4. *visit, take*

   We _____ Sabrina to our favorite seafood restaurant **when** she

   _____ us this weekend.

5. *keep, call*

   I _____ my cell* on **until** Lena _____.**

6. *miss, understand not*

   If Adam _____ the meeting, he _____ the next project.

7. *get, eat*

   If Eva _____ home early, we _____ dinner at 6:30.

□ **Exercise 27. Let's talk: pairwork.** (Chart 3-6)

Work with a partner. Read each sentence and make a follow-up sentence using *if*. Pay special attention to the verb in the *if*-clause. Share some of your partner's answers with the class.

Example: Maybe you'll go downtown tomorrow.
PARTNER A: If I **go** downtown tomorrow, I'm going to buy some new clothes.
PARTNER B: If I **go** downtown tomorrow, I'm going to look at laptop computers.

1. Maybe you'll have some free time tomorrow.
2. Maybe it'll rain tomorrow.
3. Maybe it won't rain tomorrow.
4. Maybe the teacher will be absent next week.

---

*cell = cell phone

**Time clauses beginning with *until* usually <u>follow</u> the main clause.
   Usual: I'm going to keep my cell on *until Lena calls*.
   Possible but less usual: *Until Lena calls*, I'm going to keep my cell on.

Change roles.

5. Maybe you'll be tired tonight.
6. Maybe you won't be tired tonight.
7. Maybe it'll be nice tomorrow.
8. Maybe we won't have class on Monday.

☐ **Exercise 28. Looking at grammar.** (Chart 3-6)

Look at Sue's day planner. She has a busy morning. Make sentences using the word in parentheses and the given information. Use *be going to* for the future.

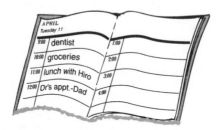

1. (after)   go to the dentist \ pick up groceries
   → *After Sue goes to the dentist, she is going to pick up groceries.*
2. (before)   go to the dentist \ pick up groceries
3. (before)   have lunch with Hiro \ pick up groceries
4. (after)   have lunch with Hiro \ pick up groceries
5. (before)   have lunch with Hiro \ take her father to his doctor's appointment

☐ **Exercise 29. Reading, grammar, and writing.** (Chart 3-6)

Part I. Read the passage.

The Home of the Future

What will the home of the future look like? Imagine life 50 years from now. What kinds of homes will people have? Here are some interesting possibilities.

The living room walls will have big plasma screens. Instead of pictures on the wall, the screens will show changing scenery. If walls have different scenes, people may not even want many windows. As you know, fewer windows will make it easier to heat a house.

The house will have special electronic features, and people will control them with a remote control. For example, a person can lie in bed at night and lock all the doors in his or her house with one push of a button. Before someone arrives home from work, the remote will turn on the lights, preheat the oven, and even turn on favorite music. The bathroom faucets will have a memory. They will remember the temperature a person likes, and when he or she turns on the water in the tub or shower, it will be at the correct temperature. Maybe bedroom closets will have racks that move automatically at the touch of a button. When the weather is cold, the racks will deliver clothes that keep a person warm, and on warm days, the racks will deliver clothes that keep a person cool.

Finally, homes will be more energy-efficient. Most of the heat will probably come from the sun. Of course, solar heat will be popular because it will be inexpensive.

Which ideas do you like? Which ones do you think you may see in your lifetime?

Part II. Complete the sentences with information from the passage. More than one answer may be possible.

1. When people look at the living room walls, they _____.

2. When a person is coming home from work, the remote _____.

3. As soon as a person gets home, _____.

4. If the bathroom faucets have a memory, they _____.

5. Before a person goes to sleep, _____.

6. When a person pushes a button, the closet racks _____.

7. When the weather is cold, the closet racks _____.

8. If a home has solar heat, the cost of heating the home _____.

Part III. Imagine you can build your dream house — 50 years from now. It can be any type of house you want. Think about the style, size, kinds of rooms, location, etc. Write a paragraph about this house. Begin with this topic sentence: *My dream house will have . . . .*

❑ **Exercise 30. Looking at grammar.** (Chapters 1, 2 and Charts 3-1 → 3-6)
Complete each sentence with a form of the words in parentheses. Read carefully for time expressions.

1. Before Tim (*go*) __goes__ to bed, he always (*brush*) __brushes__ his teeth.

2. Before Tim (*go*) _____ to bed later tonight, he (*email*) _____ his girlfriend.

3. Before Tim (*go*) _____ to bed last night, he (*take*) _____ a shower.

4. While Tim (*take*) _____ a shower last night, the phone (*ring*)

   _____ .

5. As soon as the phone (*ring*) _____ last night, Tim (*jump*) _____ out of the shower to answer it.

6. As soon as Tim (*get*) _____ up tomorrow morning, he (*brush*)

   _____ his teeth.

7. Tim always (*brush*) _____ his teeth as soon as he (*get*) _____ up.

❑ **Exercise 31. Warm-up.** (Chart 3-7)
Which sentences express future time?

1. I'm catching a train tonight. ✓
2. I'm going to take the express train. ✓
3. The trip will only take an hour. ✓

3-7 Using the Present Progressive to Express Future Time

(a) Tim *is going to come* to the party tomorrow. (b) Tim *is coming* to the party tomorrow. (c) We *'re going to go* to a movie tonight. (d) We *'re going* to a movie tonight. (e) I *'m going to stay* home this evening. (f) I *'m staying* home this evening. (g) Ann *is going to fly* to Chicago next week. (h) Ann *is flying* to Chicago next week.	The present progressive can be used to express future time. Each pair of example sentences has the same meaning. The present progressive describes *definite plans for the future, plans that were made before the moment of speaking.* A future meaning for the present progressive is indicated either by future time words (e.g., *tomorrow*) or by the situation.*
(i) You *'re going to laugh* when you hear this joke. (j) INCORRECT: *You're laughing when you hear this joke.*	The present progressive is NOT used for predictions about the future. In (i): The speaker is predicting a future event. In (j): The present progressive is not possible; laughing is a prediction, not a planned future event.

*COMPARE: Present situation: *Look! Mary's coming. Do you see her?*
Future situation: *Are you planning to come to the party? Mary's coming. So is Alex.*

□ **Exercise 32. Looking at grammar.** (Chart 3-7)

Complete the conversations with the correct form of the given verbs. Use the present progressive if possible. Discuss whether the present progressive expresses present or future time.

1. A: What (*you, do*) ___are you doing___ tomorrow afternoon?

   B: I (*go*) ___am going___ to the mall. How about you? What (*you, do*)

   ___are you going___ tomorrow afternoon?

   A: I (*go*) ___am going___ to a movie with Dan. After the movie, we (*go*)

   ___are going___ out to dinner. Would you like to meet us for dinner?

   B: No, thanks. I can't. I (*meet*) ___am meeting___ my son for dinner.

2. A: What (*you, major*) ___are your majoring___ in?

   B: I (*major*) ___am majoring___ in engineering.

   A: What courses (*you, take*) ___are you taking___ next semester?

   B: I (*take*) ___am taking___ English, math, and physics.

3. A: Stop! Paula! What (*you, do*) ___are you doing___ ?

   B: I (*cut*) ___am cutting___ my hair, Mom.

   A: Oh dear!

□ **Exercise 33. Listening.** (Chart 3-7)

Listen to the conversation and write the words you hear.

CD 1
Track 32 **Going on vacation**

A: I _____ on vacation tomorrow.

B: Where _____ you _____?

A: To San Francisco.

B: How are you getting there? _____ you _____ or _____

your car?

A: I _____. I have to be at the airport by seven tomorrow morning.

B: Do you need a ride to the airport?

A: No, thanks. I _____ a taxi.

What about you? Are you planning to go somewhere over vacation?

B: No. I _____ here.

□ **Exercise 34. Let's talk: pairwork.** (Chart 3-7)

Work with a partner. Tell each other your plans. Use the present progressive.

Example: What are your plans for this evening?
SPEAKER A: I'm staying home. How about you?
SPEAKER B: I'm going to a coffee shop to work on my paper for a while. Then I'm meeting
some friends for a movie.

What are your plans . . .
1. for the rest of today?
2. for tomorrow?
3. for this coming weekend?
4. for next month?

□ **Exercise 35. Let's write.** (Chart 3-7)

Imagine you have a week's vacation. You can go anywhere you want. Think of a place you
would like to visit. Write a paragraph in which you describe your trip. Use the present
progressive where appropriate.

Example: My friend Sara and I are taking a trip to Nashville, Tennessee. Nashville is the
home of country music, and Sara loves country music. She wants to go to lots of shows.
I don't know anything about country music, but I'm looking forward to going to Nashville.
We're leaving Friday afternoon as soon as Sara gets off work. (Etc.)

Possible questions to answer in your paragraph:
1. Where are you going?
2. When are you leaving?
3. Who are you going with, or are you traveling alone?
4. How are you getting there?
5. Where are you staying?
6. Are you visiting anyone? Who?
7. How long are you staying there?
8. When are you getting back?

□ **Exercise 36. Warm-up.** (Chart 3-8)
Circle all the possible completions.

1. Soccer season begins _____ .
   a. today   b. next week   c. yesterday

2. The mall opens _____ .
   a. next Monday   b. tomorrow   c. today

3. There is a party _____ .
   a. last week   b. tonight   c. next weekend

4. The baby cries _____ .
   a. every night   b. tomorrow night   c. in the evenings

schedualing -time

3-8 Using the Simple Present to Express Future Time

(a) My plane **arrives** at 7:35 *tomorrow evening*. (b) Tim's new job **starts** *next week*. (c) The semester **ends** *in two more weeks*. (d) There **is** a meeting at ten *tomorrow morning*.	The simple present can express future time when events are on a definite schedule or timetable. Only a few verbs are used in the simple present to express future time. The most common are **arrive, leave, start, begin, end, finish, open, close, be.**
(e) INCORRECT: *I wear my new suit to the wedding next week.* CORRECT: *I am wearing/am going to wear my new suit to the wedding next week.*	Most verbs CANNOT be used in the simple present to express future time. For example, in (e): The verb *wear* does not express an event on a schedule or timetable. It cannot be used in the simple present to express future time.

□ **Exercise 37. Looking at grammar.** (Charts 3-7 and 3-8)
Circle all the possible completions.

1. The concert _____ at eight tonight.
   a. begins   b. is beginning   c. is going to begin

2. I _____ seafood pasta for dinner tonight.
   a. make   b. am making   c. am going to make

3. I _____ to school tomorrow morning. I need the exercise.
   a. walk   b. am walking   c. am going to walk

4. The bus _____ at 8:15 tomorrow morning.
   a. leaves   b. is leaving   c. is going to leave

5. I _____ the championship game on TV at Jonah's house tomorrow.
   a. watch   b. am watching   c. am going to watch

6. The game _____ at 1:00 tomorrow afternoon.
   a. starts   b. is starting   c. is going to start

7. Alexa's plane _____ at 10:14 tomorrow morning.
    a. arrives   b. is arriving   c. is going to arrive

8. I can't pick her up tomorrow, so she _____ the airport bus into the city.
    a. takes   b. is taking   c. is going to take

9. Jonas _____ to several companies. He hopes to get a full-time job soon.
    a. applies   b. is applying   c. is going to apply

10. School _____ next Wednesday. I'm excited for vacation to begin.
    a. ends   b. is ending   c. is going to end

□ **Exercise 38. Warm-up.** (Chart 3-9)
Choose the picture that best describes this sentence: Joanne is about to leave for work.

Picture A

Picture B

3-9 Immediate Future: Using *Be About To*	
(a) Ann's bags are packed, and she is wearing her coat. She *is about to leave* for the airport. (b) Shhh. The movie *is about to begin*.	The idiom *be about to do something* expresses an activity that will happen *in the immediate future*, usually within minutes or seconds. In (a): Ann is going to leave sometime in the next few minutes. In (b): The movie is going to start in the next few minutes.

□ **Exercise 40. Game.** (Chart 3-9)

Think of an action to perform. Don't tell what it is. Get ready to do it, but just before you perform the action, ask the class to describe what you are about to do. Perform with a partner if you wish. Use your own ideas or suggestions from the list.

Example: (Students A and B hold out their hands to each other.)
Possible guess: They are about to shake hands.

Suggestions:

stand up	sneeze	pick up a pen	erase a word
open the door	fall down	close your book	look up a word
close the window	cry	write on the board	get out your wallet

□ **Exercise 41. Warm-up.** (Chart 3-10)

Circle all the possible completions for each sentence.

1. Fifteen years from now, my wife and I will retire and _____ all over the world.

   a. will travel
   b. travel
   c. traveling
   d. going to travel
   e. are traveling
   f. traveled

2. I opened the door and _____ my friend to come in.

   a. will invite
   b. invite
   c. inviting
   d. am going to invite
   e. am inviting
   f. invited

3-10 Parallel Verbs

V and V (a) Jim *makes* his bed *and* *cleans* up his room every morning. (b) Anita *called* and *told* me about her new job.	Often a subject has two verbs that are connected by *and*. We say that the two verbs are parallel: V + *and* + V *makes and cleans* = parallel verbs
(c) Ann *is cooking* dinner *and* (is) *talking* on the phone at the same time. (d) I *will stay* home *and* (will) *study* tonight. (e) I *am going to stay* home *and* (am going to) *study* tonight.	It is not necessary to repeat a helping verb (an auxiliary verb) when two verbs are the same tense and are connected by *and*.

□ **Exercise 42. Looking at grammar.** (Chart 3-10)

Complete each sentence with the correct form of the verbs in parentheses.

1. When I (*walk*) ___walked___ into the living room yesterday, Grandpa (*read*)
   ___was reading___ a newspaper and (*listen*) ___listening___ to music.

2. Helen will graduate soon. She (*move*) ___will move___ to New York and (*look*)
   ___look___ for a job after she (*graduate*) ___graduates___.
   ___adv. clause___ ___present tense___.

3. Every day my neighbor (*call*) ___calls___ me on the phone and (*complain*)
   ___complains___ about the weather.

4. Look at Erin. She (*cry*) ___is crying___ and (*laugh*) ___laughing___ at the
   same time! I wonder if she is happy or sad?

5. I'm beat.* I can't wait to get home. After I (*get*) ___get___ home, I (*take*)
   ___will take___ a hot bath and (*go*) ___go___ to bed.

6. (While Paul (*carry*) ___was carrying___ brushes and paint and (*climb*)
   ___climbing___ a ladder, *then* (a bee (*land*) ___was landing___ on his
   arm and (*sting*) ___stung___ him.) Paul (*drop*) ___dropped___ the paint and
   (*spill*) ___spilled___ it all over the ground.

☑ **Exercise 43. Looking at grammar.** (Chapters 1 → 3)
Complete each sentence with the correct form of the words in parentheses.

1. I usually (*ride*) ___ride___ my bike to work in the morning, but it (*rain*)
   ___was raining___ when I left my house early this morning, so I (*take*)
   ___took___ the bus. After I (*get*) ___got___ to work, I (*find*) ___found___
   out** that I had left my briefcase on the bus.

2. A: Are you going to take the kids to the amusement park tomorrow morning?

   B: Yes. It (*open*) ___opens___ at 10:00. If we (*leave*) ___leave___ here at 9:30,
   we'll get there at 9:55. The kids can be the first ones in the park.

3. A: Ouch! I (*cut*) ___cut___ my finger. It (*bleed*) ___is bleeding___!

   B: Put pressure on it. I (*get*) ___will get___ some antibiotics and a bandage.

   A: Thanks.

4. A: Your phone (*ring*) ___is ringing___.

   B: I (*know*) ___know___.

   A: (*you, want*) ___Do you want___ me to get it?

   B: No.

   A: Why don't you want to answer your phone?

   B: I (*answer, not*) ___don't answer___ during dinner.

---

*be beat = be very, very tired; be exhausted

**find out = discover; learn

5. A: Look! There (be) ___is___ a police car behind us. Its lights (flash)

   _____.

   B: I (know) _____. I (know) _____. I (see) _____ it.

   A: What (go) ___is going___ on? (you, speed) _____?

   B: No, I'm not. I (drive) _____ the speed limit.

   A: Oh, look. The police car (pass) ___are going to pass___ us.

   B: Whew!

□ **Exercise 44. Listening.** (Chapters 1→ 3)

Part I. Complete the sentences with the words you hear.

CD 1
Track 33

At a Chinese restaurant

   A: Okay, let's all open our fortune cookies.

   B: What _____ yours _____?

   A: Mine says, "You _____ an unexpected gift." Great! Are you

   planning to give me a gift soon?

   B: Not that I know of. Mine says, "Your life _____ long and happy."

   Good. I _____ a long life.

   C: Mine says, "A smile _____ all communication problems." Well,

   that's good! After this, when I _____ someone,

   _____ just _____ at them.

   D: My fortune is this: "If you _____ hard, you _____ successful."

   A: Well, it _____ like all of us _____ good luck in the future!

Part II. Work in small groups. Together, write a fortune for each person in your group.

□ **Exercise 45. Check your knowledge.** (Chapters 1→ 3)

Edit the paragraph. Correct errors in verb tense usage.

My Cousin Pablo

   I want to tell you about Pablo. He ~~is~~ my cousin. He ~~comes~~ *came* here four years ago. Before he

came here, he ~~study~~ *studied* statistics in Chile. He ~~leaves~~ *left* Chile and ~~move~~ *moved* here. He went to New York

and ~~stay~~ *stayed* there for three years. He graduated from New York University. Now he ~~study~~ *studies* at this

school. After he ~~finish~~ *finishes* his master's degree, he ~~return~~ *is going to* Chile.

Exercise 46. Let's write. (Chapter 3)

Pretend that you have the ability to see into the future. Choose a person you know (classmate, teacher, family member, friend) and tell this person in writing about his/her future life. Give some interesting or unusual details.

Example:

My Son's Future

My son is 15 years old now. In the future, he will have a happy and successful life. After he finishes high school, he will go to college. He really loves to study math. He also loves to build bridges out of toothpicks. He will study engineering, and he will specialize in bridge building. He likes to travel, so he will get a job with an international company and build bridges around the world. He will also work in poor villages, and his bridges will connect rural areas. This will make people's lives better. I will be very proud of him.

Chapter 4
Present Perfect and Past Perfect

☐ **Exercise 1. Warm-up.** (Chart 4-1)
Do you know the past participle form of these verbs? Complete the chart. What is the difference between the past participle forms in items 1–4 and 5–8?

Simple Form	Simple Past	Past Participle
1. stay	stayed	_stayed_
2. work	worked	_worked_
3. help	helped	_____
4. visit	visited	_____
5. go	went	_gone_
6. begin	began	_begun_
7. write	wrote	_____
8. see	saw	_____

4-1 Past Participle

	Simple Form	Simple Past	Past Participle	
REGULAR VERBS	finish stop wait	finished stopped waited	finished stopped waited	The **past participle** is one of the principal parts of a verb. (See Chart 2-3, p. 31.) The past participle is used in the PRESENT PERFECT tense and the PAST PERFECT tense.* The past participle of regular verbs is the same as the simple past form: both end in **-ed**.
IRREGULAR VERBS	see make put	saw made put	seen made put	See Chart 2-4, p. 32, or the inside front and back covers for a list of irregular verbs.

*The past participle is also used in the passive. See Chapter 10.

□ **Exercise 2. Listening.** (Charts 2-3, 2-4, and 4-1)

Write the words you hear.

CD 1
Track 34

Example: You will hear: go   went   gone

You will write: go   went   _gone_

Simple Form	Simple Past	Past Participle		Simple Form	Simple Past	Past Participle
1. call	called	_____		6. come	came	_____
2. speak	spoke	_____		7. eat	ate	_____
3. do	did	_____		8. cut	cut	_____
4. know	knew	_____		9. read	read	_____
5. meet	met	_____		10. be	was/were	_____

□ **Exercise 3. Looking at grammar.** (Charts 2-3, 2-4, and 4-1)

Make your own chart. Write the past participles.

Simple Form	Simple Past	Past Participle		Simple Form	Simple Past	Past Participle
1. finish	finished	_finished_		6. hear	heard	_____
2. have	had	_____		7. study	studied	_____
3. think	thought	_____		8. die	died	_____
4. teach	taught	_____		9. buy	bought	_____
5. live	lived	_____		10. start	started	_____

□ **Exercise 4. Warm-up.** (Chart 4-2)

Decide which sentence (a. or b.) is correct for each situation.

1. It's 10:00 A.M. Layla has been at the bus stop since 9:50.
   a. She is still there.
   b. The bus picked her up.

2. Toshi has lived in the same apartment for 30 years.
   a. After 30 years, he moved somewhere else.
   b. He still lives there.

4-2 Present Perfect with *Since* and *For*

<table>
<tr>
<td rowspan="2">
10:00 A.M. | now
</td>
<td>
(a) I **'ve been** in class *since* ten o'clock this morning.

(b) We **have known** Ben *for* ten years. We met him ten years ago. We still know him today. We are friends.
</td>
<td>
The present perfect tense is used in sentences with ***since*** and ***for*** to express situations that began in the past and continue to the present.

In (a): Class started at ten. I am still in class now, at the moment of speaking.

INCORRECT: *I am in class since ten o'clock this morning.*
</td>
</tr>
<tr>
<td>
(c)

I *have*
You *have*
She, He, It *has* } *been* here for one hour.
We *have*
They *have*
</td>
<td>
FORM: **have/has** + past participle

CONTRACTED FORMS: *I've, You've, He's, She's, It's, We've, They've.*
</td>
</tr>
</table>

Since

<table>
<tr>
<td>
(d) *I have been* here {
since eight o'clock.
since Tuesday.
since 2009
since yesterday.
since last month.
}
</td>
<td>
Since is followed by the mention of a *specific point in time:* an hour, a day, a month, a year, etc.

Since expresses the idea that something began at a specific time in the past and continues to the present.
</td>
</tr>
<tr>
<td>
(e) CORRECT: *I have lived* here since May.*
  CORRECT: *I have been* here since May.

(f) INCORRECT: *I am living here since May.*
(g) INCORRECT: *I live here since May.*
(h) INCORRECT: *I lived here since May.*
(i) INCORRECT: *I was here since May.*
</td>
<td>
Notice the incorrect sentences:

In (f): The present progressive is NOT used.

In (g): The simple present is NOT used.

In (h) and (i): The simple past is NOT used.
</td>
</tr>
<tr>
<td>
MAIN CLAUSE   SINCE-CLAUSE
(present perfect)   (simple past)
(j) *I have lived* here   since *I was* a child.

(k) Al *has met* many people   since he *came* here.
</td>
<td>
Since may also introduce a time clause (i.e., a subject and verb may follow ***since***).

Notice in the examples: The present perfect is used in the main clause; the simple past is used in the *since*-clause.
</td>
</tr>
</table>

For

<table>
<tr>
<td>
(l) *I have been* here {
for ten minutes.
for two hours.
for five days.
for about three weeks.
for almost six months.
for many years.
for a long time.
}
</td>
<td>
For is followed by the mention of a *length of time:* two minutes, three hours, four days, five weeks, etc.).

NOTE: If the noun ends in *-s* (*hours, days, weeks,* etc.), use ***for*** in the time expression, not ***since***.
</td>
</tr>
</table>

*Also correct: *I have been living* here since May. See Chart 4-6 for a discussion of the present perfect progressive.

□ **Exercise 5. Looking at grammar.** (Chart 4-2)
Complete the sentences with *since* or *for*.

Amy has been here . . .

1. _____for_____ two months.
2. ____since____ September.
3. _____ yesterday.
4. _____ the term started.
5. _____ a couple of hours.
6. _____ fifteen minutes.

Ms. Ellis has worked as a substitute teacher . . .

11. _____ school began.
12. _____ last year.
13. _____ 2008.
14. _____ about a year.
15. _____ September.
16. _____ a long time.

The Smiths have been married . . .

7. _____ two years.
8. _____ last May.
9. _____ five days.
10. _____ a long time.

I've known about Sonia's engagement . . .

17. _____ almost four months.
18. _____ the beginning of the year.
19. _____ the first of January.
20. _____ yesterday.

□ **Exercise 6. Looking at grammar.** (Chart 4-2)
Complete the sentences with information about yourself.

1. I've been in this building . . . .
   since ___*nine o'clock this morning*___.
   for ___*27 minutes*___.

2. We've been in class . . . .
   since _____.
   for _____.

3. I've been in this city . . . .
   since _____.
   for _____.

4. I've had an ID* card . . . .
   since _____.
   for _____.

5. I've had this book . . . .
   since _____.
   for _____.

---

*ID = identification

84 CHAPTER 4

Exercise 7. Looking at grammar. (Chart 4-2)
Complete each sentence with the present perfect form of the given verb.

Since 1995, Theresa, a talk-show host, . . .

1. work _____*has worked*_____ for a TV station in London.

2. interview _____ hundreds of guests.

3. meet _____ many famous people.

4. find _____ out about their lives.

5. make _____ friends with celebrities.

6. became _____ a celebrity herself.

7. sign _____ lots of autographs.

8. shake _____ hands with thousands of people.

9. write _____ two books about how to interview people.

10. think _____ a lot about the best ways to help people feel
comfortable on her show.

□ **Exercise 8. Let's talk.** (Chart 4-2)
Your teacher will ask a question. Two students will answer. Speaker A will answer with
since. Speaker B will use Speaker A's information and answer with *for*. Only the teacher's
book is open.

Example:
To SPEAKER A: How long have you been in this room?
  SPEAKER A: I've been in this room **since** (10:00).
To SPEAKER B: How long has (*Student A*) been in this room?
  SPEAKER B: She/He has been in this room **for** (15 minutes).

1. How long have you known me?
2. How long have you been up* today?
3. Where do you live? How long have you lived there?
4. Who has a cell phone? How long have you had your phone?
5. Who has a bike? How long have you had it?
6. How long have you been in this building today?
7. Who is wearing something new? What is new? How long have you had it/them?
8. Who is married? How long have you been married?

---

*be up = be awake and out of bed

□ **Exercise 9. Looking at grammar.** (Chart 4-2)
Complete the sentences with the correct form of the words in parentheses. Put brackets around the ***since***-clauses.

1. I (*know*) ___have known___ Mark Miller [ever since* we (*be*) ___were___ in college.]

2. Pedro (*change*) _____ his major three times since he (*start*)

   _____ school.

3. Ever since I (*be*) _____ a child, I (*be*) _____ afraid of snakes.

4. I can't wait to get home to my own bed. I (*sleep, not*) _____ well since

   I (*leave*) _____ home three days ago.

5. Ever since Pete (*meet*) _____ Nicole, he (*think, not*) _____

   about anything or anyone else. He's in love.

6. Otto (*have*) _____ a lot of problems with his car ever since he (*buy*)

   _____ it. It's a lemon.**

7. A: What (*you, eat*) _____ since you (*get*) _____

   up this morning?

   B: So far, I (*eat*) _____ a banana and some yogurt.***

□ **Exercise 10. Warm-up: pairwork.** (Chart 4-3)
Work with a partner. Partner A makes a true statement with a phrase from the list and then changes it to a question. Partner B gives a true answer.

climbed a tree	heard bedtime stories	ridden a tricycle
flown a kite	played in the dirt	slept with a stuffed animal

PARTNER A: Since my childhood, I haven't _____.

                 Since your childhood, have you _____?

PARTNER B: Yes, I have. OR No, I haven't.

---

*Ever since has the same meaning as *since*.

**a lemon = a car with a lot of problems

***So far + present perfect expresses situations that began in the past and continue to the present.

4-3 Negative, Question, and Short-Answer Forms

Negative

(a) I *have not* (*haven't*) *seen* Tom since lunch.	NEGATIVE: ***have/has*** + ***not*** + *past participle*
(b) Ann *has not* (*hasn't*) *eaten* for several hours.	NEGATIVE CONTRACTIONS: ***have*** + ***not*** = ***haven't*** ***has*** + ***not*** = ***hasn't***

Question

(c) *Have you seen Tom?*	QUESTION: ***have/has*** + *subject* + *past participle*
(d) *Has Ann eaten?*	
(e) How long *have you lived* here?	
(f) — Have you *ever* met a famous person? — No, I've *never* met a famous person.	In (f): ***ever*** = in your lifetime; from the time you were born to the present moment. Questions with ***ever*** frequently use the present perfect. When answering questions with ***ever***, speakers often use ***never***. ***Never*** is frequently used with the present perfect. In the answer to (f), the speaker is saying: "No, I haven't met a famous person from the time I was born to the present moment."

Short Answer

(g) — Have you seen Tom? — *Yes, I **have**.* OR *No, I **haven't**.*	SHORT ANSWER: ***have/haven't*** or ***has/hasn't*** NOTE: The helping verb in the short answer is not contracted with the pronoun. INCORRECT: *Yes, I've.* OR *Yes, he's.*
(h) — Has Ann eaten lunch? — *Yes, she **has**.* OR *No, she **hasn't**.*	

☐ **Exercise 11. Looking at grammar.** (Chart 4-3)
Complete the conversations. Use the present perfect form of the verbs in parentheses.

1. A: (*you, eat, ever*) <u>Have you ever eaten</u> an insect?

   B: No, I <u>haven't</u>. I (*eat, never*) <u>have never</u> eaten an insect.

2. A: (*you, stay, ever*) _____ in a room on the top floor of a hotel?

   B: Yes, I _____. I (*stay*) _____ in a room on the top floor of a hotel a few times.

3. A: (*you, meet, ever*) _____ a movie star?

   B: No, I _____. I (*meet, never*) _____ a movie star.

4. A: (*Ted, travel, ever*) _____ overseas?

   B: Yes, he _____. He (*travel*) _____ to several countries on business.

5. A: (*Lara, be, ever*) _____ in Mexico?

   B: No, she _____. She (*be, never*) _____ in any

   Spanish-speaking countries.

☐ **Exercise 12. Listening.** (Charts 2-3, 2-4, and 4-3)

Listen to each sentence and then the beginning of a question. Complete the question with the
past participle of the verb you heard in the first sentence. Have you ever done these things?

CD 1
Track 35 Circle *yes* or *no*.

Example: You will hear: I saw a two-headed frog once. Have you ever . . . ?
            You will write: Have you ever ___*seen*___ a two-headed frog?   yes (no)

1. Have you ever _____ a two-headed snake?		yes	no
2. Have you ever _____ in a small plane?		yes	no
3. Have you ever _____ in a limousine?		yes	no
4. Have you ever _____ volunteer work?		yes	no
5. Have you ever _____ a shirt?		yes	no
6. Have you ever _____ a scary experience on an airplane?		yes	no
7. Have you ever _____ out of a boat?		yes	no
8. Have you ever _____ so embarrassed that your face got hot?		yes	no
9. Have you ever _____ to a famous person?		yes	no
10. Have you ever _____ to be famous?		yes	no

☐ **Exercise 13. Let's talk: interview.** (Charts 2-4 and 4-3)

Interview your classmates. Make questions using the present perfect form of the given verbs.

1. you \ ever \ cut \ your own hair
2. you \ ever \ catch \ a big fish
3. you \ ever \ take care of \ an injured animal
4. you \ ever \ lose \ something very important
5. you \ ever \ sit \ on a bee
6. you \ ever \ fly \ in a private plane
7. you \ ever \ break \ your arm or your leg
8. you \ ever \ find \ something very valuable
9. you \ ever \ swim \ near a shark
10. you \ ever \ throw \ a ball \ and \ break \ a window

Exercise 14. Let's talk and write: interview. (Charts 2-3, 2-4, 4-2, and 4-3)

Part I. Work with a partner. Take turns asking and answering questions. Begin your questions with *How long have you* and the present perfect. Answer questions with *since, for,* or *never* and the present perfect.

Example: have a pet
PARTNER A: How long have you had a pet?
PARTNER B: I've had (*a cat, a dog, a bird, etc.*) for two years. OR
           I've had (*a cat, a dog, a bird, etc.*) since my 18th birthday. OR
           I've never had a pet.

1. live in (*this area*)
2. study English
3. be in this class / at this school
4. have long hair / short hair
5. have a beard / a mustache
6. wear glasses / contact lenses
7. have a roommate / a pet
8. be interested in (*a particular subject*)
9. be married

Part II. Use the information from your interview to write a paragraph about your partner. You can add some information to make it more interesting. Use the following paragraph as an example. Notice the present perfect phrases in green.

Example:

Ellie

    I'd like to tell you a little about Ellie. She has lived in Vancouver, Canada, for six months. She has studied English for five years. She has been at this school since September. She likes it here.

    She has short hair. She has worn short hair for a few years. Of course, she doesn't have a mustache! She has never worn glasses, except sunglasses.

    Ellie doesn't have a roommate, but she has a pet bird. She has had her bird for one month. Its name is Howie, and he likes to sing.

    She is interested in biology. She has been interested in biology since she was a child. She has never been married. She wants to be a doctor. She wants to become a doctor before she has a family.

❑ **Exercise 15. Warm-up.** (Chart 4-4)
Circle the correct completion (a. or b.) for each sentence.

1. Tyler has rented a house _____.
    a. last week.   b. already.

2. I have seen it _____.
    a. recently.   b. two days ago.

3. His parents haven't seen it _____.
    a. yesterday.   b. yet.

4. I have been there _____.
    a. two times.   b. yesterday.

Toshi has already eaten lunch.   Eva hasn't eaten lunch yet.

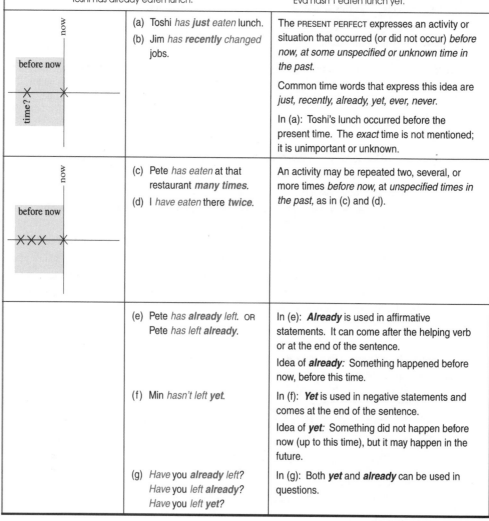

now / before now / time?	(a) Toshi *has just* eaten lunch. (b) Jim *has recently* changed jobs.	The PRESENT PERFECT expresses an activity or situation that occurred (or did not occur) *before now, at some unspecified or unknown time in the past*. Common time words that express this idea are *just, recently, already, yet, ever, never*. In (a): Toshi's lunch occurred before the present time. The *exact* time is not mentioned; it is unimportant or unknown.
now / before now	(c) Pete *has eaten* at that restaurant *many times*. (d) I *have eaten* there *twice*.	An activity may be repeated two, several, or more times *before now, at unspecified times in the past*, as in (c) and (d).
	(e) Pete *has **already** left*. OR Pete *has left **already***. (f) Min *hasn't left **yet***. (g) *Have* you ***already** left*? *Have* you *left **already***? *Have* you *left **yet***?	In (e): ***Already*** is used in affirmative statements. It can come after the helping verb or at the end of the sentence. Idea of ***already***: Something happened before now, before this time. In (f): ***Yet*** is used in negative statements and comes at the end of the sentence. Idea of ***yet***: Something did not happen before now (up to this time), but it may happen in the future. In (g): Both ***yet*** and ***already*** can be used in questions.

□ **Exercise 16. Looking at grammar.** (Chart 4-4)
Circle all the possible answers for each question. Work in small groups and then discuss your answers as a class.

SITUATION 1:
Sara is at home. At 12:00 P.M., the phone rang. It was Sara's friend from high school. They had a long conversation, and Sara hung up the phone at 12:59. It is now 1:00. Which sentences describe the situation?

    a. Sara has just hung up the phone.
    b. She has hung up the phone already.
    c. The phone has just rung.
    d. Sara hasn't finished her conversation yet.
    e. Sara has been on the phone since 12:00 P.M.

SITUATION 2:
Mr. Peters is in bed. He became sick with the flu eight days ago. Mr. Peters isn't sick very often. The last time he had the flu was one year ago. Which sentences describe the situation?

    a. Mr. Peters has been sick for a year.
    b. He hasn't gotten well yet.
    c. He has just gotten sick.
    d. He has already had the flu.
    e. He hasn't had the flu before.

SITUATION 3:
Rob is at work. His boss, Rosa, needs a report. She sees Rob working on it at his desk. She's in a hurry, and she's asking Rob questions. What questions is she going to ask him?

    a. Have you finished?
    b. Have you finished yet?
    c. Have you finished already?

□ **Exercise 17. Listening.** (Charts 2-4 and 4-4)
Richard and Lori are new parents. Their baby was born a week ago. Listen to each sentence and complete the question with the past participle of the verb you hear.

CD 1
Track 36

    1. Has Richard ___*held*___ the baby a lot yet?

    2. Has Lori _____ the baby a bath yet?

    3. Has Richard _____ a diaper yet?

    4. Has Lori _____ some pictures of the baby yet?

    5. Has Richard _____ up when the baby cries yet?

    6. Has Lori _____ some of the household chores yet?

    7. Has Richard _____ tired during the day yet?

❑ **Exercise 18. Looking at grammar.** (Chart 4-4)

Look at Andy's day planner. Write answers to the questions. Make complete sentences with *yet* and *already*.

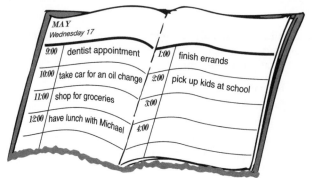

It is 11:55 A.M. right now.

1. Has Andy had his dentist appointment yet? ___*Yes, he has had his dentist*___

   ___*appointment already.*___

2. Has Andy picked up his kids at school yet? _____

   _____

3. Has Andy taken his car for an oil change already? _____

   _____

4. Has Andy finished his errands yet? _____

   _____

5. Has Andy shopped for groceries already? _____

   _____

6. Has Andy had lunch with Michael yet? _____

   _____

❑ **Exercise 19. Listening.** (Charts 4-2 → 4-4)

Both *is* and *has* can be contracted to *'s*. Listen to each sentence. Decide if the contracted verb is *is* or *has*. Before you begin, you may want to check your understanding of these words: *order, waiter*.

CD 1
Track 37

Examples: You will hear: I have to leave. My order's taking too long.
You will choose: (is)   has

You will hear: I have to leave. My order's taken too long.
You will choose: is   (has)

At a restaurant

1. is	has	3. is	has	5. is	has
2. is	has	4. is	has	6. is	has

Answer the questions and then listen to the job interview. Listen again and complete the
sentences with the words you hear. Before you begin, you may want to check your

understanding of these words: *clinic, prison, volunteer, low-income, patient, challenge.*

What types of jobs can nurses have?
Which ones could be very exciting?

A job interview

Mika is a nurse. She is interviewing for a job with the manager of a hospital emergency room.
He is looking at her résumé and asking her some general questions.

INTERVIEWER: It looks like _____ a lot of things since you became a
                                                    1

MIKA: Yes, _____ for a medical clinic. _____
                                    2   3

in a prison. _____ in several area hospitals. And
                                                4

_____ volunteer work at a community health center for
                            5

low-income patients.

INTERVIEWER: Very good. But, let me ask you, why _____
                                                                                        6

jobs so often?

MIKA: Well, I like having new challenges and different experiences.

INTERVIEWER: Why _____ for this job?
                                                    7

MIKA: Well, I'm looking for something more fast-paced,* and _____
                                                                                                8

interested in working in an E.R.** for a long time. _____
                                                                                                        9

that this hospital provides great training for its staff, and it offers excellent

patient care.

INTERVIEWER: Thank you for coming in. I'll call you next week with our decision.

MIKA: It was good to meet you. Thank you for your time.

---

more fast-paced = at a faster speed

**E.R.* = emergency room

(Chart 4-5)

❑ **Exercise 21. Warm-up.** (Chart 4-5)
Read the short conversation. Who is more likely to say the last sentence, Pamela or Jenna?

> PAMELA: I've traveled around the world several times.
> JENNA: I traveled around the world once.
>
> _____: I'm looking forward to my next trip.

4-5 Simple Past vs. Present Perfect	
SIMPLE PAST (a) I *finished* my work *two hours ago.* PRESENT PERFECT (b) I *have* already *finished* my work.	In (a): I finished my work at a specific time in the past (*two hours ago*). In (b): I finished my work at an unspecified time in the past (*sometime before now*).
SIMPLE PAST (c) I *was* in Europe *last year / three years ago / in 2006 / in 2008 and 2010 / when I was ten years old.* PRESENT PERFECT (d) I *have been* in Europe *many times / several times / a couple of times / once / (no mention of time).*	The SIMPLE PAST expresses an activity that occurred at a specific time (or times) in the past, as in (a) and (c). The PRESENT PERFECT expresses an activity that occurred at an unspecified time (or times) in the past, as in (b) and (d).
SIMPLE PAST (e) Ann *was* in Miami *for two weeks.* PRESENT PERFECT (f) Bob **has been** in Miami for *two weeks / since May 1st.*	In (e): In sentences where *for* is used in a time expression, the simple past expresses an activity that began and ended in the past. In (f): In sentences with *for* or *since,* the present perfect expresses an activity that began in the past and continues to the present.

❑ **Exercise 22. Looking at grammar.** (Chart 4-5)
Answer each question and discuss the meanings of the verb tenses in *italics.*

1. All of these verbs talk about past time, but the verb in (a) is different from the other three verbs. What is the difference?
   (a) I *have had* several bicycles in my lifetime.
   (b) I *had* a red bicycle when I was in elementary school.
   (c) I *had* a blue bicycle when I was a teenager.
   (d) I *had* a green bicycle when I lived and worked in Hong Kong.

2. What are the differences in the ideas the verb tenses express?
   (e) I *had* a wonderful bicycle last year.
   (f) I'*ve had* many wonderful bicycles.

3. What are the differences in the ideas the verb tenses express?
   (g) Ann *had* a red bike for two years.
   (h) Sue *has had* a red bike for two years.

4. Who is still alive, and who is dead?
   (i) In his lifetime, Uncle Alex *had* several red bicycles.
   (j) In his lifetime, Grandpa *has had* several red bicycles.

□ **Exercise 23. Looking at grammar.** (Chart 4-5)
Look at each verb in *italics*. Is it simple past or present perfect? Check (✓) the box that describes whether the verb expresses something that happened at a specified or unspecified time in the past.

	SPECIFIED TIME IN THE PAST	UNSPECIFIED TIME IN THE PAST
1. Ms. Parker *has been* in Tokyo many times. → *present perfect*	□	✓
2. Ms. Parker *was* in Tokyo last week. → *simple past*	✓	□
3. I'*ve met* Kaye's husband. He's a nice guy.	□	□
4. I *met* Kaye's husband at a party last week.	□	□
5. Mr. White *was* in the hospital three times last month.	□	□
6. Mr. White *has been* in the hospital many times.	□	□
7. I like to travel. I'*ve been* to more than 30 foreign countries.	□	□
8. I *was* in Morocco in 2008.	□	□
9. Venita *has never been* to Morocco.	□	□
10. Venita *wasn't* in Morocco when I was there in 2008.	□	□

□ **Exercise 24. Looking at grammar.** (Chart 4-5)
Complete the sentences. Use the present perfect or the simple past form of the verbs in parentheses.

1. A: Have you ever been to Singapore?

   B: Yes, I (*be*) __have__ . I (*be*) __have been__ to Singapore several times. In fact,

   I (*be*) __was__ in Singapore last year.

2. A: Are you going to finish your work before you go to bed?

   B: I (*finish, already**) __have already finished__ it. I (*finish*) __finished__ my work

   two hours ago.

3. A: Have you ever eaten at the Sunset Beach Café?

   B: Yes, I _____. I (*eat*) _____ there many times. In

   fact, my wife and I (*eat*) _____ lunch there yesterday.

---

*In informal spoken English, the simple past is sometimes used with **already**. Practice using the present perfect with **already** in this exercise.

4. A: Do you and Erica want to go to the movie at the Galaxy Theater with us tonight?

   B: No thanks. We (see, already) _____ it. We (see)

   _____ it last week.

5. A: When are you going to write your report for Mr. Berg?

   B: I (write, already) _____ it. I (write)

   _____ it two days ago and gave it to him.

6. A: (Antonio, have, ever) _____ a job?

   B: Yes, he _____. He (have) _____ lots of part-time

   jobs. Last summer he (have) a _____ a job at his uncle's auto shop.

7. A: This is a good book. Would you like to read it when I'm finished?

   B: Thanks, but I (read, already) _____ it. I (read)

   _____ it a couple of months ago.

8. A: What African countries (you, visit) _____?

   B: I (visit) _____ Kenya and Ethiopia. I (visit)

   _____ Kenya in 2002. I (be) _____ in

   Ethiopia last year.

☐ **Exercise 25. Let's talk: pairwork.** (Chart 4-5)
Work with a partner. Take turns asking and answering the questions. Use the present perfect
and the simple past. Share a few of your partner's answers with the class.

Example:
PARTNER A: What countries have you been to?
PARTNER B: I've been to Norway and Finland.
PARTNER A: When were you in Norway?
PARTNER B: I was in Norway three years ago. How about you? What countries have you been to?
PARTNER A: I've never been to Norway or Finland, but I've been to . . . .

1. What countries have you been to?
   When were you in . . . ?

2. Where are some interesting places you have lived?
   When did you live in . . . ?

3. What are some interesting / unusual / scary things you have done in your lifetime?
   When did you . . . ?

4. What are some helpful things (for a friend / your family / your community) you have done
   in your lifetime?
   When did you . . . ?

□ **Exercise 26. Listening.** (Charts 2-4 and 4-5)

For each item, you will hear two complete sentences and then the beginning of a third sentence. Complete the third sentence with the past participle of the verb you heard in the first two sentences.

CD 1
Track 39

Example: You will hear: I eat vegetables every day. I ate vegetables for dinner last night. I have . . .

You will write: I have ___*eaten*___ vegetables every day for a long time.

1. Since Friday, I have _____ a lot of money.

2. All week, I have _____ big breakfasts.

3. Today, I have already _____ several emails.

4. I just finished dinner, and I have _____ a nice tip.

5. Since I was a teenager, I have _____ in late on weekends.

6. All my life, I have _____ very carefully.

7. Since I was little, I have _____ in the shower.

□ **Exercise 27. Game.** (Charts 2-4 and 4-5)

Work in groups.

(1) On a piece of paper, write down two statements about yourself, one in the simple past tense and one in the present perfect tense.

(2) Make one statement true and one statement false.

(3) The other members of your group will try to guess which one is true.

(4) Tell the group the correct answers when everyone has finished guessing.

The person with the most correct guesses at the end of the game is the winner.

Example:

STUDENT A: I've never cooked dinner.
          I saw a famous person last year.

STUDENT B: *You've never cooked dinner is true.*
          You saw a famous person last year is false.

□ **Exercise 28. Warm-up.** (Chart 4-6)

Complete the sentences with time information.

1. I am sitting at my desk right now. I have been sitting at my desk since _____.

2. I am looking at my book. I have been looking at my book for _____.

4-6 Present Perfect Progressive

Al and Ann are in their car right now. They are driving home. It is now four o'clock.
 	
(a) They **have been driving** since two o'clock.
(b) They **have been driving** for two hours.
    They will be home soon.
	The PRESENT PERFECT PROGRESSIVE talks about *how long* an activity has been in progress before now.
	
	NOTE: Time expressions with **since**, as in (a), and **for**, as in (b), are frequently used with this tense.
	
	STATEMENT:
	    have/has + **been** + **-ing**

(c) How long *have they been driving*?	QUESTION: **have/has** + subject + **been** + **-ing**

Present Progressive vs. Present Perfect Progressive

Present Progressive 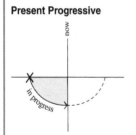	(d) Po *is sitting* in class right now.	The PRESENT PROGRESSIVE describes an activity that is in progress right now, as in (d). It does not discuss duration (length of time). INCORRECT: *Po has been sitting in class right now.*
Present Perfect Progressive 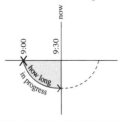	Po is sitting at his desk in class. He sat down at nine o'clock. It is now nine-thirty. (e) Po *has been sitting* in class since nine o'clock. (f) Po *has been sitting* in class for thirty minutes.	The PRESENT PERFECT PROGRESSIVE expresses the **duration** (length of time) of an activity that began in the past and is in progress right now. INCORRECT: *Po is sitting in class since nine o'clock.*

(g) CORRECT: I *know* Yoko. (h) INCORRECT: *I am knowing Yoko.* (i) CORRECT: I *have known* Yoko *for* two years. (j) INCORRECT: *I have been knowing Yoko for two years.*	NOTE: Non-action verbs (e.g., *know, like, own, belong*) are generally not used in the progressive tenses.* In (i): With non-action verbs, the present perfect is used with **since** or **for** to express the duration of a situation that began in the past and continues to the present.

*See Chart 1-6, Non-Action Verbs, p. 17.

Exercise 29. Looking at grammar. (Chart 4-6)
Complete the sentences. Use the present progressive or the present perfect progressive form of the verbs in parentheses.

1. I (*sit*) ___am sitting___ in the cafeteria right now. I (*sit*) ___have been sitting___ here since twelve o'clock.

2. Kate is standing at the corner. She (*wait*) _____ for the bus. She (*wait*) _____ for the bus for twenty minutes.

3. Scott and Rebecca (*talk*) _____ on the phone right now. They _____ (*talk*) on the phone for over an hour.

4. Right now we're in class. We (*do*) _____ an exercise. We (*do*) _____ this exercise for a couple of minutes.

5. A: You look busy right now. What (*you, do*) _____?

   B: I (*work*) _____ on my physics experiment. It's a difficult experiment.

   A: How long (*you, work*) _____ on it?

   B: I started planning it last January. I (*work*) _____ on it since then.

☐ **Exercise 30. Let's talk.** (Chart 4-6)
Answer the questions your teacher asks. Your book is closed.

Example:
TEACHER: Where are you living?
STUDENT A: I'm living in an apartment on Fourth Avenue.
TEACHER: How long have you been living there?
STUDENT A: I've been living there since last September.

1. Right now you are sitting in class. How long have you been sitting here?
2. When did you first begin to study English? How long have you been studying English?
3. I began to teach English in (*year*). How long have I been teaching English?
4. I began to work at this school in (*month or year*). How long have I been working here?
5. What are we doing right now? How long have we been doing it?
6. (*Student's name*), I see that you wear glasses. How long have you been wearing glasses?
7. Who drives? When did you first drive a car? How long have you been driving?
8. Who drinks coffee? How old were you when you started to drink coffee? How long have you been drinking coffee?

□ **Exercise 31. Listening.** (Charts 4-2 → 4-6)

Part I. When speakers use the present perfect in everyday speech, they often contract *have* and *has* with nouns. Listen to the sentences and notice the contractions.

CD 1
Track 40

1. Jane has been out of town for two days.
2. My parents have been active in politics for 40 years.
3. My friends have moved into a new apartment.
4. I'm sorry. Your credit card has expired.
5. Bob has been traveling in Montreal since last Tuesday.
6. You're the first one here. No one else* has come yet.

Part II. Listen to the sentences. Complete them with the words you hear: *noun* + **have/has**.

1. The ___*weather has*___ been warm since the beginning of April.

2. This _____ been unusually warm.

3. My _____ been living in the same house for 25 years.

4. My _____ lived in the same town all their lives.

5. You slept late. Your _____ already gotten up and made breakfast.

6. My _____ planned a going-away party for me. I'm moving back to my hometown.

7. I'm afraid your _____ been getting a little sloppy.**

8. My _____ traveled a lot. She's visited many different countries.

□ **Exercise 32. Warm-up.** (Chart 4-7)

Read the situations and answer the questions.

SITUATION 1:
Roger is having trouble with math. I am helping him with his homework tonight. I **have been helping** him since 6:00.

SITUATION 2:
Roger is moving to a new apartment. I **have helped** him move furniture several times this week.

SITUATION 3:
I sure was busy last week. I **helped** Roger with his homework, and I **helped** him move to a new apartment.

a. In which situation does the speaker emphasize the duration or the time that something continues?
b. In which situation(s) is the speaker finished with the activity?
c. Do you think the activity in situation 1 or 2 is more recent? Why?

---

*else is an adverb and is frequently contracted with *have* and *has* in phrases such as *no one else, someone else, anyone else,* etc.

***sloppy = careless or messy

4-7 Present Perfect Progressive vs. Present Perfect

Present Perfect Progressive

(a) Gina and Tarik are talking on the phone. They *have been talking* on the phone for 20 minutes.	The PRESENT PERFECT PROGRESSIVE expresses the **duration of present** *activities*, using action verbs, as in (a). The activity began in the past and is still in progress.

Present Perfect

(b) Gina *has talked* to Tarik on the phone many times (before now). (c) INCORRECT: *Gina has been talking to Tarik on the phone many times.* (d) Gina *has known* Tarik for two years. (e) INCORRECT: *Gina has been knowing Tarik for two years.*	The PRESENT PERFECT expresses (1) repeated activities that occur at **unspecified times in the past**, as in (b), OR (2) the **duration of present** *situations*, as in (d), using non-action verbs.

Present Perfect Progressive and Present Perfect

(f) I *have been living* here for six months. OR (g) I *have lived* here for six months. (h) Ed *has been wearing* glasses since he was ten. OR Ed *has worn* glasses since he was ten. (i) I *'ve been going* to school ever since I was five years old. OR I *'ve gone* to school ever since I was five years old.	For some (not all) verbs, duration can be expressed by either the present perfect or the present perfect progressive. Examples (f) and (g) have essentially the same meaning, and both are correct. Often either tense can be used with verbs that express the **duration of usual or habitual activities/situations** (things that happen daily or regularly), e.g., *live, work, teach, smoke, wear glasses, play chess, go to school, read the same newspaper every morning, etc.*

□ **Exercise 33. Looking at grammar.** (Chart 4-7)
Complete the sentences. Use the present perfect or the present perfect progressive form of the verbs in parentheses. In some sentences, either form is possible.

1. A: I'm tired. We (*hike*) ___have been hiking___ for more than an hour.
   B: Well, let's stop and rest for a while.

2. A: Is the hike to Glacier Lake difficult?
   B: No, not at all. I (*hike*) ___have hiked___ it many times with my kids.

3. A: Do you like it here?
   B: I (*live*) ___have been living / have lived___ here for only a short while. I don't know yet.

4. A: My eyes are getting tired. I (*read*) _____ for two hours. I think I'll take a break.
   B: Good idea.

5. A: I (*read*) _____ this same page in my chemistry book three times, and I still don't understand it.
   B: Maybe I can help.

6. A: Do you like the Edgewater Inn?
   B: Very much. I (*stay*) _____ there at least a dozen times. It's my favorite hotel.

7. A: The baby's crying. Shouldn't we do something? He (*cry*) _____ for several minutes.
   B: I'll go check.

8. A: Who's your daughter's teacher for next year?
   B: I think her name is Mrs. Jackson.
   A: She's one of the best teachers at the elementary school. She (*teach*) _____
   _____ kindergarten for twenty years.

9. A: Ed (*play*) _____ tennis for ten years, but he still doesn't have a good serve.
   B: Neither do I, and I (*play*) _____ tennis for twenty years.

10. A: Where does Mrs. Alvarez work?
    B: At the power company. She (*work*) _____ there for fifteen years. She likes her job.
    A: What about her husband?
    B: He's currently unemployed, but he'll find a new job soon.
    A: What kind of experience does he have?
    B: He (*work*) _____ for two different accounting firms and at one of the bigger software companies. With his work experience, he won't have any trouble finding another job.

Exercise 34. Listening. (Chart 4-7)

Listen to the weather report. Then listen again and complete the sentences with the words you hear. Before you begin, you may want to check your understanding of these words: *hail, weather system, rough.*

CD 1
Track 41

Today's Weather

The weather _____ certainly _____ today. Boy,
                              1   2

what a day! _____ already _____ rain, wind, hail, and sun. So, what's
                        3   4

in store* for tonight? As you _____ probably _____, dark clouds
                                        5   6

_____. We have a weather system moving in that is going to
                7

bring colder temperatures and high winds. _____ all week that
                                                            8

this system is coming, and it looks like tonight is it! _____ even
                                                               9

_____ snow down south of us, and we could get some snow here too. So hang
        10

onto your hats! We may have a rough night ahead of us.

☐ **Exercise 35. Looking at grammar.** (Chapters 1, 2, and 4)

Look at each pair of sentences. Compare the meanings of the verb tenses in *italics*. Check (✓) the sentences that express duration.

1. a. _____ Rachel *is taking* English classes.

   b. _____ Nadia *has been taking* English classes for two months.

2. a. _____ Ayako *has been living* in Jerusalem for two years. She likes it there.

   b. _____ Beatriz *has lived* in Jerusalem. She's also lived in Paris. She's lived in New York and Tokyo. She's lived in lots of cities.

3. a. _____ Jack *has visited* his aunt and uncle many times.

   b. _____ Matt *has been visiting* his aunt and uncle for the last three days.

4. a. _____ Cyril *is talking* on the phone.

   b. _____ Cyril *talks* on the phone a lot.

   c. _____ Cyril *has been talking* to his boss on the phone for half an hour.

   d. _____ Cyril *has talked* to his boss on the phone lots of times.

5. a. _____ Mr. Woods *walks* his dog in Forest Park every day.

   b. _____ Mr. Woods *has walked* his dog in Forest Park many times.

   c. _____ Mr. Woods *walked* his dog in Forest Park five times last week.

   d. _____ Mr. Woods *is walking* his dog in Forest Park right now.

   e. _____ Mr. Woods *has been walking* his dog in Forest Park since two o'clock.

---

what's in store = what to expect or what is coming in the future

☐ **Exercise 36. Listening.** (Charts 4-1 → 4-7)

🎧 Listen to each conversation and choose the sentence (a. or b.) that best describes it.

CD 1
Track 42

Example: You will hear: A: This movie is silly.

B: I agree. It's really dumb.

You will choose: (a.) The couple has been watching a movie.

b. The couple finished watching a movie.

1. a. The speakers listened to the radio already.

   b. The speakers have been listening to the radio.

2. a. The man lived in Dubai a year ago.

   b. The man still lives in Dubai.

3. a. The man has called the children several times.

   b. The man called the children once.

4. a. The speakers went to a party and are still there.

   b. The speakers went to a party and have already left.

☐ **Exercise 37. Listening and speaking.** (Chapters 1 → 4)

🎧 *Part I.* Listen to the phone conversation between a mother and her daughter, Lara.

CD 1
Track 43 **A common illness**

LARA: Hi, Mom. I was just calling to tell you that I can't come to your birthday party this weekend. I'm afraid I'm sick.

MOM: Oh, I'm sorry to hear that.

LARA: Yeah, I got sick Wednesday night, and it's just been getting worse.

MOM: Are you going to see a doctor?

LARA: I don't know. I don't want to go to a doctor if it's not serious.

MOM: Well, what symptoms have you been having?

LARA: I've had a cough, and now I have a fever.

MOM: Have you been taking any medicine?

LARA: Just over-the-counter* stuff.

MOM: If your fever doesn't go away, I think you need to call a doctor.

LARA: Yeah, I probably will.

MOM: Well, call me tomorrow and let me know how you're doing.

LARA: Okay. I'll call you in the morning.

---

over-the-counter = medicine you can buy without a prescription from a doctor

Part II. Work with a partner. Take turns being the parent and the sick person. Complete the conversation. Practice the new conversation with your partner.

Possible symptoms:

a fever	chills	a sore throat
a runny nose	achiness	a stomachache
a cough	a headache	sneezing
nausea		

A: Hi, Mom/Dad. I was just calling to tell you that I can't come to _____. I'm afraid I'm sick.

B: Oh, I'm sorry to hear that.

A: Yeah, I got sick Wednesday night, and it's just been getting worse.

B: Are you going to see a doctor?

A: I don't know. I don't want to go to a doctor if it's not serious.

B: Well, what symptoms have you been having?

A: I've had _____ , and now I have _____ .

B: Have you been taking any medicine?

A: Just over-the-counter stuff.

B: If your _____ doesn't go away, I think you need to call a doctor.

A: Yeah, I probably will.

B: Well, call me tomorrow and let me know how you're doing.

A: Okay. I'll call you in the morning.

☐ **Exercise 38. Looking at grammar.** (Chapter 1 and Charts 4-1→ 4-7)
Choose the correct verb. In some sentences, more than one answer may be possible. Discuss your answers.

1. I _____ the windows twice, and they still don't look clean.
    a. am washing   b. have washed   c. have been washing

2. Please tell Mira to get off the phone. She _____ for over an hour.
    a. is talking   b. has talked   c. has been talking

3. Where are you? I _____ at the mall for you to pick me up.
    a. wait   b. am waiting   c. have been waiting

4. We _____ at the Lakes Resort once. We want to go back again.
    a. stay   b. have stayed   c. have been staying

5. Where have you been? The baby _____ , and I can't comfort her.
    a. cries   b. is crying   c. has been crying

□ **Exercise 39. Reading.** (Charts 4-1 → 4-7)
Answer the questions. Then read the passage and the statements that follow. Circle "T" for
true and "F" for false.

Have you heard about the problem of disappearing honeybees?
Why are honeybees important to fruit and many other crops?

Where Have the Honeybees Gone?

Honeybees have been disappearing around the world for several years now. In the United
States, billions of bees have already died. Europe, Australia, and Brazil have also reported losses
of honeybees. This is a serious problem because bees pollinate* crops. Without pollination,
apple, orange, and other fruit trees cannot produce fruit. Other crops like nuts also need
pollination. In the United States, one-third of the food supply depends on honeybees.

Scientists have a name for this problem: colony collapse disorder (CCD). Bees live in
colonies or hives, and thousands of beekeepers have been finding their hives empty. A hive that
once held 50,000 bees may just have a few dead or dying ones left.

There have been many theories about why this has happened; for example, disease, pests,**
unnatural growing conditions, and damaged DNA.*** Scientists now think that the cause may be
a combination of a virus and a fungus, but they need to do more research to find a solution to this
very serious problem.

1. Honeybees have stopped disappearing.	T	F
2. Scientists expect that more bees will die.	T	F
3. Apples and other fruits depend on honeybees.	T	F
4. Bee hives have been disappearing.	T	F
5. There are only four reasons why honeybees have died.	T	F

---

pollinate (verb) = fertilize; *pollination* (noun) = the process that causes a plant to make a new plant

**pest* = an insect or animal that damages crops

***DNA* = deoxyribonucleic acid, a carrier of genetic information

□ **Exercise 40. Grammar and writing.** (Chapters 1, 2, and 4)

Part I. Complete the sentences with the correct form of the words in parentheses.

My name (*be*) ___is___ Surasuk Jutukanyaprateep. I (*be*) _____ from
    1   2
Thailand. Right now I (*study*) _____ English at this school. I (*be*)
                                            3
_____ at this school since the beginning of January. I (*arrive*)
            4
_____ here January 2nd, and my classes (*begin*) _____
            5   6
January 6th.

Since I (*come*) _____ here, I (*do*) _____ many
                            7   8
things, and I (*meet*) _____ many people. Last week, I (*go*)
                                9
_____ to a party at my friend's house. I (*meet*) _____ some of the
            10   11
other students from Thailand at the party. Of course, we (*speak*) _____ Thai, so
                                                                                12
I (*practice, not*) _____ my English that night. There (*be*)
                            13
_____ only people from Thailand at the party.
            14

However, since I (*come*) _____ here, I (*meet*)
                                        15
_____ a lot of other people too, including people from Latin America,
            16
Africa, the Middle East, and Asia. I enjoy meeting people from other countries. Now I (*know*)
_____ people from all these places, and they (*become*) _____
            17   18
my friends.

Part II. Write three paragraphs about yourself. Use the passage in Part I as a model. Answer
these questions:

PARAGRAPH I.
  1. What is your name?
  2. Where are you from?
  3. How long have you been here?

PARAGRAPH II.
  4. What have you done since you came here? OR
  5. What have you learned since you began studying English?

PARAGRAPH III.
  6. Who have you met in this class? OR
  7. Who have you met recently?
  8. Give a little information about these people.

☐ **Exercise 41. Warm-up.** (Chart 4-8)
Read Karen's statement. Which sequence of events (a. or b.) is correct?

> KAREN: Jane met me for lunch. She was so happy. She had passed her driver's test.
>   a. Jane talked to Karen. Then she passed her test.
>   b. Jane passed her test. Then she talked to Karen.

4-8 Past Perfect	
Situation: *Jack left his apartment at 2:00. Sue arrived at his apartment at 2:15 and knocked on the door.* (a) When Sue arrived, Jack wasn't there. He *had left*.	The PAST PERFECT is used when the speaker is talking about two different events at two different times in the past; one event ends before the second event happens. In (a): There are two events, and both happened in the past: *Jack left his apartment. Sue arrived at his apartment.* To show the time relationship between the two events, we use the past perfect (***had left***) to say that the first event (Jack leaving his apartment) was completed before the second event (Sue arriving at his apartment) occurred.

(b) Jack *had left* his apartment when Sue arrived.	FORM: ***had*** = *past participle*
(c) He *'d* left. I *'d* left. They *'d* left. Etc.	CONTRACTION: *I / you / she / he / it / we / they* + *'d*
(d) Jack *had left before* Sue arrived. (e) Jack *left before* Sue arrived. (f) Sue *arrived after* Jack had left. (g) Sue *arrived after* Jack left.	When ***before*** and ***after*** are used in a sentence, the time relationship is already clear so the past perfect is often not necessary. The simple past may be used, as in (e) and (g). Examples (d) and (e) have the same meaning. Examples (f) and (g) have the same meaning.
(h) Stella was alone in a strange city. She walked down the avenue slowly, looking in shop windows. Suddenly, she turned her head and looked behind her. Someone *had called* her name.	The past perfect is more common in formal writing such as fiction, as in (h).

□ **Exercise 42. Looking at grammar.** (Chart 4-8)
Identify which action in the past took place first (1st) and which action took place second (2nd).

1. The tennis player **jumped** in the air for joy. She **had won** the match.

   a. ___1st___ The tennis player won the match.

   b. ___2nd___ The tennis player jumped in the air.

2. Before I went to bed, I **checked** the front door. My roommate **had** already **locked** it.

   a. ___2nd___ I checked the door.

   b. ___1st___ My roommate locked the door.

3. I **looked** for Diego, but he **had left** the building.

   a. _____ Diego left the building.

   b. _____ I looked for Diego.

4. I **laughed** when I saw my son. He **had poured** a bowl of noodles on top of his head.

   a. _____ I laughed.

   b. _____ My son poured a bowl of noodles on his head.

5. Oliver **arrived** at the theater on time, but he couldn't get in. He **had left** his ticket at home.

   a. _____ Oliver left his ticket at home.

   b. _____ Oliver arrived at the theater.

6. I **handed** Betsy the newspaper, but she didn't want it. She **had read** it during her lunch hour.

   a. _____ I handed Betsy the newspaper.

   b. _____ Betsy read the newspaper.

7. After Carl arrived in New York, he **called** his mother. He **had promised** to call her as soon as he got in.

   a. _____ Carl made a promise to his mother.

   b. _____ Carl called his mother.

☐ **Exercise 43. Listening.** (Chart 4-8)

Listen to the short conversations and choose the verbs you hear.

CD 1
Track 44

Examples: You will hear: A: I'll introduce you to Professor Newton at the meeting tonight.
                                    B: You don't need to. I have already met him.

                  You will choose: has   (have)   had

                  You will hear: A: Did Jack introduce you to Professor Newton?
                                    B: No, it wasn't necessary. I had already met him.

                  You will choose: has   have   (had)

1. has   have   had   3. has   have   had
2. has   have   had   4. has   have   had

☐ **Exercise 44. Check your knowledge.** (Chapter 4)
Edit the sentences. Correct the errors in verb tense usage.

My experience with English

                    studying
1. I have been ~~studied~~ English for eight years, but I still have a lot to learn.

2. I started English classes at this school four weeks ago, and I am learning a lot of English since then.

3. I want to learn English since I am a child.

4. I have been thinking about how to improve my English skills quickly since I came here, but I hadn't found a good way.

5. Our teacher likes to give tests. We has have six tests since the beginning of the term.

6. I like learning English. When I was young, my father found an Australian girl to teach my brothers and me English, but when I move to another city, my father didn't find anyone to teach us.

7. I meet many friends in this class. I meet Abdul in the cafeteria on the first day. He was friendly and kind. We are friends since that day.

8. Abdul have been study English for three months. His English is better than mine.

Chapter 5
Asking Questions

☐ **Exercise 1. Warm-up.** (Chart 5-1)
Choose the correct completion.

A: _____ you need help?

      a. Are   c. Have

      b. Do   d. Were

B: Yes, _____.

      a. I need   c. I have

      b. I'm   d. I do

5-1 Yes/No Questions and Short Answers

Yes/No Question	Short Answer (+ Long Answer)	
(a) *Do you like* tea?	*Yes, I do.* (I like tea.) *No, I don't.* (I don't like tea.)	A **yes/no question** is a question that can be answered by *yes* or *no*.
(b) *Did Sue call?*	*Yes, she did.* (Sue called.) *No, she didn't.* (Sue didn't call.)	In an affirmative short answer (*yes*), a helping verb is NOT contracted with the subject.
(c) *Have you met* Al?	*Yes, I have.* (I have met Al.) *No, I haven't.* (I haven't met Al.)	In (c): INCORRECT: *Yes, I've.* In (d): INCORRECT: *Yes, it's.* In (e): INCORRECT: *Yes, he'll.*
(d) *Is it raining?*	*Yes, it is.* (It's raining.) *No, it isn't.* (It isn't raining.)	The spoken emphasis in a short answer is on the verb.
(e) *Will Rob be* here?	*Yes, he will.* (Rob will be here.) *No, he won't.* (Rob won't be here.)	

☐ **Exercise 2. Looking at grammar.** (Chart 5-1)
Choose the correct verbs.

A new cell phone

1. *Is, Does*   that your new cell phone? Yes, it   *is, does*.

2. *Are, Do*   you like it? Yes, I   *am, do*.

3. *Were, Did*   you buy it online? Yes, I   *was, did*.

4. *Was, Did*   it expensive? No, it   *wasn't, didn't.*

5. *Is, Does*   it ringing? Yes, it   *is, does.*

6. *Are, Do*   you going to answer it? Yes, I   *am, do.*

7. *Was, Did*   the call important? Yes, it   *was, did.*

8. *Have, Were*   you turned your phone off? No, I   *haven't, wasn't.*

9. *Will, Are*   you call me later? Yes, I   *will, are.*

□ **Exercise 3. Looking at grammar.** (Chart 5-1)
Use the information in parentheses to make yes/no questions. Complete each conversation with an appropriate short answer. Do not use a negative verb in the question.

1. A: *Do you know my brother?*

   B: No, *I don't.* (I don't know your brother.)

2. A: Do snakes have legs

   B: No, they don't (Snakes don't have legs.)

3. A: is Mexico is in north America ?

   B: Yes, It is (Mexico is in North America.)

4. A: will be at home tonight ?

   B: No, I won't (I won't be at home tonight.)

5. A: Do you have a bike ?

   B: Yes, I do (I have a bike.)*

6. A: has simon left ? yet

   B: Yes, he has (Simon has left.)

7. A: Did simon left with kate ?

   B: Yes, he did (Simon left with Kate.)

8. A: Does Acupuncture relieves Pain ?

   B: Yes, It does (Acupuncture relieves pain.)

*In American English, a form of *do* is usually used when *have* is the main verb: *Do you have a car?*
In British English, a form of *do* with the main verb *have* is not necessary: *Have you a car?*

I have been in the US since January.

□ **Exercise 4. Listening.** (Chart 5-1)

Listen to each question and choose the correct response.

CD 1
Track 45

Example: You will hear: Are you almost ready?

You will choose: a. Yes, I was.   b. Yes, I do.   (c.) Yes, I am.

Leaving for the airport

1. a. Yes, I am.   b. Yes, I do.   c. Yes, it does.

2. a. Yes, I did.   b. Yes, I was.   c. Yes, I am.

3. a. Yes, I will.   b. Yes, it will.   c. Yes, it did.

4. a. Yes, they are.   b. Yes, it did.   c. Yes, it is.

5. a. Yes, I am.   b. Yes, I will.   c. Yes, I do.

□ **Exercise 5. Let's talk: interview.** (Chart 5-1)

Interview seven students in your class. Make questions with the given words. Ask each
student a different question.

1. you \ like \ animals?   5. you \ sleep \ well last night?
2. *Have* you \ ever \ had \ a pet snake?   6. *Are* you \ be \ tired right now?
3. it \ be \ cold \ in this room?   7. you \ be \ here next year?
4. it \ rain \ right now?   *Will you*
    Is it raining right now?

□ **Exercise 6. Listening.** (Chart 5-1)

In spoken English, it may be hard to hear the beginning of a yes/no question because the words
are often reduced.*

CD 1
Track 46

Part I. Listen to these common reductions.

1. Is he absent?   →   *Ih-ze* absent? OR *Ze* absent?
2. Is she absent?   →   *Ih-she* absent?
3. Does it work?   →   *Zit* work?
4. Did it break?   →   *Dih-dit* break? OR *Dit* break?
5. Has he been sick? →   *Ze* been sick? OR *A-ze* been sick?
6. Is there enough?   →   *Zere* enough?
7. Is that okay?   →   *Zat* okay?

Part II. Complete the sentences with the words you hear. Write the non-reduced forms.

At the grocery store

1. I need to see the manager. _____ available?

2. I need to see the manager. _____ in the store today?

3. Here is one bag of apples. _____ enough?

4. I need a drink of water. _____ a drinking fountain?

5. My credit card isn't working. Hmmm. _____ expire?

_____

*See also Chapter 1, Exercise 33, p. 21, and Chapter 2, Exercise 20, p. 39.

6. Where's Simon? _____ left?

7. The price seems high. _____ include the tax?

☐ **Exercise 7. Warm-up.** (Chart 5-2)
Circle the correct answers. There may be more than one correct answer for each question.

1. Where did you go?
   a. To the hospital. b. Yes, I did. c. Outside. d. Yesterday.

2. When is James leaving?
   a. I'm not sure. b. Yes, he is. c. Yes, he does. d. Around noon.

3. Who did you meet?
   a. Tariq did. b. Sasha. c. Well, I met Sam and Mia. d. Yes, I did.

5-2 Yes/No and Information Questions

A yes/no question = a question that can be answered by "yes" or "no"
A: *Does Ann live in Montreal?*
B: *Yes, she does.* OR *No, she doesn't.*

An information question = a question that asks for information by using a question word:
where, when, why, who, whom, what, which, whose, how
A: *Where does Ann live?*
B: *In Montreal.*

(Question Word)	Helping Verb	Subject	Main Verb	(Rest of Sentence)	
(a)	*Does*	*Ann*	*live*	in Montreal?	The same subject-verb word order is used in both yes/no and information questions:
(b) Where	*does*	*Ann*	*live?*		
(c)	*Is*	*Sara*	*studying*	at the library?	*Helping Verb + Subject + Main Verb*
(d) Where	*is*	*Sara*	*studying?*		
(e)	*Will*	*you*	*graduate*	next year?	Example (a) is a yes/no question. Example (b) is an information question.
(f) When	*will*	*you*	*graduate?*		
(g)	*Did*	*they*	*see*	Jack?	
(h) Who(m)*	*did*	*they*	*see?*		In (i) and (j): Main verb *be* in simple present and simple past (*am, is, are, was, were*) precedes the subject. It has the same position as a helping verb.
(i)	*Is*	*Heidi*		at home?	
(j) Where	*is*	*Heidi?*			
(k)		*Who*	*came*	to dinner?	When the question word (e.g., *who* or *what*) is the subject of the question, usual question word order is not used. Notice in (k) and (l) that no form of *do* is used.
(l)		*What*	*happened*	yesterday?	

*See Chart 5-4 for a discussion of *who(m)*.

Read the information about Irina and Paul. Then make complete questions with the given words and choose the correct short answers.

The Simple Life

Irina and Paul live a simple life. They have a one-room cabin on a lake in the mountains. They fish for some of their food. They also raise chickens. They pick fruit from trees and berries from bushes. They don't have electricity or TV, but they enjoy their life. They don't need a lot to be happy.

1. QUESTION: where \ Irina and Paul \ live?
    Where do Irina and Paul live?

    ANSWER: a. Yes, they do.   ⓑ On a lake.

2. QUESTION: they \ live \ a simple life?
    Do

    ANSWER: a. Yes, they live.   b. Yes, they do.

3. QUESTION: what \ they \ pick \ from the trees?

    ANSWER: a. Fruit.   b. Yes, they pick.

4. QUESTION: they \ have \ electricity?
    Do

    ANSWER: a. No, they don't.   b. No, they don't have.

5. QUESTION: they \ enjoy \ their life?

    ANSWER: a. Yes, they do.   b. Yes, they enjoy.

6. QUESTION: they \ be \ happy?
    Are they happy?

    ANSWER: a. Yes, they do.   b. Yes, they are.

□ **Exercise 9. Listening.** (Chart 5-2)

Listen to the conversation. Then listen again and complete the sentences with the words you hear.

CD 1
Track 47

Where are Roberto and Isabel?

A: _____ Roberto and Isabel?
　　　　　　　　1

B: Yes, _____. They live around the corner from me.
　　　　　　　2

A: _____ them lately?
　　　　　　　3

B: No, _____. They're out of town.
　　　　　　4

A: _____ to their parents? I heard Roberto's parents are ill.
　　　　　　　5

B: Yes, _____. They went to help them.
　　　　　　6

A: _____ them soon?
　　　　　　　7

B: Yes, _____. In fact, I'm going to pick them up at the airport.
　　　　　　8

A: _____ back this weekend? I'm having a party, and I'd like
　　　　　　　9

　　to invite them.

B: No, _____. They won't be back until Monday.
　　　　　　10

□ **Exercise 10. Warm-up.** (Chart 5-3)

Complete the sentences with the most appropriate question word from the list. One sentence has two possible answers. Match the answers to the questions.

Why	What time	Where	When

QUESTIONS

1. _____where_____ do you live? _b_

2. _____why_____ are you laughing? _c_

3. _____when / what time_____ will you get here? _a_
　　what day   what month

ANSWERS

a. At noon.

b. On Fifth Street.

c. Because the joke was funny.

5-3 Where, Why, When, What Time, How Come, What ... For

Question	Answer	
(a) **Where** did he go?	Home.	**Where** asks about *place*.
(b) **When** did he leave?	Last night. Two days ago. Monday morning. Seven-thirty.	A question with **when** can be answered by any time expression, as in the sample answers in (b).
(c) **What time** did he leave?	Seven-thirty. Around five o'clock. A quarter past ten.	A question with **what time** asks about *time on a clock*.
(d) **Why** did he leave?	Because he didn't feel well.*	**Why** asks about *reason*.
(e) **What** did he leave *for*? (f) **How come** he left?	**Why** can also be expressed with the phrases **What** ... *for* and **How come**, as in (e) and (f). *what is going to.* Notice that with **How come**, usual question order is not used. The subject precedes the verb and no form of **do** is used.	

[handwritten: informal] (e) … *[handwritten: why informal]*

*See Chart 8-6, p. 221, for the use of *because*. *Because I didn't feel well* is an adverb clause. It is not a complete sentence. In this example, it is the short answer to a question.

□ **Exercise 11. Looking at grammar.** (Chart 5-3)
Complete each conversation. Make questions using the information from Speaker A.

1. A: I'm going downtown in a few minutes.
   B: I didn't catch that. When ___are you going downtown___? OR
   B: I didn't catch that. Where ___are you going in a few minutes___?

2. A: My kids are transferring to Lakeview Elementary School because it's a better school.
   B: What was that? Where ___are your kids transferring to___? OR
   B: What was that? Why ___are your kids transferring to Lakeview Elementary School___

3. A: I will meet Taka at 10:00 at the mall.
   B: I couldn't hear you. Tell me again. What time ___will you meet Taka___? OR
   B: I couldn't hear you. Tell me again. Where ___will you meet Taka at 10___?
   [handwritten: you guys meet.]

4. A: Class begins at 8:15.
   B: Are you sure? When ___does class begin___? OR
   B: Are you sure? What time ___does class begin___?

5. A: I stayed home from work because I wanted to watch the World Cup final on TV.
   B: Huh?! Why ___did you do that___? OR
   B: Huh?! What ___did you do that for___ for?
   [handwritten: How come you did that]

Asking Questions **117**

□ **Exercise 12. Looking at grammar.** (Chart 5-3)
Restate the sentences. Use *How come* and *What for*.

1. Why are you going?
2. Why did they come?
3. Why does he need more money?
4. Why are they going to leave?

□ **Exercise 13. Reading and grammar.** (Charts 5-2 and 5-3)
Read the passage about Nina's birthday. Make questions with the given words. Answer the questions in small groups or as a class.

The Birthday Present

Tom got home late last night, around midnight. His wife, Nina, was sitting on the couch waiting for him. She was quite worried because Tom is never late.

Tomorrow is Nina's birthday. Unfortunately, Tom doesn't think she will be happy with her birthday present. Yesterday, Tom bought her a bike and he decided to ride it home from the bike shop. While he was riding down a hill, a driver came too close to him, and he landed in a ditch. Tom was okay, but the bike was ruined. Tom found a bus stop nearby and finally got home.

Tom told Nina the story, but Nina didn't care about the bike. She said she had a better present: her husband.

1. When \ Tom \ get home
2. Where \ be \ his wife
3. What \ Tom \ buy
4. Why \ be \ Tom \ late
5. What present \ Nina \ get

□ **Exercise 14. Listening.** (Charts 5-2 and 5-3)
Listen to each question and choose the best answer.

CD 1
Track 48

Example: You will hear: When are you leaving?
You will choose: a. Yes, I am.   (b.) Tomorrow.   c. In the city.

1. a. I am too.   b. Yesterday.   c. Sure.

2. a. For dinner.   b. At 6:00.   c. At the restaurant.

3. a. Outside the mall. b. After lunch.   c. Because I need a ride.

4. a. At work.   b. Because traffic was heavy. c. A few hours ago.

5. a. A pair of jeans. b. At the store.   c. Tomorrow.

□ **Exercise 15. Warm-up.** (Chart 5-4)
Match each question in Column A with the correct answer in Column B.

Column A	Column B
1. Who flew to Rome? _____	a. A small plane flew to Rome.
2. Who did you fly to Rome? _____	b. Pablo flew to Rome.
3. What did you fly to Rome? _____	c. I flew a small plane to Rome.
4. What flew to Rome? _____	d. I flew Pablo to Rome.

5-4 Questions With *Who*, *Who(m)*, and *What*

Question	Answer	

(a) **Who** came?
 S
	Someone came.
	 S
		In (a): **Who** is used as the subject (S) of a question.
		 In (b): **Who**(*m*) is used as the object (O) in a question.
		 Whom is used in very formal English. In everyday spoken English, **who** is usually used instead of **whom**:
		    UNCOMMON: Whom did you see?
		    COMMON: Who did you see?

(b) **Who**(*m*) did *you* see? *O*	*I* saw *someone*. *S* *O*	

(c) **What** happened?
 S
	Something happened.
	 S
		What can be used as either the subject or the object in a question.
		 Notice in (a) and (c): When **who** or **what** is used as the subject of a question, usual question word order is not used; no form of **do** is used:
		    CORRECT: Who came?
		    INCORRECT: Who did come?

(d) **What** did *you* see? *O*	*I* saw *something*. *S* *O*	

❑ **Exercise 16. Looking at grammar.** (Chart 5-4)
Make questions with *who, who(m),* and *what*. Write "S" if the question word is the subject. Write "O" if the question word is the object.

Question	**Answer**
1. *S* *Who knows?*	*S* **Someone** knows.
2. *O* *Who(m) did you ask?*	*O* I asked **someone**.
3. _____	**Someone** knocked on the door.
4. _____	Talya met **someone**.
5. _____	Mike learned **something**.
6. _____	**Something** changed Gina's mind.
7. _____	Gina is talking about **someone**.*
8. _____	Gina is talking about **something**.

---

*A preposition may come at the beginning of a question in very formal English:
   About whom (NOT **who**) *is Tina talking?*
In everyday English, a preposition usually does not come at the beginning of a question.

□ **Exercise 17. Looking at grammar.** (Chart 5-4)
Complete the sentences with *who* or *what*.

1. A: _____ just called?
   B: That was Antonia.

2. A: _____ do you need?
   B: A pair of scissors. I'm cutting my hair.

3. A: _____ is Jae?
   B: My stepmom.

4. A: _____ is going on?
   B: Ben's having a party.

5. A: _____ did you call?
   B: Tracy.

6. A: _____ do you need?
   B: Dr. Smith or her nurse.

□ **Exercise 18. Let's talk: interview.** (Chart 5-4)
Walk around the room and ask your classmates questions with *who* or *what*.

Example: _____ are you currently reading?
SPEAKER A: What are you currently reading?
SPEAKER B: A book about a cowboy.

1. _____ do you like to do in your free time?
2. _____ is your idea of the perfect vacation?
3. _____ is your best friend?
4. _____ was the most memorable event of your childhood?
5. _____ stresses you out?
6. _____ do you need that you don't have?
7. _____ would you most like to invite to dinner? Why? (*The person can be living or dead.*)

□ **Exercise 19. Listening.** (Chart 5-4)
Listen to the conversation. Listen again and complete the sentences with the words you hear.

CD 1
Track 49 **A secret**

A: John told me something.

B: _____ tell you?
               1
A: It's confidential. I can't tell you.

B: _____ anyone else?
               2
A: He told a few other people.

B: _____ tell?
               3
A: Some friends.

B: Then it's not a secret. _____ say?
                         4
A: I can't tell you.

B: _____ can't _____ me?
          5   6
A: Because it's about you. But don't worry. It's nothing bad.

B: Gee. Thanks a lot. That sure makes me feel better.

□ **Exercise 20. Let's read and talk.** (Chart 5-4)
Work in small groups. Ask your classmates for the meaning of the *italicized* words in the passage. Refer to a dictionary as necessary.

Example: type
STUDENT A: What does *type* mean?
STUDENT B: *Type* means *kind* or *category.*

Types of Books

There are several different *types* of books. You may be familiar with the categories of *fiction* and *nonfiction*. These are the two main types. *Fiction* includes *mysteries, romance, thrillers, science fiction,* and *horror. Nonfiction* includes *biographies, autobiographies, history,* and *travel.* There are other types, but these are some of the more common ones. Which type do you like best?

□ **Exercise 21. Warm-up.** (Chart 5-5)
Answer the questions with information about yourself.

1. What do you do on weekends? I . . .
2. What did you do last weekend? I . . .
3. What are you going to do this weekend? I'm going to . . .
4. What will you do the following weekend? I will . . .

5-5 Using *What* + a Form of *Do*

Question	Answer	
(a) What *does* Bob *do* every morning?	He *goes to class.*	***What*** + *a form of do* is used to ask questions about activities.
(b) What *did* you *do* yesterday?	I *went downtown.*	
(c) What *is* Anna *doing* (right now)?	She*'s studying.*	Examples of forms of ***do:*** *am doing, will do, are going to do, did, etc.*
(d) What *are* you *going to do* tomorrow?	I*'m going to go to the beach.*	
(e) What *do* you *want to do* tonight?	I *want to go to a movie.*	
(f) What *would* you *like to do* tomorrow?	I *would like to visit Jim.*	

□ **Exercise 22. Looking at grammar.** (Chart 5-5)
Make questions beginning with ***What*** + a form of ***do.***

1. A: _What are you doing_____ right now?

   B: I'm working on my monthly report.

2. A: _What did you do_____ last night?

   B: I worked on my monthly report.

3. A: _What are you going to do_____ tomorrow?

   B: I'm going to visit my relatives.

4. A: _What do you want to do_ _____ tomorrow?

   B: I want to go to the beach.

5. A: _What would you like to go_ _____ this evening?

   B: I would like to go to a movie.

6. A: _What are you going to do_ _____ tomorrow?

   B: I'm staying home and relaxing most of the day.

7. A: _What do you do_ _____ in your history class every day?

   B: We listen to the teacher talk.

8. A: _What do you do_ _____ (for a living)?*

   B: I'm a teacher.

   A: _What does_ _____ your wife _do_ ?

   B: She designs websites. She works for an Internet company.

□ **Exercise 23. Let's talk: interview.** (Chart 5-5)
Interview your classmates. Make questions with the given words and *what* + a form of *do*.
More than one verb tense may be possible. Share a few of your classmates' answers with the
class.

Example: tomorrow
SPEAKER A: What are you going to do tomorrow? / What do you want to do tomorrow? / What
would you like to do tomorrow? / Etc.
SPEAKER B: I'm going to buy a new video game. / I want to buy a new video game. / I'd like to
buy a new video game. / Etc.

 1. last night
 2. right now
 3. next Saturday
 4. this afternoon
 5. tonight
 6. last weekend
 7. after class yesterday
 8. every morning
 9. since you arrived in this city
10. on weekends

□ **Exercise 24. Warm-up.** (Chart 5-6)
Answer the questions about ice-cream flavors.

blackberry	chocolate	coffee	lemon	strawberry
caramel	coconut	green tea	mint	vanilla

1. Which ice-cream flavors are popular in your country?
2. What kind of ice cream do you like?

---

*__What do you do?__ has a special meaning. It means: *What is your occupation, your job?* Another way of asking the same
question: *What do you do for a living?*

5-6 Using *Which* and *What Kind Of*

Which

(a) TOM: May I borrow a pen from you? ANN: Sure. I have two pens. This pen has black ink. That pen has red ink. **Which pen** do you want? OR **Which one** do you want? OR **Which** do you want?	In (a): Ann uses **which** (not **what**) because she wants Tom to choose. **Which** is used when the speaker wants someone to make a choice, when the speaker is offering alternatives: *this one or that one; these or those.*
(b) SUE: I like these earrings, and I like those too. BOB: **Which** (*earrings* / *ones*) are you going to buy? SUE: I think I'll get these.	**Which** can be used with either singular or plural nouns.
(c) JIM: Here's a photo of my daughter's class. KIM: Very nice. **Which one** is your daughter?	**Which** can be used to ask about people as well as things.
(d) SUE: My aunt gave me some money for my birthday. I'm going to take it with me to the mall. BOB: **What** are you going to buy with it? SUE: I haven't decided yet.	In (d): The question doesn't involve choosing from a particular group of items, so Bob uses **what**, not **which**.

What kind of

QUESTION	ANSWER	*What kind of* asks for information about a specific type (a specific kind) in a general category.
(e) **What kind of** *shoes* did you buy?	Boots. Sandals. Tennis shoes. Loafers. Running shoes. High heels. Etc.	In (e): general category = shoes specific kinds = boots sandals tennis shoes etc.
(f) **What kind of** *fruit* do you like best?	Apples. Bananas. Oranges. Grapefruit. Strawberries. Etc.	In (f): general category = fruit specific kinds = apples bananas oranges etc.

❑ **Exercise 25. Looking at grammar.** (Chart 5-6)
Make questions beginning with **Which** or **What**.

1. A: I have two books. ___Which book / Which one / Which do you want?___

   B: That one. (I want that book.)

2: A: ___What did you buy when you went shopping?___

   B: A book. (I bought a book when I went shopping.)

3. A: Could I borrow your pen for a minute?

    B: Sure. I have two. _____

    A: That one. (I would like that one.)

4. A: _____

    B: A pen. (Hassan borrowed a pen from me.)

5. A: _____

    B: Two pieces of hard candy. (I have two pieces of hard candy in my hand.) Would you like one?

    A: Yes. Thanks.

    B: _____

    A: The yellow one. (I'd like the yellow one.)

6. A: Tony and I went shopping. I got some new shoes.

    B: _____

    A: A tie. (Tony got a tie.)

7. A: Did you enjoy your trip to South America?

    B: Yes, I did. Very much.

    A: _____

    B: Peru, Brazil, and Venezuela. (I visited Peru, Brazil, and Venezuela.)*

    A: _____

    B: Peru. (I enjoyed Peru the most. I have family there.)

□ **Exercise 26. Let's talk: interview.** (Chart 5-6)
Make questions. Ask one of your classmates each question and write the answer. Share some of their answers with the class.

1. A: What kind of ___*shoes*___ are you wearing?

    B: Boots. *Classmate's answer:* _____

2. A: What kind of ___*meat*___ do you eat most often?

    B: Beef. *Classmate's answer:* _____

3. A: What kind of _____ do you like best?

    B: Rock 'n roll. *Classmate's answer:* _____

4. A: What kind of _____ do you like to watch?

    B: Comedy. *Classmate's answer:* _____

5. A: What kind of _____ do you like best?

    B: *Classmate's answer:* _____

---

*The difference between **what** *country* and **which** *country* is often very small.

□ **Exercise 27. Warm-up.** (Chart 5-7)
Answer the questions.

1. This is Ted's daughter. Whose daughter is that?
   a. That's Terry.   b. That's Terry's.

2. This is Ted. Who's next to him?
   a. That's Terry.   b. That's Terry's.

5-7 Using *Whose*

Question	Answer	
(a) *Whose* (*book*) is this?	It's John's (book).	*Whose* asks about possession.*
(b) *Whose* (*books*) are those?	They're mine (OR my books).	Notice in (a): The speaker of the question
(c) *Whose car* did you borrow?	I borrowed Karen's (car).	may omit the noun (*book*) if the meaning is clear to the listener.
COMPARE:		*Who's* and *whose* have the same pronunciation.
(d) *Who's* that?	Mary Smith.	
(e) *Whose* is that?	Mary's.	*Who's* is a contraction of *who is*. *Whose* asks about possession.

*See Charts 6-11, p. 166, and 6-12, p. 168, for ways of expressing possession.

□ **Exercise 28. Let's talk: pairwork.** (Chart 5-7)
Work with a partner. Partner B looks at the picture below and tries to remember what the women are wearing. Then Partner B closes his/her book. Partner A asks questions by pointing to an item on page 126 and using *whose*. Partners should change roles after four items.

Example:
PARTNER A: Whose purse is that?
PARTNER B: It's Rita's.

Nina   Rita

□ **Exercise 29. Listening.** (Chart 5-7)

Listen to the questions and circle the correct completions.

CD 1
Track 50

| 1. Who's | Whose | 3. Who's | Whose | 5. Who's | Whose |
| 2. Who's | Whose | 4. Who's | Whose | 6. Who's | Whose |

□ **Exercise 30. Listening.** (Chart 5-7)

Listen to the questions. Decide if the speaker is saying *whose* or *who's.*

CD 1
Track 51

An old vacation photo

| 1. whose | who's | 3. whose | who's | 5. whose | who's |
| 2. whose | who's | 4. whose | who's | 6. whose | who's |

□ **Exercise 31. Warm-up.** (Chart 5-8)

Match each question in Column A with the correct answer in Column B.

Column A

1. How tall is your sister? _____

2. How old is your brother? _____

3. How did you get here? _____

4. How soon do we need to go? _____

5. How well do you know Kazu? _____

Column B

a. By bus.

b. In five minutes.

c. I don't. I only know his sister.

d. Fifteen.

e. Five feet (1.52 meters).

5-8 Using *How*

Question	Answer	
(a) *How* did you get here?	I drove. / By car. I took a taxi. / By taxi. I took a bus. / By bus. I flew. / By plane. I took a train. / By train. I walked. / On foot.	*How* has many uses. One use of *how* is to ask about means (ways) of transportation.
(b) *How old* are you? (c) *How tall* is he? (d) *How big* is your apartment? (e) *How sleepy* are you? (f) *How hungry* are you? (g) *How soon* will you be ready? (h) *How well* does he speak English? (i) *How quickly* can you get here?	Twenty-one. About six feet. It has three rooms. Very sleepy. I'm starving. In five minutes. Very well. I can get there in 30 minutes.	*How* is often used with adjectives (e.g., *old, big*) and adverbs (e.g., *well, quickly*).

❑ **Exercise 32. Reading and grammar.** (Chart 5-8)
Read the passage about John and then answer the questions.

Long John

John is 14 years old. He is very tall for his age. He is 6 foot, 6 inches (2 meters). His friends call him "Long John." People are surprised to find out that he is still a teenager. Both his parents are average height, so John's height seems unusual.

It causes problems for him, especially when he travels. Beds in hotels are too short, and there is never enough leg room on airplanes. He is very uncomfortable. When he can, he prefers to take a train because he can walk around and stretch his legs.

1. How tall is John? _____.

2. How old is John? _____.

3. How well do you think he sleeps in hotels? _____.

4. How comfortable is he on airplanes? _____.

5. How does he like to travel? _____.

Exercise 33. Looking at grammar. (Chart 5-8)
Make questions with *How*.

1. A: <u>How old is your daughter?</u>
   B: Ten. (My daughter is ten years old.)

2. A: _____
   B: Very important. (Education is very important.)

3. A: _____
   B: By bus. (I get to school by bus.)

4. A: _____
   B: Very, very deep. (The ocean is very, very deep.)

5. A: _____
   B: By plane. (I'm going to get to Buenos Aires by plane.)

6. A: _____
   B: Not very. (The test wasn't very difficult.)

7. A: _____
   B: It's 29,029 feet high. (Mt. Everest is 29,029 feet high.)★

8. A: _____
   B: I ran. (I ran here.)

□ **Exercise 34. Listening.** (Chart 5-8)
Complete the conversations with the words you hear.

CD 1
Track 52

1. A: _____ are these eggs?
   B: I just bought them at the Farmers' Market, so they should be fine.

2. A: _____ were the tickets?
   B: They were 50% off.

3. A: _____ was the driver's test?
   B: Well, I didn't pass, so that gives you an idea.

4. A: _____ is the car?
   B: There's dirt on the floor. We need to vacuum it inside.

5. A: _____ is the frying pan?
   B: Don't touch it! You'll burn yourself.

6. A: _____ is the street you live on?
   B: There is a lot of traffic, so we keep the windows closed a lot.

7. A: _____ are you about interviewing for the job?
   B: Very. I already scheduled an interview with the company.

★29,029 feet = 8,848 meters

□ **Exercise 35. Warm-up: trivia.** (Chart 5-9)
Match each question in Column A with the best answer in Column B.*

Column A

1. How often does the earth go completely
   around the sun? ____
2. How often do the summer Olympics
   occur? ____
3. How often do earthquakes occur? ____
4. How many times a year can a healthy
   person safely donate blood? ____
5. How many times a day do the hands
   on a clock overlap? ____

Column B

a. About six times a year.
b. Several hundred times a day.
c. Once a year.
d. Every four years.
e. Exactly 22 times a day.

5-9	Using *How Often*	
Question	**Answer**	
(a) *How often* do you go shopping?	Every day. Once a week. About twice a week. Every other day or so.* Three times a month.	***How often*** asks about frequency.
(b) *How many times a day* do you eat?	Three or four.	Other ways of asking ***how often:***
How many times a week do you go shopping?	Two.	
How many times a month do you go to the post office?	Once.	***how many times*** { a day / a week / a month / a year
How many times a year do you take a vacation?	Once or twice.	

Frequency Expressions		
a lot	every	
occasionally	every other	
once in a while	once a	} day / week / month / year
not very often	twice a	
hardly ever	three times a	
almost never	ten times a	
never		

Every other day means "Monday yes, Tuesday no, Wednesday yes, Thursday no," etc.
Or so means "approximately."

---

*See *Trivia Answers,* p. 421.

□ **Exercise 36. Let's talk: pairwork.** (Chart 5-9)
Work with a partner. Take turns asking and answering questions with *How often* or *How many times a day/week/month/year*.

Example: eat lunch at the cafeteria
SPEAKER A: How often do you eat lunch at the cafeteria?
SPEAKER B: About twice a week. How about you? How often do you eat at the cafeteria?
SPEAKER A: I don't. I bring my own lunch.

1. check email
2. listen to podcasts
3. go out to eat
4. cook your own dinner
5. buy a toothbrush
6. go swimming
7. attend weddings
8. download music from the Internet

□ **Exercise 37. Reading and listening.** (Charts 5-8 and 5-9)
Read the short paragraph about Ben. Then complete the questions with the words you hear.

CD 1
Track 53

Ben's Sleeping Problem

Ben has a problem with insomnia. He's unable to fall asleep at night very easily. He also wakes up often in the middle of the night and has trouble getting back to sleep. Right now he's talking to a nurse at a sleep disorders clinic. The nurse is asking him some general questions.

1. _____ you?

2. _____ you?

3. _____ you weigh?

4. In general, _____ you sleep at night?

5. _____ you fall asleep?

6. _____ you wake up during the night?

7. _____ you in the mornings?

8. _____ you exercise?

9. _____ you feeling right now?

10. _____ you come in for an overnight appointment?

□ **Exercise 38. Warm-up.** (Chart 5-10)
Look at the map and answer the questions about flying distances to these cities.

1. How far is it from London to Madrid?
2. How many miles is it from London to Paris?
3. How many kilometers is it from Paris to Madrid?

5-10 Using *How Far*

(a) *It is* 489 miles *from* Oslo *to* Helsinki by air.*	The most common way of expressing distance: *It is* + distance + *from/to* + *to/from*
(b) *It is* 3,605 miles { *from* Moscow *to* Beijing. *from* Beijing *to* Moscow. *to* Beijing *from* Moscow. *to* Moscow *from* Beijing.	In (b): All four expressions with *from* and *to* have the same meaning.
(c) — *How far is it* from Mumbai to Delhi? — 725 miles. (d) — *How far do you* live from school? — Four blocks.	*How far* is used to ask questions about distance.
(e) *How many miles* is it from London to Paris? (f) *How many kilometers* is it to Montreal from here? (g) *How many blocks* is it to the post office?	Other ways to ask *how far*: • how many miles • how many kilometers • how many blocks

*1 mile = 1.60 kilometers; 1 kilometer = 00.614 mile

□ **Exercise 39. Looking at grammar.** (Chart 5-10)
Make questions with *How far*.

1. A: ___How far is it from Prague to Budapest?___
   B: 276 miles. (It's 276 miles to Prague from Budapest.)

2. A: _____

   B: 257 kilometers. (It's 257 kilometers from Montreal to Quebec.)

3. A: _____

   B: Six blocks. (It's six blocks from here to the post office.)

4. A: _____

   B: A few miles. (I live a few miles from work.)

☐ **Exercise 40. Looking at grammar.** (Chart 5-10)
Write four questions with **How far** and words from the list. Use this model: **How far is it
from (___) to (___)?** Look up the correct distances. Ask other students your questions.

the sun	the moon	the earth	Mars
Venus	Jupiter	Saturn	Neptune

☐ **Exercise 41. Warm-up.** (Chart 5-11)
Complete the sentences. Then ask three different classmates about their nighttime routine.
Begin with **How long does it take you to . . . ?** Share some of their answers with the class.

1. It takes me _____ minutes to get ready for bed.

2. It takes me _____ minutes to brush my teeth.

3. It usually takes me _____ minutes/hour(s) to fall asleep.

5-11 Length of Time: *It + Take* and *How Long*

IT + TAKE + (SOMEONE) + LENGTH OF TIME + INFINITIVE				*It + take* is often used with time words
(a) *It* takes		20 minutes	*to cook* rice.	and an infinitive to express **length of time**, as in (a) and (b).
(b) *It* took	Al	two hours	*to drive* to work.	An infinitive = *to + the simple form of a verb.**
				In (a): *to cook* is an infinitive.

(c) *How long* does it take to cook rice? Twenty minutes.	*How long* asks about *length of time*.
(d) *How long* did it take Al to drive to work today? Two hours.	
(e) *How long* did you study last night? Four hours.	
(f) *How long* will you be in Hong Kong? Ten days.	

(g) *How many days* will you be in Hong Kong?	Other ways of asking *how long:*
	how many + { minutes, hours, days, weeks, months, years }

*See Chart 13-3, p. 346.

❑ **Exercise 42. Let's talk: pairwork.** (Chart 5-11)
Work with a partner. Take turns asking and answering questions using *it* + *take*. Share a few of your answers with the class.

1. How long does it take you to . . .
   a. eat breakfast? → *It takes me ten minutes to eat breakfast.*
   b. get to class?
   c. write a short paragraph in English?
   d. read a 300-page book?

2. Generally speaking, how long does it take to . . .
   a. fly from (*a city*) to (*a city*)?
   b. get from here to your hometown?
   c. get used to living in a foreign country?
   d. commute from (*a local place*) to (*a local place*) during rush hour?

❑ **Exercise 43. Looking at grammar.** (Chart 5-11)
Make questions with *How long*.

1. A: ___How long did it take you to drive to İstanbul?___
   B: Five days. (It took me five days to drive to Istanbul.)

2. A: _____
   B: A week. (Mr. McNally will be in the hospital for a week.)

3. A: _____
   B: A long time. (It takes a long time to learn a second language.)

4. A: _____
   B: Six months. (I've been living here for six months.)

5. A: _____
   B: Six years. (I lived in Oman for six years.)

6. A: _____
   B: A couple of years. (I've known Mr. Pham for a couple of years.)

7. A: _____
   B: Since 2005. (He's been living in Canada since 2005.)

□ **Exercise 44. Warm-up: listening.** (Chart 5-12)

Listen to the questions. The verbs in *italics* are contracted with the question word. Choose the correct verb from the list for each question.

CD 1
Track 54

does	did	is	are	will

A birthday

1. *When's* your birthday?   _____

2. *When'll* your party be?   _____

3. *Where'd* you decide to have it?   _____

4. *Who're* you inviting?   _____

5-12 Spoken and Written Contractions with Question Words

	Spoken Only	
is	(a) "*When's* he coming?" "*Why's* she late?"	**Is**, **are**, **does**, **did**, **has**, **have**, and **will** are usually contracted with question words in speaking.
are	(b) "*What're* these?" "*Who're* they talking to?"	
does	(c) "*When's* the movie start?" "*Where's* he live?"	
did	(d) "*Who'd* you see?" "*What'd* you do?"	
has	(e) "*What's* she done?" "*Where's* he gone?"	
have	(f) "*How've* you been?" "*What've* I done?"	
will	(g) "*Where'll* you be?" "*When'll* they be here?"	
	(h) **What do you** → Whaddaya think? (i) **What are you** → Whaddaya thinking?	**What do you** and **What are you** both can be reduced to "Whaddaya" in spoken English.
	Written	
is	(j) *Where's* Ed? *What's* that? *Who's* he?	Only contractions with **where**, **what**, or **who** + **is** are commonly used in writing, such as in letters to friends or emails. They are generally not appropriate in more formal writing, such as in magazine articles or reference material.

□ **Exercise 45. Listening.** (Chart 5-12)

Listen to the contractions in these questions.

CD 1
Track 55

1. Where is my key?
2. Where are my keys?
3. Who are those people?
4. What is in that box?
5. What are you doing?
6. Where did Bob go last night?
7. Who will be at the party?

8. Why is the teacher absent?
9. Who is that?
10. Why did you say that?
11. Who did you talk to at the party?
12. How are we going to get to work?
13. What did you say?
14. How will you do that?

□ **Exercise 46. Listening.** (Chart 5-12)

Complete the sentences with the words you hear. Write the non-contracted forms.

CD 1
Track 56
On an airplane

Example: You will hear: When's the plane land?

You will write: ___*When does*___ the plane land?

1. _____ you going to sit with?

2. _____ you going to get your suitcase under the seat?

3. _____ the flight attendant just say?

4. _____ we need to put our seat belts back on?

5. _____ the plane descending?

6. _____ we going down?

7. _____ the pilot tell us what's going on?

8. _____ meet you when you land?

9. _____ our connecting flight?

10. _____ we get from the airport to our hotel?

□ **Exercise 47. Listening.** (Chart 5-12)

Complete the questions with the words you hear. Write the non-contracted forms.

CD 1
Track 57
A mother talking to her teenage daughter

1. _____ going?

2. _____ going with?

3. _____ that?

4. _____ known him?

5. _____ meet him?

6. _____ go to school?

7. _____ a good student?

8. _____ be back?

9. _____ wearing that outfit?

10. _____ giving me that look?

11. _____ asking so many questions?

      Because I love you!

❑ Exercise 48. Listening. (Chart 5-12)

Listen to the questions and circle the correct non-reduced forms of the words you hear.

CD 1
Track 58

Example: You will hear: Whaddya want?

           You will choose: What are you (What do you)

1. What are you   What do you

2. What are you   What do you

3. What are you   What do you

4. What are you   What do you

5. What are you   What do you

6. What are you   What do you

7. What are you   What do you

8. What are you   What do you

❑ Exercise 49. Warm-up. (Chart 5-13)

Part I. Both sentences in each pair are grammatically correct. Which question in each pair do you think is more common in spoken English?

1. a. How do you spell "Hawaii?"
   b. What is the spelling for "Hawaii?"

2. a. How do you pronounce G-A-R-A-G-E?
   b. What is the pronunciation for G-A-R-A-G-E?

Part II. Which two questions have the same meaning?

1. How are you doing?
2. How's it going?
3. How do you do?

5-13 More Questions with *How*

Question		Answer	
(a) *How do you spell* "coming"?		C-O-M-I-N-G.	To answer (a): Spell the word.
(b) *How do you say* "yes" in Japanese?		Hai.	To answer (b): Say the word.
(c) *How do you say /pronounce* this word?		———	To answer (c): Pronounce the word.
(d) *How are you getting along?*	Great.		In (d), (e), and (f): How is your life? Is your life okay? Do you have any problems?
(e) *How are you doing?*	Fine.		
(f) *How's it going?*	Okay.		NOTE: Example (f) is also used in greetings: *Hi, Bob. How's it going?*
	So-so.		
(g) *How do you feel?* *How are you feeling?*	Terrific! Wonderful! Great! Fine. Okay. So-so. A bit under the weather. Not so good. Terrible! / Lousy. / Awful!		The questions in (g) ask about health or about general emotional state.
(h) *How do you do?*	How do you do?		***How do you do?*** is used by two speakers when they meet each other for the first time in a somewhat formal situation, as in (h).*

*A: *Dr. Erickson, I'd like to introduce you to a friend of mine, Rick Brown. Rick, this is my biology professor, Dr. Erickson.*
B: ***How do you do,*** *Mr. Brown?*
C: ***How do you do,*** *Dr. Erickson? I'm pleased to meet you.*

☐ **Exercise 50. Game.** (Chart 5-13)
Divide into two teams. Take turns spelling the words your teacher gives you. The team with the most correct answers wins. Your book is closed.

Example: country
TEACHER: How do you spell "country"?
TEAM A: C-O-U-N-T-R-Y.
TEACHER: Good. (*If the answer is incorrect, the other team gets a try.*)

1. together
2. people
3. daughter
4. beautiful
5. foreign
6. neighbor
7. beginning
8. intelligent
9. Mississippi
10. purple
11. rained
12. different

□ **Exercise 51. Let's talk.** (Chart 5-13)

Walk around the room and ask your classmates how to say each item in another language (Japanese, Arabic, German, French, Korean, etc). If someone doesn't know, ask another person. Use this question: **How do you say (___) in (___)?**

Example:
SPEAKER A: How do you say "yes" in French?
SPEAKER B: "Yes" in French is "oui."

1. No.	3. Okay.	5. Good-bye.
2. Thank you.	4. How are you?	6. Excuse me.

□ **Exercise 52. Warm-up.** (Chart 5-14)

In the conversation, the speakers are making suggestions. Underline their suggestions.

A: Let's invite the Thompsons over for dinner.

B: Good idea! How about next Sunday?

A: Let's do it sooner. What about this Saturday?

5-14 Using *How About* and *What About*

(a) A: We need one more player. 　　B: *How about/What about Jack?* 　　　 Let's ask him if he wants to play.	*How about* and *what about* have the same meaning and usage. They are used to make suggestions or offers.
(b) A: What time should we meet? 　　B: *How about/What about three o'clock?*	*How about* and *what about* are followed by a noun (or pronoun) or the *-ing* form of a verb (gerund).
(c) A: What should we do this afternoon? 　　B: *How about going* to the zoo? (d) A: *What about asking* Sally over for dinner next 　　　 Sunday? 　　B: Okay. Good idea.	NOTE: *How about* and *what about* are frequently used in informal spoken English, but are usually not used in writing.
(e) A: I'm tired. *How about you?* 　　B: Yes, I'm tired too. (f) A: Are you hungry? 　　B: No. *What about you?* 　　A: I'm a little hungry.	*How about you?* and *What about you?* are used to ask a question that refers to the information or question that immediately preceded it. In (e): *How about you?* = *Are you tired?* In (f): *What about you?* = *Are you hungry?*

□ **Exercise 53. Grammar and listening.** (Chart 5-14)

Choose the best response. Then listen to each conversation and check your answer.

CD 1
Track 59

Example:
SPEAKER A: What are you going to do over vacation?
SPEAKER B: I'm staying here. What about you?
SPEAKER A: a. Yes, I will. I have a vacation too.
　　　　　　 (b.) I'm going to Jordan to visit my sister.
　　　　　　 c. I did too.

1. A: Did you like the movie?
   B: It was okay, I guess. How about you?
   A: a. I thought it was pretty good.
      b. I'm sure.
      c. I saw it last night.

2. A: Are you going to the company party?
   B: I haven't decided yet. What about you?
   A: a. I didn't know that.
      b. Why aren't you going?
      c. I think I will.

3. A: Do you like living in this city?
   B: Sort of. How about you?
   A: a. I'm living in the city.
      b. I'm not sure. It's pretty noisy.
      c. Yes, I have been.

4. A: What are you going to have?
   B: Well, I'm not really hungry. I think I might order just a salad. How about you?
   A: a. I'll have one too.
      b. I'm eating at a restaurant.
      c. No, I'm not.

☐ **Exercise 54. Let's talk: pairwork.** (Chart 5-14)
Work with a partner. The given questions are common ways to begin casual conversations or make "small talk." Partner A asks the question and Partner B answers. Both speakers look at each other, not the book, when speaking.

Example: What kind of books do you like to read?
PARTNER A: What kind of books do you like to read?
PARTNER B: I like biographies. How about you?
PARTNER A: Thrillers are my favorite.

1. How long have you been living in (*this city or country*)?
2. What are you going to do after class today?
3. What kind of movies do you like to watch?

Change roles.
4. Do you come from a large family?
5. What kind of sports do you enjoy?
6. Do you speak a lot of English outside of class?

☐ **Exercise 55. Warm-up.** (Chart 5-15)
What is the <u>expected</u> response? Circle *yes* or *no*.

1. You're studying English, aren't you?   yes   no

2. You're not a native speaker of English, are you?   yes   no

5-15 Tag Questions

(a) Jill is sick, ***isn't she?*** (b) You didn't know, ***did you?*** (c) There's enough time, ***isn't there?*** (d) I'm not late, ***am I?*** (e) I'm late, ***aren't I?***	A tag question is a question that is added onto the end of a sentence. An auxiliary verb is used in a tag question. Notice that ***I am*** becomes ***aren't I*** in a negative tag, as in (e). (*Am I not* is also possible, but it is very formal and rare.)

Affirmative (+)	**Negative (−)**	**Affirmative Expected Answer**	When the main verb is affirmative, the tag question is negative, and the expected answer agrees with the main verb.
(d) You ***know*** Bill,	***don't*** you?	Yes.	
(e) Marie ***is*** from Paris,	***isn't*** she?	Yes.	

Negative (−)	**Affirmative (+)**	**Negative Expected Answer**	When the main verb is negative, the tag question is affirmative, and the expected answer agrees with the main verb.
(f) You ***don't know*** Tom,	***do*** you?	No.	
(g) Marie ***isn't*** from Athens,	***is*** she?	No.	

THE SPEAKER'S QUESTION	THE SPEAKER'S IDEA
	Tag questions have two types of intonation: rising and falling. The intonation determines the meaning of the tag.
(h) It will be nice tomorrow, ***won't it?*** ↗	A speaker uses rising intonation to make sure information is correct. In (h): the speaker has an idea; the speaker is checking to see if the idea is correct.
(i) It will be nice tomorrow, ***won't it?*** ↘	Falling intonation is used when the speaker is seeking agreement. In (i): the speaker thinks it will be nice tomorrow and is almost certain the listener will agree.
YES/NO QUESTIONS (j) — Will it be nice tomorrow? — ***Yes, it will.*** OR ***No, it won't.***	In (j): The speaker has no idea. The speaker is simply looking for information. Compare (h) and (i) with (j).

☐ **Exercise 56. Listening and grammar.** (Chart 5-15)

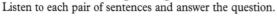

Listen to each pair of sentences and answer the question.

CD 1
Track 60

1. a. You're Mrs. Rose, aren't you?
   b. Are you Mrs. Rose?

   QUESTION: In which sentence is the speaker checking to see if her information is correct?

2. a. Do you take cream with your coffee?
   b. You take cream with your coffee, don't you?

   QUESTION: In which sentence does the speaker have no idea?

3. a. You don't want to leave, do you?
   b. Do you want to leave?

   QUESTION: In which sentence is the speaker looking for agreement?

□ **Exercise 57. Grammar and listening.** (Chart 5-15)

Complete the tag questions with the correct verbs. Then listen to the questions and check your answers.

CD 1
Track 61

1. **Simple Present**

   a. You *like* strong coffee, ___don't___ you?

   b. David *goes* to Ames High School, _____ he?

   c. Leila and Sara *live* on Tree Road, _____ they?

   d. Jane *has* the keys to the storeroom, _____ she?

   e. Jane*'s* in her office, _____ she?

   f. You*'re* a member of this class, _____ you?

   g. Oleg *doesn't* have a car, _____ he?

   h. Lisa *isn't* from around here, _____ she?

   i. I*'m* in trouble, _____ I?

2. **Simple Past**

   a. Paul *went* to Indonesia, _____ he?

   b. You *didn't talk* to the boss, _____ you?

   c. Ted's parents *weren't* at home, _____ they?

   d. That *was* Pat's idea, _____ it?

3. **Present Progressive, *Be Going To*, and Past Progressive**

   a. You*'re studying* hard, _____ you?

   b. Greg *isn't working* at the bank, _____ he?

   c. It *isn't going to rain* today, _____ it?

   d. Michelle and Yoko *were helping*, _____ they?

   e. He *wasn't listening*, _____ he?

4. **Present Perfect**

   a. It *has been* warmer than usual, _____ it?

   b. You*'ve had* a lot of homework, _____ you?

   c. We *haven't spent* much time together, _____ we?

   d. Fatima *has started* her new job, _____ she?

   e. Bruno *hasn't finished* his sales report yet, _____ he?

   f. Steve*'s had to leave* early, _____ he?

□ **Exercise 58. Let's talk: pairwork.** (Chart 5-15)

Work with a partner. Make true statements for your partner to agree with. Remember, if your partner makes an affirmative statement before the tag, the expected answer is "yes." If your partner makes a negative statement before the tag, the expected answer is "no."

1. The weather is _____ today, isn't it?

2. This books costs _____, doesn't it?

3. I'm _____, aren't I?

4. The classroom isn't _____, is it?

5. Our grammar homework wasn't _____,was it?

6. Tomorrow will be _____, won't it?

□ **Exercise 59. Listening.** (Chart 5-15)

Listen to the tag questions and choose the <u>expected</u> responses.

CD 1
Track 62 **Checking in at a hotel**

Example: You will hear: Our room's ready, isn't it?

You will choose: (yes)   no

1. yes	no	6. yes	no
2. yes	no	7. yes	no
3. yes	no	8. yes	no
4. yes	no	9. yes	no
5. yes	no	10. yes	no

□ **Exercise 60. Check your knowledge.** (Chapter 5)

Edit the sentences. Correct the errors in question formation.

1. Who you saw? → *Who did you see?*

2. Where I buy subway tickets?

3. Whose is that backpack?

4. What kind of tea you like best?

5. It's freezing out and you're not wearing gloves, aren't you?

6. Who you studied with at school?

7. She is going to work this weekend, doesn't she?

8. How long take to get to the airport from here?

9. How much height your father have?

10. It's midnight. Why you so late? Why you forget to call?

□ **Exercise 61. Listening.** (Chapter 5)

Part I. Listen to the questions and choose the correct answers.

CD 1
Track 63

Example: You will hear: How often do you brush your teeth?
You will choose: (a.) Three times a day.
b. Yes, I do.
c. In the evening.

1. a. I love it.
   b. Jazz and rock.
   c. The radio.

2. a. I was really tired.
   b. At 7:30.
   c. A package.

3. a. A little sick.
   b. No, I'm not.
   c. Howard's fine.

4. a. Two miles.
   b. Three blocks.
   c. Ten minutes.

5. a. Amy is.
   b. Amy's.
   c. That is Amy.

6. a. Next week.
   b. A few days ago.
   c. On Fifth Street.

Part II. Listen to each conversation and choose the sentence that best completes it.

7. a. My wallet.
   b. At the box office.
   c. I think so.

8. a. It usually comes by noon.
   b. By truck.
   c. One time a day.

9. a. Yes, I am.
   b. My company is moving to another city.
   c. I loved my job.

10. a. It's great.
    b. I'm a construction supervisor.
    c. We're doing really well.

□ **Exercise 62. Let's listen and talk: pairwork.** (Chapter 5)

Listen to the conversation. Then work with a partner. Take turns being the cashier and the customer. Complete the sentences with items from the menu and practice the conversation.

CD 1
Track 64

burger	chicken strips	soft drinks: *cola, lemon soda, iced tea*
cheeseburger	fish burger	milkshakes: *vanilla, strawberry, chocolate*
double cheeseburger	veggie burger	*(small, medium, large)*
fries	salad	

Ordering at a fast-food restaurant

CASHIER: So, what'll it be?

CUSTOMER: I'll have a _____.

CASHIER: Would you like fries or a salad with your burger?

CUSTOMER: I'll have (a) _____.

CASHIER: What size?

CUSTOMER: _____.

CASHIER: Anything to drink?

CUSTOMER: I'll have a _____.

CASHIER: Size?

CUSTOMER: _____.

CASHIER: Okay. So that's _____

_____.

CUSTOMER: About how long'll it take?

CASHIER: We're pretty crowded right now. Probably 10 minutes or so. That'll be $6.50. Your number's on the receipt. I'll call the number when your order's ready.

CUSTOMER: Thanks.

□ **Exercise 63. Let's read and write.** (Chapters 1 → 5)

Part I. Read the fairy tale and answer the questions at the end.

The Frog Prince

Once upon a time, there was a king with three unmarried daughters. One day while the king was thinking about his daughters' futures, he had an idea. He thought, "I'm going to drop three jewels among the young men in the village center. The men who find* the jewels will become my daughters' husbands." He announced his plan to all of the people of his kingdom.

The next day, the king took an emerald, a ruby, and a diamond into the village. He walked among the young men and dropped the jewels. A handsome man picked up the emerald. Then a wealthy prince found the ruby. But a frog hopped toward the diamond and took it. He said to the king, "I am the Frog Prince. I claim your third daughter as my wife."

When the king told Trina, his third daughter, about the Frog Prince, she refused to marry him. She hid from her friends and grew sadder every day. Meanwhile, her two sisters had grand weddings.

---

*The simple present is used here because the story is giving the king's exact words in a quotation. Notice that quotation marks ("...") are used. See Chart 14-8, p. 000, for more information about quotations.

Eventually, Trina ran away and went to live in the woods, but she was very lonely and unhappy. One day Trina went swimming in a lake. Trina became tired in the cold water and decided to give up. She didn't want to live anymore. As she was drowning, the frog suddenly appeared and pushed Trina to the shore.

"Why did you save my life, Frog?"

"Because you are very young, and you have a lot to live for."

"No, I don't," said the princess. "I am the most miserable person in the world."

"Let's talk about it," said the frog. Trina and the Frog Prince sat together for hours and hours. Frog listened and understood. He told her about his own unhappiness and loneliness. They shared their deepest feelings with each other.

One day while they were sitting near the lake, Trina felt great affection for the frog. She bent down and kissed him on his forehead. Suddenly the frog turned into a man! He took Trina in his arms and said, "You saved me with your kiss. An evil wizard changed me from a prince into a frog. I needed to find the love of a woman with a truly good heart to set me free.* You looked inside me and found the real me."

Trina and the prince returned to the castle and got married. Her two sisters, she discovered, were very unhappy because their husbands treated them poorly. But Trina and her Frog Prince lived happily ever after.

Questions:
1. What did the king want for his daughters?
2. Why did a frog claim Trina for his wife?
3. What did Trina do to escape the marriage?
4. Where did she meet the frog again?
5. Why did she kiss the frog?
6. What did an evil wizard do to the frog?
7. What kind of lives did her sisters have?
8. What kind of life did Trina and the Frog Prince have?

Part II. Write a story that begins ***Once upon a time***. Use one of the given topics.

Topics:
1. Read the story again and then retell it in your own words. Write one or two paragraphs. Do not look at the story when you write.

2. Write a fairy tale that you are familiar with, perhaps one that is well known in your culture.

3. Create a story with your classmates. Each student writes one or two sentences at a time. One student begins the story. Then he or she passes the paper on to another student, who then writes a sentence or two and passes the paper on — until everyone in the class has had a chance to write part of the story, or until the story has an ending. This story can then be reproduced for the class to edit together. The class may want to add art and "publish" the final product as a small book.

---

set me free = give me my freedom

Chapter 6
Nouns and Pronouns

□ **Exercise 1. What do I already know?** (Chapter 6)
This exercise previews grammar terms used in this chapter. Identify the *italicized* word in each sentence as a noun, adjective, preposition, or pronoun.

1. Miki is a *student* at my school. _____ noun _____

2. *She* is from Kyoto, Japan. _____ pronoun _____

3. Kyoto is south *of* Tokyo. _____ preposition _____

4. It is a *beautiful* city. _____ adjective _____

5. This summer *I* am going there with Miki. _____ pronoun. _____

6. I am looking forward to this *trip*. _____ n _____

7. My parents are *happy* for me. _____ a. _____

8. I will stay *with* Miki's family. _____ prep _____

9. They have a *small* hotel. _____ a _____

10. *It* is near a popular park. _____ pron. _____

11. The park has lovely *gardens*. _____ n. _____

12. Miki has shown me postcards *of* them. _____ prep. _____

□ **Exercise 2. Warm-up.** (Chart 6-1)
Write the word **one** before the singular nouns and the word **two** before the plural nouns.

1. _____ trips   4. _____ way

2. _____ vacation   5. _____ cities

3. _____ classes   6. _____ knives

6-1 Plural Forms of Nouns

Singular	Plural	
(a) one bird one street one rose	two *birds* two *streets* two *roses*	To make most nouns plural, add *-s*.
(b) one dish one match one class one box	two *dishes* two *matches* two *classes* two *boxes*	Add *-es* to nouns ending in *-sh*, *-ch*, *-ss*, and *-x*.
(c) one baby one city	two *babies* two *cities*	If a noun ends in a consonant + *-y*, change the *y* to *i* and add *-es*, as in (c).
(d) one toy one key	two *toys* two *keys*	If *-y* is preceded by a vowel, add only *-s*, as in (d).
(e) one knife one shelf	two *knives* two *shelves*	If a noun ends in *-fe* or *-f*, change the ending to *-ves*. EXCEPTIONS: beliefs, chiefs, roofs, cuffs, cliffs.
(f) one tomato one zoo one zero	two *tomatoes* two *zoos* two *zeroes/zeros*	The plural form of nouns that end in *-o* is sometimes *-oes* and sometimes *-os*. *-oes*: tomatoes, potatoes, heroes, echoes *-os*: zoos, radios, studios, pianos, solos, sopranos, photos, autos, videos *-oes* or *-os*: zeroes/zeros, volcanoes/volcanos, tornadoes/tornados, mosquitoes/mosquitos.
(g) one child one foot one goose one man one mouse one tooth one woman one person	two *children* two *feet* two *geese* two *men* two *mice* two *teeth* two *women* two *people*	Some nouns have irregular plural forms. NOTE: The singular form of *people* can be *person, woman, man, child*. For example, one *man* and one *child* = two *people*. (Two *persons* is also possible.)
(h) one deer one fish one sheep	two *deer* two *fish* two *sheep*	The plural form of some nouns is the same as the singular form.
(i) one bacterium one crisis	two *bacteria* two *crises*	Some nouns that English has borrowed from other languages have foreign plurals.

☐ **Exercise 3. Looking at grammar.** (Chart 6-1)
Write the correct singular or plural form of the given words.

1. one chair   two _chairs_

2. a _window_   a lot of windows

3. one wish   several _wishes_

a few 3 or 4
several 6-8

4. a _dish_   two dishes

5. a tax   a lot of _taxes_ (2)

6. one boy   two _boys (2)_

7. a hobby   several _hobbies_ (2)

8. one leaf   two _leaves_ (2)

9. a _half_   two halves

10. a belief   many _beliefs_

11. one wolf   two _wolves_ (2)

12. a radio   several _radios_ (2)

13. one _sheep_   a lot of sheep

14. one _foot_   two feet

Exercise 4. Looking at grammar. (Chart 6-1)

Write the plural form of each noun under the correct heading. The number of words for each column is given in parentheses. NOTE: *fish* and *thief* can go in two places.

✓butterfly	child	hero	mouse	thief
baby	city	library	✓museum	tomato
boy	fish	✓man	potato	woman
✓bean	girl	mosquito	sandwich	zoo

People (8)	Food (5)	Things people catch (5)	Places people visit (4)
men	beans	butterflies	museums
babies			
boys			
children			
cities			
girls			

☐ **Exercise 5. Check your knowledge.** (Chart 6-1)
Edit the newspaper ad by making the appropriate nouns plural. There are eight errors.

ON SALE (while supply last)

shirt   jean   pant   dress

Outfit and shoe for babys 50% off

☐ **Exercise 6. Warm-up: listening.** (Chart 6-2)
Listen to the nouns. Circle *yes* if you hear a plural ending. If not, circle *no*.

CD 2
Track 1

Example: You will hear: books
You will choose: (yes)   no

You will hear: class
You will choose: yes   (no)

1. yes   no   3. yes   no   5. yes   no

2. yes   no   4. yes   no   6. yes   no

6-2 Pronunciation of Final -s/-es

Final **-s/-es** has three different pronunciations: /s/, /z/, and /əz/.

(a)	seats	=	seat/s/	Final **-s** is pronounced /s/ after voiceless sounds. In (a): /s/ is the sound of "s" in "bus."
	maps	=	map/s/	
	lakes	=	lake/s/	Examples of voiceless* sounds: /t/, /p/, /k/.
(b)	seeds	=	seed/z/	Final **-s** is pronounced /z/ after voiced sounds. In (b): /z/ is the sound of "z" in "buzz."
	stars	=	star/z/	
	holes	=	hole/z/	Examples of voiced* sounds: /d/, /r/, /l/, /m/, /b/, and all vowel sounds.
	laws	=	law/z/	
(c)	dishes	=	dish/əz/	Final **-s/-es** is pronounced /əz/ after *-sh, -ch, -s, -z, -ge/-dge* sounds. In (c): /əz/ adds a syllable to a word.
	matches	=	match/əz/	
	classes	=	class/əz/	
	sizes	=	size/əz/	
	pages	=	page/əz/	
	judges	=	judge/əz/	

*See Chart 2-5, p. 39, for more information about voiceless and voiced sounds.

□ **Exercise 7. Listening.** (Chart 6-2)

Listen to the words. Circle the sound you hear at the end of each word: /s/, /z/, or /əz/.

CD 2
Track 2

1. pants	/s/	/z/	/əz/		4. pens	/s/	/z/	/əz/
2. cars	/s/	/z/	/əz/		5. wishes	/s/	/z/	/əz/
3. boxes	/s/	/z/	/əz/		6. lakes	/s/	/z/	/əz/

□ **Exercise 8. Listening.** (Chart 6-2)

Listen to each pair of words. Decide if the endings have the same sound or a different sound.

CD 2
Track 3

Example: You will hear: maps   streets
You will choose: (same) different

You will hear: knives   forks
You will choose: same (different)

1. same	different		5. same	different
2. same	different		6. same	different
3. same	different		7. same	different
4. same	different		8. same	different

□ **Exercise 9. Listening and pronunciation.** (Chart 6-2)

Listen to the words. Write the pronunciation of each ending you hear: /s/, /z/, or /əz/. Practice pronouncing the words.

CD 2
Track 4

1. names = name/z/   4. boats = boat/ /   7. lips = lip/ /
2. clocks = clock/s/   5. eyelashes = eyelash/ / 8. bridges = bridge/ /
3. eyes = eye/ /   6. ways = way/ /   9. cars = car/ /

□ **Exercise 10. Listening.** (Chart 6-2)

Listen to the sentences and circle the words you hear.

CD 2
Track 5

1. size	sizes		3. fax	faxes		5. glass	glasses
2. fax	faxes		4. price	prices		6. prize	prizes

□ **Exercise 11. Warm-up** (Chart 6-3)

Part I. Work in small groups. Make lists.

1. Name things people need to take with them when they travel. *money. water. food.*
2. Name things you do when you have free time. *exercise*
3. Name important people in your life. *your family.*

Part II. Read your lists. Make sentences using the following information. Share some of your sentences with the class.

1. People need to take _money_ with them when they travel.
2. I _listen to music_ when I have free time.
3. _____ have been important in my life.
   My mom and dad.

Part III. Answer these questions about your answers in Part II.

1. In which sentence did you write verbs?
2. In which two sentences did you write nouns?
3. In which sentence did you write subjects?
4. In which sentence did you write objects?

6-3 Subjects, Verbs, and Objects

S   V
(a) The   *sun*   *shines*.
   (noun) (verb)
 	
   S   V
(b) *Plants*   *grow*.
   (noun) (verb)
	An English sentence has a SUBJECT (S) and a VERB (V).
	
	The SUBJECT is a **noun**. In (a): *sun* is a noun; it is the subject of the verb *shines*.

S   V   O
(c) *Plants* *need* *water*.
   (noun) (verb) (noun)
 	
   S   V   O
(d) *Bob*   *is reading* *a book*.
   (noun)   (verb)   (noun)
	Sometimes a VERB is followed by an OBJECT (O).
	
	The OBJECT of a verb is a **noun**. In (c): *water* is the object of the verb *need*.

❑ **Exercise 12. Looking at grammar.** (Chart 6-3)
Complete each diagram with the correct subject, verb, and object.

1. The carpenter built a table.

The carpenter	built	a table
subject	verb	object of verb

2. Birds fly.

Birds	fly	(none)
subject	verb	object of verb

3. Cows eat grass.

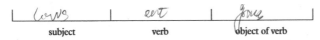

subject	verb	object of verb

4. The actor sang.

subject	verb	object of verb

5. The actor sang a song.

| The actor | sang | a song |
| subject | verb | object of verb |

6. Accidents happen frequently.

| Accidents | happe | none |
| subject | verb | object of verb |

7. The accident injured a woman.

| The accident | injured | a woman |
| subject | verb | object of verb |

☑ **Exercise 13. Looking at grammar.** (Charts 6-2 and 6-3)
If the word in *italics* is used as a noun, circle "N." If the word in *italics* is used as a verb, circle "V."

1. People *smile* when they're happy.   N   (V)
2. Maryam has a nice *smile* when she's happy.   (N)   V
3. Please don't sign your *name* in pencil.   (N)   V
4. People often *name* their children after relatives.   N   (V)
5. Airplanes *land* on runways at the airport.   N   (V)
6. The *land* across the street from our house is vacant.   (N)   V
7. People usually *store* milk in the refrigerator.   N   (V)
8. We went to the *store* to buy some milk.   (N)   V
9. I took the express *train* from New York to Washington, D.C., last week.   (N)   V
10. Lindsey *trains* horses as a hobby.   N   (V)

❑ **Exercise 14. Warm-up: pairwork.** (Chart 6-4)
Work with a partner. Make true sentences about yourself using *like* or *don't like*. Share a few of your partner's answers with the class.

I like/don't like to do my homework . . .

1. at the library.
2. at the kitchen table.
3. in my bedroom.
4. on my bed.
5. with a friend.
6. in the evening.
7. on weekends.
8. after dinner.
9. before class.
10. during class.

6-4 Objects of Prepositions

S	V	O	PREP	O OF PREP	Many English sentences have prepositional phrases.
(a) Ann put her books			*on*	*the*	*desk.*

(a) Ann put her books *on* *the* *desk.*
(noun)

In (a): *on the desk* is a prepositional phrase.

A prepositional phrase consists of a PREPOSITION (PREP) and an OBJECT OF A PREPOSITION (O of PREP). The object of a preposition is a NOUN.

S V PREP   O OF PREP
(b) A leaf fell *to* *the* *ground.*
(noun)

Reference List of Prepositions

about	before	despite	of	to
above	behind	down	off	toward(s)
across	below	during	on	under
after	beneath	for	out	until
against	beside	from	over	up
along	besides	in	since	upon
among	between	into	through	with
around	beyond	like : *for example*	throughout	within
at	by	near *next to*	till	without

I buy fruits like apples and bananas.

□ **Exercise 15. Looking at grammar.** (Chart 6-4)

Check (✓) the prepositional phrases, and <u>underline</u> the noun in each phrase that is the object of the preposition.

1. __✓__ across the <u>street</u>   5. __✓__ next to the phone
2. __✓__ in a minute   6. _____ doing work
3. _____ daily   7. __✓__ in a few hours *n.*
4. __✓__ down the hill   8. __✓__ from my parents

□ **Exercise 16. Looking at grammar.** (Charts 6-3 and 6-4)

Check (✓) the sentences that have objects of prepositions. Identify the preposition (P) and the object of the preposition (Obj. of P).

1. a. _____ Emily waited quietly.

                                 P   Obj. of P
    b. __✓__ Emily waited quietly for her mother.

                                   P Obj. of P
    c. __✓__ Emily's mother was talking to a friend.

2. a. _____ Kimiko saw a picture on the wall.

    b. _____ Kimiko recognized the people.

    c. _____ Kimiko looked at the picture closely.

3. a. _____ Annika lost her ring yesterday.

   b. _✓_ Annika lost her ring in the sand.

   c. _✓_ Annika lost her ring in the sand at the beach.

4. a. _✓_ A talkative woman sat with her husband.

   b. _✓_ We were at a meeting.

   c. _____ She talked to her husband the entire time.

☐ **Exercise 17. Let's talk.** (Chart 6-4)

Review prepositions of place by using the given phrases in complete sentences. Demonstrate the meaning of the preposition with an action while you say the sentence. Work in pairs, in small groups, or as a class.

Example: across the room
            → *I'm walking across the room.* OR *I'm looking across the room.*

1. above the door	9. below the window
2. against the wall	10. beside my book
3. toward(s) the door	11. near the door
4. between two pages of my book	12. far from the door
5. in the room	13. off my desk
6. into the room	14. out the window
7. on my desk	15. behind me
8. at my desk	16. through the door

☐ **Exercise 18. Game: trivia.** (Chart 6-4)

Work in small groups. Answer the questions without looking at a map. After you have finished, look at a map to check your answers.* The team with the most correct answers wins.

1. Name a country directly under Russia.
2. Name the country directly above Germany.
3. What river flows through London?
4. What is a country near Haiti?
5. Name a country next to Vietnam.
6. Name a city far from Sydney, Australia.
7. What is the country between Austria and Switzerland?
8. Name the city within Rome, Italy.
9. Name two countries that have a river between them.
10. Name a country that is across from Saudi Arabia.

---

*See *Trivia Answers*, p. 421.

☐ **Exercise 19. Reading.** (Chart 6-4)
Read the passage and then answer the questions.

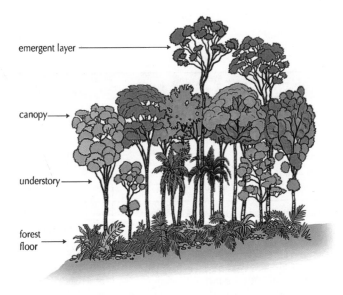

emergent layer

canopy→

understory→

forest
floor

The Habitats of a Rainforest

Rainforests have different areas where animals live. These areas are called *habitats*.
Scientists have given names to the four main habitats or layers of a rainforest.

Some animals live in the tops of giant trees. The tops of these trees are much higher than
the other trees, so this layer is called the *emergent* layer*. Many birds and insects live there.

Under the emergent layer is the *canopy*. The canopy is the upper part of the trees. It is
thick with leaves and vines, and it forms an umbrella over the rainforest. Most of the animals in
the rainforest live in the canopy.

The next layer is the *understory*. The understory is above the ground and under the leaves.
In the understory, it is very dark and cool. It gets only 2–5% of the sunlight that the canopy
gets. The understory has the most insects of the four layers, and a lot of snakes and frogs also
live there.

Finally, there is the *forest floor*. On the surface of this floor are fallen leaves, branches, and
other debris.** In general, the largest animals in the rainforest live in this layer. Common
animals in this habitat are tigers and gorillas.

1. Name two types of animals that live in the tops of giant trees.
2. Where is the understory?
3. Where do you think most mosquitoes live?
4. What are some differences between the emergent layer and the forest floor?

---

*emergent = in botany, a plant that is taller than other plants around it, like a tall tree in a forest

**debris = loose, natural material, like dirt

□ **Exercise 20. Warm-up.** (Chart 6-5)
Complete the sentences with information about yourself.

I was born . . .

1. in ___Sep___ (*month*).
2. on ___Sep 30th___ (*date*).
   ___May 6th___
3. on ___Thursday___ (*weekday*).
4. at ___5am___ (*time*).

6-5 Prepositions of Time

in	(a) Please be on time **in** the future. (b) I usually watch TV **in** the evening.	**in** + the past, the present, the future* **in** + the morning, the afternoon, the evening
	(c) I was born **in** October. (d) I was born **in** 1995. (e) I was born **in** the 20th century. (f) The weather is hot **in** (the) summer. *spring*	**in** + { a month a year a century a season }
on	(g) I was born **on** October 31st, 1995. (h) I went to a movie **on** Thursday. (i) I have class **on** Thursday morning(s).	**on** + a date **on** + a weekday **on** + (a) weekday morning(s), afternoon(s), evening(s)
at	(j) We sleep at night. I was asleep **at** midnight. (k) I fell asleep **at** 9:30 (nine-thirty). (l) He's busy **at** the moment. Can I take a message?	**at** + noon, night, midnight **at** + "clock time" **at** + the moment, the present time, present

*Possible in British English: *in future* (e.g., *Please be on time in future.*).

□ **Exercise 21. Looking at grammar.** (Chart 6-5)
Complete the sentences with *in, at,* or *on.* All the sentences contain time expressions.
study a lot
Studious Stan has college classes . . .

1. ___in___ the morning.
2. ___in___ the afternoon.
3. ___in___ the evening.
4. ___at___ night.
5. ___on___ weekdays.
6. ___on___ Saturdays.
7. ___on___ Saturday mornings.
8. ___at___ noon.
9. ___at___ midnight.

Unlucky Lisa has a birthday every four years. She was born . . .

10. ___on___ February 29th.
11. ___on___ February 29th, 2000.
12. ___in___ February.
13. ___in___ 2000.
14. ___in___ February 2000.
15. ___in___ the winter.

Cool Carlos is a fashion designer. He's thinking about clothing designs . . .

16. ___at___ the moment.
17. ___at___ the present time.
18. ___in___ the past.

156 CHAPTER 6

Exercise 22. Let's talk: interview. (Chart 6-5)

Complete each question with an appropriate preposition. Interview seven classmates. Ask each person one question.

1. What do you like to do _____ the evening?

2. What do you usually do _____ night before bed?

3. What do you like to do _____ Saturday mornings?

4. What did you do _____ January 1st of this year?

5. What were you doing _____ January 1st, 2000 (the beginning of the new millennium)?

6. How do you spend your free time _____ January?

7. What will you do with your English skills _____ the future?

❏ **Exercise 23. Warm-up.** (Chart 6-6)

Check (✓) all the grammatically correct sentences.

1. a. ✓ I left Athens in 2005.   2. a. ✓ Lee sold his car yesterday.

   b. ___ I left in 2005 Athens.   b. ✓ Yesterday Lee sold his car.

   c. ✓ In 2005, I left Athens.   c. ___ Lee sold yesterday his car.

6-6 Word Order: Place and Time

S V PLACE TIME (a) Ann moved *to Paris* *in 2008.* We went *to a movie* *yesterday.*	In a typical English sentence, "place" comes before "time," as in (a). *INCORRECT: Ann moved in 2008 to Paris.*
S V O P T (b) We bought a house in Miami in 2005.	S-V-O-P-T = Subject-Verb-Object-Place-Time (basic English sentence structure)
TIME S V PLACE (c) *In 2008,* Ann moved to Paris. (d) *Yesterday* we went to a movie.	Expressions of time can also come at the beginning of a sentence, as in (c) and (d). A time phrase at the beginning of a sentence is often followed by a comma, as in (c).

❏ **Exercise 24. Looking at grammar.** (Chart 6-6)

Put the given phrases in correct sentence order.

1. to Paris \ next month

   Monique's company is going to transfer her _to Paris next month_.

2. last week \ through Turkey

   William began a bike trip _through Turkey last week_.

3. at his uncle's bakery \ Alexi \ on Saturday mornings \ works

   Alexi works at his uncle's bakery on Saturday mornings

4. arrived \ in the early morning \ at the airport \ my plane

   My plane arrived at the airport in the early morning

☐ **Exercise 25. Warm-up.** (Chart 6-7)
Add *-s* where appropriate. If no final *-s* is necessary, write Ø.

1. Lions roar __Ø__.
2. A lion roar __s__.
3. Lions and tigers roar __Ø__.

4. A tiger in the jungle roar __s__.
5. Tigers in the jungle roar __Ø__.
6. Tigers in jungles roar __Ø__.

6-7 Subject-Verb Agreement

SINGULAR SINGULAR (a) The *sun* shine*s*. PLURAL PLURAL (b) *Birds* sing.	A singular subject takes a singular verb, as in (a). A plural subject takes a plural verb, as in (b). Notice: *verb* + *-s* = singular (*shines*) *noun* + *-s* = plural (*birds*)
SINGULAR SINGULAR (c) *My brother* ***lives*** in Jakarta. PLURAL PLURAL (d) *My brother **and** sister* ***live*** in Jakarta.	Two subjects connected by **and** take a plural verb, as in (d).
(e) The ***glasses*** over there under the window by the sink ***are*** clean. (f) The ***information*** in those magazines about Vietnamese culture and customs ***is*** very interesting.	Sometimes phrases come between a subject and a verb. These phrases do not affect the agreement of the subject and verb.
V S (g) *There **is** a **book** on the desk.* V S (h) *There **are** some **books** on the desk.*	***There*** + ***be*** + *subject* expresses that something exists in a particular place. The verb agrees with the noun that follows **be**.
(i) ***Every student is*** sitting down. (j) ***Everybody/Everyone hopes*** for peace.	***Every*** is a singular word. It is used with a singular, not plural, noun. *INCORRECT: Every students . . .* Subjects with ***every*** take singular verbs, as in (i) and (j).
(k) ***People*** in my country ***are*** friendly.	***People*** is a plural noun and takes a plural verb.

❑ **Exercise 26. Looking at grammar.** (Chart 6-7)
Work in small groups. Complete the sentences with the correct form of the verb from the list.
Discuss the words you use to describe different animal sounds in your native language.

bark	chirp	hiss	meow	roar

What sounds do these animals make?

1. A dog _barks_ . ruff. woof
2. Dogs _bark_ .
3. Lions in the wild _roar_ .
4. Lions, tigers, and leopards _roar_ .
5. Every snake _hisses_ . sss
6. A bird _chirps_ . cheep .
7. Cats _meow_ .
8. Sea lions on a beach _bark_ .
9. A lizard _hisses_ .
10. Baby chickens _chirp_ .

❑ **Exercise 27. Looking at grammar.** (Chart 6-7)
Underline and identify the subject (S) and the verb (V). Correct errors in agreement.

        S   V

1. The students in this class speaks English very well.

2. My aunt and uncle speak Spanish. → OK (*no error*).

3. ~~Every~~ The students in my class speak English well.

4. There are five students from Korea in Mr. Ahmad's class.

5. There's a vacant apartment in my building. ✓

6. Does people in your neighborhood know each other?

7. The neighbors in the apartment next to mine is very friendly and helpful. *are*

❑ **Exercise 28. Listening.** (Charts 6-2 and 6-7)
Listen to the passage. Listen a second time and add *-s* where necessary. Before you begin,
you may want to check your understanding of these words: *sweat, fur, paw, flap, mud*.

CD 2
Track 6

How Some Animals Stay Cool

How do animal _s_ stay cool in hot weather? Many animal _s_ don't sweat like
human ____, so they have other way ____ to cool themselves.
   3   4

Dog ____, for example, have a lot of fur ____ and can become very hot. They stay ____
  5   6   7
cool mainly by panting. By the way, if you don't know what *panting* means, this is the sound of
panting.

Cat ___ lick ___ their paw ___ and chest ___. When their fur ___ is wet, they
   8   9   10   11   12
become cooler.

Elephant ___ have very large ear ___. When they are hot, they can flap their huge
       13   14
ear ___. The flapping ear ___ act ___ like a fan and it cool ___ them. Elephant ___ also
   15   16   17   18   19
like to roll in the mud ___ to stay cool.
                20

❑ **Exercise 29. Warm-up.** (Chart 6-8)
Think about the very first teacher you had. Choose words from below to describe him/her.

young	friendly ✓	serious
middle-aged ✓	unfriendly	patient ✓
elderly	fun	impatient

6-8 Using Adjectives to Describe Nouns

ADJECTIVE NOUN (a) Bob is reading a **good** book.	Words that describe nouns are called ADJECTIVES. In (a): **good** is an adjective; it describes the book.
(b) The **tall** woman wore a **new** dress. (c) The **short** woman wore an **old** dress. (d) The **young** woman wore a **short** dress.	We say that adjectives "modify" nouns. *Modify* means "change a little." An adjective changes the meaning of a noun by giving more information about it.
(e) Roses are **beautiful** flowers. INCORRECT: Roses are beautifuls flowers.	Adjectives are neither singular nor plural. They do NOT have a plural form.
(f) He wore a **white** shirt. INCORRECT: He wore a shirt white. (g) Roses are **beautiful**. (h) His shirt was **white**.	Adjectives usually come immediately before nouns, as in (f). Adjectives can also follow main verb **be**, as in (g) and (h).

❑ **Exercise 30. Looking at grammar.** (Chart 6-8)
Check (✓) the phrases that have adjectives. <u>Underline</u> the adjectives.

1. ✓ a <u>scary</u> story
2. ___ on Tuesday
3. ✓ going to a <u>famous</u> place
4. ✓ a <u>small, dark, smelly</u> room
5. ___ quickly and then slowly
6. ✓ <u>long</u> or <u>short</u> hair

❑ **Exercise 31. Looking at grammar.** (Chart 6-8)
Add the given adjectives to the sentences. Choose *two* of the three adjectives in each item to add to the sentence.

Example: hard, heavy, strong   A man lifted the box.
    → A strong man lifted the heavy box.

1. beautiful, safe, red   Roses are flowers.

2. empty, wet, hot   The waiter poured coffee into my cup.
3. fresh, clear, hungry   Mrs. Fields gave the kids a snack.
4. dirty, modern, delicious   After our dinner, Frank helped me with the dishes.
        dirty

☐ **Exercise 32. Looking at grammar.** (Chart 6-8)
Work in small groups.

Part I. Add your own nouns, adjectives, and prepositions to the list. Don't look at Part II.

1. an adjective _____old_____   6. an adjective ___funny___
2. a person's name ___Amy___   7. an adjective ___good___
3. a plural noun ___pictures___   8. a preposition of place ___on___
4. a plural noun ___clothes___   9. an adjective ___excellent___
5. a singular noun ___paper___   10. a plural noun ___dogs___

Part II. Complete the sentences with the same words you added in Part I. Some of your completions might sound a little odd or funny. Read your completed passage aloud to another group or to the rest of the class.

One day a/an _____old_____ girl was walking in the city. Her name was
        1

___Amy___. She was carrying a package for her grandmother. It contained some
        2

___pictures___, some ___clothes___, and a/an ___paper___, among other
        3   4   5

things.

As she was walking down the street, a/an ___funny___ thief stole her package.
        6

The ___good___ girl pulled out her cell phone and called the police, who caught the
        7

thief ___on___ a nearby building and returned her package to her. She took it
        8

immediately to her ___excellent___ grandmother, who was glad to get the package
        9

because she really needed some new ___dogs___.
        10

☐ **Exercise 33. Warm-up.** (Chart 6-9)
Combine the word *chicken* with the words in the list.

| ✓fresh | hot | ✓legs | recipe | soup |

1. ___chicken legs___   4. ___hot chicken___
2. ___fresh chicken___   5. ___chicken soup___
3. ___chicken recipe___

Nouns and Pronouns **161**

6-9 Using Nouns as Adjectives

(a) I have a *flower* garden. (b) The *shoe* store also sells socks.	Sometimes words that are usually used as nouns are used as adjectives. For example, *flower* is usually a noun, but in (a), it's used as an adjective to modify *garden*.
(c) INCORRECT: a flowers garden (d) INCORRECT: the shoes store	When a noun is used as an adjective, it is singular in form, NOT plural.

☐ **Exercise 34. Looking at grammar.** (Chart 6-9)

<u>Underline</u> and identify the nouns (N). Use one of the nouns in the first sentence as an adjective in the second sentence.

        N   N

1. This <u>book</u> is about <u>grammar</u>. It's a __grammar book*__.

2. My garden has vegetables. It's a __vegetable garden__.

3. The soup has beans. It's __bean soup__.

4. I read a lot of articles in magazines. I read a lot of __magazine articles__.

5. The factory makes toys. It's a __toy factory__.

6. The villages are in the mountains. They are __mountain villages__.

7. The lesson was about art. It was an __art lesson__.

8. Flags fly from poles. Many government buildings have __flag poles__.

☐ **Exercise 35. Looking at grammar.** (Chart 6-9)

Add **-s** to the *italicized* nouns if necessary. Then agree or disagree with each statement. Circle *yes* or *no*.

1. One day, *computer* programs will make it possible for computers to think.   yes   no

2. *Computer* make life more stressful.   yes   no

3. *Airplane* trips are enjoyable nowadays.   yes   no

4. *Airplane* don't have enough legroom.   yes   no

5. *Bicycle* are better than cars for getting around in a crowded city.   yes   no

6. It's fun to watch *bicycle* races like the *Tour de France* on TV.   yes   no

7. *Vegetable* soups are delicious.   yes   no

8. Fresh *vegetable* are my favorite food.   yes   no

---

*When one noun modifies another noun, the spoken stress is usually on the first noun: a **grammar** book.

□ **Exercise 36. Listening and speaking.** (Charts 6-1 → 6-9)

Part I. Listen to two friends talking about finding an apartment.

CD 2
Track 7

Part II. Complete your own conversation. Perform it for the class. You can use words from the list. NOTE: This conversation is slightly different from Part I.

air-conditioning	an elevator	near a bus stop	a studio
a balcony	an exercise room	near a freeway	a two-bedroom
close to my job	a laundry room	parking	a walk-up

A: I'm looking for a new place to live.

B: How come?

A: _____. I need _____.

B: I just helped a friend find one. I can help you. What else do you want?

A: I want _____. Also, I _____.

I don't want _____.

B: Anything else?

A: _____ would be nice.

B: That's expensive.

A: I guess I'm dreaming.

□ **Exercise 37. Warm-up.** (Chart 6-10)

Read the conversation. Look at the personal pronouns in green. Decide if they are subject or object pronouns.

A: Did you hear? Ivan quit his job.
        1

B: I know. I don't understand him. Between you and me, I think it's a bad decision.
   2   3   4   5

1. you   subject   object
2. I   subject   object
3. him   subject   object
4. you   subject   object
5. me   subject   object

6-10 Personal Pronouns: Subjects and Objects

Personal Pronouns

SUBJECT PRONOUNS:	*I*	*we*	*you*	*he, she, it*	*they*
OBJECT PRONOUNS:	*me*	*us*	*you*	*him, her, it*	*them*

S (a) **Kate** is married. **She** has two children.	A pronoun refers to a noun. In (a): **she** is a pronoun; it refers to **Kate**. In (b): **her** is a pronoun; it refers to **Kate**.
O (b) **Kate** is my friend. I know **her** well.	In (a): **She** is a SUBJECT PRONOUN. In (b): **her** is an OBJECT PRONOUN.
(c) Mike has *a new blue bike*. He bought *it* yesterday.	A pronoun can refer to a single noun (e.g., **Kate**) or to a noun phrase. In (c): *it* refers to the whole noun phrase *a new blue bike*.
S (d) Eric and *I* are good friends.	Guidelines for using pronouns following *and*: If the pronoun is used as part of the subject, use a subject pronoun, as in (d).
O (e) Ann met Eric and *me* at the museum.	If the pronoun is part of the object, use an object pronoun, as in (e) and (f).
O of PREP (f) Ann walked between Eric and *me*.	INCORRECT: Eric and me are good friends. INCORRECT: Ann met Eric and I at the museum.

SINGULAR PRONOUNS:	*I*	*me*	*you*	*he, she, it*	*him, her*
PLURAL PRONOUNS:	*we*	*us*	*you*	*they*	*them*

(g) **Mike** is in class. **He** is taking a test.	Singular = one. Plural = more than one.
(h) The **students** are in class. **They** are taking a test.	Singular pronouns refer to singular nouns; plural pronouns refer to plural nouns, as in the examples.
(i) **Kate and Tom** are married. **They** have two children.	

□ **Exercise 38. Looking at grammar.** (Chart 6-10)
Write the nouns that the pronouns in **boldface** refer to.

1. The apples were rotten, so the children didn't eat **them** even though **they** were really hungry.

   a. them = _____

   b. they = _____

2. Do bees sleep at night? Or do **they** work in the hive all night long? You never see **them** after dark. What do **they** do after night falls?

   a. they = _bees_

   b. them = _bees_

   c. they = _bees_

3. Table tennis began in England in the late 1800s. Today **it** is an international sport. My brother and I played **it** a lot when we were teenagers. I beat **him** sometimes, but **he** was a better player and usually won.

a. it = _table tennis_

b. it = _table tennis_

c. him = _my brother_

d. he = _my brother_

☐ **Exercise 39. Looking at grammar.** (Chart 6-10)
Circle the correct words in *italics*.

1. Toshi ate dinner with   *I,* (*me.*)

2. Toshi ate dinner with Mariko and   *I,* (*me.*)

3. (*I,*) *me* had dinner with Toshi last night.

4. Jay drove Eva and   *I,* (*me*) to the store. He waited for   *we,* (*us*) in the car.

5. A: I want to get tickets for the soccer game.

   B: You'd better get   *it,* (*them*) right away. *It,* (*They*) *is,* (*are*) selling fast.

☐ **Exercise 40. Looking at grammar.** (Chart 6-10)
Complete the sentences with **she, he, it, her, him, they,** or **them**.

1. I have a grammar book. ___*It*___ is black.

2. Brian borrowed my books. ___*He*___ returned ___*them*___ yesterday.

3. Sonya is wearing some new earrings. ___*She*___ look good on ___*them*___.

4. Don't look directly at the sun. Don't look at _____ directly even if you are wearing sunglasses. The intensity of its light can injure your eyes.

5. Recently, I read about "micromachines." _____ are machines that are smaller than a grain of sand. One scientist called _____ "the greatest scientific invention of our time."

□ **Exercise 41. Warm-up.** (Chart 6-11)
Match the phrases to the pictures that describe them.

Picture A   Picture B

1. _____ the teacher's office
2. _____ the teachers' office

6-11 Possessive Nouns

SINGULAR: (a) I know the *student's* name. PLURAL: (b) I know the *students'* names. PLURAL: (c) I know the *children's* names.	An apostrophe (') and an **-s** are used with nouns to show possession.
SINGULAR (d) the student → the *student's* name my baby → my *baby's* name a man → a *man's* name (e) James → *James'/James's* name	SINGULAR POSSESSIVE NOUN: *noun + apostrophe (') + -s* A singular noun that ends in **-s** has two possible possessive forms: *James'* OR *James's*.

PLURAL
(f) the students → the *students'* names
my babies → my *babies'* names
(g) men → *men's* names
the children → the *children's* names
	PLURAL POSSESSIVE NOUN:
	  noun + -s + apostrophe (')
	
	IRREGULAR PLURAL POSSESSIVE NOUN:
	  noun + apostrophe (') + -s
	
	(An irregular plural noun is a plural noun that does not end in **-s**: *children, men, people, women*. See Chart 6-1.)

Compare: (h) *Tom's* here. (i) *Tom's* brother is here.	In (h): **Tom's** is not a possessive noun. It is a contraction of *Tom is*, used in informal writing. In (i): **Tom's** is a possessive noun.

□ **Exercise 42. Looking at grammar.** (Chart 6-11)
Decide if the meaning of the *italicized* word is "one" or "more than one."

1. The teacher answered the *student's* questions.   (one)   more than one
2. The teacher answered the *students'* questions.   one   more than one
3. Our *daughters'* bedroom is next to our room.   one   more than one

166 CHAPTER 6

4. Our *son's* room is downstairs.   one   more than one

5. *Men's* clothing is on sale at the department store.   one   more than one

6. This looks like a *woman's* shirt.   one   more than one

❏ **Exercise 43. Looking at grammar.** (Chart 6-11)
Look at the Nelson's family tree. Complete the sentences using the correct possessive form.

1. ___Ned's___ wife is Ella.

2. ___Lisa's___ husband is Sam.

3. Howard is ___Lisa's___ brother.

4. Howard is ___Monia's___ husband.

5. ___William's___ grandmother is Ella.

6. ___William's___ parents are Sam and Lisa.

7. Ella and ___Ned's___ grandson is William.

8. Howard and Monica are ___William's___ aunt and uncle.

Nelson Family Tree

Ella + Ned

Lisa + Sam   Howard + Monic

William

❏ **Exercise 44. Game: trivia.** (Chart 6-11)
Work in small groups. Use the correct possessive form of the given nouns to complete the sentences. Decide if the information is true or false. The group with the most correct answers wins.*

1. earth   The ___earth's___ surface is about 70% water.   T   F

2. elephant An ___elephant's___ skin is pink and wrinkled.   T   F

3. man   Pat is a ___man's___ name.   T   F

4. woman   Pat is a ___woman's___ name.   T   F

5. women   The area for language is larger in ___women's___ brains.   T   F

6. Men   ___Men's___ brains are bigger than women's brains.   T   F

7. person   A ___person's___ eyes blink more if he/she is nervous.   T   F

8. People   ___people's___ voices always get lower as they age.   T   F

❏ **Exercise 45. Warm-up.** (Chart 6-12)
Check (✓) all the grammatically correct responses.

Whose camera is this?

1. __✓__ It's my camera.   5. __✓__ It's your camera.

2. __✓__ It's mine.   6. ____ It's your's.

3. ____ It's my.   7. __✓__ It's theirs.

4. __✓__ It's yours.   8. __✓__ It's their camera.

---

*See *Trivia Answers*, p. 421.

6-12 Possessive Pronouns and Adjectives

This pen belongs to me. (a) It's *mine.* (b) It is *my* pen.	Examples (a) and (b) have the same meaning; they both show possession. *Mine* is a *possessive pronoun; my* is a *possessive adjective.*
POSSESSIVE PRONOUNS POSSESSIVE ADJECTIVES (c) I have *mine.* I have *my* pen. (d) You have *yours.* You have *your* pen. (e) She has *hers.* She has *her* pen. (f) He has *his.* He has *his* pen. (g) We have *ours.* We have *our* pens. (h) You have *yours.* You have *your* pen. (i) They have *theirs.* They have *their* pens. (j) —— I have a book. *Its* cover is black.	A POSSESSIVE PRONOUN is used alone, without a noun following it. A POSSESSIVE ADJECTIVE is used only with a noun following it. INCORRECT: *I have mine pen.* INCORRECT: *I have my.*
COMPARE *its* vs. *it's:* *adj.* (k) Sue gave me a book. I don't remember *its* title. (l) Sue gave me a book. *It's* a novel.	In (k): *its* (NO apostrophe) is a possessive adjective modifying the noun *title.* In (l): *It's* (with an apostrophe) is a contraction of *it + is.*

COMPARE *their* vs. *there* vs. *they're:*
(m) The students have *their* books.
(n) My books are over *there.*
(o) Where are the students? *They're* in class.
	Their, there, and *they're* have the same pronunciation, but not the same meaning.
	    their = possessive adjective, as in (m)
	    there = an expression of place, as in (n)
	    they're = *they are,* as in (o)

□ **Exercise 46. Looking at grammar.** (Chart 6-12)
Circle the correct completions.

1. Alice called (*her,*) *hers* friend.

2. Hasan wrote a letter to *his, he's* mother.

3. *It's, Its* normal for a dog to chase *it's, its* tail.

4. The bird cleaned (*its,*) *it's* feathers with *its, it's* beak.

5. Paula had to drive my car to work. *Hers, Her* had a flat tire.

6. Junko fell off her bike and broke *hers, her* arm.

7. Anastasia is a good friend of *me, mine.★*

8. I met a friend of *you, yours* yesterday.

9. A: Excuse me. Is this *my, mine* pen or *your, yours?*

    B: This one is *my, mine. Your, Yours* is on *your, yours* desk.

★*A friend of* + possessive pronoun (e.g., *a friend of mine*) is a common expression.

10. a. Adam and Amanda are married. *They, Them* live in an apartment building.
    b. *Their, There, They're* apartment is on the fifth floor.
    c. We live in the same building. *Our, Ours* apartment has one bedroom, but *their, theirs* has two.
    d. *Their, There, They're* sitting *their, there, they're* now because *their, there, they're* waiting for a visit from *their, there, they're* son.

□ **Exercise 47. Warm-up.** (Chart 6-13)
Work in small groups. Use a mirror to demonstrate the following sentences. Take turns saying the sentences while students perform the actions.

1. I am looking at myself.
2. You are looking at yourself.
3. You are looking at yourselves.
4. He is looking at himself.

5. They are looking at themselves.
6. She is looking at herself.
7. We are looking at ourselves.

6-13 Reflexive Pronouns

myself	(a) *I* saw *myself* in the mirror.	Reflexive pronouns end in **-self/-selves**. They are used when the subject (e.g., *I*) and the object (e.g., *myself*) are the same person.
yourself	(b) *You* (one person) saw *yourself*.	
herself	(c) *She* saw *herself*.	
himself	(d) *He* saw *himself*.	INCORRECT: *I saw me in the mirror.*
itself	(e) *It* (e.g., the kitten) saw *itself*.	
ourselves	(f) *We* saw *ourselves*.	
yourselves	(g) *You* (plural) saw *yourselves*.	
themselves	(h) *They* saw *themselves*.	

(i) *Greg* lives **by himself**.	**By** + *a reflexive pronoun* = alone
(j) *I* sat **by myself** on the park bench.	In (i): Greg lives alone, without family or roommates.
(k) *I* **enjoyed myself** at the fair.	*Enjoy* and a few other verbs are commonly followed by a reflexive pronoun. See the list below.

Common Expressions with Reflexive Pronouns

believe in yourself	help yourself	pinch yourself	tell yourself
blame yourself	hurt yourself	be proud of yourself	work for yourself
cut yourself	give yourself (something)	take care of yourself	wish yourself (luck)
enjoy yourself	introduce yourself	talk to yourself	
feel sorry for yourself	kill yourself	teach yourself	

□ **Exercise 48. Looking at grammar.** (Chart 6-13)

Complete the sentences with reflexive pronouns.

1. Are you okay, Heidi? Did you hurt __*yourself*__?

2. Leo taught _____ to play the piano. He never had a teacher.

3. Do you ever talk to _____? Most people talk to

   _____ sometimes.

4. A newborn baby can't take care of _____.

5. It is important for all of us to have confidence in our own abilities. We need to believe in

   _____.

6. Isabel always wishes _____ good luck before a big test.

7. Kazu, there's plenty of food on the table. Please help _____.

8. I couldn't believe my good luck! I had to pinch _____ to make sure I
   wasn't dreaming.

□ **Exercise 49. Listening.** (Chart 6-13)

Listen to the sentences and complete them with reflexive pronouns.

CD 2
Track 8

Example: You will hear: The accident was my fault. I caused it. I was responsible. In other
                              words, I blamed . . .

   You will write: __*myself*__

1. _____   4. _____

2. _____   5. _____

3. _____   6. _____

□ **Exercise 50. Let's talk: interview.** (Chart 6-13)

Interview six students in your class. Ask each student a different question. Share some of
their answers with the class.

1. In this town, what is a good way to enjoy yourself?
2. How do people introduce themselves in your country? What do they say?
3. Have you ever wished yourself good luck? When or why?
4. Have you ever felt sorry for yourself? Or, have you ever felt proud of yourself? If so, why?
5. When athletes talk to themselves before an important event, what do you imagine they say?
6. In your country, at what age does a person usually begin living by himself or herself?

Choose the picture that matches the description.

One flower is red. Another is yellow. The other is pink.

Picture A   Picture B

6-14 Singular Forms of *Other: Another* vs. *The Other*

Another

(a) There is a large bowl of apples on the table. Paul is going to eat one apple. If he is still hungry after that, he can eat *another* apple. There are many apples to choose from.	**Another** means "one more out of a group of similar items, one in addition to the one(s) already mentioned." **Another** is a combination of *an + other*, written as one word.

The Other

(b) There are two apples on the table. Paul is going to eat one of them. Sara is going to eat *the other* apple.	**The other** means "the last one in a specific group; the only one that remains from a given number of similar items."
(c) Paul ate one apple. Then he ate { *another* apple. *another* one. *another*.	**Another** and **the other** can be used as adjectives in front of a noun (e.g., *apple*) or in front of the word *one*. **Another** and **the other** can also be used alone as pronouns.
(d) Paul ate one apple. Sara ate { *the other* apple. *the other* one. *the other*.	

☐ **Exercise 52. Looking at grammar.** (Chart 6-14)
Complete the sentences with *another* or *the other*.

1. There are two birds in Picture A. One is an eagle. <u>*The other*</u> is a chicken.

Picture A   Picture B

2. There are three birds in Picture B. One is an eagle.

   a. _____ one is a chicken.

   b. _____ bird is a crow.

3. There are many kinds of birds in the world. One kind is an eagle.

   a. _____ kind is a chicken.

   b. _____ kind is a crow.

   c. _____ kind is a sea gull.

   d. What is the name of _____ kind of bird in the world?

4. It rained yesterday, and from the look of those dark clouds, we're going to have

   _____ rainstorm today.

5. Nicole and Michelle are identical twins. The best way to tell them apart is by looking at
   their ears. One of them has pierced ears, and _____ doesn't.

6. France borders several countries. One is Spain. _____ is Italy.

☐ **Exercise 53. Warm-up.** (Chart 6-15)
Match the sentences to the correct pictures.

Picture A   Picture B

1. ____ Some are red. Others are yellow.
2. ____ Some are red. The others are yellow.

172 CHAPTER 6

6-15 Plural Forms of *Other*: *Other(s)* vs. *The Other(s)*

Other(s)

There are many apples in Paul's kitchen. Paul is holding one apple.	***Other(s)*** (without ***the***) means "several more out of a group of similar items, several in addition to the one(s) already mentioned."
(a) There are ***other*** *apples* in a bowl. (adjective) + (noun)	The adjective ***other*** (without an ***-s***) can be used with a plural noun (e.g., *apples*) or with the word ***ones***.
(b) There are ***other*** *ones* on a plate. (adjective) + *ones*	***Others*** (with an ***-s***) is a plural pronoun; it is not used with a noun.
(c) There are ***others*** on a chair. (pronoun)	In (c): ***others*** = ***other apples***

The Other(s)

There are four apples on the table. Paul is going to take one of them.	***The other(s)*** means "the last ones in a specific group, the remains from a given number of similar items."
(d) Sara is going to take ***the other*** *apples*. (adjective) + (noun)	***The other*** (without an ***-s***) can be used as an adjective in front of a noun or the word ***ones***, as in (d) and (e).
(e) Sara is going to take ***the other*** *ones*. (adjective) + *ones*	***The others*** (with an ***-s***) is a plural pronoun; it is not used with a noun.
(f) Sara is going to take ***the others***. (pronoun)	In (f): ***the others*** = ***the other apples***

□ **Exercise 54. Looking at grammar.** (Charts 6-14 and 6-15)
Perform these actions.

1. Hold two pens. Use a form of *other* to describe the second pen.
   → *I'm holding two pens. One is mine, and the other belongs to Ahmed.*
2. Hold three pens. Use a form of *other* to describe the second and third pens.
3. Hold up your two hands. One of them is your right hand. Tell us about your left hand, using a form of *other*.
4. Hold up your right hand. One of the five fingers is your thumb. Using forms of *other*, tell us about your index finger, then your middle finger, then your ring finger, and then your little finger, the last of the five fingers on your right hand.

□ **Exercise 55. Looking at grammar.** (Chart 6-15)
Complete the sentences with *other(s)* or *the other(s)*.

1. There are many kinds of animals in the world. The elephant is one kind. Some

   ___others___ are tigers, horses, and bears.

2. There are many kinds of animals in the world. The elephant is one kind. Some

   _____ kinds are tigers, horses, and bears.

3. There are three colors in the Italian flag. One of the colors is red.

   _____ are green and white.

4. There are three colors in the Italian flag. One of the colors is red.

   _____ colors are green and white.

5. Many people like to get up very early in the morning. _____ like to sleep until noon.

6. There are many kinds of geometric figures. Some are circles. _____ figures are squares. Still _____ are rectangular.

7. There are four geometric figures in the above drawing. One is a square.

   _____ figures are a rectangle, a circle, and a triangle.

8. Of the four geometric figures in the drawing, only the circle has curved lines.

   _____ have straight lines.

□ **Exercise 56. Let's read and write.** (Charts 6-13 → 6-15)
Part I. Read the passage and answer the questions.

Calming Yourself

When was the last time you felt nervous or anxious? Were you able to calm yourself? There are a variety of techniques that people use to calm themselves. Here are three that many people have found helpful.

One way that people relax is by imagining a peaceful place, such as a tropical beach. Thinking about the warm water, cool breezes, and steady sounds of the ocean waves helps people calm themselves. Another popular method is deep breathing. Inhaling deeply and then slowly exhaling is an easy way for people to slow their heart rate and relax their body. Still other people find exercise helpful. Some people benefit from a slow activity like a 20-minute walk. Others prefer activities that make them tired, like running or swimming.

How about you? How do you calm yourself when you feel nervous? Do any of these methods help you, or do you do other things to relax?

1. What are three ways people relax when they are nervous? (Use *one* and *another* in your answer.)
2. Why do some people choose activities like running and swimming as a way to relax?
3. Imagine you are trying to relax by thinking of a peaceful place. What place would you think of?
4. How do you relax when you are nervous?

Part II. Read this paragraph by one student who tells how he relaxes when he's nervous.

How I Calm Down

Sometimes I feel nervous, especially when I have to give a speech. My body begins to shake, and I realize that I have to calm myself down. This is the technique I use: I imagine myself in a peaceful place. My favorite place in the world is the sea. I imagine myself on the water. I am floating. I feel the warm water around me. The sounds around me are very relaxing. I only hear the waves and maybe a few birds. I don't think about the past or the future. I can feel my heart rate decrease a little, and my body slowly starts to calm down.

Part III. Write a paragraph about how you relax when you are nervous. Follow the model. Give specific details about how you relax and what the results are.

Sometimes I feel nervous, especially when I have to _____. My _____ and I realize that I have to calm myself down. This is the technique I use: _____.

6-16 Summary of Forms of *Other*

	Adjective	Pronoun	
SINGULAR	another apple	another	Notice that the word ***others*** (***other*** + *final -s*) is used only as a plural pronoun.
PLURAL	other apples	others	
SINGULAR	the other apple	the other	
PLURAL	the other apples	the others	

❏ **Exercise 57. Looking at grammar.** (Charts 6-15 and 6-16)
Complete the sentences with correct forms of *other: another, other, others, the other, the others*.

1. Juan has only two suits, a blue one and a gray one. His wife wants him to buy

   ___another___ one.

2. Juan has two suits. One is blue, and _____ is gray.

3. Some suits are blue. _____ are gray.

4. Some jackets have zippers. _____ jackets have buttons.

5. Some people keep dogs as pets. _____ have cats. Still

   _____ people have fish or birds as pets.

6. My boyfriend gave me a ring. I tried to put it on my ring finger, but it didn't fit. So I had

   to put it on _____ finger.

7. People have two thumbs. One is on the right hand. _____ is on the

   left hand.

8. Sometimes when I'm thirsty, I'll have a glass of water, but often one glass isn't enough, so

   I'll have _____ one.

9. There are five letters in the word *fresh*. One of the letters is a vowel. _____

   are consonants.

10. Smith is a common last name in English. _____ common names are

    Johnson, Jones, Miller, Anderson, Moore, and Brown.

❏ **Exercise 58. Listening.** (Charts 6-15 and 6-16)
Listen to each conversation and circle the correct statement (a. or b.).

CD 2
Track 9

1. a. The speaker was looking at two jackets.
   b. The speaker was looking at several jackets.

2. a. The speakers have only two favorite colors.
   b. The speakers have more than two favorite colors.

3. a. There are several roads the speakers can take.
   b. There are two roads the speakers can take.

4. a. There are only two ways to get downtown.
   b. There are more than two ways to get downtown.

5. a. The speaker had more than four pets.
   b. The speaker had only four pets.

□ **Exercise 59. Listening.** (Charts 6-15 and 6-16)

Listen to the conversation about dealing with loneliness. Complete the sentences with the
words you hear.

CD 2
Track 10

A: What do you do when you're feeling lonely?

B: I go someplace where I can be around _____ people. Even if they

are strangers, I feel better when there are _____ around me. How

about you?

A: That doesn't work for me. For example, if I'm feeling lonely and I go to a movie by

myself, I look at all _____ people who are there with their friends

and family, and I start to feel even lonelier. So I try to find _____

things to do to keep myself busy. When I'm busy, I don't feel lonely.

□ **Exercise 60. Check your knowledge.** (Chapter 6)

Edit the sentences. Correct errors in nouns, pronouns, adjectives, and subject-verb agreement.

                    wishes
1. Jimmy had three ~~wish~~ for his birthday.

2. I had some black beans soup for lunch.

3. The windows in our classroom is dirty.

4. People in Brazil speaks Portuguese.

5. Are around 8,600 types of birds in the world.

6. My mother and father work in Milan. Their teacher's.

7. Today many womens are carpenter, pilot, and doctor.

8. Is a new student in our class. Have you met her?

9. There are two pool at the park. The smaller one is for childs. The another is for adults.

10. The highways in my country are excellents.

11. I don't like my apartment. Its in a bad neighborhood. Is a lot of crime. I'm going to

    move to other neighborhood.

Chapter 7
Modal Auxiliaries

□ **Exercise 1. Warm-up.** (Chart 7-1)
Check (✓) the sentences that are grammatically correct.

1. _____ I can speak English well.

2. _____ He cans speaks English well.

3. _____ She can to speak English well.

4. _____ Our neighbors can speak some English.

5. _____ My parents can't speaking English at all.

7-1 The Form of Modal Auxiliaries

The verbs listed below are called "modal auxiliaries." They are helping verbs that express a wide range of meanings (ability, permission, possibility, necessity, etc.). Most of the modals have more than one meaning.

Auxiliary + the Simple Form of a Verb

can	(a) Olga *can speak* English.	*Can, could, may, might, should, had better, must, will,*
could	(b) He *couldn't come* to class.	and *would* are immediately followed by the simple form
may	(c) It *may rain* tomorrow.	of a verb.
might	(d) It *might rain* tomorrow.	• They are not followed by *to*.
should	(e) Mary *should study* harder.	*INCORRECT: Olga can to speak English.*
had better	(f) I *had better study* tonight.	• The main verb does not have a final *-s*.
must	(g) Billy! You *must listen* to me!	*INCORRECT: Olga can speaks English.*
will	(h) I *will be* in class tomorrow.	• The main verb is not in a past form.
would	(i) *Would* you please *close* the door?	*INCORRECT: Olga can spoke English.*
		• The main verb is not in its *-ing* form.
		INCORRECT: Olga can speaking English.

Auxiliary + *to* + the Simple Form of a Verb

have to	(j) I *have to study* tonight.	*To* + *the simple form* is used with these auxiliaries:
have got to	(k) I *have got to study* tonight.	*have to, have got to, be able to,* and *ought to.*
be able to	(l) Kate *is able to study* harder.	
ought to	(m) Kate *ought to study* harder.	

Exercise 2. Looking at grammar. (Chart 7-1)
Make sentences with the given verbs + *come*. Add *to* where necessary. Use this model:
Leo _____ tonight.

Example: can → *Leo can come tonight.*

1. may
2. should
3. ought
4. will not
5. could not

6. might
7. had better
8. has
9. has got
10. is not able

□ **Exercise 3. Listening.** (Chart 7-1)
Listen to the sentences. Add *to* where necessary. If *to* isn't necessary, write Ø.
Notice that *to* may sound like "ta."

CD 2
Track 11

1. I have _*to*_ go downtown tomorrow.

2. You must _Ø_ fasten your seat belt.

3. Could you please _____ open the window?

4. May I _____ borrow your eraser?

5. I'm not able _____ sign the contract today.

6. Today is the deadline. You must _____ sign it!

7. I have got _____ go to the post office this afternoon.

8. Shouldn't you _____ save some of your money for emergencies?

9. I feel bad for Elena. She has _____ have more surgery.

10. Alexa! Stop! You must not _____ run into the street!

□ **Exercise 4. Warm-up.** (Chart 7-2)
Circle the best completion for each sentence. Discuss your answers.

1. A newborn baby *can / can't* roll over.

2. A baby of four months *can / can't* smile.

3. A newborn baby *is able to / isn't able to* see black and white shapes.

4. A baby of six months *is able to / isn't able to* see colors.

5. When I was nine months old, I *could / couldn't* crawl.

6. When I was nine months old, I *could / couldn't* walk.

7-2 Expressing Ability: *Can* and *Could*

(a) Bob *can play* the piano. (b) You *can buy* a screwdriver at a hardware store. (c) I *can meet* you at Ted's tomorrow afternoon.	*Can* expresses *ability* in the present or future.
(d) I $\left\{\begin{array}{l}\text{can't}\\\text{cannot}\\\text{can not}\end{array}\right\}$ understand that sentence.	The negative form of *can* may be written *can't*, *cannot*, or *can not*.
(e) I can gó. (f) I cán't go.	In spoken English, *can* is usually unstressed and pronounced /kən/ = "kun." *Can't* is stressed and pronounced /kæn?/, with the final sound being a glottal stop.* The glottal stop replaces the /t/ in spoken English. Occasionally native speakers have trouble hearing the difference between *can* and *can't* and have to ask for clarification.
(g) Our son *could walk* when he was one year old.	The past form of *can* is *could*.
(h) He *couldn't walk* when he was six months old.	The negative of *could* is *couldn't* or *could not*.
(i) He *can read*. (j) He *is able to read*. (k) She *could read*. (l) She *was able to read*.	Ability can also be expressed with a form of *be able to*. Examples (i) and (j) have the same meaning. Examples (k) and (l) have the same meaning.

*A glottal stop is the sound you hear in the negative "unh-uh." The air is stopped by the closing of your glottis in the back of your throat. The phonetic symbol for the glottal stop is /ʔ/.

☐ **Exercise 5. Looking at grammar.** (Chart 7-2)
   Part I. Complete the sentences with *can* or *can't*.

   1. A dog _____ swim, but it _____ fly.

   2. A frog _____ live both on land and in water, but a cat _____.

   3. A bilingual person _____ speak three languages, but a trilingual person

      _____.

   4. People with a Ph.D. degree _____ use "Dr." in front of their name, but people

      with a master's degree _____.

   Part II. Restate the sentences in Part I. Use *be able to*.

☐ **Exercise 6. Let's talk: interview.** (Chart 7-2)
   Interview your classmates. Ask each student a different question. If the answer is "yes,"
   ask the follow-up question in parentheses. Share some of your answers with the class.

Can you . . .
1. speak more than two languages? (Which ones?)
2. play chess? (How long have you played?)
3. fold a piece of paper in half more than six times? (Can you show me?)
4. draw well — for example, draw a picture of me? (Can you do it now?)

Are you able to . . .
5. write clearly with both your right and left hands?
   (Can you show me?)
6. pat the top of your head with one hand and rub your
   stomach in a circle with the other hand at the same time?
   (Can you show me?)
7. drive a stick-shift car? (When did you learn?)
8. play a musical instrument? (Which one?)

❑ **Exercise 7. Listening.** (Chart 7-2)

Listen to the conversation. You will hear reductions for *can* and *can't*. Write the words you hear.

CD 2
Track 12

In the classroom

A: I _____ this math assignment.
　　　　　　　　　　1

B: I _____ you with that.
　　　　　　2

A: Really? _____ this problem to me?
　　　　　　　　　　3

B: Well, we _____ out the answer unless we do this part first.
　　　　　　　　　4

A: Okay! But it's so hard.

B: Yeah, but I know you _____ it. Just go slowly.
　　　　　　　　　　　　5

A: Class is almost over. _____ me after school today to finish this?
　　　　　　　　　　　　　　6

B: Well, I _____ you right after school, but how about at 5:00?
　　　　　　　　7

A: Great!

❑ **Exercise 8. Let's talk.** (Chart 7-2)

Complete the sentences with *could/couldn't/be able to/not be able to* and your own words.

Example: A year ago I ____, but now I can.
　　　　→ *A year ago I couldn't speak English, but now I can.*

1. When I was a child, I ____, but now I can.
2. When I was six, I ____, but I wasn't able to do that
   when I was three.
3. Five years ago, I ____, but now I can't.
4. In the past, I ____, but now I am.

□ **Exercise 9. Warm-up.** (Chart 7-3)
Check (✓) the sentences in each group that have the same meaning.

GROUP A

1. ____ Maybe it will be hot tomorrow.

2. ____ It might be hot tomorrow.

3. ____ It may be hot tomorrow.

GROUP B

4. ____ You can have dessert, now.

5. ____ You may have dessert, now.

GROUP C

6. ____ She can't stay up late.

7. ____ She might not stay up late.

7-3 Expressing Possibility: *May, Might,* and *Maybe;* Expressing Permission: *May* and *Can*

(a) It *may rain* tomorrow. (b) It *might rain* tomorrow. (c) — Why isn't John in class? — I don't know. He $\left\{ \begin{array}{c} may \\ might \end{array} \right\}$ be sick today.	*May* and *might* express *possibility* in the present or future. They have the same meaning. There is no difference in meaning between (a) and (b).
(d) It *may not rain* tomorrow. (e) It *might not rain* tomorrow.	Negative: *may not* and *might not* (Do not contract *may* and *might* with *not*.)
(f) *Maybe* it will rain tomorrow. COMPARE: (g) *Maybe* John is sick. (*adverb*) (h) John *may be* sick. (*verb*)	In (f) and (g): *maybe* (spelled as one word) is an adverb. It means "possibly." It comes at the beginning of a sentence. INCORRECT: *It will maybe rain tomorrow.* In (h): *may be* (two words) is a verb form: the auxiliary *may* + *the main verb* *be*. Examples (g) and (h) have the same meaning. INCORRECT: *John maybe sick.*
(i) Yes, children, you *may have* a cookie after dinner. (j) Okay, kids, you *can have* a cookie after dinner.	*May* is also used to give *permission*, as in (i). *Can* is often used to give *permission*, too, as in (j). NOTE: Examples (i) and (j) have the same meaning, but *may* is more formal than *can*.
(k) You *may not have* a cookie. You *can't have* a cookie.	*May not* and *cannot* (*can't*) are used to deny permission (i.e., to say "no").

□ **Exercise 10. Looking at grammar.** (Chart 7-3)

Complete the sentences with *can, may,* or ***might.*** Identify the meaning expressed by the modals: possibility or permission.

In a courtroom for a speeding ticket

1. No one speaks without the judge's permission. You __*may / can*__ not speak until the

    judge asks you a question. *Meaning:* __*permission*__

2. The judge _____ reduce your fine for your speeding ticket, or she

    _____ not. It depends. *Meaning:* _____

3. You _____ not argue with the judge. If you argue, you will get a fine.

    Meaning: _____

4. You have a strong case, but I'm not sure if you will convince the judge. You _____

    win or you _____ lose. *Meaning:* _____

□ **Exercise 11. Looking at grammar.** (Chart 7-3)

Rewrite the sentences with the words in parentheses.

1. It may snow tonight.

    (might) _____

    (Maybe) _____

2. You might need to wear your boots.

    (may) _____

    (Maybe) _____

3. Maybe there will be a blizzard.

    (may) _____

    (might) _____

Exercise 12. Let's talk. (Chart 7-3)

Answer each question with **may, might,** and **maybe**. Include at least three possibilities in each answer. Work in pairs, in small groups, or as a class.

Example: What are you going to do tomorrow?

→ *I don't know. I **may** go downtown.* OR *I **might** go to the laundromat.*
***Maybe** I'll study all day. Who knows?*

1. What are you going to do tomorrow night?
2. What's the weather going to be like tomorrow?
3. What is our teacher going to do tonight?
4. (_____) isn't in class today. Where is he/she?
5. What is your occupation going to be ten years from now?

❑ **Exercise 13. Listening.** (Charts 7-2 and 7-3)

You will hear sentences with **can, may,** or **might**. Decide if the speakers are expressing ability, possibility, or permission.

CD 2
Track 13

Example: You will hear: A: Where's Victor?

B: I don't know. He may be sick.

You will choose: ability (possibility) permission

1. ability	possibility	permission		4. ability	possibility	permission
2. ability	possibility	permission		5. ability	possibility	permission
3. ability	possibility	permission				

❑ **Exercise 14. Warm-up.** (Chart 7-4)

In which sentence is the speaker expressing a past ability? a present possibility? a future possibility?

A soccer game

1. There is five minutes left and the score is 3–3. Our team could win.
2. The goalie is on the ground. He could be hurt.
3. Our team didn't win. We couldn't score another goal.

7-4 Using *Could* to Express Possibility

(a) — How was the movie? *Could* you **understand** the English? — Not very well. I *could* only **understand** it with the help of subtitles.	One meaning of *could* is *past ability*, as in (a).* Another meaning of *could* is *possibility*. In (b): **He could be sick** has the same meaning as *He may/might be sick*, i.e., *It is possible that he is sick.*
(b) — Why isn't Greg in class? — I don't know. He *could be* sick.	In (b): *could* expresses a *present* possibility.
(c) Look at those dark clouds. It *could start* raining any minute.	In (c): *could* expresses a *future* possibility.

*See also Chart 7-2.

☐ **Exercise 15. Looking at grammar.** (Charts 7-2 and 7-4)

Does *could* express past, present, or future time? What is the meaning: ability or possibility?

Sentence	Past	Present	Future	Ability	Possibility
1. I *could be* home late tonight. Don't wait for me for dinner.			x		x
2. Thirty years ago, when he was a small child, David *could speak* Swahili fluently. Now he's forgotten a lot of it.					
3. A: Where's Alicia? B: I don't know. She *could be* at the mall.					
4. When I was a child, I *could climb* trees, but now I'm too old.					
5. Let's leave for the airport now. Yuki's plane *could arrive* early, and we want to be there when she arrives.					
6. A: What's that on the carpet? B: I don't know. It looks like a bug. Or it *could be* a piece of fuzz.					

☐ **Exercise 16. Let's talk.** (Chart 7-4)

Suggest possible solutions for each situation. Use *could*. Work in pairs, in small groups, or as a class.

Example: Tim has to go to work early tomorrow. His car is completely out of gas. His bicycle is broken.
→ *He could take the bus to work.*
→ *He could get a friend to take him to a gas station to get gas.*
→ *He could try to fix his bike.*
→ *He could get up very early and walk to work.*
    Etc.

1. Lisa walked to school today. Now she wants to go home. It's raining hard. She doesn't have an umbrella, and she's wearing sandals.

2. Joe and Joan want to get some exercise. They have a date to play tennis this morning, but the tennis court is covered with snow.

3. Roberto just bought a new camera. He has it at home now. He has the instruction manual. It is written in Japanese. He can't read Japanese. He doesn't know how to operate the camera.

4. Albert likes to travel around the world. He is 22 years old. Today he is alone in Paris. He needs to eat, and he needs to find a place to stay overnight. But while he was asleep on the train last night, someone stole his wallet. He has no money.

Exercise 17. Listening. (Charts 7-3 and 7-4)

Listen to the conversation between a husband and wife. Listen again and complete the sentences with the words you hear.

CD 2
Track 14

In a home office

A: Look at this cord. Do you know what it's for?

B: I don't know. We have so many cords around here with all our electronic equipment. It

_____ for the printer, I guess.
        1

A: No, I checked. The printer isn't missing a cord.

B: It _____ for one of the kid's toys.
              2

A: Yeah, I _____. But they don't have many electronic toys.
                3

B: I have an idea. It _____ for the cell phone. You know — the one I
                        4
had before this one.

A: I bet that's it. We _____ probably throw this out.
                        5

B: Well, let's be sure before we do that.

Exercise 18. Warm-up. (Chart 7-5)

Check (✓) all the sentences that have the same meaning.

1. ____ May I use your cell phone?

2. ____ Can I use your cell phone?

3. ____ Could I use your cell phone?

7-5 Polite Questions: *May I, Could I, Can I*

Polite Question	Possible Answers	
(a) **May I** please borrow your pen? (b) **Could I** please borrow your pen? (c) **Can I** please borrow your pen?	Yes. Yes. Of course. Yes. Certainly. Of course. Certainly. Sure. (*informal*) Okay. (*informal*) Uh-huh (*meaning "yes"*) I'm sorry, but I need to use it myself.	People use **may I, could I,*** and **can I** to ask polite questions. The questions ask for someone's permission or agreement. Examples (a), (b), and (c) have basically the same meaning. NOTE: **can I** is less formal than **may I** and **could I**.
(d) **Can I** borrow your pen, *please?* (e) **Can I** borrow your pen?		**Please** can come at the end of the question, as in (d). **Please** can be omitted from the question, as in (e).

*In a polite question, **could** is NOT the past form of **can**.

☐ **Exercise 19. Looking at grammar.** (Chart 7-5)
Complete the phone conversations. Use *may I, could I,* or *can I* + a verb from the list.
NOTE: The caller is always Speaker B.

ask	help	leave	speak/talk	take

1. A: Hello?

   B: Hello. Is Ahmed there?

   A: Yes, he is.

   B: _____ to him?

   A: Just a minute. I'll get him.

2. A: Hello. Mr. Black's office.

   B: _____ to Mr. Black?

   A: _____ who is calling?

   B: Susan Abbott.

   A: Just a moment, Ms. Abbott. I'll transfer you.

3. A: Hello?

   B: Hi. This is Bob. _____ to Pedro?

   A: Sure. Hold on.

4. A: Good afternoon. Dr. Wu's office. _____ you?

   B: Yes. I have an appointment that I need to change.

   A: Just a minute, please. I'll transfer you to our appointment desk.

5. A: Hello?

   B: Hello. _____ to Emily?

   A: She's not at home right now. _____ a message?

   B: No, thanks. I'll call later.

6. A: Hello?

   B: Hello. _____ to Maria?

   A: She's not here right now.

   B: Oh. _____ a message?

   A: Sure. Just let me get a pen.

□ **Exercise 20. Let's talk: pairwork.** (Chart 7-5)
Work with a partner. Ask and answer polite questions. Begin with *May I, Could I*, or *Can I*.
Make conversations you can role-play for the class.

Example: (A), you want to see (B)'s grammar book for a minute.
SPEAKER A: May/Could/Can I (please) see your grammar book for a minute?
SPEAKER B: Of course. / Sure. / Etc.
SPEAKER A: Thank you. / Thanks. I forgot to bring mine to class today.

1. (A), you want to see (B)'s dictionary for a minute.

2. (A), you are at a restaurant. (B) is your server. You have finished your meal. You want the check.

3. (B), you run into (A) on the street. (A) is carrying some heavy packages. What are you going to say to him/her?

4. (A), you are speaking to (B), who is one of your teachers. You want to leave class early today.

5. (B), you are in a store with your good friend (A). The groceries cost more than you expected. You don't have enough money. What are you going to say to your friend?

□ **Exercise 21. Warm-up.** (Chart 7-6)
Check the questions that are grammatically correct. Which two questions do you think are more polite than the others?

In the kitchen

1. _____ Will you help me with the dishes?

2. _____ Would you load the dishwasher?

3. _____ May you load the dishwasher?

4. _____ Can you unload the dishwasher?

5. _____ Could you unload the dishwasher?

7-6 Polite Questions: *Would You, Could You, Will You, Can You*

Polite Question	Possible Answers	
(a) *Would you* please open the door? (b) *Could you* please open the door? (c) *Will you* please open the door? (d) *Can you* please open the door?	Yes. Yes. Of course. Certainly. I'd be happy to. Of course. I'd be glad to. Sure. (informal) Okay. (informal) Uh-huh. (meaning "yes") I'm sorry. I'd like to help, but my hands are full.	People use *would you*, *could you*, *will you*, and *can you* to ask polite questions. The questions ask for someone's help or cooperation. Examples (a), (b), (c), and (d) have basically the same meaning. *Would* and *could* are generally considered more polite than *will* and *can*.
		NOTE: *May* is NOT used when *you* is the subject of a polite question. INCORRECT: *May you please open the door?*

□ **Exercise 22. Looking at grammar.** (Chart 7-6)
Make two different questions for each situation. Use *you*.

1. You're in a room and it's getting very hot.

   Formal: ___*Would you please open the window?*___

   Informal: ___*Can you turn on the air-conditioner?*___

2. You're trying to listen to the news on TV, but your friends are talking too loud, and you can't hear it.

   Formal: _____

   Informal: _____

3. You're in a restaurant. You are about to pay and notice the bill is more than it should be. The server has made a mistake.

   Formal: _____

   Informal: _____

□ **Exercise 23. Let's talk: pairwork.** (Charts 7-5 and 7-6)
Work with a partner. Make a conversation for one (or more) of the given situations. Perform your conversation for the rest of the class.

Example: You're in a restaurant. You want the server to refill your coffee cup.
You catch the server's eye and raise your hand slightly. He approaches your table and says: "Yes? What can I do for you?"

PARTNER A: Yes? What can I do for you?
PARTNER B: Could I please have some more coffee?
PARTNER A: Of course. Right away. Could I get you anything else?

PARTNER B: No thanks. Oh, on second thought, yes. Would you bring some cream too?
PARTNER A: Certainly.
PARTNER B: Thanks.

1. You've been waiting in a long line at a busy bakery. Finally, it's your turn. The clerk turns toward you and says: "Next!"

2. You are at work. You feel sick and you have a slight fever. You really want to go home. You see your boss, Mr. Jenkins, passing by your desk. You say: "Mr. Jenkins, could I speak with you for a minute?"

3. The person next to you on the plane has finished reading his newspaper. You would like to read it. He also has a bag on the floor that is in your space. You would like him to move it. You say: "Excuse me."

□ **Exercise 24. Warm-up.** (Chart 7-7)
Your friend Paula has a terrible headache. What advice would you give her? Check (✓) the sentences you agree with.

1. _____ You should lie down.

2. _____ You should take some medicine.

3. _____ You ought to call the doctor.

4. _____ You should go to the emergency room.

5. _____ You ought to put an ice-pack on your forehead.

7-7 Expressing Advice: *Should* and *Ought To*

(a) My clothes are dirty. I { *should* / *ought to* } wash them.	**Should** and **ought to** have the same meaning: "This is a good idea. This is good advice."

(b) INCORRECT: *I should to wash them.*
(c) INCORRECT: *I ought washing them.*
	FORMS:
	    should + simple form of a verb (no **to**)
	    ought + **to** + simple form of a verb

(d) You need your sleep. You **should not** (**shouldn't**) stay up late.	NEGATIVE: **should** + **not** = **shouldn't** (*Ought to* is usually not used in the negative.)
(e) A: I'm going to be late for the bus. What **should I do**? B: Run!	QUESTION: **should** + subject + main verb (*Ought to* is usually not used in questions.)
(f) A: I'm tired today. B: You **should/ought to** go home and take a nap. (g) A: I'm tired today. B: **Maybe** you **should/ought to** go home and take a nap.	The use of **maybe** with **should** and **ought to** "softens" advice. COMPARE: In (f): Speaker B is giving definite advice. He is stating clearly that he believes going home for a nap is a good idea and is the solution to Speaker A's problem. In (g): Speaker B is making a suggestion: going home for a nap is one possible way to solve Speaker A's problem.

Exercise 25. Let's talk: pairwork. (Chart 7-7)
Work with a partner. Partner A states the problem. Partner B gives advice using *should* or
ought to. Include *maybe* to soften the advice if you wish.

Example: I'm sleepy.
PARTNER A: I'm sleepy.
PARTNER B: (Maybe) You should/ought to drink a cup of tea.

1. I can't fall asleep at night.
2. I have a sore throat.
3. I have the hiccups.
4. I sat on my friend's sunglasses. Now the frames are bent.

Change roles.
5. I'm starving.*
6. I dropped my sister's camera, and now it doesn't work.
7. Someone stole my lunch from the refrigerator in the staff lounge at work.
8. I bought some shoes that don't fit. Now my feet hurt.

□ **Exercise 26. Warm-up.** (Chart 7-8)
Marco has lost his passport. Here are some suggestions. Check (✓) the sentences you agree
with. Which sentences seem more serious or urgent?

1. _____ He had better go to the embassy.

2. _____ He should wait and see if someone returns it.

3. _____ He had better report it to the police.

4. _____ He should ask a friend to help him look for it.

7-8 Expressing Advice: *Had Better*	
(a) My clothes are dirty. I { *should* / *ought to* / *had better* } wash them.	***Had better*** has the same basic meaning as *should* and *ought to:* "This is a good idea. This is good advice."
(b) You're driving too fast! You *'d better slow* down.	***Had better*** has more of a sense of urgency than *should* or *ought to*. It often implies a warning about possible bad consequences. In (b): If you don't slow down, there could be a bad result. You could get a speeding ticket or have an accident.
(c) You *'d better not eat* that meat. It looks spoiled.	NEGATIVE: ***had better not***
(d) I *'d better send* my boss an email right away.	In conversation, ***had*** is usually contracted: *'d.*

---

starving (informal English) = very, very hungry

Exercise 27. Looking at grammar. (Chart 7-8)
Give advice using *had better*. What are some possible bad consequences if your advice is not followed? Work in pairs, in small groups, or as a class.

1. I haven't paid my electric bill.
   → *You'd better pay it by tomorrow. If you don't pay it, the electric company will turn off the power.*
2. Joe oversleeps a lot. This week he has been late to work three times. His boss is very unhappy about that.
3. I don't feel good right now. I think I'm coming down with something.*
4. I can't remember if I locked the front door when I left for work.
5. My ankle really hurts. I think I've sprained it.
6. I can't find my credit card, and I've looked everywhere.

□ **Exercise 28. Check your knowledge.** (Chapter 7)
Edit the sentences. Correct the verb form errors.

      had
1. You ~~will~~ better not be late.

2. Anna shouldn't wears shorts to work.

3. I should to go to the post office today.

4. I ought paying my bills today.

5. You'd had better to call the doctor today.

6. You don't should stay up too late tonight.

7. You better not leaving your key in the door.

8. Mr. Lim is having a surprise party for his wife. He ought told people soon.

□ **Exercise 29. Let's talk.** (Charts 7-7 and 7-8)
Work in small groups. Give advice using *should, ought to*, and *had better*. The leader states the problem, and others in the group offer suggestions. Select a different leader for each item.

Example:
LEADER: I study, but I don't understand my physics class. It's the middle of the term, and I'm failing the course. I need a science course in order to graduate. What should I do?**
SPEAKER A: You**'d better** get a tutor right away.
SPEAKER B: You **should** make an appointment with your teacher and see if you can get some extra help.
SPEAKER C: Maybe you **ought to** drop your physics course and take a different science course next term.

---

*The idiom *come down with something* = get a sickness, like a cold or the flu

**Should* (NOT *ought to* or *had better*) is usually used in a question that asks for advice. The answer, however, can contain *should, ought to*, or *had better*. For example:
  A: *My houseplants always die. What **should** I do?*
  B: *You'd **better** get a book on plants. You **should** try to find out why they die. Maybe you **ought to** look on the Internet and see if you can find some information.*

1. I forgot my dad's birthday yesterday. I feel terrible about it. What should I do?

2. I just discovered that I made dinner plans for tonight with two different people. I'm supposed to meet my parents at one restaurant at 7:00, and I'm supposed to meet my boss at a different restaurant across town at 8:00. What should I do?

3. Samira accidentally left the grocery store with an item she didn't pay for. Her young daughter put it in Samira's shopping bag, but she didn't see it. What should Samira do?

4. I borrowed Karen's favorite book of poetry. It was special to her. A note on the inside cover said "To Karen." The author's signature was under it. Now I can't find the book. I think I lost it. What should I do?

□ **Exercise 30. Warm-up.** (Chart 7-9)
Which of these statements about writing a résumé are true in your country? Check (✓) them and then decide which sentence is more common in writing and which sentences are more common in speaking.

Writing a résumé

1. _____ You must list all your previous employers.

2. _____ You have to provide references.

3. _____ You have got to include personal information, for example, whether you are married or not.

7-9 Expressing Necessity: *Have to, Have Got to, Must*

(a) I have a very important test tomorrow. I { have to / have got to / must } study tonight.	***Have to, have got to***, and ***must*** have basically the same meaning. They express the idea that something is necessary.
(b) I'd like to go with you to the movie this evening, but I can't. I ***have to go*** to a meeting. (c) Bye now! I ***'ve got to go***. My wife's waiting for me. I'll call you later. (d) All passengers ***must present*** their passports at customs upon arrival. (e) Tommy, you ***must hold*** onto the railing when you go down the stairs.	***Have to*** is used much more frequently in everyday speech and writing than ***must***. ***Have got to*** is typically used in informal conversation, as in (c). ***Must*** is typically found in written instructions or rules, as in (d). Adults also use it when talking to younger children, as in (e). It sounds very strong.
(f) ***Do*** we ***have to bring*** pencils to the test? (g) Why ***did*** he ***have to leave*** so early?	QUESTIONS: ***Have to*** is usually used in questions, not ***must*** or ***have got to***. Forms of ***do*** are used with ***have to*** in questions.
(h) I ***had to study*** last night.	The PAST form of ***have to, have got to***, and ***must*** (meaning necessity) is ***had to***.
(i) I ***have to*** ("hafta") *go* downtown today. (j) Rita ***has to*** ("hasta") *go* to the bank. (k) I've ***got to*** ("gotta") *study* tonight.	Notice that ***have to, has to***, and ***have got to*** are commonly reduced, as in (i) through (k).

Exercise 31. Let's talk. (Charts 7-7 and 7-9)

Answer the questions. Work in pairs, in small groups, or as a class.

1. What are some things you *have to do* today? tomorrow? every day?
2. What is something you *had to do* yesterday?
3. What is something you*'ve got to do* soon?
4. What is something you*'ve got to do* after class today or later tonight?
5. What is something a driver *must do,* according to the law?
6. What is something a driver *should always do* to be a safe driver?
7. What are some things a person *should do* to stay healthy?
8. What are some things a person *must do* to stay alive?

□ **Exercise 32. Listening.** (Chart 7-9)

Complete the sentences with the words you hear. Before you begin, you may want to check your understanding of these words: *apply, applicable, legal, nickname, previous, employer.*

CD 2
Track 15

EMPLOYMENT APPLICATION

Applications are considered for all positions without regard to race, color, religion, sex, national origin, age, marital or veteran status, or in the presence of a non-related medical condition or handicap.

Donna	*N/A*	*Frost*	*May 4, 2011*
First Name	Middle Initial	Last Name	Date

1443 Maple Ridge Heights	*555-545-5454*
Address	Phone #

Happyville	*PA*	*05055*	*123-000-7890*
City	State	Zip Code	Social Security #

Filling out a job application

1. The application _____ be complete. You shouldn't skip any parts. If a section doesn't fit your situation, you can write N/A (not applicable).

2. _____ type it, but your writing _____ be easy to read.

3. _____ use your full legal name, not your nickname.

4. _____ list the names and places of your previous employers.

5. _____ list your education, beginning with either high school or college.

6. _____ always _____ apply in person. Sometimes you can do it online.

7. _____ write some things, like the same telephone number, twice. You can write "same as above."

8. All spelling _____ be correct.

Read the passage and then give advice.

A Family Problem

Mr. and Mrs. Hill don't know what to do about their 15-year-old son, Mark. He's very intelligent but has no interest in learning. His grades are getting worse, and he won't do any homework. Sometimes he skips school and spends the day at the mall.

His older sister Kathy is a good student, and she never causes any problems at home. Kathy hasn't missed a day of school all year. Mark's parents keep asking him why he can't be more like Kathy. Mark is jealous of Kathy and picks fights* with her.

All Mark does when he's home is stay in his room and listen to loud music. He often refuses to eat meals with his family. He argues with his parents, his room is a mess, and he won't** help around the house.

This family needs advice. Tell them what changes they should make. What should they do? What shouldn't they do?

Use each of these words at least once in the advice you give:

should	ought to
shouldn't	have to/has to
have got to/has got to	must
had better	

❑   **Exercise 34. Warm-up.** (Chart 7-10)
Which sentence (a. or b.) completes the idea of the given sentence?

We have lots of time.

    a. You must not drive so fast!
    b. You don't have to drive so fast.

7-10 Expressing Lack of Necessity: *Do Not Have To;* Expressing Prohibition: *Must Not*	
(a) I finished all of my homework this afternoon. I *don't have to study* tonight.	***Don't/doesn't have to*** expresses the idea that something is *not necessary*.
(b) Tomorrow is a holiday. Mary *doesn't have to go* to class.	
(c) Bus passengers *must not talk* to the driver.	***Must not*** expresses *prohibition* (DO NOT DO THIS!).
(d) Children, you *must not play* with matches!	
(e) You *mustn't play* with matches.	***Must + not = mustn't*** (NOTE: The first "t" is not pronounced.)

---

*pick a fight = start a fight

**won't is used here to express refusal: *He refuses to help around the house.*

☐ **Exercise 35. Looking at grammar.** (Chart 7-10)
Complete the sentences with **don't have to, doesn't have to,** or **must not**.

1. You ___*must not*___ drive when you are tired. It's dangerous.

2. I live only a few blocks from my office. I ___*don't have to*___ drive to work.

3. Liz finally got a car, so now she drives to work. She _____ take the bus.

4. Mr. Murphy is very wealthy. He _____ work for a living.

5. You _____ tell Daddy about the birthday party. We want it to be a surprise.

6. A: Did Professor Acosta give an assignment?

    B: Yes, she assigned Chapters 4 and 6, but we _____ read Chapter 5.

7. A: Listen carefully, Kristen. If a stranger offers you a ride, you _____ get in the car. Never get in a car with a stranger. Do you understand?

    B: Yes, Mom.

☐ **Exercise 36. Warm-up.** (Chart 7-11)
Read the situation and the conclusions that follow. Which conclusion(s) seems logical to you? Explain your answers, if necessary.

SITUATION: Mr. Ellis is a high school gym teacher. He usually wears gym clothes to work. Today he is wearing a suit and tie.

1. He must have an important meeting.
2. He must be rich.
3. He must need new clothes.
4. He must want to make a good impression on someone.
5. His gym clothes must not be clean.

7-11 Making Logical Conclusions: *Must*

(a) A: Nancy is yawning. B: She ***must be*** sleepy.	In (a): Speaker B is making a logical guess. He bases his guess on the information that Nancy is yawning. His logical conclusion, his "best guess," is that Nancy is sleepy. He uses ***must*** to express his logical conclusion.
(b) LOGICAL CONCLUSION: Amy plays tennis every day. She ***must like*** to play tennis. (c) NECESSITY: If you want to get into the movie theater, you ***must buy*** a ticket.	COMPARE: ***Must*** can express • a logical conclusion, as in (b). • necessity, as in (c).
(d) NEGATIVE LOGICAL CONCLUSION: Eric ate everything on his plate except the pickle. He ***must not like*** pickles. (e) PROHIBITION: There are sharks in the ocean near our hotel. We ***must not go*** swimming there.	COMPARE: ***Must not*** can express • a negative logical conclusion, as in (d). • prohibition, as in (e).

❑ **Exercise 37. Looking at grammar.** (Chart 7-11)
Complete the conversations with ***must*** or ***must not***.

1. A: Did you offer our guests something to eat?

    B: Yes, but they didn't want anything. They __*must not*__ be hungry yet.

2. A: You haven't eaten since breakfast? That was hours ago. You __*must*__ be
    hungry.

    B: I am.

3. A: Gregory has already had four glasses of water, and now he's having another.

    B: He _____ be really thirsty.

4. A: I offered Holly something to drink, but she doesn't want anything.

    B: She _____ be thirsty.

5. A: The dog won't eat.

    B: He _____ feel well.

6. A: Brian has watery eyes and has been coughing and sneezing.

    B: Poor guy. He _____ have a cold.

7. A: Erica's really smart. She always gets above 95 percent on her math tests.

    B: I'm sure she's pretty bright, but she _____ also study a lot.

8. A: Listen. Someone is jumping on the floor above us.

    B: It _____ be Sam. Sometimes he does exercises in his apartment.

Exercise 38. Looking at grammar. (Chart 7-11)
Make a logical conclusion for each situation. Use ***must***.

1. Alima is crying. → *She must be unhappy.*
2. Mrs. Chu has a big smile on her face.
3. Samantha is shivering.
4. Olga watches ten movies a week.
5. James is sweating.
6. Toshi can lift one end of a compact car by himself.

Exercise 39. Let's talk. (Chart 7-11)
Make logical conclusions with ***must*** or ***must not***. Use the suggested completions and/or your own words.

1. I am at Cyril's apartment door. I've knocked on the door and have rung the doorbell several times. Nobody has answered the door. *be at home? be out somewhere?*
   → *Cyril must not be at home. He must be out somewhere.*

2. Jennifer reads all the time. She sits in a quiet corner and reads even when people come to visit her. *love books? like books better than people? like to talk to people?*

3. Lara has a full academic schedule, plays on the volleyball team, has the lead in the school play, is a volunteer at the hospital, takes piano lessons, and has a part-time job at an ice-cream store. *be busy all the time? have a lot of spare time? be a hard worker?*

4. Simon gets on the Internet every day as soon as he gets home from work. He stays at his computer until he goes to bed. *be a computer addict? have a happy home life? have a lot of friends?*

Exercise 40. Looking at grammar. (Charts 7-9 and 7-11)
Complete the sentences with ***must, have to,*** or ***had to*** and the correct form of the verbs in parentheses.

At work

A: Your eyes are red. You (*be*) _____ really tired.
                                            1

B: Yeah, I (*stay*) _____ up all night working on a project.
                        2

A: Did you finish?

B: No, I (*work*) _____ on it later today, but I have a million other
                          3

things to do.

A: You (*be*) _____ really busy.
                        4

B: I am!

□ **Exercise 41. Warm-up.** (Chart 7-12)

Complete the questions with the correct words from the list. Two words don't fit any questions.

can't	couldn't	do	does	will	wouldn't

1. You can work this weekend, _____ you?

2. He won't be late, _____ he?

3. We'd like you to stay, _____ we?

4. They don't have to leave, _____ they?

7-12 Tag Questions with Modal Auxiliaries

(a) You *can* come, ***can't you*** ? (b) She *won't* tell, ***will she*** ? (c) He *should* help, ***shouldn't he*** ? (d) They *couldn't* do it, ***could they*** ? (e) We *would* like to help, ***wouldn't we*** ?	Tag questions are common with these modal auxiliaries: ***can, will, should, could***, and ***would***.*
(f) They *have to* leave, ***don't they*** ? (g) They *don't have to* leave, ***do they*** ? (h) He *has to* leave, ***doesn't he*** ? (i) He *doesn't have to* leave, ***does he*** ? (j) You *had to* leave, ***didn't you*** ? (k) You *didn't have to* leave, ***did you*** ?	Tag questions are also common with ***have to, has to***, and ***had to***. Notice that forms of ***do*** are used for the tag in (f) through (k).

*See Chart 5-15, p. 140, for information on how to use tag questions.

□ **Exercise 42. Looking at grammar.** (Chart 7-12)

Complete the tag questions.

1. You can answer these questions, _____ you?

2. Melinda won't tell anyone our secret, _____ she?

3. Alice would like to come with us, _____ she?

4. I don't have to do more chores, _____ I?

5. Steven shouldn't come to the meeting, _____ he?

6. Flies can fly upside down, _____ they?

7. You would rather have your own apartment, _____ you?

8. Jill has to renew her driver's license, _____ she?

9. If you want to catch your bus, you should leave now, _____ you?

10. Ms. Baxter will be here tomorrow, _____ she?

11. You couldn't hear me, _____ you?

12. We have to be at the doctor's early tomorrow, _____ we?

☐ **Exercise 43. Warm-up.** (Chart 7-13)
Read each group of sentences. Decide who the speaker is and a possible situation for each group.

GROUP A
1. Show me your driver's license.
2. Take it out of your wallet, please.
3. Step out of the car.

GROUP B
1. Open your mouth.
2. Stick out your tongue.
3. Say "ahhh."
4. Let me take a closer look.
5. Don't bite me!

7-13 Giving Instructions: Imperative Sentences

COMMAND:
(a) Captain: *Open* the door!
  Soldier: Yes, sir!
 	
REQUEST:
(b) Teacher: *Open* the door, please.
  Student: Sure.
 	
DIRECTIONS:
(c) Barbara: Could you tell me how to get to the post office?
  Stranger: Certainly. *Walk* two blocks down this **street. *Turn* left and *walk* three more blocks.** It's on the right-hand side of the street.
	Imperative sentences are used to give commands, make polite requests, and give directions. The difference between a command and a request lies in the speaker's tone of voice and the use of *please*.
	
	Please can come at the beginning or end of a request:
	  Open the door, please.
	  Please open the door.

(d) *Close* the window. (e) Please *sit* down. (f) *Be* quiet! (g) *Don't walk* on the grass. (h) Please *don't wait* for me. (i) *Don't be* late.	The simple form of a verb is used in imperative sentences. In (d): The understood subject of the sentence is *you* (meaning the person the speaker is talking to): *Close the window = You close the window.* NEGATIVE FORM: *Don't* + the simple form of a verb

Exercise 44. Let's talk. (Chart 7-13)

Part I. Read the steps for cooking rice. Put them in a logical order (1–9). Work with a partner or in small groups.

1. Measure the rice. _____

2. Cook for 20 minutes. _____

3. Pour water into a pan. _____

4. Bring the water to a boil. _____

5. Put the rice in the pan. _____

6. Don't burn yourself. _____

7. Set the timer. _____

8. Turn off the heat. _____

9. Take the pan off the stove. _____

Part II. Write instructions for cooking something simple. Share your recipe with the class.

□ **Exercise 45. Listening.** (Chart 7-13)

Part I. Listen to the steps in this number puzzle and write the verbs you hear.
Before you begin, you may want to check your understanding of these words: *add, subtract,*
CD 2
Track 16 *multiply, double.*

Puzzle steps:

1. _____ down the number of the month you were born. For example,

   _____ the number 2 if you were born in February.

   _____ 3 if you were born in March, etc.

2. _____ the number.

3. _____ 5 to it.

4. _____ it by 50.

5. _____ your age.

6. _____ 250.

Part II. Now follow the steps in Part I to complete the puzzle. In the final number, the last two digits on the right will be your age, and the one or two digits on the left will be the month you were born.

❏ **Exercise 46. Reading and writing.** (Chart 7-13)

Part I. Read the passage. Cross out suggestions that don't work for a job interview in your country. Then add more suggestions until there are ten.

How to Make a Good Impression in a Job Interview

Do you want to know how to make a good impression when you interview for a job? Here are some suggestions for you to consider.

1. Dress appropriately for the company. Flip-flops and shorts, for example, are usually not appropriate.
2. Be sure to arrive early. Employers like punctual workers.
3. Bring extra copies of your résumé and references. There may be more than one interviewer.
4. Make eye contact with the interviewer. It shows confidence.
5. Don't chew gum during the interview.
6. Research the company before you go. That way you can show your knowledge and interest in the company.

If you follow these suggestions, you will have a better chance of making a good impression when you go for a job interview.

Part II. Write three paragraphs. Use the topic in Part I, or give general advice to people who want to . . .

1. improve their health.
2. get good grades.
3. improve their English.
4. find a job.
5. get a good night's sleep.
6. protect the environment by recycling.

Use this model.
  I. Introductory paragraph: *Do you want to . . . ? Here are some suggestions for you to consider.*
 II. Middle paragraph: (List the suggestions and add details.)
III. Final paragraph: *If you follow these suggestions, you will . . . .*

□ **Exercise 47. Warm-up.** (Chart 7-14)
Check (✓) the items that are suggestions.

1. ____ Why do bears hibernate?
2. ____ I have a day off. Why don't we take the kids to the zoo?
3. ____ Let's go see the bears at the zoo.

7-14 Making Suggestions: *Let's* and *Why Don't*

(a) — It's hot today. *Let's go to the beach.* — Okay. Good idea. (b) — It's hot today. *Why don't we go to the beach?* — Okay. Good idea.	*Let's* and *Why don't we* are used to make suggestions about activities for you and another person to do. Examples (a) and (b) have the same meaning. *Let's* = *let us*
(c) — I'm tired. — *Why don't you take a nap?* — That's a good idea. I think I will.	In (c): *Why don't you* is used to make a friendly suggestion or to give friendly advice.

□ **Exercise 48. Let's talk.** (Chart 7-14)
Make suggestions beginning with *Let's* and *Why don't we*.

1. Where should we go for dinner tonight?
2. Who should we ask to join us for dinner tonight?
3. What time should we meet at the restaurant?
4. Where should we go afterwards?

□ **Exercise 49. Let's talk.** (Chart 7-14)
Work in small groups. The leader states the problem, and then others in the group offer suggestions beginning with *Why don't you*.

1. I'm freezing.
2. I'm feeling dizzy.
3. I feel like doing something interesting and fun this weekend. Any ideas?
4. I need to get more exercise, but I get bored with indoor activities. Any suggestions?
5. I haven't done my assignment for Professor Lopez. It will take me a couple of hours, and class starts in an hour. What am I going to do?
6. I've lost the key to my apartment, so I can't get in. My roommate is at the library. What am I going to do?
7. My friend and I had an argument, and now we aren't talking to each other. I've had some time to think about it, and I'm sorry for what I said. I miss her friendship. What should I do?

□ **Exercise 50. Listening.** (Chart 7-14)

Listen to the conversation about a couple making suggestions for the evening. Listen a second time and put the suggestions in the correct order (1–3).

CD 2
Track 17

Suggestions:

1. go to a restaurant _____

2. go dancing _____

3. go to a movie _____

□ **Exercise 51. Warm-up.** (Chart 7-15)

Check (✓) the statements that are true for you.

1. _____ I prefer fruit to vegetables.

2. _____ I like raw vegetables better than cooked.

3. _____ I would rather eat vegetables than meat.

7-15 Stating Preferences: *Prefer, Like ... Better, Would Rather*

(a) I *prefer* apples *to* oranges. (b) I *prefer* watching TV *to* studying.	***prefer*** + *noun* + ***to*** + *noun* ***prefer*** + ***-ing*** *verb* + ***to*** + ***-ing*** *verb*
(c) I *like* apples *better than* oranges. (d) I *like* watching TV *better than* studying.	***like*** + *noun* + ***better than*** + *noun* ***like*** + ***-ing*** *verb* + ***better than*** + ***-ing*** *verb*
(e) Ann *would rather have* an apple than an orange. (f) INCORRECT: *Ann would rather has an apple.* (g) I'd rather visit a big city *than live* there. (h) INCORRECT: *I'd rather visit a big city than to live there.* INCORRECT: *I'd rather visit a big city than living there.*	***Would rather*** is followed immediately by the simple form of a verb (e.g., *have, visit, live*), as in (e). Verbs following ***than*** are also in the simple form, as in (g).
(i) *I'd / You'd / She'd / He'd / We'd / They'd* rather have an apple.	Contraction of ***would*** = ***'d***
(j) ***Would you rather*** have an apple *or* an orange?	In (j): In a polite question, ***would rather*** can be followed by ***or*** to offer someone a choice.

□ **Exercise 52. Looking at grammar.** (Chart 7-15)

Complete the sentences with *than* or *to*.

1. When I'm hot and thirsty, I **prefer** cold drinks ___to___ hot drinks.

2. When I'm hot and thirsty, I **like** cold drinks **better** ___than___ hot drinks.

3. When I'm hot and thirsty, I'**d rather have** a cold drink ___than___ a hot drink.

4. I **prefer** tea _____ coffee.

5. I **like** tea **better** _____ coffee.

6. I'd **rather** drink tea _____ coffee.

7. When I choose a book, I **prefer** nonfiction _____ fiction.

8. I **like** folk music music **better** _____ rock and roll.

9. My parents **would rather work** _____ retire. They enjoy their jobs.

10. Do you **like** spring **better** _____ fall?

11. I **prefer visiting** my friends in the evening _____ watching TV by myself.

12. I **would rather read** a book in the evening _____ visit with friends.

□ **Exercise 53. Let's talk: pairwork.** (Chart 7-15)
Work with a partner. Take turns asking and answering questions. Be sure to answer in complete sentences.

Examples: Which do you prefer: apples or oranges?*
    → *I prefer oranges to apples.*

    Which do you like better: bananas or strawberries?
    → *I like bananas better than strawberries.*

    Which would you rather have right now: an apple or a banana?
    → *I'd rather have a banana.*

1. Which do you like better: rice or potatoes?
2. Which do you prefer: peas or corn?
3. Which would you rather have for dinner tonight: fish or chicken?
4. Name two sports. Which do you like better?
5. Name two movies. Which one would you rather see?
6. What kind of music would you rather listen to: rock or classical?
7. Name two vegetables. Which do you prefer?
8. Name two TV programs. Which do you like better?

□ **Exercise 54. Let's talk: interview.** (Chart 7-15)
Interview your classmates. Use **would rather . . . than** in your answers.

Would you rather . . .
1. live in an apartment or in a house?** Why?
2. be an author or an artist? Why?
3. drive a fast car or fly a small plane? Why?
4. be rich and unlucky in love or poor and lucky in love? Why?
5. surf the Internet or watch TV? Why?
6. have a big family or a small family? Why?
7. be a bird or a fish? Why?
8. spend your free time with other people or be by yourself? Why?

---

*Use a rising intonation on the first choice and a falling intonation on the second choice: *Which do you prefer, apples or oranges?*

It is possible but not necessary to repeat a preposition after **than.
   CORRECT: *I'd rather live in an apartment **than in a house**.*
   CORRECT: *I'd rather live in an apartment **than a house**.*

Choose the best completion for each sentence.

Example: A: My cat won't eat.
B: You _____ call the vet.
a. will (b.) had better c. may

1. A: Does this pen belong to you?
   B: No. It _____ be Susan's. She was sitting at that desk.
   a. had better b. will c. must

2. A: Let's go to a movie this evening.
   B: That sounds like fun, but I can't. I _____ finish a report before I go to bed tonight.
   a. have got to b. would rather c. ought to

3. A: Hey, Pietro. What's up* with Ken? Is he upset about something?
   B: He's angry because you recommended Ann instead of him for the promotion. You _____ sit down with him and explain your reasons. At least that's what I think.
   a. should b. will c. can

4. A: Does Omar want to go with us to the film festival tonight?
   B: No. He _____ go to a wrestling match than the film festival.
   a. could b. would rather c. prefers

5. A: I did it! I did it! I got my driver's license!
   B: Congratulations, Michelle. I'm really proud of you.
   A: Thanks, Dad. Now _____ I have the car tonight? Please, please?
   B: No. You're not ready for that quite yet.
   a. will b. should c. may

6. A: I just tripped on your carpet and almost fell. It's loose right by the door. You _____ fix it before someone gets hurt.
   B: Yes, Uncle Ben. I should. I will. I'm sorry. Are you all right?
   a. can b. ought to c. may

7. A: Are you going to the conference in Atlanta next month?
   B: I _____. It's sort of iffy** right now. I've applied for travel money, but who knows what my supervisor will do.
   a. will b. have to c. might

8. A: What shall we do after the meeting this evening?
   B: _____ pick Jan up and all go out to dinner together.
   a. Why don't b. Let's c. Should

9. A: What shall we do after that?
   B: _____ we go back to my place for dessert.
   a. Why don't b. Let's c. Should

---

*What's up? = What's going on?

**iffy = uncertain; doubtful

10. A: Have you seen my denim jacket? I ____ find it.
    B: Look in the hall closet.
        a. may not   b. won't   c. can't

11. A: Bye, Mom. I'm going to go play soccer with my friends.
    B: Wait a minute, young man! You ____ do your chores first.
        a. had better not   b. have to   c. would rather

12. A: Do you think that Scott will quit his job?
    B: I don't know. He ____ . He's very angry. We'll just have to wait and see.
        a. must   b. may   c. will

13. A: The hotel provides towels, you know. You ____ pack a towel in your suitcase.
    B: This is my bathrobe, not a towel.
        a. don't have to   b. must not   c. couldn't

14. A: Did you climb to the top of the Statue of Liberty when you were in New York?
    B: No, I didn't. My knee was very sore, and I ____ climb all those stairs.
        a. might not   b. couldn't   c. must not

15. A: Rick, ____ work for me this evening? I'll take your shift tomorrow.
    B: Sure. I was going to ask you to work for me tomorrow anyway.
        a. should you   b. could you   c. do you have to

16. A: What are you children doing? Stop! You ____ play with sharp knives.
    B: Why not?
        a. must not   b. couldn't   c. don't have to

17. A: Don't wait for me. I ____ late.
    B: Okay.
        a. maybe   b. can be   c. may be

18. A: The Bensons are giving their daughter a new skateboard for her birthday.
    B: They ____ give her a helmet, too. She does some dangerous things on a skateboard.
        a. had better   b. can't   c. would rather

Chapter 8
Connecting Ideas

☐ **Exercise 1. Warm-up.** (Chart 8-1)
Check (✓) the sentences that have the correct punctuation.

1. _____ I ate an apple, and an orange.
2. _____ I ate an apple and an orange.
3. _____ I ate an apple, an orange, and a banana.
4. _____ I ate an apple, Nina ate a peach.
5. _____ I ate an apple, and Nina ate a peach.

8-1 Connecting Ideas with *And*

Connecting Items within a Sentence	
(a) NO COMMA: I saw a cat *and* a mouse. (b) COMMAS: I saw a cat, a mouse, *and* a dog.	When *and* connects only TWO WORDS (or phrases) within a sentence, NO COMMA is used, as in (a). When *and* connects THREE OR MORE items within a sentence, COMMAS are used, as in (b).*
Connecting Two Sentences	
(c) COMMA: I saw a cat, *and* you saw a mouse.	When *and* connects TWO COMPLETE SENTENCES (also called "independent" clauses), a COMMA is usually used, as in (c).
(d) PERIOD: I saw a cat. You saw a mouse. (e) INCORRECT: *I saw a cat, you saw a mouse.*	Without *and*, two complete sentences are separated by a period, as in (d), *not* a comma.** A complete sentence begins with a capital letter; note that *You* is capitalized in (d).

*In a series of three or more items, the comma before *and* is optional.
    ALSO CORRECT: *I saw a cat, a mouse and a dog.*
**A "period" (the dot used at the end of a sentence) is called a "full stop" in British English.

☐ **Exercise 2. Looking at grammar.** (Chart 8-1)
Underline and label the words (noun, verb, adjective) connected by **and**. Add commas as necessary.

                 noun + noun
1. My mom puts <u>milk</u> and <u>sugar</u> in her tea. → *(no commas needed)*

               noun + noun + noun
2. My mom puts <u>milk,</u> <u>sugar,</u> and <u>lemon</u> in her tea. → *(commas needed)*

3. The river is wide and deep.

4. The river is wide deep and dangerous.

5. The teenage girls at the slumber* party played music ate pizza and told ghost stories.

6. The teenage girls played music and ate pizza.

7. My mom dad sister and grandfather came to the party to see my son and daughter

   celebrate their fourth birthday.

8. When he wanted to entertain the children, my husband mooed like a cow roared like a lion

   and barked like a dog.

☐ **Exercise 3. Let's talk and write: interview.** (Chart 8-1)
Interview another student in your class. Take notes and then write complete sentences using **and**. Share some of the answers with the class.

What are . . .
1. your three favorite sports?
2. three adjectives that describe the weather today?
3. four cities that you would like to visit?
4. two characteristics that describe this city or town?
5. five things you did this morning?
6. three things you are afraid of?
7. two or more things that make you happy?
8. three or more adjectives that describe the people in your country?
9. the five most important qualities of a good parent?

★slumber = sleep; at a slumber party, friends sleep overnight together.

❑ **Exercise 4. Looking at grammar.** (Chart 8-1)
Add commas and periods where appropriate. Capitalize as necessary.

1. The rain fell. ᴛthe wind blew.

2. The rain fell, and the wind blew.*

3. I talked he listened.

4. I talked to Ryan about his school grades and he listened to me carefully.

5. The five most common words in English are *the and of to* and *a*.

6. The man asked a question the woman answered it.

7. The man asked a question and the woman answered it.

8. Rome is an Italian city it has a mild climate and many interesting attractions.

9. You should visit Rome its climate is mild and there are many interesting attractions.

❑ **Exercise 5. Warm-up.** (Chart 8-2)
Complete the sentences with your own ideas. Make true statements.

1. When I'm not sure of the meaning of a word in English, I _____

   _____ or _____.

2. Sometimes I don't understand native speakers of English, but I _____

   _____.

8-2 Connecting Ideas with *But* and *Or*

(a) I *went* to bed *but couldn't sleep*.	***And, but,*** and ***or*** are called "coordinating conjunctions."
(b) Is a lemon *sweet **or** sour*?	Like ***and, but*** and ***or*** can connect items within a sentence.
(c) Did you order *coffee, tea,* ***or*** *milk*?	Commas are used with a series of three or more items, as in (c).
I dropped the vase. = a sentence It didn't break. = a sentence (d) I dropped the vase, ***but*** it didn't break. (e) Do we have class on Monday, ***or*** is Monday a holiday?	A comma is usually used when ***but*** or ***or*** combines two complete (independent) sentences into one sentence, as in (d) and (e). A conjunction can also come at the beginning of a sentence, except in formal writing. ALSO CORRECT: I dropped the vase. But it didn't break. I saw a cat. And you saw a mouse.

---

*Sometimes the comma is omitted when ***and*** connects two very short independent clauses.
ALSO CORRECT: *The rain fell **and** the wind blew.* (NO COMMA)
In longer sentences, the comma is helpful and usual.

□ **Exercise 6. Looking at grammar.** (Charts 8-1 and 8-2)
Complete the sentences with *and*, *but*, or *or*. Add commas as necessary.

1. I washed my shirt, _*but*_ it didn't get clean.

2. Would you like some water _*or*_ some fruit juice?

3. I bought some paper, a birthday card, _*and*_ some envelopes.

4. The flight attendants served dinner _____ I didn't eat it.

5. I was hungry _____ didn't eat on the plane. The food didn't look appetizing.

6. I washed my face, brushed my teeth _____ combed my hair.

7. Golf _____ tennis are popular sports.

8. Sara is a good tennis player _____ she's never played golf.

9. Which would you prefer? Would you like to play tennis _____ golf Saturday?

10. Who made the call? Did Bob call you _____ did you call Bob?

□ **Exercise 7. Looking at grammar.** (Charts 8-1 and 8-2)
Add commas, periods, and capital letters as necessary.

Electronic devices* on airplanes

1. Laptops are electronic devices. ¢ell phones are electronic devices.

2. Laptops and portable DVD players are electronic devices but flashlights aren't.

3. Passengers can't use these electronic devices during takeoffs and landings they can use them the rest of the flight.

4. During takeoffs and landings, airlines don't allow passengers to use laptops DVD players electronic readers or PDAs.**

5. The devices may cause problems with the navigation system and they may cause problems with the communication system.

□ **Exercise 8. Warm-up.** (Chart 8-3)
Match the sentences in Column A with a logical idea from Column B.

Column A	**Column B**
1. I was tired, so I _____.	a. didn't sleep
2. I was tired, but I _____.	b. slept

---

*device = a thing, often electric or electronic, that has a specific purpose

**PDA = personal digital assistant; a small device that has some computer functions

8-3 Connecting Ideas with *So*	
(a) The room was dark, *so* I turned on a light.	*So* can be used as a conjunction, as in (a). It is preceded by a comma. It connects the ideas in two independent clauses. *So* expresses **results**: cause: *The room was dark.* result: *I turned on a light.*
(b) COMPARE: The room was dark, *but* I didn't turn on a light.	*But* often expresses an unexpected result, as in (b).

❑ **Exercise 9. Looking at grammar.** (Charts 8-2 and 8-3)
Complete the sentences with *so* or *but*.

1. It began to rain, ___*so*___ I opened my umbrella.

2. It began to rain, ___*but*___ I didn't open my umbrella.

3. I didn't have an umbrella, _____ I got wet.

4. I didn't have an umbrella, _____ I didn't get wet because I was wearing my raincoat.

5. The water was cold, _____ I went swimming anyway.

6. The water was cold, _____ I didn't go swimming.

7. Scott's directions to his apartment weren't clear, _____ Sonia got lost.

8. The directions weren't clear, _____ I found Scott's apartment anyway.

9. My friend lied to me, _____ I still like and trust her.

10. My friend lied to me, _____ I don't trust her anymore.

❑ **Exercise 10. Looking at grammar.** (Charts 8-1 → 8-3)
Add commas, periods, and capital letters as necessary.

Surprising animal facts:

1. Some tarantulas* can go two and a half years without food. $\overset{W}{\cancel{w}}$hen they eat, they like grasshoppers beetles small spiders and sometimes small lizards.

2. A female elephant is pregnant for approximately twenty months and almost always has only one baby a young elephant stays close to its mother for the first ten years of its life.

---

tarantula = a big, hairy spider

3. Dolphins sleep with one eye open they need to be conscious or awake in order to breathe if they fall asleep when they are breathing, they will drown so they sleep with half their brain awake and one eye open.

❑ **Exercise 11. Listening and grammar.** (Charts 8-1 → 8-3)

Listen to the passage. Then add commas, periods, and capital letters as necessary. Listen again as you check your answers. Before you begin, you may want to check your understanding of these words: *blinker, do a good deed, motioned, wave someone on.*

CD 2
Track 18

Paying It Forward*

(1)   A̸ few days ago, a friend and I were driving from Benton Harbor to Chicago.

(2)   W̸e didn't have any delays for the first hour but we ran into some highway construction

(3)   near Chicago the traffic wasn't moving my friend and I sat and waited we talked about

(4)   our jobs our families and the terrible traffic slowly it started to move

(5)   ˙ we noticed a black sports car on the shoulder its blinker was on the driver

(6)   obviously wanted to get back into traffic car after car passed without letting him in I

(7)   decided to do a good deed so I motioned for him to get in line ahead of me he waved

(8)   thanks and I waved back at him

(9)   all the cars had to stop at a toll booth a short way down the road I held out my

(10)   money to pay my toll but the toll-taker just smiled and waved me on she told me that the

(11)   man in the black sports car had already paid my toll wasn't that a nice way of saying

(12)   thank you?

---

*paying it forward = doing something nice for someone after someone does something nice for you. For example, imagine you are at a coffee stand waiting to buy a cup of coffee. The person in front of you is chatting with you and pays for your cup of coffee. You then buy a cup of coffee for the next person in line. You are *paying it forward.*

Paying it forward means the opposite of *paying it back* (repaying a debt or an obligation).

Exercise 12. Warm-up. (Chart 8-4)

Complete the sentences. Make true statements.

1. I like ___*fish*___, but ___*my sister*___ doesn't.

2. I don't like _____, but _____ does.

3. I've seen _____, but _____ hasn't.

4. I'm not _____, but _____ is.

8-4 Using Auxiliary Verbs after *But*

(a) I **don't like** coffee, but my husband **does**.	After **but**, often only an auxiliary verb is used. It has the same tense or modal as the main verb.
(b) I **like** tea, but my husband **doesn't**.	
(c) I **won't be** here tomorrow, but Sue **will**.	In (a): **does** = likes coffee
(d) I'**ve seen** that movie, but Joe **hasn't**.	Notice in the examples:
(e) He **isn't** here, but she **is**.*	negative + **but** + affirmative
	affirmative + **but** + negative

*A verb is not contracted with a pronoun at the end of a sentence after **but** and **and**:
    CORRECT: . . . *but she is.*
    INCORRECT: . . . *but she's.*

❑ **Exercise 13. Looking at grammar.** (Chart 8-4)

Part I. Complete each sentence with the correct negative auxiliary verb.

1. Alan reads a lot of books, but his brother ___*doesn't*___.

2. Alan reads a lot of books, but his brothers ___*don't*___.

3. Alan is reading a book, but his brother _____.

4. Alan is reading a book, but his brothers _____.

5. Alan read a book last week, but his brother(s) _____.

6. Alan has read a book recently, but his brother _____.

7. Alan has read a book recently, but his brothers _____.

8. Alan is going to read a book soon, but his brother _____.

9. Alan is going to read a book soon, but his brothers _____.

10. Alan will read a book soon, but his brother(s) _____.

Part II. Complete each sentence with the correct affirmative auxiliary verb.

1. Nicole doesn't eat red meat, but her sister ___*does*___.

2. Nicole doesn't eat red meat, but her sisters ___*do*___.

3. Nicole isn't eating red meat, but her sister _____.

4. Nicole isn't eating red meat, but her sisters _____.

5. Nicole didn't eat red meat last night, but her sister(s) _____.

6. Nicole hasn't eaten red meat recently, but her sister _____.

7. Nicole hasn't eaten red meat recently, but her sisters _____.

8. Nicole isn't going to eat red meat soon, but her sister _____.

9. Nicole isn't going to eat red meat soon, but her sisters _____.

10. Nicole won't eat red meat soon, but her sister(s) _____.

☐ **Exercise 14. Let's talk.** (Chart 8-4)
Complete the sentences with true statements about your classmates. You may need to interview them to get more information. Use appropriate auxiliary verbs.

1. ___Kira_____ has long hair, but ___Yuki doesn't_____.

2. _____ isn't hungry right now, but _____.

3. _____ lives nearby, but _____.

4. _____ can speak (*a language*) _____, but _____.

5. _____ plays a musical instrument, but _____.

6. _____ wasn't here last year, but _____.

7. _____ will be at home tonight, but _____.

8. _____ doesn't wear a ring, but _____.

9. _____ didn't study here last year, but _____.

10. _____ has lived here for a long time, but _____.

☐ **Exercise 15. Listening.** (Chart 8-4)
Complete the sentences with appropriate auxiliary verbs.

CD 2
Track 19 **A strong storm**

Example: You will hear: My husband saw a tree fall, but I . . .
You will write: ___didn't___.

1. _____.   5. _____.

2. _____.   6. _____.

3. _____.   7. _____.

4. _____.   8. _____.

□ **Exercise 16. Warm-up.** (Chart 8-5)
Match each sentence with the correct picture. NOTE: One picture doesn't match any of the sentences.

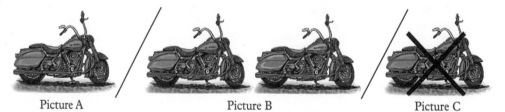

Picture A   Picture B   Picture C

1. ____ Alice has a motorcycle, and her husband does too.

2. ____ Alice has a motorcycle, and so does her husband.

3. ____ Alice doesn't have a motorcycle, and her husband doesn't either.

4. ____ Alice doesn't have a motorcycle, and neither does her husband.

8-5 Using *And* + *Too, So, Either, Neither*

S + AUX + *TOO*
(a) Sue works, *and* **Tom does** too.
 	
SO + AUX + S
(b) Sue works, *and* **so** **does Tom**.
	In affirmative statements, an auxiliary verb + **too** or **so** can be used after **and**.
	
	Examples (a) and (b) have the same meaning.
	
	Word order:
	    subject + *auxiliary* + **too**
	    so + *auxiliary* + *subject*

S + AUX   + *EITHER*
(c) Ann doesn't work, *and* **Joe doesn't** either.
 	
NEITHER + AUX + S
(d) Ann doesn't work, *and* **neither** **does Joe**.
	An auxiliary verb + **either** or **neither** are used with negative statements.
	
	Examples (c) and (d) have the same meaning.
	Word order:
	    subject + *auxiliary* + **either**
	    neither + *auxiliary* + *subject*
	
	NOTE: An affirmative auxiliary is used with *neither*.

(e) — I'm hungry.
    — *I am too. / So am I.*
 	
(f) — I don't eat meat.
    — *I don't either. / Neither do I.*
	And is not usually used when there are two speakers.

(g) — I'm hungry.
    — *Me too.* (*informal*)
 	
(h) — I don't eat meat.
    — *Me* (*n*)*either.* (*informal*)
	Me too, me either, and **me neither** are often used in informal spoken English.

□ **Exercise 17. Looking at grammar.** (Chart 8-5)
Complete the sentences with the given words. Pay special attention to word order.

Omar   James   Marco   Ivan

1. a. too   Marco has a mustache, and __James does too_____.

   b. so   Marco has a mustache, and _____.

2. a. either   Omar doesn't have a mustache, and _____.

   b. neither   Omar doesn't have a mustache, and _____.

3. a. too   Marco is wearing a hat, and _____.

   b. so   Marco is wearing a hat, and _____.

4. a. either   Ivan isn't wearing a hat, and _____.

   b. neither   Ivan isn't wearing a hat, and _____.

□ **Exercise 18. Looking at grammar.** (Chart 8-5)
Part I. Complete each sentence with the correct affirmative auxiliary verb.

1. Andy walks to work, and his roommate __*does*__ too.

2. Andy walks to work, and his roommates _____ too.

3. Andy is walking to work, and his roommate _____ too.

4. Andy is walking to work, and his roommates _____ too.

5. Andy walked to work last week, and his roommate(s) _____ too.

6. Andy has walked to work recently, and so _____ his roommate.

7. Andy has walked to work recently, and so _____ his roommates.

8. Andy is going to walk to work tomorrow, and so _____ his roommate.

9. Andy is going to walk to work tomorrow, and so _____ his roommates.

10. Andy will walk to work tomorrow, and so _____ his roommate(s).

Part II. Complete each sentence with the correct negative auxiliary verb.

1. Karen doesn't watch TV, and her sister ___*doesn't*___ either.

2. Karen doesn't watch TV, and her sisters _____ either.

3. Karen isn't watching TV, and her sister _____ either.

4. Karen isn't watching TV, and her sisters _____ either

5. Karen didn't watch TV last night, and her sister(s) _____ either.

6. Karen hasn't watched TV recently, and neither _____ her sister.

7. Karen hasn't watched TV recently, and neither _____ her sisters.

8. Karen isn't going to watch TV tomorrow, neither _____ her sister.

9. Karen isn't going to watch TV tomorrow, and neither _____ her sisters.

10. Karen won't watch TV tomorrow, and neither _____ her sister(s).

❑ **Exercise 19. Let's talk and write.** (Chart 8-5)
Work in small groups. Complete the sentences with *too, so, either,* or *neither.* Make true statements. You may need to research your answers.

1. Haiti is a small country, and ___*Cuba is too*_____.

2. Japan produces rice, and _____.

3. Turkey has had many strong earthquakes, and _____.

4. Iceland doesn't grow coffee, and _____.

5. Most Canadian children will learn more than one language, and _____

   _____.

6. Norway joined the United Nations in 1945, and _____.

7. Argentina doesn't lie on the equator, and _____.

8. Somalia lies on the Indian Ocean, and _____.

9. Monaco has never* hosted the Olympic Games, and _____.

10. South Korea had a Nobel Prize winner in 2000, and _____.

*****Never** makes a sentence negative: *The teacher is **never** late, and **neither** am I.* OR *I'm **not either**.*

❑ **Exercise 20. Let's talk: pairwork.** (Chart 8-5)
Work with a partner. Speaker A says the given sentence. Speaker B agrees with Speaker A's statement by using *so* or **neither**.

Example: I'm confused.
SPEAKER A (*book open*): I'm confused.
SPEAKER B (*book closed*): So am I.

1. I studied last night.
2. I study grammar every day.
3. I'd like a cup of coffee.
4. I'm not hungry.
5. I've never seen a vampire.
6. Running is an aerobic activity.
7. Snakes don't have legs.
8. Coffee contains caffeine.

Change roles.
9. I overslept this morning.
10. I don't like mushrooms.
11. Swimming is an Olympic sport.
12. Denmark doesn't have any volcanoes.
13. I've never touched a crocodile.
14. Chickens lay eggs.
15. Elephants can swim.
16. I'd rather go to (*name of a place*) than (*name of a place*).

❑ **Exercise 21. Let's listen and talk.** (Chart 8-5)
There are responses you can use if you don't agree with someone else's statement.

CD 2
Track 20
Part I. Listen to the examples. As you listen, pay special attention to the sentence stress in items 4–6 when Speaker B is disagreeing.

To get more information:
1. A: I'm going to drop this class.
   B: **You are? Why? What's the matter?**

2. A: My laptop doesn't have enough memory for this application.
   B: **Really? Are you sure?**

3. A: I can read Braille.
   B: **You can? How did you learn to do that?**

To disagree:
4. A: I love this weather.
   B: **I don't.**

5. A: I didn't like the movie.
   B: **I did!**

6. A: I'm excited about graduation.
   B: **I'm not.**

Part II. Work with a partner. Partner A will make a statement, and Partner B will ask for more information. Take turns saying the sentences.

1. I'm feeling tired.
2. I don't like grammar.
3. I've seen a ghost.
4. I didn't eat breakfast this morning.
5. I haven't slept well all week.
6. I'm going to leave class early.

Part III. Now take turns disagreeing with the given statements.

7. I believe in ghosts.
8. I didn't study hard for the last test.
9. I'm going to exercise for an hour today.
10. I like strawberries.
11. I haven't worked very hard this week.
12. I don't enjoy birthdays.

❑ **Exercise 22. Let's talk.** (Charts 8-4 and 8-5)
Make true statements about your classmates using *and* and *but*. You may need to interview them to get more information. Use the appropriate auxiliary verbs.

1. ___Kunio___ lives in an apartment, and ___Boris does too___ .

2. ___Ellen___ is wearing jeans, but ___Ricardo isn't___ .

3. _____ is absent today, but _____ .

4. _____ didn't live here last year, and _____ either.

5. _____ can cook, and _____ too.

6. _____ has a baseball cap, and _____ too.

7. _____ doesn't have a motorcycle, and _____ either.

8. _____ doesn't have a pet, but _____ .

9. _____ will get up early tomorrow, but _____ .

10. _____ has studied English for more than a year, and _____ too.

❑ **Exercise 23. Warm-up.** (Chart 8-6)
Circle all the logical completions.

Because Roger felt tired, _____.

a. he took a nap.   c. he went to bed early.
b. he didn't take a nap.   d. he didn't go to bed early.

8-6 Connecting Ideas with *Because*

(a) He drank water *because* he was thirsty.	*Because* expresses a cause; it gives a reason. Why did he drink water? *Reason:* He was thirsty.
(b) MAIN CLAUSE: *He drank water.*	A main clause is a complete sentence: ***He drank water*** = a complete sentence
(c) ADVERB CLAUSE: *because he was thirsty*	An adverb clause is NOT a complete sentence: ***because he was thirsty*** = NOT a complete sentence ***Because*** introduces an adverb clause: ***because*** + *subject* + *verb* = *an adverb clause*
(d) MAIN CLAUSE ADVERB CLAUSE He drank water ***because*** he was thirsty. (no comma) (e) ADVERB CLAUSE MAIN CLAUSE ***Because*** he was thirsty, he drank water. (comma)	An adverb clause is connected to a main clause, as in (d) and (e). In (d): *main clause* + *no comma* + *adverb clause* In (e): *adverb clause* + *comma* + *main clause* Examples (d) and (e) have exactly the same meaning.
(f) *INCORRECT IN WRITING:* He drank water. *Because he was thirsty.*	Example (f) is incorrect in written English: ***Because he was thirsty*** cannot stand alone as a sentence that starts with a capital letter and ends with a period. It has to be connected to a main clause, as in (d) and (e).
(g) CORRECT IN SPEAKING: — Why did he drink some water? — Because he was thirsty.	In spoken English, an adverb clause can be used as the short answer to a question, as in (g).

□ **Exercise 24. Looking at grammar.** (Chart 8-6)
Combine each pair of sentences in two different orders. Use *because*. Punctuate carefully.

1. We didn't have class. \ The teacher was absent.
   - → *We didn't have class because the teacher was absent.*
   - → *Because the teacher was absent, we didn't have class.*

2. The children were hungry. \ There was no food in the house.

3. The bridge is closed. \ We can't get across the river.

4. My car didn't start. \ The battery was dead.

5. Talya and Patti laughed hard. \ The joke was very funny.

□ **Exercise 25. Looking at grammar.** (Chart 8-6)
Add periods, commas, and capital letters as necessary.

1. Jimmy is very young. ꞵecause he is afraid of the dark, he likes to have a light on in his bedroom at night.

2. Mr. El-Sayed had a bad cold because he was not feeling well he stayed home from the office.

3. Judy went to bed early because she was tired she likes to get at least eight hours of sleep a night.

4. Frank put his head in his hands he was angry and upset because he had lost a lot of work on his computer.

☐ **Exercise 26. Looking at grammar.** (Charts 8-3 and 8-6)
Make sentences with the same meaning as the given sentence. Use commas where appropriate.

Part I. Restate the sentences. Use *so.*

1. Wendy lost her job because she never showed up for work on time.

    → *Wendy never showed up for work on time,* so she lost her job.

2. I opened the window because the room was hot.

3. Because it was raining, I stayed indoors.

Part II. Restate the sentences. Use *because.*

4. Jason was hungry, so he ate.

    → *Because Jason was hungry,* he ate. OR *Jason ate because he was hungry.*

5. The water in the river is polluted, so we shouldn't go swimming there.

6. My alarm clock didn't go off,* so I was late for my job interview.

☐ **Exercise 27. Looking at grammar.** (Charts 8-1 → 8-6)
Add commas, periods, and capital letters where appropriate. Don't change any of the words or the order of the words.

1. Jim was hot. ~~h~~ He sat in the shade.

2. Jim was hot and tired so he sat in the shade.

3. Jim was hot tired and thirsty.

4. Because he was hot Jim sat in the shade.

5. Because they were hot and thirsty Jim and Susan sat in the shade and drank iced-tea.

6. Jim and Susan sat in the shade and drank iced-tea because they were hot and thirsty.

7. Jim sat in the shade drank iced-tea and fanned himself with his cap because he was hot tired and thirsty.

8. Because Jim was hot he stayed under the shade of the tree but Susan went back to work.

---

*go off = ring

Exercise 28. Listening. (Charts 8-1 → 8-6)

Listen to the passage. Then add commas, periods, and capital letters where appropriate.
Listen again as you check your answers.

CD 2
Track 21

Understanding the Scientific Term *Matter*

The word *matter* is a chemical term. M̶atter is anything that has weight this book your

finger water a rock air and the moon are all examples of matter heat and radio waves are not matter

because they do not have weight happiness dreams and fears have no weight and are not matter.

❑ **Exercise 29. Warm-up.** (Chart 8-7)
In which sentences is the result (in green) the opposite of what you expect?

1. Even though I didn't eat dinner last night, I wasn't hungry this morning.
2. Because I didn't eat dinner last night, I was hungry this morning.
3. Although I didn't eat dinner last night, I wasn't hungry this morning.

8-7 Connecting Ideas with *Even Though/Although*

(a) *Even though* I was hungry, I did not eat. I did not eat *even though* I was hungry.	*Even though* and *although* introduce an adverb clause.
(b) *Although* I was hungry, I did not eat. I did not eat *although* I was hungry.	Examples (a) and (b) have the same meaning: *I was hungry, but I did not eat.*
COMPARE: (c) *Because* I was hungry, *I ate.* (d) *Even though* I was hungry, *I did not eat.*	*Because* expresses an expected result, as in (c). *Even though/although* expresses an unexpected or opposite result, as in (d).

❑ **Exercise 30. Looking at grammar.** (Chart 8-7)
Complete the sentences with the given words.

1. *is, isn't*

    a. Because Dan is sick, he _____ going to work.

    b. Although Dan is sick, he _____ going to work.

    c. Even though Dan is sick, he _____ going to work.

2. *went, didn't go*

    a. Even though it was late, we _____ home.

    b. Although it was late, we _____ home.

    c. Because it was late, we _____ home.

Exercise 31. Looking at grammar. (Chart 8-7)
Complete the sentences with *even though* or *because*.

1. ___Even though_____ the weather is cold, Rick isn't wearing a coat.

2. ___Because_____ the weather is cold, Ben is wearing a coat.

3. _____ Jane was sad, she smiled.

4. _____ Jane was sad, she cried.

5. _____ it was cold outside, we went swimming in the lake.

6. _____ our friends live on an island, it isn't easy to get there by car.

7. People ask Kelly to sing at weddings _____ she has a good voice.

8. _____ I'm training for the Olympics, I biked up the mountain

   _____ it was starting to snow.

9. George sings loudly _____ he can't carry a tune.

□ **Exercise 32. Looking at grammar.** (Charts 8-6 and 8-7)
Choose the best completion for each sentence.

1. Even though the test was fairly easy, most of the class _____ .
   a. failed
   b. passed
   c. did pretty well

2. Jack hadn't heard or read about the bank robbery even though _____ .
   a. he was the robber
   b. it was on the front page of every newspaper
   c. he was out of town when it occurred

3. Although _____ , she finished the race in first place.
   a. Miki was full of energy and strength
   b. Miki was leading all the way
   c. Miki was far behind in the beginning

4. We can see the light from an airplane at night before we can hear the plane because _____ .
    a. light travels faster than sound
    b. airplanes travel at high speeds
    c. our eyes work better than our ears at night

5. My partner and I worked all day and late into the evening. Even though _____ , we stopped at our favorite restaurant before we went home.
    a. we were very hungry
    b. we had finished our report
    c. we were very tired

6. In the mountains, melting snow in the spring runs downhill into rivers. The water carries soil and rocks. In the spring, mountain rivers become muddy rather than clear because _____ .
    a. mountain tops are covered with snow
    b. the water from melting snow brings soil and rocks to the river
    c. ice is frozen water

□ **Exercise 33. Listening.** (Charts 8-6 and 8-7)

Choose the best completion for each sentence.

CD 2
Track 22

Example: You will hear: Because there was a sale at the mall, . . .
You will choose: a. it wasn't busy.
                  (b.) there were a lot of shoppers.
                  c. prices were very high.

1. a. they were under some mail.
   b. my roommate helped me look for them.
   c. I never found them.

2. a. the rain had stopped.
   b. a storm was coming.
   c. the weather was nice.

3. a. he was sick.
   b. he had graduated already.
   c. he was happy for me.

4. a. I mailed it.
   b. I decided not to mail it.
   c. I sent it to a friend.

5. a. the coaches celebrated afterwards.
   b. the fans cheered loudly.
   c. the players didn't seem very excited.

Exercise 34. Let's talk. (Charts 8-6 and 8-7)
Answer the questions in complete sentences, using either *because* or *even though*. Work in pairs, in small groups, or as a class.

Example: Last night you were tired. Did you go to bed early?
→ *Yes, I went to bed early because I was tired.* OR
→ *Yes, because I was tired, I went to bed before nine.* OR
→ *No, I didn't go to bed early even though I was really sleepy.* OR
→ *No, even though I was really tired, I didn't go to bed until after midnight.*

1. Last night you were tired. Did you stay up late?
2. Vegetables are good for you. Do you eat a lot of them?
3. Space exploration is exciting. Would you like to be an astronaut?
4. What are the winters like here? Do you like living here in the winter?
5. (*A recent movie*) has had good reviews. Do you want to see it?
6. Are you a good artist? Will you draw a picture of me on the board?
7. Where does your family live? Are you going to visit them over the next holiday?

☐ **Exercise 35. Reading and grammar.** (Chapter 8)
Part I. Read the passage.

The Importance of Water

What is the most common substance on earth? It isn't wood, iron, or sand. The most common substance on earth is water. Every living thing contains water. For example, a person's body is about 67 percent water, a bird's is about 75 percent water, and most fruit contains about 90 percent water.

In addition, 70 percent of the earth's surface is water. Besides being in lakes, rivers, and oceans, water is in the ground and in the air. However, most of the water in the world is saltwater. Only 3 percent of the earth's water is fresh, and just one percent of that is available for human use. The rest is saltwater, and people can't drink it or grow food with it.

Water is essential to life, but human beings often poison it with chemicals from industry and farming. When people pollute water, the quality of all life — plant life, animal life, and human life — suffers. Life cannot exist without fresh water, so it is essential that people take care of this important natural resource.

Part II. Complete the sentences with *because/although/even though/so*.

1. _____ 70 percent of the earth's surface is water and water is in every living thing, it is the most common substance on earth.

2. _____ 70 percent of the earth's surface is water, only 3 percent is fresh.

3. _____ water is everywhere, not much is available for human use.

4. Chemicals pollute water, _____ it is important to keep them out of the water supply.

5. _____ water is essential to human life, people need to take care of it.

6. Water is essential to human life, _____ people need to take care of it.

□ **Exercise 36. Check your knowledge.** (Chapter 8)
Edit the sentences. Correct the errors in sentence structure. Pay special attention to punctuation.

1. Even though I was sick**,** ~~but~~ I went to work.

2. Gold silver and copper. They are metals.

3. The children crowded around the teacher. Because he was doing a magic trick.

4. I had a cup of coffee, and so does my friend.

5. My roommate didn't go. Neither I went either.

6. Even I was exhausted, I didn't stop working until after midnight.

7. Although I like chocolate, but I can't eat it because I'm allergic to it.

8. I like to eat raw eggs for breakfast and everybody else in my family too.

9. A hardware store sells tools and nails and plumbing supplies and paint.

10. Most insects have wings, spiders do not.

□ **Exercise 37. Let's write.** (Chapter 8)
Write about an animal that interests you. Follow these steps:

1. Choose an animal you want to know more about.

   Hint: If you are doing your research on the Internet, type in "interesting facts about _____ ."

2. Take notes on the information you find. For example, here is some information about giraffes from an Internet site.

   Sample notes:

   Giraffes
   → have long necks (6 feet or 1.8 meters)
   → can reach tops of trees
   → need very little sleep (20 minutes to two hours out of 24 hours)
   → eat about 140 pounds of food a day
   → can go for weeks without drinking water
   → get a lot of water from the plants they eat
   → can grab and hold onto objects with their tongues
   → don't have vocal cords
   → can communicate with one another
     (but humans can't hear them)

3. Write sentences based on your facts. Combine some of the ideas using **and, but, or, so, because, although, even though**.

   Sample sentences:

   Giraffes
   → Giraffes have long necks, so they can reach the tops of trees.
   → Although they eat about 140 pounds of food a day, they can go for weeks without drinking water.
   → Even though giraffes don't have vocal cords, they can communicate with one another.
   → Giraffes can communicate, but people can't hear their communication.

4. Put your sentences into a paragraph.

   Sample paragraph:

   ## Interesting Facts About Giraffes

   Giraffes are interesting animals. They have long necks, so they can reach the tops of trees. They eat flowers, fruit, climbing plants, and the twigs and leaves from trees. Although they eat about 140 pounds of food a day, they can go for weeks without drinking water. They get a lot of water from the plants they eat too. They have very long tongues and these tongues are useful. Because they are so long, they can grab objects with them. Even though giraffes don't have vocal cords, they can communicate, but people can't hear their communication.

Chapter 9
Comparisons

❑ **Exercise 1. Warm-up.** (Chart 9-1)
Compare the lengths of the lines.

1. Line D is as long as Line _____ .
2. Line A isn't as long as Line _____ .
3. Line E is almost as long as Line _____ .

Line A _____

Line B _____

Line C _____

Line D _____

Line E _____

9-1 Making Comparisons with *As . . . As*	
(a) Tina is 21 years old. Sam is also 21. Tina is *as old as* Sam (is). (b) Mike came *as quickly as* he could.	*As . . . as* is used to say that the two parts of a comparison are equal or the same in some way. In (a): *as* + *adjective* + *as* In (b): *as* + *adverb* + *as*
(c) Ted is 20. Tina is 21. Ted is *not as old as* Tina. (d) Ted is *not quite as old as* Tina. (e) Amy is 5. She is *not nearly as old as* Tina.	Negative form: *not as . . . as.* * *Quite* and *nearly* are often used with the negative. In (d): *not quite as . . . as* = a small difference. In (e): *not nearly as . . . as* = a big difference.
(f) Sam is *just as old as* Tina. (g) Ted is *nearly/almost as old as* Tina.	Common modifiers of *as . . . as* are *just* (meaning "exactly") and *nearly/almost.*

Tina	Sam	Ted	Amy
21	21	20	5

*Also possible: *not so . . . as: Ted is **not so** old as Tina.*

□ **Exercise 2. Looking at grammar.** (Chart 9-1)

Complete the sentences, with *just as, almost as/not quite as,* or *not nearly as.*

Part I. Compare the fullness of the glasses.

1. Glass 4 is ___*almost as / not quite as*___ full as Glass 2.

2. Glass 3 is _____ full as Glass 2.

3. Glass 1 is _____ full as Glass 2.

Part II. Compare the size of the boxes.

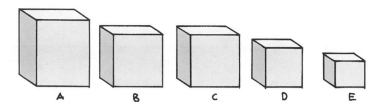

4. Box B is _____ big as Box A.

5. Box E is _____ big as Box A.

6. Box C is _____ big as Box B.

7. Box E is _____ big as Box D.

□ **Exercise 3. Looking at grammar.** (Chart 9-1)

Complete the sentences with *as . . . as* and words from the list. Give your own opinion. Use negative verbs where appropriate.

a housefly / an ant	good health / money
a lake / an ocean	honey / sugar
a lemon / a watermelon	monkeys /people
a lion / a tiger	reading a book / listening to music
a shower / a bath	the sun / the moon

1. <u>An ant isn't as</u>   big as <u>a housefly</u>   .

2. <u>A lion is as</u>   dangerous and wild as <u>a tiger</u>   .

3. _____ large as _____ .

4. _____ sweet as _____ .

5. _____ important as _____ .

6. _____ quiet as _____ .

7. _____ hot as _____ .

8. _____ good at climbing trees as _____ .

9. _____ relaxing as _____ .

CD 2
Track 23

☐ **Exercise 4. Listening.** (Chart 9-1)

Complete the sentences with the words you hear.

Sylvia   Brigita   Lara   Tanya
30   28   50   50

Example: You will hear: Brigita isn't as old as Lara.

You will write: <u>isn't as old as</u>

1. Lara _____ Tanya.

2. Sylvia _____ Lara.

3. Sylvia and Brigita _____ Tanya.

4. Brigita _____ Sylvia.

5. Brigita _____ Sylvia.

□ **Exercise 5. Game.** (Chart 9-1)

As . . . as is used in many traditional phrases. These phrases are generally spoken rather than written. See how many of them you're familiar with by completing the sentences with the given words. Work in teams. The team with the most correct answers wins.

✓a bear	a cat	a hornet	a mule	an ox
a bird	a feather	a kite	a rock	the hills

ox

mule

1. When will dinner be ready? I'm **as** hungry **as** ___a bear___ .

2. Did Toshi really lift that heavy box all by himself? He must be **as** strong **as**

   _____ .

3. It was a lovely summer day. School was out, and there was nothing in particular that I had to do. I felt **as** free **as** _____ .

4. Marco won't change his mind. He's **as** stubborn **as** _____ .

5. How can anyone expect me to sleep in this bed? It's **as** hard **as** _____ .

6. Of course I've heard that joke before! It's **as** old **as** _____ .

7. Why are you walking back and forth? What's the matter? You're **as** nervous **as**

   _____ .

8. Thanks for offering to help, but I can carry the box alone. It looks heavy, but it isn't. It's **as** light **as** _____ .

9. When Erica received the good news, she felt **as** high **as** _____ .

10. A: Was he angry?

    B: You'd better believe it! He was **as** mad **as** _____ .

hornet

☐ **Exercise 6. Warm-up.** (Chart 9-2)
Compare the people.

David

Paolo

Matt

1. Paolo looks younger than _____.

2. Matt looks younger than _____.

3. _____ looks the youngest of all.

9-2 Comparative and Superlative

(a) "A" is *older than* "B." (b) "A" and "B" are *older than* "C" and "D." (c) Ed is *more generous than* his brother.	The comparative compares *this* to *that* or *these* to *those*. Form: *-er* or *more* (See Chart 9-3.) Notice: A comparative is followed by *than*.
(d) "A," "B," "C," and "D" are sisters. "A" is *the oldest* of all four sisters. (e) A woman in Turkey claims to be *the oldest person* in the world. (f) Ed is *the most generous person* in his family.	The superlative compares one part of a whole group to all the rest of the group. Form: *-est* or *most* (See Chart 9-3 for forms.) Notice: A superlative begins with *the*.

☐ **Exercise 7. Game.** (Chart 9-2)
Work in teams. Decide if the sentences are true (T) or false (F). The team with the most correct answers wins.

1. Canada is larger than France.   T   F

2. Russia and Canada are the largest countries in the world.   T   F

3. The South Pole is generally colder than the North Pole.   T   F

4. The Pacific Ocean is the coldest ocean in the world.   T   F

5. The Mediterranean Sea is the biggest sea of all.   T   F

6. In general, Libya is hotter than Mexico.   T   F

7. Africa is larger than Asia.   T   F

8. Argentina has the highest and lowest points in South America.   T   F

9. The nearest continent to Antarctica is Australia.   T   F

10. The longest country in the world is Chile.   T   F

□ **Exercise 8. Listening.** (Charts 9-1 and 9-2)

Listen to the statements. Do you agree or disagree? Circle *yes* or *no*. Before you begin, you may want to check your understanding of these words: *talkative, cooked, tasty, raw.*

CD 2
Track 24

1. yes   no

2. yes   no

3. yes   no

4. yes   no

5. yes   no

6. yes   no

7. yes   no

8. yes   no

□ **Exercise 9. Warm-up.** (Chart 9-3)

Compare the three handwriting samples.

A: *The meeting starts at eight!*

B: *The meeting starts at eight :*

C: *The meeting starts at eight!*

1. _C_ is neater than _A (or B)_.

2. ___ is messier than _____.

3. ___ is more readable than _____.

4. ___ is better than _____.

5. ___ is the best.

6. ___ is the worst.

7. ___ wrote more carefully than _____.

9-3 Comparative and Superlative Forms of Adjectives and Adverbs

		Comparative	Superlative	
ONE-SYLLABLE ADJECTIVES	old wise	older wiser	the oldest the wisest	For most one-syllable adjectives, **-er** and **-est** are added.
TWO-SYLLABLE ADJECTIVES	famous pleasant	more famous more pleasant	the most famous the most pleasant	For most two-syllable adjectives, **more** and **most** are used.
	clever gentle friendly	cleverer more clever gentler more gentle friendlier more friendly	the cleverest the most clever the gentlest the most gentle the friendliest the most friendly	Some two-syllable adjectives use either **-er/-est** or **more/most**: *able, angry, clever, common, cruel, friendly, gentle, handsome, narrow, pleasant, polite, quiet, simple, sour.*
	busy pretty	busier prettier	the busiest the prettiest	**-Er** and **-est** are used with two-syllable adjectives that end in **-y**. The **-y** is changed to **-i**.
ADJECTIVES WITH THREE OR MORE SYLLABLES	important fascinating	more important more fascinating	the most important the most fascinating	**More** and **most** are used with long adjectives.
IRREGULAR ADJECTIVES	good bad	better worse	the best the worst	**Good** and **bad** have irregular comparative and superlative forms.
-LY ADVERBS	carefully slowly	more carefully more slowly	the most carefully the most slowly	**More** and **most** are used with adverbs that end in **-ly**.*
ONE-SYLLABLE ADVERBS	fast hard	faster harder	the fastest the hardest	The **-er** and **-est** forms are used with one-syllable adverbs.
IRREGULAR ADVERBS	well badly far	better worse farther/further	the best the worst the farthest/furthest	Both **farther** and **further** are used to compare physical distances: *I walked farther than my friend did.* OR *I walked further than my friend did.* **Further** also means "additional": *I need further information.* NOTE: **Farther** cannot be used when the meaning is "additional."

*Exception: **early** is both an adjective and an adverb. Forms: *earlier, earliest.*

❑ **Exercise 10. Looking at grammar.** (Charts 9-2 and 9-3)
Write the comparative and superlative forms of the following adjectives and adverbs.

1. high   _higher, the highest_   8. dangerous   _____

2. good   _____   9. slowly   _____

3. lazy   _____   10. common   _____

4. hot*   _____   11. friendly   _____

5. neat*   _____   12. careful   _____

6. late*   _____   13. bad   _____

7. happy   _____   14. far   _____

❑ **Exercise 11. Looking at grammar.** (Charts 9-2 and 9-3)
Complete the sentences with the correct comparative form (***more/-er***) of the adjectives in
the list.

clean	dangerous	funny	✓sweet
confusing	dark	pretty	wet

1. Oranges are __sweeter__ than lemons.

2. I heard some polite laughter when I told my jokes, but everyone laughed loudly when Janet
   told hers. Her jokes are always much _____ than mine.

3. Many more people die in car accidents than in plane accidents. Statistics show that
   driving your own car is _____ than flying in an airplane.

4. Professor Sato speaks clearly, but I have trouble understanding Professor Larson's lectures.
   Her lectures are much _____ than Professor Sato's.

5. Is there a storm coming? The sky looks _____ than it did an hour ago.

6. That tablecloth has some stains on it. Take this one. It's _____.

7. We're having another beautiful sunrise. It looks like an orange fireball. The sky is even
   _____ than yesterday.

8. If a cat and a duck are out in the rain, the cat will get much _____ than
   the duck. The water will just roll off the duck's feathers, but it will soak into the cat's hair.

---

*Spelling notes:
  • When a one-syllable adjective ends in *one vowel* + *a consonant,* double the consonant and add ***-er/-est: sad, sadder,***
    saddest.
  • When an adjective ends in two *vowels* + *a consonant,* do NOT double the consonant: ***cool, cooler, coolest.***
  • When an adjective ends in *-e,* do NOT double the consonant: ***wide, wider, widest.***

❑ **Exercise 12. Listening.** (Chart 9-3)

Listen to the sentences and choose the words that you hear.

CD 2
Track 25 *Example:* You will hear: I am the shortest person in our family.

You will choose: short   shorter   ⬭shortest⬭

My family

1. young   younger   youngest

2. tall   taller   tallest

3. happy   happier   happiest

4. happy   happier   happiest

5. old   older   oldest

6. funny   funnier   funniest

7. hard   harder   hardest

8. hard   harder   hardest

❑ **Exercise 13. Looking at grammar.** (Chart 9-3)

Choose the correct completion(s) for each sentence.

1. Ron and his friend went jogging. Ron ran two miles, but his friend got tired after one
   mile. Ron ran _____ than his friend did.
   ⓐ farther   ⓑ further

2. If you have any _____ questions, don't hesitate to ask.
   a. farther   b. further

3. I gave my old computer to my younger sister because I had no _____ use for it.
   a. farther   b. further

4. Paris is _____ north than Tokyo.
   a. farther   b. further

5. I like my new apartment, but it is _____ away from school than my old apartment was.
   a. farther   b. further

6. Thank you for your help, but I'll be fine now. I don't want to cause you any _____ trouble.
   a. farther   b. further

7. Which is _____ from here: the subway or the train station?
   a. farther   b. further

□ **Exercise 14. Let's talk: pairwork.** (Charts 9-2 and 9-3)

Work with a partner. Make comparison sentences with *more/-er* and adjectives in the list. Share some of your answers with the class.

beautiful	enjoyable	light	soft
cheap	expensive	relaxing	stressful
deep	fast	shallow	thick
easy	heavy	short	thin

1. traveling by air \ traveling by train
   → *Traveling by air is faster than traveling by train.*
   → *Traveling by air is more stressful than traveling by train.*
      Etc.
2. a pool \ a lake
3. an elephant's neck \ a giraffe's neck
4. taking a trip \ staying home
5. iron \ wood
6. going to the doctor \ going to the dentist
7. gold \ silver
8. rubber \ wood
9. an emerald \ a diamond
10. a feather \ a blade of grass

□ **Exercise 15. Listening.** (Charts 9-1 → 9-3)

Listen to each sentence and choose the statement (a. or b.) that has a similar meaning.

CD 2
Track 26

Example: You will hear: I need help! Please come as soon as possible.
          You will choose: (a.) Please come quickly.
                            b. Please come when you have time.

1. a. Business is better this year.
   b. Business is worse this year.

2. a. Steven is a very friendly person.
   b. Steven is an unfriendly person.

3. a. The test was difficult for Sam.
   b. The test wasn't so difficult for Sam.

4. a. We can go farther.
   b. We can't go farther.

5. a. Jon made a very good decision.
   b. Jon made a very bad decision.

6. a. I'm going to drive faster.
   b. I'm not going to drive faster.

7. a. Your work was careful.
   b. Your work was not careful.

8. a. I am full.
   b. I would like more to eat.

9. a. My drive and my flight take
      the same amount of time.
   b. My drive takes more time.

❑ **Exercise 16. Warm-up.** (Chart 9-4)

Complete the sentences with the names of people you know. Make true statements.

1. I'm older than _____ is.

2. I live nearer to/farther from school than _____ does.

3. I got to class earlier/later than _____ did.

4. _____'s hair is longer/shorter than mine.

9-4 Completing a Comparative

(a) I'm older *than **my brother*** (*is*). (b) I'm older *than **he** is*. (c) I'm older *than **him**. (informal)*	In formal English, a subject pronoun (e.g., *he*) follows ***than***, as in (b). In everyday, informal spoken English, an object pronoun (e.g., *him*) often follows ***than***, as in (c).
(d) He works harder *than **I do***. (e) I arrived earlier *than **they did***.	Frequently an auxiliary verb follows the subject after ***than***. In (d): *than I do = than I work*
(f) *Ann's* hair is longer *than **Kate's***. (g) *Jack's* apartment is smaller *than **mine***.	A possessive noun (e.g., *Kate's*) or pronoun (e.g., *mine*) may follow ***than***.

❑ **Exercise 17. Looking at grammar.** (Chart 9-4)

Complete the sentences. Use pronouns in the completions.

1. My sister is only six. She's much younger than ___*I am* OR *(informally) me*___ .

2. Peggy is thirteen, and she feels sad. She thinks most of the other girls in school are far more popular than _____.

3. The kids can't lift that heavy box, but Mr. El-Sayid can. He's stronger than

   _____.

4. Jared isn't a very good speller. I can spell much better than _____.

5. I was on time. Carlo was late. I got there earlier than _____.

6. Mariko is out of shape. I can run a lot faster and farther than _____.

7. Isabel's classes are difficult, but my classes are easy. Isabel's classes are more difficult than _____. My classes are easier than _____.

8. Our neighbor's house is very large. Our house is much smaller than

   _____. Their house is larger than _____.

Exercise 18. Warm-up. (Chart 9-5)

Do you agree or disagree with these statements? Circle *yes* or *no*.

1. I enjoy very cold weather.   yes   no

2. It's cooler today than yesterday.   yes   no

3. It's much warmer today than yesterday.   yes   no

4. It's a little hotter today than yesterday.   yes   no

9-5 Modifying Comparatives

(a) Tom is *very* old. (b) Ann drives *very* carefully.	*Very* often modifies adjectives, as in (a), and adverbs, as in (b).
(c) INCORRECT: Tom is very older than I am. 　　INCORRECT: Ann drives very more carefully 　　　　　than she used to.	*Very* is NOT used to modify comparative adjectives and adverbs.
(d) Tom is *much / a lot / far* older than I am. (e) Ann drives *much / a lot / far* more carefully than she used to.	Instead, *much*, *a lot*, or *far* are used to modify comparative adjectives and adverbs, as in (d) and (e).
(f) Ben is *a little* (*bit*) older than I am OR (*informally*) me.	Another common modifier is *a little/a little bit*, as in (f).

□ **Exercise 19. Looking at grammar.** (Chart 9-5)

Add *very, much, a lot,* or *far* to the sentences.

1. It's hot today. → *It's **very** hot today.*
2. It's hotter today than yesterday. → *It's **much/a lot/far** hotter today than yesterday.*
3. An airplane is fast.
4. Taking an airplane is faster than driving.
5. Learning a second language is difficult for many people.
6. Learning a second language is more difficult than learning chemistry formulas.
7. You can live more inexpensively in student housing than in a rented apartment.
8. You can live inexpensively in student housing.

□ **Exercise 20. Warm-up.** (Chart 9-6)

Complete the sentences with your own words.

1. Compare the cost of two cars:

   (*A*/*An*) _____ is more expensive than (*a*/*an*) _____.

2. Compare the cost of two kinds of fruit:

   _____ are less expensive than _____.

3. Compare the cost of two kinds of shoes (boots, sandals, tennis shoes, flip-flops, etc.):

   _____ are not as expensive as _____ .

4. Compare the cost of two kinds of heat: (gas, electric, solar, wood, coal, etc.):

_____ heat is not as cheap as _____ heat.

9-6 Comparisons with *Less ... Than* and *Not As ... As*

MORE THAN ONE SYLLABLE: (a) A pen is *less expensive than* a book. (b) A pen is *not as expensive as* a book.	The opposite of *-er/more* is expressed by *less* or *not as ... as.* Examples (a) and (b) have the same meaning.
	Less and *not as ... as* are used with adjectives and adverbs of **more than one syllable**.
ONE SYLLABLE: (c) A pen is *not as large as* a book. INCORRECT: *A pen is less large than a book.*	Only *not as ... as* (NOT *less*) is used with **one-syllable adjectives or adverbs**, as in (c).

❑ **Exercise 21. Looking at grammar.** (Chart 9-6)
Circle the correct completion(s) for each sentence.

1. My nephew is _____ old _____ my niece.
   a. less ... than   b. not as ... as

2. My nephew is _____ hard-working _____ my niece.
   a. less ... than   b. not as ... as

3. A bee is _____ big _____ a bird.
   a. less ... than   b. not as ... as

4. My brother is _____ interested in computers _____ I am.
   a. less ... than   b. not as ... as

5. Some students are _____ serious about their schoolwork _____ others.
   a. less ... than   b. not as ... as

6. I am _____ good at repairing things _____ Diane is.
   a. less ... than   b. not as ... as

❑ **Exercise 22. Game.** (Charts 9-1 → 9-6)
Work in teams. Compare the given words using (*not*) *as ... as, less,* and *more/-er.* How many comparison sentences can you think of? The team with the most correct sentences wins.

Example: trees and flowers (*big, colorful, useful, etc.*)
→ *Trees are bigger than flowers.*
→ *Flowers are usually more colorful than trees.*
→ *Flowers are less useful than trees.*
→ *Flowers aren't as tall as trees.*

1. the sun and the moon
2. teenagers and adults
3. two restaurants in this area
4. two famous people in the world

Exercise 23. Listening. (Charts 9-1 → 9-6)
Listen to each sentence and the statements that follow it. Choose "T" for true or "F" for false.

CD 2
Track 27

Example: France \ Brazil

You will hear: a. France isn't as large as Brazil.
You will choose: (T)   F

You will hear: b. France is bigger than Brazil.
You will choose: T   (F)

1. a sidewalk \ a road
   a. T   F
   b. T   F

2. a hill \ a mountain
   a. T   F
   b. T   F

3. a mountain path \ a mountain peak
   a. T   F
   b. T   F

4. toes \ fingers
   a. T   F
   b. T   F
   c. T   F

5. basic math \ algebra
   a. T   F
   b. T   F
   c. T   F
   d. T   F

□ **Exercise 24. Warm-up: trivia.** (Chart 9-7)
Compare Manila, Seattle, and Singapore. Which two cities have more rain in December?*

_____ and _____ have more rain

than _____ in December.

9-7 Using *More* with Nouns	
(a) Would you like some *more coffee*? (b) Not everyone is here. I expect *more people* to come later.	In (a): *Coffee* is a noun. When *more* is used with nouns, it often has the meaning of "additional." It is not necessary to use *than*.
(c) There are *more people* in China *than* there are in the United States.	*More* is also used with nouns to make complete comparisons by adding *than*.
(d) Do you have enough coffee, or would you like some *more*?	When the meaning is clear, the noun may be omitted and *more* can be used by itself.

*See *Trivia Answers*, p. 421.

□ **Exercise 25. Game: trivia.** (Chart 9-7)
Work in teams. Write true sentences using the given information. The team with the most correct sentences wins.*

1. more kinds of mammals: South Africa \ Kenya
   → *Kenya has more kinds of mammals than South Africa.*
2. more volcanoes: Indonesia \ Japan
3. more moons: Saturn \ Venus
4. more people: Saõ Paulo, Brazil \ New York City
5. more islands: Greece \ Finland
6. more mountains: Switzerland \ Nepal
7. more sugar (per 100 grams): an apple \ a banana
8. more fat (per 100 grams): the dark meat of a chicken \ the white meat of a chicken

□ **Exercise 26. Looking at grammar.** (Charts 9-2, 9-3, and 9-7)
First, underline the words in the list that are nouns. Second, use *-er/more* and the words in the list to complete the sentences.

doctors	information	responsible
happily	mistakes	responsibly
happiness	responsibilities	✓traffic
happy		

1. A city has ___more traffic___ than a small town.

2. There is _____ available on the Internet today than there was one year ago.

3. I used to be sad, but now I'm a lot _____ about my life than I used to be.

4. Unhappy roommates can live together _____ if they learn to respect each other's differences.

5. Maggie's had a miserable year. I hope she finds _____ in the future.

6. I made _____ on the last test than I did on the first one, so I got a worse grade.

7. My daughter Layla is trustworthy and mature. She behaves much _____ than my nephew Jakob.

8. A twelve-year-old has _____ at home and in school than an eight-year-old.

9. My son is _____ about doing his homework than his older sister is.

10. Health care in rural areas is poor. We need _____ to treat people in rural areas.

*See *Trivia Answers*, p. 421.

Exercise 27. Warm-up. (Chart 9-8)

Do you agree or disagree with these statements? Circle *yes* or *no*.

1. The grammar in this book is getting harder and harder.   yes   no

2. The assignments in this class are getting longer and longer.   yes   no

3. My English is getting better and better.   yes   no

9-8 Repeating a Comparative

(a) Because he was afraid, he walked *faster and faster*. (b) Life in the modern world is getting *more and more complicated*.	Repeating a comparative gives the idea that something becomes progressively greater, i.e., it increases in intensity, quality, or quantity.

☐ **Exercise 28. Looking at grammar.** (Chart 9-8)

Complete the sentences by repeating a comparative. Use the words in the list.

big	✓fast	hard	loud	warm
discouraged	good	long	tired	wet

1. When I get excited, my heart beats _____faster and faster_____.

2. When you blow up a balloon, it gets _____.

3. Brian's health is improving. It's getting _____
   every day.

4. As the ambulance came closer to us, the siren became _____.

5. The line of people waiting to get into the theater got _____
   _____ until it went around the building.

6. Thank goodness winter is over. The weather is getting _____
   _____ with each passing day.

7. I've been looking for a job for a month and still haven't been able to find one. I'm getting

   _____.

8. The rain started as soon as I left my office. As I walked to the bus stop, it rained

   _____, and I got _____.

9. I started to row the boat across the lake, but my arms got _____
   _____, so I turned back.

Exercise 29. Warm-up. (Chart 9-9)

Do you agree or disagree with the following idea? Why?

If you pay more money for something, you will get better quality. In other words, the more expensive something is, the better the quality will be.

9-9 Using Double Comparatives

(a) *The harder* you study, *the more* you will learn.	A double comparative has two parts; both parts begin with *the*, as in the examples. The second part of the comparison is the **result** of the first part.
(b) *The more* she studied, *the more* she learned.	
(c) *The warmer* the weather (is), *the better* I like it.	In (a): If you study harder, the result will be that you will learn more.
(d) — Should we ask Jenny and Jim to the party too? — Why not? *The more, the merrier.*	*The more, the merrier* and *the sooner, the better* are two common expressions.
	In (d): It is good to have more people at the party.
(e) — When should we leave? — *The sooner, the better.*	In (e): It is good if we leave as soon as we can.

□ **Exercise 30. Looking at grammar.** (Chart 9-9)

Part I. Complete the sentences with double comparatives (*the more/-er . . . the more/-er*) and the words in *italics*.

1. If the fruit is *fresh,* it tastes *good.*

   _____The fresher_____ the fruit (is), ___the better_____ it tastes.

2. We got *close* to the fire. We felt *warm.*

   _____ we got to the fire, _____ we felt.

3. If a knife is *sharp,* it is *easy* to cut something with.

   _____ a knife (is), _____ it is to cut something.

4. The party got *noisy* next door. I got *angry.*

   _____ it got, _____ I got.

5. If a flamingo eats a lot of *shrimp,* it becomes very *pink.*

   The _____ a flamingo eats,

   the _____ it gets.

   SHRIMP,
   ALL YOU
   CAN EAT

Part II. Combine each pair of sentences. Use double comparatives (*the more/-er . . . the more/-er*) and the words in *italics*.

6. She drove *fast*. \ I became *nervous*.

   Rosa offered to take me to the airport, and I was grateful. But we got a late start, so she began to drive faster. → *The faster she drove, the more nervous I became.*

7. He *thought* about his family. \ He became *homesick*.

   Pierre tried to concentrate on his studies, but he kept thinking about his family and home. →

8. The sky grew *dark*. \ We ran *fast* to reach the house.

   A storm was threatening. →

❑ **Exercise 31. Warm-up.** (Chart 9-10)
Complete the sentences with your own ideas.

1. _____ is the most expensive city I have ever visited.

2. _____ is one of the most expensive cities in the world.

3. _____ is one of the least expensive cities in the world.

9-10 Using Superlatives

(a) Tokyo is one of *the largest cities in the world*.	Typical completions when a superlative is used:
(b) David is *the most generous person I have ever known*.	In (a): *superlative* + *in* a place (*the world, this class, my family, the corporation*, etc.)
(c) I have three books. These two are quite good, but this one is the *best* (book) *of all*.	In (b): *superlative* + *adjective clause** In (c): *superlative* + *of all*
(d) I took four final exams. The final in accounting was *the least difficult* of all.	*The least* has the opposite meaning of *the most*.
(e) Ali is *one of* the best *students* in this class. (f) *One of* the best *students* in this class *is* Ali.	Notice the pattern with *one of*: *one of* + *plural noun* (+ *singular verb*)
(g) I've *never* taken a *harder* test. (h) I've *never* taken a *hard* test.	*Never* + comparative = superlative Example (g) means "It was the hardest test I've ever taken." Compare (g) and (h).

*See Chapter 12 for more information about adjective clauses.

❑ **Exercise 32. Looking at grammar.** (Chart 9-10)
Complete the sentences with superlatives of the words in *italics* and the appropriate preposition, *in* or *of*.

1. Kyle is *lazy*. He is ___the laziest___ student ___in___ the class.

2. Mike and Julie were *nervous*, but Amanda was ___*the most nervous of*___ all.

3. Costa Rica is *beautiful*. It is one of _____

   countries _____ the world.

4. Scott got a *bad* score on the test. It was one of _____ scores

   _____ the class.

5. Neptune is *far* from the sun. Is it _____ planet from the

   sun _____ our solar system?

6. There are a lot of *good* cooks in my family, but my mom is _____ cook

   _____ all.

7. My grandfather is very *old*. He is _____ person _____ the town

   where he lives.

8. That chair in the corner is *comfortable*. It is _____

   chair _____ the room.

9. Everyone who ran in the race was *exhausted*, but I was _____ all.

□ **Exercise 33. Looking at grammar.** (Chart 9-10)
Complete the sentences with the superlative form of the given phrases.

> big bird
> two great natural dangers
> ✓deep ocean
> high mountains on earth
>
> long river in South America
> popular forms of entertainment
> three common street names

1. The Pacific is ___*the deepest ocean*___ in the world.

2. _____ are in the Himalayan Range

   in Asia.

3. Most birds are small, but not the flightless North African ostrich. It is

   _____ in the world.

4. _____ to ships are fog and icebergs.

5. One of _____ throughout the world

   is movies.

6. _____ in the United States are Park,

   Washington, and Maple.

7. _____ is the Amazon.

□ **Exercise 34. Looking at grammar.** (Chart 9-10)
Complete the sentences with the superlative form of the words in *italics*.

1. I have had many *good experiences*. Of those, my vacation to Honduras was one of

_____ I have ever had.

2. Ayako has had many *nice times,* but her birthday party was one of _____

_____ she has ever had.

3. I've taken many *difficult courses,* but statistics is one of _____

_____ I've ever taken.

4. I've made some *bad mistakes* in my life, but lending money to my cousin was one of

_____ I've ever made.

5. We've seen many *beautiful buildings* in the world, but the Taj Mahal is one of _____

_____ I've ever seen.

6. The *final exam* I took was pretty *easy.* In fact, it was one of _____

_____ I've ever taken.

□ **Exercise 35. Let's talk: pairwork.** (Chart 9-10)
Work with a partner. Take turns asking and answering questions. Use superlatives in your
answers. Pay special attention to the use of plural nouns after *one of*.

Example:
SPEAKER A: You have known many interesting people. Who is one of them?
SPEAKER B: ***One of* the most interesting people** I've ever known *is* (_____). OR
(_____) *is one of* **the most interesting people** I've ever known.

1. There are many beautiful countries in the world. What is one of them?
2. There are many famous people in the world. Who is one of them?
3. You've probably seen many good movies. What is one of them?
4. You've probably done many interesting things in your life. What is one of them?
5. Think of some happy days in your life. What was one of them?
6. There are a lot of interesting animals in the world. What is one of them?
7. You have probably had many good experiences. What is one of them?
8. You probably know several funny people. Who is one of them?

□ **Exercise 36. Grammar and listening.** (Chart 9-10)
Part I. Circle the sentence (a. or b.) that is closest in meaning to the given sentence.

1. I've never been on a bumpier plane ride.
   a. The flight was bumpy.   b. The flight wasn't bumpy.

2. I've never tasted hot chili peppers.
   a. The peppers are hot.   b. I haven't eaten hot chili peppers.

3. The house has never looked cleaner.

    a. The house looks clean.   b. The house doesn't look clean.

4. We've never visited a more beautiful city.

    a. The city was beautiful.   b. The city wasn't beautiful.

Part II. Listen to the sentences. Circle the sentence (a. or b.) that is closest in meaning to the one you hear.

5. a. His jokes are funny.   b. His jokes aren't funny.

6. a. It tastes great.   b. It doesn't taste very good.

7. a. The mattress is hard.   b. I haven't slept on hard mattresses.

8. a. The movie was scary.   b. I haven't watched scary movies.

☐ Exercise 37. Let's talk: interview. (Chart 9-10)

Make questions with the given words and the superlative form, and then interview your classmates. Share some of their answers with the class.

1. what \ bad movie \ you have ever seen

    → *What is the worst movie you have ever seen?*

2. what \ interesting sport to watch \ on TV

3. what \ crowded city \ you have ever visited

4. where \ good restaurant to eat \ around here

5. what \ fun place to visit \ in this area

6. who \ kind person \ you know

7. what \ important thing \ in life

8. what \ serious problem \ in the world

9. who \ most interesting person \ in the news right now

☐ Exercise 38. Game. (Charts 9-1 → 9-10)

Work in teams. Compare each list of items using the words in *italics*. Write sentences using **as . . . as**, the comparative (**-er/more**), and the superlative (**-est/most**). The group with the most correct sentences wins.

Example: streets in this city: *wide / narrow / busy / dangerous*

    → *First Avenue is **wider** than Market Street.*

    → *Second Avenue is **nearly as wide as** First Avenue.*

    → *First Avenue is **narrower** than Interstate Highway 70.*

    → ***The busiest** street is Main Street.*

    → *Main Street is **busier** than Market Street.*

    → ***The most dangerous street** in the city is Olive Boulevard.*

1. a lemon, a grapefruit, and an orange: *sweet / sour / large / small*

2. a kitten, a cheetah, and a lion: *weak / powerful / wild / gentle / fast*

3. boxing, soccer, and golf: *dangerous / safe / exciting / boring*

4. the food at (*three places in this city where you have eaten*): *delicious / appetizing / inexpensive / good / bad*

Complete the sentences with any appropriate form of the words in parentheses. Add any other necessary words. In some cases, more than one completion may be possible.

1. Lead is a very heavy metal. It is (*heavy*) ___heavier than___ gold or silver. It is one of (*heavy*) ___the heaviest___ metals ___of___ all.

2. Mrs. Cook didn't ask the children to clean up the kitchen. It was (*easy*) _____ for her to do it herself _____ to nag them to do it.

3. A car has two (*wheels*) _____ a bicycle.

4. Crocodiles and alligators are different. The snout of a crocodile is (*long*) _____ and (*narrow*) _____ than an alligator's snout. An alligator has a (*wide*) _____ upper jaw than a crocodile.

5. Although both jobs are important, being a teacher requires (*education*) _____ _____ being a bus driver.

6. The Great Wall of China is (*long*) _____ structure that has ever been built.

7. Hannah Anderson is one of (*friendly*) _____ and (*delightful*) _____ people I've ever met.

8. One of (*famous*) _____ volcanoes _____ the world is Mount Etna in Sicily.

9. It's possible that the volcanic explosion of Krakatoa near Java in 1883 was (*loud*) _____ noise _____ recorded history. People heard it 2,760 miles/4,441 kilometers away.

10. (*hard*) _____ I tried, (*impossible*) _____
    the math problem seemed.

11. World Cup Soccer is (*big*) _____ sporting event _____ the world.
    It is viewed on TV by (*people*) _____ any other event in sports.

12. When the temperature stays below freezing for a long period of time, the Eiffel Tower
    becomes six inches or fifteen centimeters (*short*) _____.

13. Young people have (*high*) _____ rate of automobile accidents
    _____ all drivers.

14. You'd better buy the tickets for the show soon. (*long*) _____
    you wait, (*difficult*) _____ it will be for you to get
    good seats.

15. No animals can travel (*fast*) _____ birds. Birds are (*fast*)
    _____ animals of all.

16. (*great*) _____ variety of birds _____ a single area can be
    found in the rainforests of Southeast Asia and India.

☐ **Exercise 40. Warm-up.** (Chart 9-11)
Solve the math problems* and then complete the sentences.

PROBLEM A: $2 + 2 =$
PROBLEM B: $\sqrt{900} + 20 =$
PROBLEM C: $3 \times 127 =$
PROBLEM D: $2 + 3 =$
PROBLEM E: $127 \times 3 =$

1. Problem ____ and Problem ____ have the same answers.

2. Problem ____ and Problem ____ have similar answers

3. Problem ____ and Problem ____ have different answers.

4. The answer to Problem ____ is the same as the answer to Problem ____.

5. The answers to Problem ____ and Problem ____ are similar.

6. The answers to Problem ____ Problem ____ are different.

7. Problem ____ has the same answer as Problem ____.

8. Problem ____ is like Problem ____.

9. Problem ____ and Problem ____ are alike.

*See *Trivia Answers*, p. 421, for answers to the math problems.

9-11 Using *The Same, Similar, Different, Like, Alike*

(a) John and Mary have *the same books*. (b) John and Mary have *similar books*. (c) John and Mary have *different books*. (d) Their books are *the same*. (e) Their books are *similar*. (f) Their books are *different*.	*The same, similar*, and *different* are used as adjectives. Notice: *the* always precedes *same*.

(g) This book is *the same as* that one.
(h) This book is *similar to* that one.
(i) This book is *different from* that one.
	Notice: *the same* is followed by *as;*
	       similar is followed by *to;*
	       different is followed by *from*.*

(j) She is *the same age as* my mother. My shoes are *the same size as* yours.	A noun may come between *the same* and *as*, as in (j).

(k) My pen *is like* your pen.
(l) My pen *and* your pen *are alike*.
	Notice in (k) and (l):
	    noun + *be like* + *noun*
	    noun **and** *noun* + *be alike*

(m) She *looks like* her sister.
    It *looks like* rain.
    It *sounds like* thunder.
    This material *feels like* silk.
    That *smells like* gas.
    This chemical *tastes like* salt.
    Stop *acting like* a fool.
    He *seems like* a nice guy.
	In addition to following *be, like* also follows certain verbs, primarily those dealing with the senses.
	
	Notice the examples in (m).

(n) The twins *look alike*.
    We *think alike*.
    Most four-year-olds *act alike*.
    My sister and I *talk alike*.
    The little boys are *dressed alike*.
	Alike may follow a few verbs other than *be*.
	
	Notice the examples in (n).

*In informal speech, native speakers might use *than* instead of *from* after *different*. *From* is considered correct in formal English, unless the comparison is completed by a clause: *I have a different attitude now than I used to have.*

❑ **Exercise 41. Looking at grammar.** (Chart 9-11)
Complete the sentences with *as, to, from,* or *Ø.*

1. Geese are similar __to__ ducks. They are both large water birds.

2. But geese are not the same _____ ducks. Geese are usually larger and have longer necks.

3. Geese are different _____ ducks.

4. Geese are like _____ ducks in some ways, but geese and ducks are not exactly alike _____ .

5. An orange is similar _____ a peach. They are both round, sweet, and juicy.

6. However, an orange is not the same _____ a peach.

7. An orange is different _____ a peach.

8. An orange is like _____ a peach in some ways, but they are not exactly alike

_____.

☐ **Exercise 42. Listening.** (Charts 9-3 and 9-11)

CD 2
Track 29

Listen to each passage. Complete the sentences with the words you hear.

Gold vs. Silver

Gold is similar _____ silver. They are both valuable metals that people use for
                        1

jewelry, but they aren't _____ same. Gold is not _____ same color
                          2   3

_____ silver. Gold is also different _____ silver in cost: gold is
    4   5

_____ expensive _____ silver.
    6   7

Two Zebras

Look at the two zebras in the picture. Their names are Zee and Bee. Zee looks

_____ Bee. Is Zee exactly _____ same _____ Bee? The pattern of
    8   9   10

the stripes on each zebra in the world is unique. No two zebras are exactly _____.
                                                                              11

Even though Zee and Bee are similar _____ each other, they are different
                                      12

_____ each other in the exact pattern of their stripes.
    13

Exercise 43. Looking at grammar. (Chart 9-11)
Compare the figures. Complete the sentences with *the same (as)*, *similar (to)*, *different* *(from)*, *like*, or *alike*.

A   B

C   D

1. All of the figures are ___similar to___ each other.

2. Figure A is _____ Figure B.

3. Figure A and Figure B are _____.

4. A and C are _____.

5. A and C are _____ D.

6. C is _____ A.

7. B isn't _____ D.

□ **Exercise 44. Looking at grammar.** (Chart 9-11)
Complete the sentences with *the same (as)*, *similar (to)*, *different (from)*, *like*, or *alike*. In some cases, more than one completion may be possible.

1. Jennifer and Jack both come from Rapid City. In other words, they come from

   ___the same___ town.

2. This city is ___the same as / similar to / like___ my hometown. Both are quiet and conservative.

3. You and I don't agree. Your ideas are _____ mine.

4. Sergio never wears _____ clothes two days in a row.

5. A male mosquito is not _____ size _____ a female mosquito. The female is larger.

6. I'm used to stronger coffee. I think the coffee at this cafe tastes _____ dishwater!

7. *Meet* and *meat* are homonyms; in other words, they have _____ pronunciation.

8. *Flower* has _____ pronunciation _____ *flour.*

9. My twin sisters act _____, but they don't look _____.

10. Trying to get through school without studying is _____ trying to go swimming without getting wet.

❑ **Exercise 45. Reading.** (Chapter 9)
Part I. Read the passage and the statements that follow it. NOTE: *He* and *she* are used interchangeably.

Birth Order

In your family, are you the oldest, youngest, middle, or only child? Some psychologists believe your place in the family, or your birth order, has a strong influence on your personality. Let's look at some of the personality characteristics of each child.

The oldest child has all the parents' attention when she is born. As she grows up, she may want to be the center of attention. Because she is around adults, she might act more like an adult around other children and be somewhat controlling. As the oldest, she might have to take care of the younger children, so she may be more responsible. She may want to be the leader when she is in groups.

The middle child (or children) may feel a little lost. Middle children have to share their parents' attention. They may try to be different from the oldest child. If the oldest child is "good," the second child may be "bad." However, since they need to get along with both the older and younger sibling(s), they may be the peacekeepers of the family.

The youngest child is the "baby" of the family. Other family members may see him as weaker, smaller, or more helpless. If the parents know this is their last child, they may not want the child to grow up as quickly as the other children. As a way to get attention, the youngest child may be the funniest child in the family. He may also have more freedom and turn out to be more artistic and creative.

An only child (no brothers or sisters) often grows up in an adult world. Such children may use adult language and prefer adult company. Only children may be more intelligent and serious than other children their age. They might also be more self-centered because of all the attention they get, and they might have trouble sharing with others.

Of course, these are general statements. A lot depends on how the parents raise the child, how many years are between each child, and the culture the child grows up in. How about you? Do you see any similarities to your family?

Part II. Read the statements. Circle "T" for true and "F" for false according to the information in the passage.

1.	The two most similar children are the oldest and only child.	T	F
2.	The middle child often wants to be like the oldest child.	T	F
3.	The youngest child likes to control others.	T	F
4.	Only children may want to spend time with adults.	T	F
5.	All cultures share the same birth order characteristics.	T	F

□ **Exercise 46. Writing.** (Chapter 9)
Part I. The word list contains personality characteristics. Do you know all these words?

artistic	funny	rebellious
competitive	hard-working	relaxed
controlling	immature	secretive
cooperative	loud	sensitive
creative	mature	serious
flexible	outgoing	shy

Part II. Compare yourself to other members of your family. Write sentences using the structures below:

Structures:
1. not as . . . as
2. more . . . than
3. -er . . . than
4. the most . . .

Part III. Write a paragraph comparing your personality to that of another member of your family. Follow these steps:

1. Write an introductory sentence: *I am different from / similar to my . . .*
2. Choose at least four characteristics from the list. For each one, make some type of comparison.
3. Write a few details that explain each comparison.
4. Write one or two concluding sentences.

Sample paragraph:

My Father and I

  I am different from my father in several ways. He is more hard-working than I am. He is a construction worker and has to get up at 6:00 A.M. He often doesn't get home until late in the evening. I'm a student, and I don't work as hard. Another difference is that I am funnier than he is. I like to tell jokes and make people laugh. He is serious, but he laughs at my jokes. My father was an athlete when he was my age, and he is very competitive. I don't like playing competitive sports, but we watch them together on TV. My father and I are different, but we like to spend time with each other. Our differences make our time together interesting.

Exercise 47. Check your knowledge. (Chapter 9)
Edit the sentences. Correct the errors in comparison structures.

1. Did you notice? My shoes and your shoes are *the* ̷a̷ same.

2. Alaska is largest state in the United States.

3. A pillow is soft, more than a rock.

4. Who is most generous person in your family?

5. The harder you work, you will be more successful.

6. One of a biggest disappointment in my life was when my soccer team lost the championship.

7. My sister is very taller than me.

8. A firm mattress is so comfortable for many people than a soft mattress.

9. One of the most talkative student in the class is Frederick.

10. Professor Bennett's lectures were the confusing I have ever heard.

Chapter 10
The Passive

❑ **Exercise 1. Warm-up.** (Charts 10-1 and 10-2)
Choose the sentence in each item that describes the picture above it. More than one answer may be correct.

1. a. The worm is watching the bird.
   b. The bird is watching the worm.

2. a. The bird caught the worm.
   b. The worm was caught by the bird.

3. a. The bird ate the worm.
   b. The worm was eaten.

10-1 Active Sentences and Passive Sentences

Active (a) The mouse *ate* the cheese. **Passive** (b) The cheese *was eaten* by the mouse.	Examples (a) and (b) have the same meaning.

Active	**Passive**

Active
     s   o
 (c) `Bob`   mailed   `the package.`
 	
 Passive
     s   by + o
 (d) `The package` was mailed `by Bob.`
	In (c): The object in an active sentence becomes the subject in a passive sentence.
	
	 In (d): The subject in an active sentence is the object of *by* in a passive sentence.

10-2 Form of the Passive

	be	+	past participle		Form of all passive verbs:
(a) Corn	is		grown	by farmers.	**be** + *past participle*
(b) Sara	was		surprised	by the news.	**Be** can be in any of its forms: *am, is, are, was, were,*
(c) The report	will be		written	by Mary.	*has been, have been, will be, etc.*

	Active	Passive
SIMPLE PRESENT	Farmers *grow* corn. ⟶	Corn *is grown* by farmers.
SIMPLE PAST	The news *surprised* Sara. ⟶	Sara *was surprised* by the news.
PRESENT PROGRESSIVE	Diana *is copying* the letters. ⟶	The letters *are being copied* by Diana.
PAST PROGRESSIVE	Diana *was copying* the letters. ⟶	The letters *were being copied* by Diana.
PRESENT PERFECT	Jack *has mailed* the letter. ⟶	The letter *has been mailed* by Jack.
FUTURE	Mr. Lee *will plan* the meeting. ⟶	The meeting *will be planned* by Mr. Lee.
	Sue *is going to write* the report. ⟶	The report *is going to be written* by Sue.

□ **Exercise 2. Looking at grammar.** (Charts 10-1 and 10-2)
Change the active verbs to passive by adding the correct form of *be*. Include the subject of the passive sentence.

1. SIMPLE PRESENT
   a. The teacher *helps* **me**.   __I__   __am__   **helped** by the teacher.
   b. The teacher *helps* **Eva**.   __Eva__   __is__   **helped** by the teacher.
   c. The teacher *helps* **us**.   _____   _____   **helped** by the teacher.

2. SIMPLE PAST
   a. The teacher *helped* **him**.   _____   _____   **helped** by the teacher.
   b. The teacher *helped* **them**.   _____   _____   **helped** by the teacher.

3. PRESENT PROGRESSIVE
   a. The teacher *is helping* **us**.   _____   _____   **helped** by the teacher.
   b. The teacher *is helping* **her**.   _____   _____   **helped** by the teacher.

4. PAST PROGRESSIVE
   a. The teacher *was helping* **me**.   _____   _____   **helped** by the teacher.
   b. The teacher *was helping* **him**.   _____   _____   **helped** by the teacher.

5. PRESENT PERFECT
   a. The teacher *has helped* **Yoko**.   _____   _____   **helped** by the teacher.
   b. The teacher *has helped* **Joe**.   _____   _____   **helped** by the teacher.

6. FUTURE

    a. The teacher *will help* **me**.   _____ _____ **helped** by the teacher.

    b. The teacher *is going to help* **us**.   _____ _____ **helped** by the teacher.

CD 2
Track 30

☐ **Exercise 3. Listening.** (Charts 10-1 and 10-2)
Listen to the sentences and write the words and endings you hear. Listen to the sentences again as you check your answers.

An office building at night

1. The janitors *clean* the building at night.

    The building __*is*__ clean *ed* by the janitors at night.

2. Window washers *wash* the windows.

    The windows _____ wash ____ by window washers.

3. A window washer *is washing* a window right now.

    A window _____ wash ____ by a window washer right now.

4. The security guard *has checked* the offices.

    The offices _____ check ____ by the security guard.

5. The security guard *discovered* an open window.

    An open window _____ discover ____ by the security guard.

6. The security guard *found* an unlocked door.

    An unlocked door _____ found by the security guard.

7. The owner *will visit* the building tomorrow.

    The building _____ visit ____ by the owner tomorrow.

8. The owner *is going to announce* new parking fees.

    New parking fees _____ announce ____ by the owner.

Exercise 4. Looking at grammar. (Charts 10-1 and 10-2)
Check (✓) the sentences that are passive.

At the dentist

1. _____ The dental assistant cleaned your teeth.
2. _____ Your teeth were cleaned by the dental assistant.
3. _____ The dentist is checking your teeth.
4. _____ Your teeth are being checked by the dentist.
5. _____ You have a cavity.
6. _____ You are going to need a filling.
7. _____ The filling will be done by the dentist.
8. _____ You will need to schedule another appointment.

□ **Exercise 5. Looking at grammar.** (Charts 10-1 and 10-2)
Change the verbs from active to passive. Do not change the tenses.

		be	+	**past participle**	

1. Leo *mailed* the package.

   The package ___was___ _____mailed_____ by Leo.

2. That company *employs* many people.

   Many people _____ _____ by that company.

3. That company *has hired* Ellen.

   Ellen _____ _____ by that company.

4. The secretary *is going to fax* the letter.

   The letters _____ _____ by the secretary.

5. A college student *bought* my old car.

   My old car _____ _____ by a college student.

6. Mrs. Adams *will do* the work.

   The work _____ _____ by Mrs. Adams.

7. The doctor *was examining* the patient.

   The patient _____ _____ by the doctor.

❑ **Exercise 6. Looking at grammar.** (Charts 10-1 and 10-2)
Change the sentences from active to passive.

Active	Passive	
1. a. The news surprised Carlo.	_____Carlo was surprised_____	by the news.
b. Did the news surprise you?	_____Were you surprised_____	by the news?
2. a. The news surprises Erin.	_____	by the news.
b. Does the news surprise you?	_____	by the news?
3. a. The news will shock Greta.	_____	by the news.
b. Will the news shock Pat?	_____	by the news?
4. a. Liz is signing the birthday card.	_____	by Liz.
b. Is Ricardo signing it?	_____	by Ricardo?
5. a. Jill signed the card.	_____	by Jill.
b. Did Ryan sign it?	_____	by Ryan?
6. a. Sami was signing it.	_____	by Sami.
b. Was Vicki signing it?	_____	by Vicki?
7. a. Rob has signed it.	_____	by Rob.
b. Has Kazu signed it yet?	_____	by Kazu yet?
8. a. Luis is going to sign it.	_____	by Luis.
b. Is Carole going to sign it?	_____	by Carole?

❑ **Exercise 7. Looking at grammar.** (Charts 10-1 and 10-2)
Change these hotel questions from active to passive.

1. Has the maid cleaned our room yet?
   → *Has our room been cleaned by the maid yet?*
2. Does the hotel provide hair dryers?
3. Did housekeeping bring extra towels?
4. Has room service brought our meal?
5. Is the bellhop* bringing our luggage to our room?
6. Is maintenance going to fix the air-conditioning?
7. Will the front desk upgrade** our room?

---

*bellhop = a person who carries luggage for hotel guests

**upgrade = make better; in this case, provide a better room than the original one. *Upgrade* is a regular verb.

Check (✓) the sentences that have objects. <u>Underline</u> the objects.

1. ____ The tree fell over.
2. ____ The tree hit the truck.
3. ____ The tree fell on the truck.
4. ____ Fortunately, the driver didn't die.
5. ____ The tree didn't kill the driver.

10-3 Transitive and Intransitive Verbs

Transitive			A TRANSITIVE verb is a verb that is followed by an object. An object is a noun or a pronoun.
S	V	O	
(a) Bob	*mailed*	*the letter.*	
(b) Mr. Lee	*signed*	*the check.*	
(c) A cat	*killed*	*the bird.*	
Intransitive			An INTRANSITIVE verb is a verb that is NOT followed by an object.
S	V		
(d) Something	*happened.*		
(e) Kate	*came*	to our house.	
(f) The bird	*died.*		

Common Intransitive Verbs*				
agree	die	happen	rise	stand
appear	exist	laugh	seem	stay
arrive	fall	live	sit	talk
become	flow	occur	sleep	wait
come	go	rain	sneeze	walk

Transitive Verbs	Only transitive verbs can be used in the passive.
(g) ACTIVE: Bob *mailed* the letter.	
(h) PASSIVE: The letter *was mailed* by Bob.	
Intransitive Verbs	An intransitive verb is NOT used in the passive.
(i) ACTIVE: Something *happened.*	
(j) PASSIVE: (*not possible*)	
(k) INCORRECT: *Something was happened.*	

*To find out if a verb is transitive or intransitive, look in your dictionary. The usual abbreviations are v.t. (transitive) and v.i. (intransitive). Some verbs have both transitive and intransitive uses. For example:
  transitive: *Students study books.*
  intransitive: *Students study.*

☐ **Exercise 9. Looking at grammar.** (Chart 10-3)
Underline the verbs and identify them as transitive (v.t.) or intransitive (v.i.). If possible, change the sentences to the passive.

     v.i.
1. Omar <u>walked</u> to school yesterday. (*no change*)

     v.t.
2. Alexa <u>broke</u> the window. → *The window was broken by Alexa.*

3. The leaves fell to the ground.

4. I slept at my friend's house last night.

5. Many people felt an earthquake yesterday.

6. Dinosaurs existed millions of years ago.

7. I usually agree with my sister.

8. Many people die during a war.

9. Scientists will discover a cure for cancer someday.

10. Did the Italians invent spaghetti?

☐ **Exercise 10. Game: trivia.** (Charts 10-1 → 10-3)
Work in teams. Make true statements by matching the information in Column A with the information in Column B. Some sentences are active and some are passive. Add **was/were** as necessary. The team with the most answers wins.* A sentence is correct when both the facts and the grammar are correct.

Example: 1. Alexander Eiffel **designed** the Eiffel Tower.
    2. Anwar Sadat **was shot** in 1981.

Column A
1. Alexander Eiffel __h__
2. Anwar Sadat __c__
3. Princess Diana ____
4. Marie and Pierre Curie ____
5. Oil ____
6. Mahatma Gandhi and Martin Luther King Jr. ____
7. Michael Jackson ____
8. Leonardo da Vinci ____
9. John F. Kennedy ____
10. Nelson Mandela ____

Column B
a. killed in a car crash in 1997.
b. died in 2009.
✓c. shot in 1981.
d. painted the *Mona Lisa*.
e. elected president of the United States in 1960.
f. discovered in Saudi Arabia in 1938.
g. arrested** several times for peaceful protests.
✓h. designed the Eiffel Tower.
i. released from prison in 1990.
j. discovered radium.

*See *Trivia Answers*, p. 421.

**arrested = taken to jail

Exercise 11. Warm-up. (Chart 10-4)
Complete the sentences with information from the front of this book.

1. This book, *Fundamentals of English Grammar,* was published by _____.

2. It was written by _____ and _____.

3. The illustrations were drawn by _____ and _____.

10-4 Using the *by*-Phrase

(a) This sweater *was made* **by my aunt.**	The *by*-phrase is used in passive sentences when it is important to know who performs an action. In (a): **by my aunt** is important information.
(b) My sweater *was made* in Korea. (c) Spanish *is spoken* in Colombia. (d) That house *was built* in 1940. (e) Rice *is grown* in many countries.	Usually there is no *by*-phrase in a passive sentence. The passive is used when it is **not known or not important to know exactly who performs an action**. In (b): The exact person (or people) who made the sweater is not known and is not important to know, so there is no *by*-phrase in the passive sentence.

(f) **My aunt** is very skillful. **She** *made* this sweater.
 (g) A: I like your sweaters.
  B: Thanks. **This sweater** *was made by* my aunt.
  That sweater *was made by* my mother.
	Usually the active is used when the speaker knows who performed the action, as in (f), where the focus of attention is on **my aunt.**
	
	 In (g): Speaker B uses the passive WITH a *by*-phrase because he wants to focus attention on the subjects of the sentences. The focus of attention is on the two sweaters. The *by*-phrases add important information.

❑ **Exercise 12. Looking at grammar.** (Chart 10-4)
Change the sentences from active to passive. Include the *by*-phrase only as necessary.

1. Bob Smith built that house.
   → *That house was built by Bob Smith.*

2. Someone built this house in 1904.

3. People grow rice in India.

4. Do people speak Spanish in Peru?

5. Alexander Graham Bell invented the telephone.

6. When did someone invent the first computer?

7. People sell hammers at a hardware store.

8. Has anyone ever hypnotized you?

9. Someone published *The Origin of Species* in 1859.

10. Charles Darwin wrote *The Origin of Species*.

☐ **Exercise 13. Looking at grammar.** (Chart 10-4)
Underline the passive verbs in each pair of sentences and then answer the questions.

1. a. The mail <u>is</u> usually <u>delivered</u> to Hamid's apartment around ten o'clock.
   b. The mail carrier usually delivers the mail to Hamid's apartment around ten o'clock.

   QUESTIONS: Is it important to know who delivers the mail? → No.
   Which sentence do you think is more common? → Sentence a.

2. a. Construction workers built our school in the 1980s.
   b. Our school was built in the 1980s.

   QUESTIONS: Is it important to know who built the school?
   Which sentence do you think is more common?

3. a. That office building was designed in 1990.
   b. That office building was designed by an architect in 1990.
   c. That office building was designed by my husband in 1990.

   QUESTIONS: What additional information do the *by*-phrases provide?
   Which sentence has important information in the *by*-phrase?

4. a. *Thailand* means "land of the free."
   b. The country of Thailand has never been ruled by a foreign power.

   QUESTION: What happens to the meaning of the second sentence if there is no
   by-phrase?

☐ **Exercise 14. Looking at grammar.** (Charts 10-1 → 10-4)
Make sentences with the given words, either orally or in writing. Some sentences are active
and some are passive. Use the past tense. Do not change the order of the words.

A traffic stop

1. The police \ stop \ a speeding car
   → *The police stopped a speeding car.*

2. The driver \ tell \ to get out of the car \ by the police

3. The driver \ take out \ his license

4. The driver \ give \ his license \ to the police officer

5. The license \ check

6. The driver \ give \ a ticket

7. The driver \ tell \ to drive more carefully

Exercise 15. Listening. (Charts 10-1 → 10-4)

Complete the sentences with the words you hear. Before you begin, you may want to check your understanding of these words: *treated, bruises, reckless.*

CD 2
Track 31

A bike accident

A: Did you hear about the accident outside the dorm entrance?

B: No. What _____?
     _____
         1

A: A guy on a bike _____ by a taxi.
                          _____
                              2

B: _____ he _____?
        _____   _____
            3   4

A: Yeah. Someone _____ an ambulance. He _____ to
                          _____   _____
                              5   6

     City Hospital and _____ in the emergency room for cuts and
                             _____
                                 7

     bruises.

B: What _____ to the taxi driver?
              _____
                  8

A: He _____ for reckless driving.
            _____
                9

B: He's lucky that the bicyclist _____.
                                         _____
                                            10

□ **Exercise 16. Looking at grammar.** (Charts 10-1 → 10-4)

Complete the sentences with the correct form (active or passive) of the verb in parentheses.

1. Yesterday our teacher (*arrive*) ___*arrived*___ five minutes late.

2. Last night my favorite TV program (*interrupt*) _____

    by breaking news.

3. That's not my coat. It (*belong*) _____ to Lara.

4. Our mail (*deliver*) _____ before noon every day.

5. The "b" in *comb* (*pronounce, not*) _____. It is silent.

6. What (*happen*) _____ to John? Where is he?

7. When I (*arrive*) _____ at the airport yesterday, I (*meet*)

    _____ by my cousin and a couple of her friends.

8. Yesterday Lee and I (*hear*) _____ about Scott's divorce. I (*surprise, not*)

    _____ by the news, but Lee (*shock*)

    _____.

9. A new house (*build*) _____ next to ours next year.

10. Roberto (*write*) _____ that composition last week. This one (*write*)

    _____ yesterday.

11. At the soccer game yesterday, the winning goal (*kick*) _____ by
    Luigi. Over 100,000 people (*attend*) _____ the soccer game.

12. A: I think American football is too violent.

    B: I (*agree*) _____ with you. I (*prefer*) _____ baseball.

13. A: When (*your bike, steal*) _____?

    B: Two days ago.

14. A: (*you, pay*) _____ your electric bill yet?

    B: No, I haven't, but I'd better pay it today. If I don't, my electricity (*shut off*)

    _____ by the power company.

□ **Exercise 17. Listening.** (Charts 10-1 → 10-4)

CD 2
Track 32 Listen to the passage with your book closed. Listen again and complete the sentences with the
verbs you hear. Before you begin, you may want to check your understanding of these words:
ancient, athlete, designed, wealthy.

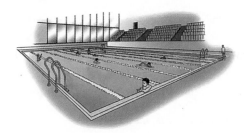

Swimming Pools

Swimming pools ___are___ very popular nowadays, but can you guess when swimming
                      1

pools _____ first _____? _____ it 100 years ago? Five hundred
          2   3   4

years ago? A thousand years ago? Actually, ancient Romans and Greeks _____
                                                                              5

the first swimming pools. Male athletes and soldiers _____ in them for training.
                                                              6

Believe it or not, as early as 1 B.C., a heated swimming pool _____ for
                                                                    7

a wealthy Roman. But swimming pools _____ popular until the
                                              8

middle of the 1800s. The city of London _____ six indoor swimming pools.
                                                9

Soon after, the modern Olympic games _____, and swimming races _____
                                              10   11

included in the events. After this, swimming pools _____ even more popular,
                                                            12

and now they _____ all over the world.
                      13

❏ **Exercise 18. Warm-up.** (Chart 10-5)
Read the paragraph and then the statements. Circle "T" for true and "F" for false.

Getting a Passport

Jerry is applying for a passport. He needs to bring proof of citizenship, two photographs, and the application to the passport office. He also needs money for the fee. He will receive his passport in the mail about three weeks after he applies for it.

1.	The application process can be completed by mail.	T	F
2.	Proof of citizenship must be provided.	T	F
3.	A fee has to be paid.	T	F
4.	Photographs should be taken before Jerry goes to the passport office.	T	F
5.	The passport will be sent by mail.	T	F

10-5 Passive Modal Auxiliaries

Active Modal Auxiliaries	Passive Modal Auxiliaries (*modal* + ***be*** + *past participle*)	Modal auxiliaries are often used in the passive.
Bob *will mail* it. Bob *can mail* it. Bob *should mail* it. Bob *ought to mail* it. Bob *must mail* it. Bob *has to mail* it. Bob *may mail* it. Bob *might mail* it. Bob *could mail* it.	It ***will be mailed*** by Bob. It ***can be mailed*** by Bob. It ***should be mailed*** by Bob. It ***ought to be mailed*** by Bob. It ***must be mailed*** by Bob. It ***has to be mailed*** by Bob. It ***may be mailed*** by Bob. It ***might be mailed*** by Bob. It ***could be mailed*** by Bob.	FORM: *modal* + ***be*** + *past participle* (See Chapter 7 for information about the meanings and uses of modal auxiliaries.)

❏ **Exercise 19. Looking at grammar.** (Chart 10-5)
Complete the sentences by changing the active modals to passive.

1. Someone must send this letter immediately.

   This letter ___must be sent___ immediately.

2. People should plant tomatoes in the spring.

   Tomatoes _____ in the spring.

3. People cannot control the weather.

   The weather _____.

4. Someone had to fix our car before we left for Chicago.

   Our car _____ before we left for Chicago.

5. People can reach me on my cell at 555-3815.

   I _____ on my cell at 555-3815.

The Passive **269**

6. Someone ought to wash these dirty dishes soon.

These dirty dishes _____ soon.

7. People may cook carrots or eat them raw.

Carrots _____ or _____ raw.

8. Be careful! If that email file has a virus, it could destroy your reports.

Your reports _____ if that email file has a virus.

9. You must keep medicine out of the reach of children.

Medicine _____ out of the reach of children.

☐ **Exercise 20. Reading.** (Charts 10-1 → 10-5)
Part I. Read the questions and then the passage about jeans.

Are you wearing jeans right now, or do you have a pair at home?
If so, who were they made by?

The Origin of Jeans

Around the world, a very popular pant for men, women, and children is jeans. Did you know that jeans were created more than 100 years ago? They were invented by Levi Strauss during the California Gold Rush.

In 1853, Levi Strauss, a 24-year-old immigrant from Germany, traveled from New York to San Francisco. His brother was the owner of a store in New York and wanted to open another one in San Francisco. When Strauss arrived, a gold miner* asked him what he had to sell. Levi said he had strong canvas for tents and wagon covers. The miner told him he really needed strong pants because he couldn't find any that lasted very long.

So Levi Strauss took the canvas and designed a pair of overall pants. The miners liked them except that they were rough on the skin. Strauss exchanged the canvas for a cotton cloth from France called *serge de Nimes*. Later, the fabric was called "denim" and the pants were given the nickname "blue jeans."

Eventually, Levi Strauss & Company was formed. Strauss and tailor David Jacobs began putting rivets** in pants to make them stronger. In 1936, a red tab was added to the rear pocket. This was done so "Levis" could be more easily identified. Nowadays the company is very well known, and for many people, all jeans are known as Levis.

Part II. Answer the questions in complete sentences.

1. Who was Levi Strauss?
2. Why did Strauss go to California?
3. Who were jeans first created for?
4. What is denim?
5. What two changes were later made to jeans?
6. Why were rivets put in jeans?
7. Why was a red tab added to the rear pocket?
8. Many people have a different name for blue jeans. What is it?

---

*gold miner = a person who digs for gold

**rivet* = a very strong pin to hold the seams of clothing together

❑ **Exercise 21. Warm-up: trivia.** (Chart 10-6)
Do you know this trivia?* Complete the sentences with words from the list.

> China   monkeys   sand   spiders
> Mongolia   Nepal   small spaces whales

1. Glass is composed mainly of _____.

2. Dolphins are related to _____.

3. The Gobi Desert is located in two countries: _____ and

   _____.

4. People with claustrophobia are frightened by _____.

10-6 Using Past Participles as Adjectives (Non-Progressive Passive)

	be +	*adjective*	**Be** can be followed by an adjective, as in (a)–(c). The adjective describes or gives information about the subject of the sentence.
(a) Paul	*is*	*young.*	
(b) Paul	*is*	*tall.*	
(c) Paul	*is*	*hungry.*	
	be +	*past participle*	**Be** can be followed by a past participle (the passive form), as in (d)–(f). The past participle is often like an adjective. The past participle describes or gives information about the subject of the sentence. Past participles are used as adjectives in many common, everyday expressions.
(d) Paul	*is*	*married.*	
(e) Paul	*is*	*tired.*	
(f) Paul	*is*	*frightened.*	

(g) Paul *is married **to*** Susan.	Often the past participles in these expressions are followed by particular prepositions + an object. For example:
(h) Paul *was excited **about*** the game.	In (g): **married** is followed by **to** (+ *an object*)
(i) Paul *will be prepared **for*** the exam.	In (h): **excited** is followed by **about** (+ *an object*)
	In (i): **prepared** is followed by **for** (+ *an object*)

Some Common Expressions with Be + Past Participle

be acquainted (*with*)	be excited (*about*)	be opposed (*to*)
be bored (*with, by*)	be exhausted (*from*)	be pleased (*with*)
be broken	be finished (*with*)	be prepared (*for*)
be closed	be frightened (*of, by, about*)	be qualified (*for*)
be composed of	be gone (*from*)	be related (*to*)
be crowded (*with*)	be hurt	be satisfied (*with*)
be devoted (*to*)	be interested (*in*)	be scared (*of, by*)
be disappointed (*in, with*)	be involved (*in, with*)	be shut
be divorced (*from*)	be located in / south of / etc.	be spoiled
be done (*with*)	be lost	be terrified (*of, by*)
be drunk (*on*)	be made of	be tired (*of, from*)*
be engaged (*to*)	be married (*to*)	be worried (*about*)

*I'm **tired** *of* the cold weather. = *I've had enough cold weather. I want the weather to get warm.*
I'm **tired** *from* working hard all day. = *I'm tired because I worked hard all day.*

---

*See *Trivia Answers*, p. 421.

□ **Exercise 22. Looking at grammar.** (Chart 10-6)
Choose all the correct completions.

1. Roger is disappointed with _____.
   a. his job   b. in the morning   c. his son's grades

2. Are you related to _____?
   a. the Browns   b. math and science   c. me

3. Finally! We are done with _____.
   a. finished   b. our chores   c. our errands

4. My boss was pleased with _____.
   a. my report   b. thank you   c. the new contract

5. The baby birds are gone from _____.
   a. away   b. their nest   c. yesterday

6. Taka and JoAnne are bored with _____.
   a. their work   b. this movie   c. their marriage

7. Are you tired of _____?
   a. work   b. asleep   c. the news

□ **Exercise 23. Looking at grammar.** (Chart 10-6)
Complete each sentence with an appropriate preposition.

Nervous Nick is . . .

1. worried _____ almost everything in life.

2. frightened _____ being around people.

3. also scared _____ snakes, lizards, and dogs.

4. terrified _____ going outside and seeing a dog.

5. exhausted _____ worrying so much.

Steady Steve is . . .

6. excited _____ waking up every morning.

7. pleased _____ his job.

8. interested _____ having a good time.

9. involved _____ many community activities.

10. satisfied _____ just about everything in his life.

❑ **Exercise 24. Looking at grammar.** (Chart 10-6)
Complete the sentences with the present form of the given verbs. Note the **boldface** prepositions that follow them.

compose	interest	oppose	satisfy
finish	marry	prepare	✓scare

1. Most children ___are scared___ **of** loud noises.

2. Jane _____ **in** ecology.

3. Don't clear the table yet. I _____ not _____ **with** my meal.

4. I _____ **with** my progress in English.

5. Tony _____ **to** Sonia. They have a happy marriage.

6. Roberta's parents _____ **to** her marriage. They don't like her fiancé.

7. The test is tomorrow. _____ you _____ **for** it?

8. A digital picture _____ **of** thousands of tiny dots called pixels.

❑ **Exercise 25. Looking at grammar.** (Chart 10-6)
Complete each sentence with an appropriate preposition.

1. Because of the sale, the mall was crowded _____ shoppers.

2. Do you think you are qualified _____ that job?

3. Mr. Ahmad loves his family very much. He is devoted _____ them.

4. My sister is married _____ a law student.

5. I'll be finished _____ my work in another minute or two.

6. The workers are opposed _____ the new health-care plan.

7. Are you acquainted _____ this writer? I can't put her books down!*

8. Janet doesn't take good care of herself. I'm worried _____ her health.

*can't put a book down = can't stop reading a book because it's so exciting/interesting

□ **Exercise 26. Listening.** (Chart 10-6)

Listen to the sentences and write the prepositions you hear.

CD 2
Track 33

Example: You will hear: Linda loves her grandchildren. She is devoted to them.

You will write: ___to___

1. _____   5. _____

2. _____   6. _____

3. _____   7. _____

4. _____   8. _____

□ **Exercise 27. Looking at grammar.** (Chart 10-6)

Complete the sentences with expressions in the list. Use the present and add prepositions as necessary.

be acquainted	be exhausted	be qualified
be composed	be located	be spoiled
be crowded	be made	✓be worried
be disappointed		

1. Dennis isn't doing well in school this semester. He ___is worried about___ his grades.

2. My shirt _____ cotton.

3. I live in a three-room apartment with six other people. Our apartment _____

    _____ .

4. Vietnam _____ Southeast Asia.

5. I'm going to go straight to bed tonight. It's been a hard day. I _____ .

6. The kids _____ . I had promised to take them to the

    beach today, but now we can't go because it's raining.

7. This milk doesn't taste right. I think it _____ . I'm not going to

    drink it.

8. Water _____ hydrogen and oxygen.

9. According to the job description, an applicant must have a master's degree and at least five

    years of teaching experience. Unfortunately, I _____ not _____

    that job.

10. A: Have you ever met Mrs. Novinsky?

    B: No, I _____ not _____ her.

Exercise 28. Listening. (Chart 10-6)

Complete the sentences with the words you hear.

CD 2
Track 34

Example: You will hear: My earrings are made of gold.

You will write: *are made of*

1. This fruit _____ . I think I'd better throw it out.

2. When we got to the post office, it _____ .

3. Oxford University _____ Oxford, England.

4. Haley doesn't like to ride in elevators. She's _____ small spaces.

5. What's the matter? _____ you _____?

6. Excuse me. Could you please tell me how to get to the bus station from here?

   I _____ .

7. Your name is Tom Hood? _____ you _____ Mary Hood?

8. Where's my wallet? It's _____! Did someone take it?

9. Oh, no! Look at my sunglasses. I sat on them and now they _____ .

10. It's starting to rain. _____ all of the windows _____?

Exercise 29. Warm-up. (Chart 10-7)

Match three of the sentences with the pictures. One sentence does not match either picture.

Picture A   Picture B

1. The shark is terrifying. ____

2. The shark is terrified. ____

3. The swimmer is terrifying. ____

4. The swimmer is terrified. ____

The Passive **275**

10-7 Participial Adjectives: -ed vs. -ing

Art **interests** me.
 	
(a) I am *interested* in art.
   INCORRECT: *I am interesting in art.*
 	
(b) Art is *interesting*.
   INCORRECT: *Art is interested.*
 	
The news **surprised** Kate.
(c) Kate was *surprised*.
(d) The news was *surprising*.
	The past participle (**-ed**)* and the present participle (**-ing**) can be used as adjectives.
	
	In (a): The past participle (***interested***) describes how a person feels.
	
	In (b): The present participle (***interesting***) describes the **cause** of the feeling. The cause of the interest is art.
	
	In (c): ***surprised*** describes how Kate felt. The past participle carries a passive meaning: *Kate was surprised **by the news***.
	
	In (d): ***the news*** was the cause of the surprise.

(e) Did you hear the *surprising news?* (f) Roberto fixed the *broken window.*	Like other adjectives, participial adjectives may follow **be**, as in examples (a) through (d), or they may come in front of nouns, as in (e) and (f).

*The past participle of regular verbs ends in **-ed**. For verbs that have irregular forms, see the inside front and back covers.

☐ **Exercise 30. Looking at grammar.** (Chart 10-7)
Complete the sentences with the correct word: *girl, man,* or *roller coaster.*

1. The _____ is frightened.

2. The _____ is frightening.

3. The _____ is excited.

4. The _____ is exciting.

5. The _____ is thrilling.

6. The _____ is delighted.

☐ **Exercise 31. Listening.** (Chart 10-7)
Listen to the statements and choose the words you hear.

CD 2
Track 35

Example: You will hear: It was a frightening experience.

        You will choose: frighten   (frightening)   frightened

1. bore   boring   bored

2. shock   shocking   shocked

3. confuse   confusing   confused

4. embarrass   embarrassing   embarrassed

5. surprise   surprising   surprised

6. scare   scary*   scared

*The adjective ending is **-y**, not **-ing**.

❑ **Exercise 32. Looking at grammar.** (Chart 10-7)

Complete the sentences with the **-ed** or **-ing** form of the verbs in *italics*.

1. Talal's classes *interest* him.

   a. Talal's classes are ___interesting___.

   b. Talal is an ___interested___ student.

2. Emily is going to Australia. The idea of going on this trip *excites* her.

   a. Emily is _____ about going on this trip.

   b. She thinks it is going to be an _____ trip.

3. I like to study sea life. The subject of marine biology *fascinates* me.

   a. Marine biology is a _____ subject.

   b. I'm _____ by marine biology.

4. Mike heard some bad news. The bad news *depressed* him.

   a. Mike is very sad. In fact, he is _____.

   b. The news made Mike feel very sad. The news was _____.

5. The exploration of space *interests* me.

   a. I'm _____ in the exploration of space.

   b. The exploration of space is _____ to me.

❑ **Exercise 33. Listening.** (Chart 10-7)

CD 2
Track 36

Listen to each sentence and circle the word you hear.

SITUATION: Julie was walking along the edge of the fountain outside her office building. She was with her co-worker and friend Paul. Suddenly she lost her balance and accidentally fell into the water.

1. embarrassed	embarrassing	6. surprised	surprising
2. embarrassed	embarrassing	7. upset*	upsetting
3. shocked	shocking	8. depressed	depressing
4. shocked	shocking	9. interested	interesting
5. surprised	surprising	10. interested	interesting

☐ **Exercise 34. Warm-up.** (Chart 10-8)
Are any of these statements true for you? Circle *yes* or *no*.

Right now ...

1. I am getting tired.   yes   no

2. I am getting hungry.   yes   no

3. I am getting confused.   yes   no

10-8 *Get* + Adjective; *Get* + Past Participle

Get + Adjective	**Get** can be followed by an adjective. **Get** gives the idea of change — the idea of becoming, beginning to be, growing to be.
(a) I **am getting hungry**. Let's eat.	
(b) Eric **got nervous** before the job interview.	In (a): **I'm getting hungry**. = I wasn't hungry before, but now I'm beginning to be hungry.
Get + Past Participle	Sometimes **get** is followed by a past participle. The past participle after **get** is like an adjective; it describes the subject of the sentence.
(c) I **'m getting tired**. Let's stop working.	
(d) Steve and Rita **got married** last month.	

Get + **Adjective**

get angry	get dry	get quiet
get bald	get fat	get rich
get big	get full	get serious
get busy	get hot	get sick
get close	get hungry	get sleepy
get cold	get interested	get thirsty
get dark	get late	get well
get dirty	get nervous	get wet
get dizzy	get old	

Get + **Past Participle**

get acquainted	get drunk	get involved
get arrested	get engaged	get killed
get bored	get excited	get lost
get confused	get finished	get married
get crowded	get frightened	get scared
get divorced	get hurt	get sunburned
get done	get interested	get tired
get dressed	get invited	get worried

---

*There is no *-ed* ending.

Exercise 35. Looking at grammar. (Chart 10-8)

Complete the sentences with the words in the list.

bald	dirty	hurt	lost	rich
busy	✓full	late	nervous	serious

1. This food is delicious, but I can't eat any more. I'm getting ___*full*___.

2. This work has to be done before we leave. We'd better get _____ and stop wasting time.

3. I didn't understand Mariam's directions very well, so on the way to her house last night I got _____. I couldn't find her house.

4. It's hard to work on a car and stay clean. Paul's clothes always get _____ from all the grease and oil.

5. Tim doesn't like to fly. As soon as he sits down, his heart starts to beat quickly. He gets really _____.

6. We'd better go home. It's getting _____, and you have school tomorrow.

7. Simon wants to get _____, but he doesn't want to work. That's not very realistic.

8. If you plan to go to medical school, you need to get _____ about the time and money involved and start planning now.

9. Mr. Andersen is losing some of his hair. He's slowly getting _____.

10. Was the accident serious? Did anyone get _____?

□ **Exercise 36. Let's talk: interview.** (Chart 10-8)

Interview your classmates. Share some of their answers with the class.

1. Have you ever gotten hurt? What happened?
2. Have you ever gotten lost? What happened?
3. When was the last time you got dizzy?
4. How long does it take you to get dressed in the morning?
5. In general, do you get sleepy during the day? When?
6. Do you ever get hungry in the middle of the night? What do you do?
7. Have you ever gotten involved with a charity? Which one?

□ **Exercise 37. Listening.** (Chart 10-8)

Listen to the sentences and complete them with any adjectives that make sense.

CD 2
Track 37

Example: You will hear: This towel is soaking wet. Please hang it up so it will get . . .

You will write: __dry__

1. _____

2. _____

3. _____

4. _____

5. _____

6. _____

□ **Exercise 38. Looking at grammar.** (Chart 10-8)

Complete the sentences with appropriate forms of **get** and the words in the list.

angry	dressed	kill	tired
cold	dry	lost	well
crowd	hungry	marry	worry
dark	involve	✓sunburn	

1. When I stayed out in the sun too long yesterday, I ___got sunburned___.

2. If you're sick, stay home and take care of yourself. You won't _____ if you don't take care of yourself.

3. Alima and Hasan are engaged. They are going to _____ a year from now.

4. Sarah doesn't eat breakfast, so she always _____ by ten or ten-thirty.

5. In the winter, the sun sets early. It _____ outside by six or even earlier.

6. Put these towels back in the dryer. They didn't _____ the first time.

7. Let's stop working for a while. I'm _____. I need a break.

8. Anastasia has to move out of her apartment next week, and she hasn't found a new place to live. She's _____.

9. Toshiro was in a terrible car wreck and almost _____. He's lucky to be alive.

10. The temperature is dropping. Brrr! I'm _____. Can I borrow your sweater?

11. Sorry we're late. We took a wrong turn and _____.

280 CHAPTER 10

12. Good restaurants _____ around dinner time. It's hard to find a seat because there are so many people.

13. Calm down! Take it easy! You shouldn't

    _____ so _____. It's not good for your blood pressure.

14. I left when Ellen and Joe began to argue. I never

    _____ in other people's quarrels.

15. Sam is wearing one brown sock and one blue sock today.

    He _____ in a hurry this morning and didn't pay attention to the color of his socks.

□ **Exercise 39. Reading.** (Chart 10-8)
Read the passage and the statements that follow it. Circle "T" for true and "F" for false.

A Blended Family

Lisa and Thomas live in a blended family. They are not related to each other, but they are brother and sister. Actually, they are stepbrother and stepsister. This is how they came to be in the same family.

Lisa's mother got divorced when Lisa was a baby. Thomas' father was a widower. His wife had died seven years earlier. Lisa and Thomas' parents met five years ago at a going-away party for a friend. After a year of dating, they got engaged and a year later, they got married. Lisa and Thomas are about the same age and get along well. Theirs is a happy, blended family.

1. Lisa's mother got married. Then she got divorced.
   Then she got remarried.   T F

2. Thomas' father got married, and then he got divorced.
   After he got divorced, he got engaged, and then he got remarried.   T F

3. Lisa and Thomas became stepsister and stepbrother when
   their parents got remarried.   T F

□ **Exercise 40. Warm-up.** (Chart 10-9)
Circle the words in *italics* that make these sentences true for you.

1. I am *used to, not used to* speaking English with native speakers.

2. I am *accustomed to, not accustomed to* speaking English without translating from my language.

3. I am *getting used to, not getting used to* English slang.

4. I am *getting accustomed to, not getting accustomed to* reading English without a dictionary.

10-9 Using *Be Used/Accustomed To* and *Get Used/Accustomed To*

(a) I *am used to* hot weather. (b) I *am accustomed to* hot weather.	Examples (a) and (b) have the same meaning: "Living in a hot climate is usual and normal for me. I'm familiar with what it is like to live in a hot climate. Hot weather isn't strange or different to me."
(c) I *am used to living* in a hot climate. (d) I *am accustomed to living* in a hot climate.	Notice in (c) and (d): *to* (a preposition) is followed by the *-ing* form of a verb (a gerund).
(e) I just moved from Florida to Alaska. I have never lived in a cold climate before, but I *am getting used to (accustomed to)* the cold weather here.	In (e): *I'm getting used to/accustomed to* = something is beginning to seem usual and normal to me.

□ **Exercise 41. Looking at grammar.** (Chart 10-9)

Part I. Complete the sentences with *be used to*, affirmative or negative.

1. Juan is from Mexico. He ___is used to___ hot weather. He ___isn't used to___ cold weather.

2. Alice was born and raised in Chicago. She _____ living in a big city.

3. My hometown is New York City, but this year I'm going to school in a town with a population of 10,000. I _____ living in a small town. I _____ living in a big city.

4. We do a lot of exercises in class. We _____ doing exercises.

Part II. Complete the sentences with *be accustomed to*, affirmative or negative.

5. Spiro recently moved to Hong Kong from Greece. He ___is accustomed to___ eating Greek food. He ___isn't accustomed to___ eating Chinese food.

6. I always get up around 6:00 A.M. I _____ getting up early. I _____ sleeping late.

7. Our teacher always gives us a lot of homework. We _____ having a lot of homework every day.

8. Young schoolchildren rarely take multiple-choice tests. They _____ taking that kind of test.

□ **Exercise 42. Listening and speaking.** (Chart 10-9)

Part I. Complete the questions with the words you hear.

CD 2
 Track 38 *Example:* You will hear: What time are you accustomed to getting up?

You will write: ___are you accustomed to___

1. What _____ doing in the evenings?

2. What time _____ going to bed?

3. What _____ having for breakfast?

4. _____ living in this area?

5. Do you live with someone or do you live alone? _____ that?

6. _____ speaking English every day?

7. What _____ doing on weekends?

8. What do you think about the weather here? _____ it?

Part II. Work with a partner. Take turns asking and answering the questions in Part I.

☐ **Exercise 43. Let's talk: interview.** (Chart 10-9)
Ask your classmates questions with **be used to/accustomed to**.

Example: buy \ frozen food
→ *Are you used to / accustomed to buying frozen food?*

1. get up \ early
2. sleep \ late
3. eat \ breakfast
4. skip \ lunch
5. eat \ a late dinner

6. drink \ coffee in the morning
7. have \ dessert at night
8. live \ in a big city
9. live \ in a small town
10. pay \ for all your expenses

☐ **Exercise 44. Let's talk.** (Chart 10-9)
Work in small groups. Discuss one or more of the given topics. Make a list of your answers. Share some of them with the class.

Topics:
1. Junko is going to leave her parents' house next week. She is going to move in with two of her cousins who work in the city. Junko will be away from her home for the first time in her life. What is she going to have to get accustomed to?

2. Think of a time you traveled in or lived in a foreign country. What weren't you used to? What did you get used to? What didn't you ever get used to?

3. Think of the first day of a job you have had. What weren't you used to? What did you get used to?

☐ **Exercise 45. Warm-up.** (Chart 10-10)
Complete the sentences about food preferences. Make statements that are true for you.

1. There are some foods I liked when I was younger, but now I don't eat them. I used to eat

_____, but now I don't.

2. There are some foods I didn't like when I first tried them, but now they're okay. For

example, the first time I ate _____, I didn't like it, but now I'm

used to eating them.

10-10 Used To vs. Be Used To

(a) I *used to* **live** in Chicago, but now I live in Tokyo. INCORRECT: *I used to living in Chicago.* INCORRECT: *I am used to live in a big city.*	In (a): *Used to* expresses the habitual past (see Chart 2-8, p. 53). It is followed by the **simple form of a verb.**
(b) I am *used to* **living** in a big city.	In (b): **be used to** is followed by the **-ing form of a verb** (a gerund).*

*NOTE: In both **used to** (habitual past) and **be used to**, the "d" is not pronounced.

□ **Exercise 46. Looking at grammar.** (Chart 10-10)
Complete the sentences with an appropriate form of **be**. If no form of **be** is necessary, use Ø.

1. I have lived in Malaysia for a long time. I ___am___ used to warm weather.

2. I ___Ø___ used to live in Portugal, but now I live in Spain.

3. I _____ used to sitting at this desk. I sit here every day.

4. I _____ used to sit in the back of the classroom, but now I prefer to sit in the front row.

5. When I was a child, I _____ used to play games with my friends in a big field near my house after school every day.

6. It's hard for my kids to stay inside on a cold, rainy day. They _____ used to playing outside in the big field near our house. They play there almost every day.

7. A teacher _____ used to answering questions. Students, especially good students, always have a lot of questions.

8. People _____ used to believe the world was flat.

□ **Exercise 47. Looking at grammar.** (Chart 10-10)
Complete the sentences with **used to/be used to** and the correct form of the verb in parentheses.

1. Nick stays up later now than he did when he was in high school. He (*go*) ___used to go___ to bed at ten, but now he rarely gets to bed before midnight.

2. I got used to going to bed late when I was in college, but now I have a job and I need my sleep. These days I (*go*) ___am used to going___ to bed around ten-thirty.

3. I am a vegetarian. I (*eat*) _____ meat, but now I eat only meatless meals.

4. Ms. Wu has had a vegetable garden all her life. She (*grow*) _____ her own vegetables.

5. Oscar has lived in Brazil for ten years. He (*eat*) _____

   Brazilian food. It's his favorite.

6. Georgio moved to Germany to open his own restaurant. He (*have*) _____

   _____ a small bakery in Italy.

7. I have taken the bus to work every day for the past five years. I (*take*) _____

   _____ the bus.

8. Juanita travels by train on company business. She (*go*) _____

   by plane, but now it's too expensive.

❑ **Exercise 48. Warm-up.** (Chart 10-11)
Complete the sentences about airline passengers.

1. Before getting on the plane, passengers are expected to _____.

2. After boarding the plane, passengers are supposed to _____.

3. During landing, passengers are not supposed to _____.

10-11 Using *Be Supposed To*

(a) Mike *is supposed to call* me tomorrow. (IDEA: I expect Mike to call me tomorrow.)	*Be supposed to* is used to talk about an activity or event that is expected to occur.
(b) We *are supposed to write* a composition. (IDEA: The teacher expects us to write a composition.)	In (a): The idea of *is supposed to* is that Mike is expected (by me) to call me. I asked him to call me. He promised to call me. I expect him to call me.
(c) Alice *was supposed to be* home at ten, but she didn't get in until midnight. (IDEA: Someone expected Alice to be home at ten.)	In the past form, *be supposed to* often expresses the idea that an expected event did not occur, as in (c).

❑ **Exercise 49. Looking at grammar.** (Chart 10-11)
Make a sentence with a similar meaning to the given sentence. Use *be supposed to*.

1. The teacher expects us to be on time for class.

   → *We are supposed to be on time for class.*

2. People expect the weather to be cold tomorrow.

3. People expect the plane to arrive at 6:00.

4. My boss expects me to work late tonight.

5. I expected the mail to come an hour ago, but it didn't.

Exercise 50. Let's talk. (Chart 10-11)

Summarize each conversation with a statement. Use *be supposed to*. Work in pairs, in small groups, or as a class.

1. TOM'S BOSS: Mail this package.
     TOM: Yes, sir.

   → *Tom is supposed to mail a package.*

2. LENA: Call me at nine.
     ANN: Okay.

3. MS. MARTINEZ: Please make your bed before you go to school.
     JOHNNY: Okay, Mom.

4. PROF. THOMPSON: Read the test directions carefully and raise your hand if you have any questions.
     STUDENTS: (*no response*)

5. DR. KEMPER: You should take one pill every eight hours.
     PATIENT: Right. Anything else?
     DR. KEMPER: Drink plenty of fluids.

Exercise 51. Listening. (Chart 10-11)

Listen to the statements with *be supposed to*. Choose "T" for true and "F" for false. Notice that *to* in *be supposed to* sounds like "ta."

CD 2
Track 39

Example: You will hear: Visitors at a museum are not supposed to touch the art.
     You will choose: (T)   F

1. T   F   5. T   F
2. T   F   6. T   F
3. T   F   7. T   F
4. T   F   8. T   F

Exercise 52. Reading, grammar, and listening. (Chapter 10)

Part I. Answer the questions and then read the passage on zoos.

Have you visited a zoo recently?
What was your opinion of it?
Were the animals well-taken care of?
Did they live in natural settings or in cages?

Zoos

Zoos are common around the world. The first zoo was established around 3,500 years ago by an Egyptian queen for her enjoyment. Five hundred years later, a Chinese emperor established a huge zoo to show his power and wealth. Later, zoos were established for the purpose of studying animals.

Zoos were supposed to take good care of animals, but some of the early ones were dark holes or dirty cages. At that time, people became disgusted with the poor care the animals were given. Later, these early zoos were replaced by scientific institutions. Animals were studied and kept in better conditions there. These research centers became the first modern zoos.

Because zoos want to treat animals well and encourage breeding, animals today are put in large, natural settings instead of small cages. They are fed a healthy diet and are watched carefully for any signs of disease. Most zoos have specially trained veterinarians and a hospital for their animals. Today, animals in these zoos are treated well, and zoo breeding programs have saved many different types of animals.

Part II. Circle all the grammatically correct statements.

1. a. The first zoo was established around 3,500 years ago.
    b. The first zoo established around 3,500 years ago.
    c. An Egyptian queen established the first zoo.

2. a. Zoos supposed to take good care of animals.
    b. Zoos were supposed to take good care of animals.
    c. Zoos were suppose to take good care of animals.

3. a. The animals was poorly cared for in some of the early zoos.
    b. The animals were poorly cared for in some of the early zoos.
    c. The early zoos didn't take good care of the animals.

4. a. Today, animals are kept in more natural settings.
    b. Today, zoos keep animals in more natural settings.
    c. Today, more natural settings are provided for animals.

5. a. Nowadays, animals are treated better in zoos than before.
    b. Nowadays, animals are taken better care of in zoos than before.
    c. Nowadays, animals take care of in zoos than before.

CD 2
Track 40

Part III. Listen to the passage. Complete the sentences with the verbs you hear and then answer the questions.

Zoos

Zoos are common around the world. The first zoo ___was___ established around 3,500
                                                      1

years ago by an Egyptian queen for her enjoyment. Five hundred years later, a Chinese

emperor _____ a huge zoo to show his power and wealth. Later, zoos
                    2

_____ for the purpose of studying animals.
          3

    Zoos _____ take good care of animals, but some of
                        4

the early ones were dark holes or dirty cages. At that time, people _____
                                                                              5

disgusted with the poor care the animals _____. Later, these early
                                                      6

zoos _____ replaced by scientific institutions. Animals _____
           7   8

and _____ in better conditions there. These research centers became the first
           9

modern zoos.

Because zoos want to treat animals well and encourage breeding, animals today

_____ in large, natural settings instead of small cages. They
             10

_____ a healthy diet and _____ carefully for any signs of
             11   12

disease. Most zoos _____ specially trained veterinarians and a hospital for their
                              13

animals. Today, animals in these zoos _____ well, and zoo breeding
                                                        14

programs _____ many different types of animals.
                    15

1. Why was the first zoo established?
2. What were some of the early zoos like?
3. What was the purpose of the first modern zoos?
4. What are zoos doing to encourage breeding?
5. Why do zoos want to encourage breeding?

❑ **Exercise 53. Check your knowledge.** (Chapter 10)
Edit the sentences.

1. I ~~am~~ agree with him.

2. Something was happened.

3. This pen is belong to me.

4. I'm interesting in that subject.

5. He is marry with my cousin.

6. Mary's dog was died last week.

7. Were you surprise when you heard the news?

8. When I went downtown, I am get lost.

9. The bus was arrived ten minutes late.

10. We're not suppose to have pets in our apartment.

❑ **Exercise 54. Reading and writing.** (Chapter 10)

Part I. Read the passage and <u>underline</u> the passive verbs.

My Favorite Holiday

(1) New Year's is the most important holiday of the year in my country. New Year's <u>is</u> <u>celebrated</u> for fifteen days, but my favorite day is the first day.

(2) The celebration actually begins at midnight. Fireworks are set off, and the streets are filled with people. Neighbors and friends greet each other and wish one another good luck for the year. The next morning, gifts are exchanged. Children are given money. It is wrapped in red envelopes because red is the color for good luck. When I was younger, this was always my favorite part of the holiday.

(3) On New Year's Day, everyone wears new clothes. These clothes are bought especially for the holiday. People are very polite to each other. It is considered wrong to yell, lie, or use bad language on the first day of the year. It is a custom for younger generations to visit their elders. They wish them good health and a long life.

Part II. Choose a holiday you like. Describe the activities on this day. What do you do in the morning? afternoon? evening? Which activities do you enjoy the most? Make some of your sentences passive.

Chapter **11**

Count/Noncount Nouns and Articles

☐ **Exercise 1. Warm-up.** (Chart 11-1)
Check (✓) all the items you have with you right now. Do you know why some nouns have *a* before them and others have *an?*

1. _____ **a** pen
2. _____ **an** eraser
3. _____ **a** notebook
4. _____ **an** umbrella
5. _____ **an** interesting book
6. _____ **a** university map

11-1 *A* vs. *An*	
(a) I have *a pencil*. (b) I live in *an apartment*. (c) I have *a small apartment*. (d) I live in *an old building*.	*A* and *an* are used in front of a singular noun (e.g., *pencil, apartment*). They mean "one." If a singular noun is modified by an adjective (e.g., *small, old*), *a* or *an* comes in front of the adjective, as in (c) and (d). *A* is used in front of words that begin with a consonant (*b, c, d, f, g*, etc.): *a boy, a bad day, a cat, a cute baby*. *An* is used in front of words that begin with the vowels *a, e, i*, and *o*: *an apartment, an angry man, an elephant, an empty room*, etc.

(e) I have *an umbrella*.
(f) I saw *an ugly picture*.
(g) I attend *a university*.
(h) I had *a unique experience*.
	For words that begin with the letter *u:*
	   (1) *An* is used if the *u* is a vowel sound, as in *an umbrella, an uncle, an unusual day*.
	   (2) *A* is used if the *u* is a consonant sound, as in *a university, a unit, a usual event*.

(i) He will arrive in *an hour*.
(j) New Year's Day is *a holiday*.
	For words that begin with the letter *h:*
	   (1) *An* is used if the *h* is silent: *an hour, an honor, an honest person*.
	   (2) *A* is used if the *h* is pronounced: *a holiday, a hotel, a high grade*.

□ **Exercise 2. Looking at grammar.** (Chart 11-1)
Add *a* or *an* to these words.

1. _a_ mistake
2. _an_ abbreviation
3. _a_ dream
4. _an_ interesting dream
5. _an_ empty box
6. _a_ box
7. _a_ uniform
8. _an_ email
9. _an_ untrue story

10. _an_ urgent message
11. _a_ universal problem
12. _an_ unhappy child
13. _an_ hour or two
14. _a_ hole in the ground
15. _a_ hill
16. _a_ handsome man
17. _an_ honest man
18. _an_ honor

□ **Exercise 3. Listening.** (Chart 11-1)
Listen to the sentences. Decide if you hear *a, an,* or Ø (no article).

CD 2
Track 41

Example: You will hear: I have a bad toothache.
You will choose: (a)   an   Ø

1. a   an   Ø
2. a   an   Ø
3. a   an   Ø
4. a   an   Ø
5. a   an   Ø

6. a   an   Ø
7. a   an   Ø
8. a   an   Ø
9. a   an   Ø
10. a   an   Ø

□ **Exercise 4. Warm-up.** (Chart 11-2)
Circle all the correct completions.

1. I need one ____.
a. chair   b. chairs

2. There are two ____ in the room.
a. chairs   b. furniture

3. I found some ____ in the storage room.
a. chairs   b. furniture

4. I found ____ in the storage room.
a. chairs   b. furniture

11-2 Count and Noncount Nouns

	Singular	Plural	
COUNT NOUN	*a* chair *one* chair	Ø chairs *two* chairs *some* chairs	A count noun: (1) can be counted with numbers: *one chair, two chairs, ten chairs,* etc. (2) can be preceded by *a/an* in the singular: *a chair.* (3) has a plural form ending in *-s* or *-es: chairs.**

NONCOUNT NOUN	Ø furniture
	some furniture
		Ø
		Ø
			A noncount noun:
			(1) cannot be counted with numbers.
			   INCORRECT: *one furniture*
			(2) is NOT immediately preceded by *a/an.*
			   INCORRECT: *a furniture*
			(3) does NOT have a plural form (no final *-s*).
			   INCORRECT: *furnitures*

*See Chart 1-5, p. 14, and Chart 6-1, p. 147, for the spelling and pronunciation of *-s/-es*.

☐ **Exercise 5. Looking at grammar.** (Chart 11-2)
Check (✓) the correct sentences. Correct the sentences with errors. Use *some* with the noncount nouns.

some furniture

one chair

two chairs

some chairs

1. __✓__ I bought one chair for my apartment.
2. _____ I bought ~~one~~ *some* furniture for my apartment.*
3. __✓__ I bought four chairs for my apartment.
4. _____ I bought ~~four furnitures~~ for my apartment.
5. __✓__ I bought a chair for my apartment.
6. _____ I bought ~~a~~ furniture for my apartment.
7. _____ I bought some chair for my apartment.
8. _____ I bought some furnitures for my apartment.

☐ **Exercise 6. Warm-up.** (Chart 11-3)
Write the words under the correct categories.

bracelets	ideas	letters	postcards	rings	suggestions

Advice	Mail	Jewelry
ideas	letters	bracelets
suggestions	postcards	rings

---

*CORRECT: *I bought **some furniture** for my apartment.* OR *I bought **furniture** for my apartment.* See Chart 11-8 for more information about the use of Ø and *some*.

11-3 Noncount Nouns

Individual Parts → The Whole		Noncount nouns usually refer to a whole group of things that is made up of many individual parts, a whole category made of different varieties.
(Count Nouns)	(Noncount Nouns)	
(a) letters, postcards, bills, etc.	→ *mail*	For example, *furniture* is a noncount noun; it describes a whole category of things: *chairs, tables, beds, etc.*
(b) apples, bananas, oranges, etc.	→ *fruit*	chairs, tables, beds, etc. → *furniture*
(c) rings, bracelets, necklaces, etc.	→ *jewelry*	*Mail, fruit,* and *jewelry* are other examples of noncount nouns that refer to a whole category made up of individual parts.

Some Common Noncount Nouns: Whole Groups Made up of Individual Parts

A. clothing, equipment, food, fruit, furniture, jewelry, mail, money, scenery, stuff, traffic	B. homework, housework, work C. advice, information D. history, literature, music, poetry	E. grammar, slang, vocabulary F. Arabic, Chinese, English, German, Indonesian, Spanish, Etc.	G. corn, dirt, flour, hair, pepper, rice, salt, sand, sugar

❑ **Exercise 7. Looking at grammar.** (Charts 11-2 and 11-3)

Complete the sentences with *a/an* or *some*. Decide if the **boldface** nouns are count or noncount.

1. I often have __some__ **fruit** for dessert.   count (noncount)

2. I had __a__ **banana** for dessert.   (count) noncount

3. I got __a__ **letter** today.   count noncount

4. I got _some / ∅_ **mail** today.   count (noncount)

5. Anna wears __a__ **ring** on her left hand.   count noncount

6. Maria is wearing _some / ∅_ **jewelry** today.   count (noncount)

7. I have _some / ∅_ **homework** to finish.   count (noncount)

8. I have __a__ **assignment** to finish.   (count) noncount

9. I needed _some / ∅_ **information**.   count (noncount)

10. I asked __a__ **question**.   (count) noncount

□ **Exercise 8. Grammar and speaking.** (Charts 11-2 and 11-3)
Add final *-s/-es* if possible. Otherwise, write Ø. Then decide if you agree or disagree with the statement. Discuss your answers.

1. I'm learning a lot of **grammar** _Ø_ this term. yes no

2. Count and noncount **noun** _s_ are easy. yes no

3. A good way to control **traffic** _✓_ is to charge people money
   to drive in the city. yes no

4. Electric **car** _s_ will replace gas **car** _s_ . yes no

5. **Information** _✓_ from the Internet is usually reliable. yes no

6. **Fact** _s_ are always true. / A fact is always true. yes no

7. Many **word** _s_ in English are similar to those in my language. yes no

8. The best way to learn new **vocabulary** _✓_ is to memorize it. yes no

9. I enjoy singing karaoke **song** _s_ . yes no

10. I enjoy listening to classical **music** _✓_ . yes no

11. I like to read good **literature** _✓_ . yes no

12. I like to read mystery **novel** _s_ . yes no

13. **Beach** _es_ are relaxing places to visit. yes no

14. Walking on **sand** _✓_ is good exercise for your legs. yes no

15. Parents usually have helpful **suggestion** _s_ for their kids. yes no

16. Sometimes kids have helpful **advice** _✓_ for their parents. yes no

□ **Exercise 9. Warm-up.** (Chart 11-4)
Complete the sentences with words from the list. Make sentences that are true for you.

beauty	health	milk	pollution	traffic
coffee	honesty	money	smog	violence
happiness	juice	noise	tea	water

1. During the day, I drink __milk__ or __coffee__ .

2. Two things I don't like about big cities are __pollution__ and
   __traffic__ .

3. __Health__ is more important than __money__ .

11-4 More Noncount Nouns

(a) Liquids		Solids and Semi-Solids				Gases
coffee	soup	bread	meat	chalk	paper	air
milk	tea	butter	beef	glass	soap	pollution
oil	water	cheese	chicken	gold	toothpaste	smog
		ice	fish	iron	wood	smoke

(b) Things That Occur in Nature						
weather	darkness	thunder				
rain	light	lightning				
snow	sunshine					

(c) Abstractions*						
beauty	fun	health	ignorance	luck	selfishness	
courage	generosity	help	kindness	patience	time	
experience	happiness	honesty	knowledge	progress	violence	

*An abstraction is an idea. It has no physical form. A person cannot touch it.

❑ **Exercise 10. Looking at grammar.** (Charts 11-2 → 11-4)

Add final -s/-es if possible. Otherwise, write Ø. Choose verbs in parentheses as necessary.

1. I made some **mistake** _s_ on my algebra test.

2. In winter in Siberia, there ((is), are) **snow** _Ø_ on the ground. _nc_

3. Siberia has very cold **weather** _/_.

4. Be sure to give the new couple my best **wish** _es_.

5. I want to wish them good **luck** _/_.

6. **Silver** _is_ ((is, are) expensive. **Diamond** _s_ (is, (are) expensive too.

7. I admire Professor Yoo for her extensive **knowledge** _/_ of organic farming methods.

8. Professor Yoo has a lot of good **idea** _s_ and strong **opinion** _s_.

9. Teaching children to read requires **patience** _/_.

10. Doctors take care of **patient** _s_.

11. Mr. Fernandez's English is improving. He's making **progress** _/_.

12. Wood stoves are a source of **pollution** _/_ in many cities.

Exercise 11. Listening. (Charts 11-2 → 11-4)

Listen to the sentences. Add *-s* if the given nouns have plural endings. Otherwise, write Ø.

CD 2
Track 42
Example: You will hear: Watch out! There's ice on the sidewalk.
You will write: ice __Ø__

1. chalk____   6. storm_____

2. soap____   7. storm_____

3. suggestion_____   8. toothpaste____

4. suggestion_____   9. stuff_____

5. gold_____   10. equipment_____

□ **Exercise 12. Let's talk.** (Chart 11-4)

Work in small groups. These common sayings use abstract nouns. Choose two sayings to explain to the class.

Example: Ignorance is bliss.
→ ***Ignorance*** *means you don't know about something.* ***Bliss*** *means happiness.*
This saying means that you are happier if you don't know about a problem.

1. Honesty is the best policy.   4. Knowledge is power.
2. Time is money.   5. Experience is the best teacher.
3. Laughter is the best medicine.

□ **Exercise 13. Let's talk.** (Chart 11-4)

Complete the sentences. Give two to four answers for each item. Share your answers with a partner. See how many of your answers are the same. *Note:* Abstract nouns are usually noncount. To find out if a noun is count or noncount, check your dictionary or ask your teacher.

1. Qualities I admire in a person are . . . .
2. Bad qualities people can have are . . . .
3. Some of the most important things in life are . . . .
4. Certain bad conditions exist in the world. Some of them are . . . .

□ **Exercise 14. Game.** (Charts 11-1 → 11-4)

Work in small teams. Imagine your team is at one of the given places. Make a list of the things you see. Share your team's list with the class. The team with the most complete and grammatically correct list wins.

Example: a teacher's office
→ *two windows*
→ *a lot of grammar books*
→ *office equipment — a computer, a printer, a photocopy machine*
→ *office supplies — a stapler, paper clips, pens, pencils, a ruler*
→ *some pictures*
    etc.

Places:

a restaurant	an island
a museum	a hotel
a popular department store	an airport

❑ **Exercise 15. Warm-up.** (Chart 11-5)
Complete the sentences with *apples* or *fruit*.

1. I bought several ___apples___ yesterday.

2. Do you eat a lot of ___fruit___?

3. Do you eat many ___apples___?

4. Do you eat much ___fruit___?

5. I eat a few ___apples___ every week.

6. I eat a little ___fruit___ for breakfast.

11-5 Using *Several, A Lot Of, Many/Much,* and *A Few/A Little*

	Count	Noncount	
(a)	*several* chairs	Ø	*Several* is used only with count nouns.
(b)	*a lot of* chairs	*a lot of* furniture	*A lot of* is used with both count and noncount nouns.
(c)	*many* chairs	*much* furniture	*Many* is used with count nouns. *Much* is used with noncount nouns.
(d)	*a few* chairs	*a little* furniture	*A few* is used with count nouns. *A little* is used with noncount nouns.

❑ **Exercise 16. Looking at grammar.** (Charts 11-2 and 11-5)
Check (✓) the correct sentences. Correct the sentences that have mistakes. One sentence has a spelling error.

                     some / Ø
1. _____ Jakob learned ~~several~~ new vocabulary.

2. __✓__ He learned several new words.

3. __✓__ Takashi learned a lot of new words.

4. __✓__ Sonia learned a lot of new vocabulary too.

5. __✓__ Lydia doesn't like learning too much new vocabulary in one day.

6. _____ She can't remember too ~~much~~ *many* new words.

7. _____ Mr. Lee assigned a few vocabulary to his class.

8. _____ He assigned a few new words.

9. _____ He explained several new vocabulary.

10. _____ There is alot of new words at this level.

11. _____ There are a lot of new vocabulary at this level.

☐ **Exercise 17. Looking at grammar: pairwork.** (Charts 11-1 → 11-5)
Work with a partner. Take turns completing the questions with *how many* or *how much*.*
Make nouns plural as necessary.

1. How _____ does Mr. Miller have?

    a. son → *many sons*   d. car
    b. child → *many children*   e. stuff
    c. work → *much work*   f. experience

2. How _____ did you buy?

    a. fruit   d. tomato
    b. vegetable   e. orange
    c. banana   f. food

3. How _____ did you have?

    a. fun   d. information
    b. help   e. fact
    c. time   f. money

☐ **Exercise 18. Let's talk: interview.** (Chart 11-5)
Interview your classmates. Begin your questions with *How much* or *How many*. Share some of your answers with the class.

How much/How many . . .

1. pages does this book have?
2. coffee do you drink every day?
3. cups of tea do you drink every day?
4. homework do you have to do tonight?
5. assignments have you had this week?
6. provinces does Canada have?
7. countries does Africa have?
8. snow does this area get in the winter?

---

*__Much__ and __many__ are more commonly used in questions than in affirmative statements.

□ **Exercise 19. Looking at grammar.** (Charts 11-1 → 11-5)
Complete the sentences with *a few* or *a little* and the given noun. Use the plural form of the noun as necessary.

1. music   I feel like listening to ___*a little music*___ tonight.

2. song   We sang ___*a few songs*___ at the party.

3. help   Do you need _____ with that?

4. pepper   My grandfather doesn't use salt, but he always puts
              _____ on his eggs.

5. thing   I need to pick up _____ at the store on my way
              home from work tonight.

6. apple   I bought _____ at the store.*

7. fruit   I bought _____ at the store.

8. advice   I need _____.

9. money   If I accept that job, I'll make _____ more _____.

10. friend   _____ came by last night to visit us.

11. rain   It looks like we might get _____ today. I
              think I'll take my umbrella with me.

12. French   I can speak _____, but I don't know any
              Italian at all.

13. hour   Ron's plane will arrive in _____ more _____.

□ **Exercise 20. Warm-up.** (Chart 11-6)
Match the sentences to the pictures.

   Picture A   Picture B   Picture C

1. Do you need one glass or two? C
2. Your glasses fit nicely. A
3. A: What happened? B
   B: Some neighborhood kids were playing baseball, and their ball went through the glass.

---

*I bought a few apples. = I bought a small number of apples.
I bought a little apple. = I bought one apple, and it was small, not large.

11-6 Nouns That Can Be Count or Noncount

Quite a few nouns can be used as either count or noncount nouns. Examples of both count and noncount usages for some common nouns follow.

Noun	Used as a Noncount Noun	Used as a Count Noun
glass	(a) Windows are made of *glass*.	(b) I drank *a glass* of water. (c) Janet wears *glasses* when she reads.
hair	(d) Rita has brown *hair*.	(e) There's *a hair* on my jacket.
iron	(f) *Iron* is a metal.	(g) I pressed my shirt with *an iron*.
light	(h) I opened the curtain to let in *some light*.	(i) Please turn off *the lights* (*lamps*).
paper	(j) I need *some paper* to write a note.	(k) I wrote *a paper* for Professor Lee. (l) I bought *a paper* (a *newspaper*).
time	(m) How *much time* do you need to finish your work?	(n) How *many times* have you been to Mexico?
work	(o) I have *some work* to do tonight.	(p) That painting is *a work* of art.
coffee	(q) I had *some coffee* after dinner.	(r) *Two coffees*, please.
chicken/fish	(s) I ate *some chicken/some fish*.	(t) She drew a picture of *a chicken/a fish*.
experience	(u) I haven't had *much experience* with computers. (I don't have much knowledge or skill in using computers.)	(v) I had *many* interesting *experiences* on my trip. (Many interesting events happened to me on my trip.)

☐ **Exercise 21. Looking at grammar.** (Chart 11-6)
Match the correct picture to each sentence on page 301. Discuss the differences in meaning.

Picture A   Picture B   Picture C

Picture D   Picture E   Picture F

1. That was a great meal. I ate a lot of chicken. Now I'm stuffed.* ___E___
2. Are you hungry? How about a little chicken for lunch? ___B___
3. When I was a child, we raised a lot of chickens. ___F___
4. I bought a few chickens so I can have fresh eggs. ___C___
5. There's a little chicken in your yard. ___A___
6. That's a big chicken over there. Who does it belong to? ___D___

□ **Exercise 22. Looking at grammar.** (Chart 11-6)
Complete the sentences with the given words. Make words plural as necessary. Choose words in parentheses as necessary. Discuss the differences in meaning.

1. time   It took a lot of ___time___ to write my composition.

2. time   I really like that movie. I saw it three ___times___ .

3. paper   Students in Professor Young's literature class have to write a lot of
             ___papers___ .

4. paper   Students who take careful lecture notes can use a lot of ___paper___ .

5. paper   The *New York Times* is ((a) some) famous ___paper___ .

6. work   Van Gogh's painting *Irises* is one of my favorite ___works___ of art.

7. work   I have a lot of ___work___ NC to do tomorrow at my office.

8. hair   Erin has straight ___hair___ , and Mariam has curly
             ___hair___ .

9. hair   Brian has a white cat. When I stood up from Brian's sofa, my black slacks
             were covered with short white ___hairs___ .

10. glass   I wear ___glasses___ for reading.

11. glass   In some countries, people use ___glasses___ for their tea; in other
             countries, they use cups.

12. glass   Many famous paintings are covered with ___glass___ to protect them.

13. iron   NC. ___Iron is___ ((is) are) necessary to animal and plant life.

14. iron   CN ___Irons___ (is, (are)) used to make clothes look neat.

*stuffed = very full

15. experience   My grandfather had a lot of interesting ___experiences___ in his long
career as a diplomat.

16. experience   You should apply for the job at the electronics company because you have a
lot of ___experience___ in that field.

17. chicken   Joe, would you like (a, *some*) more ___chicken___?

18. chicken   My grandmother raises ___chickens___ in her yard.

19. light   There (is, *are*) a lot of ___lights___ ^{CN} on the ceilings of the school
building.

20. light   A: If you want to take a picture outside now, you'll need a flash. The
___light isn't___ (*isn't*, aren't) good here.

B: Or, we could wait an hour. (*It*, They) will be brighter then.

❑ **Exercise 23. Warm-up.** (Chart 11-7)
Which of the following do you have in your kitchen? Check (✓) the items.

1. ____ a can* of tuna

2. ____ a bag of flour

3. ____ a jar of olive oil

4. ____ a bottle of soda pop

5. ____ a box of tea bags

6. ____ a bowl of sugar

11-7 Using Units of Measure with Noncount Nouns

(a) I had some tea. (b) I had **two cups of** tea.	To mention a specific quantity of a noncount noun, speakers use units of measure such as *two cups of* or *one piece of.*
(c) I ate some toast. (d) I ate **one piece of** toast.	A unit of measure usually describes **the container** (*a cup of, a bowl of*), **the amount** (*a pound of, a quart of*),* or **the shape** (*a bar of soap, a sheet of paper*).

*Weight measure: *one pound* = 0.45 kilograms/kilos.
 Liquid measure: *one quart* = 0.95 litres/liters; four quarts = one gallon = 3.8 litres/liters.

---

*a can in American English = a tin in British English

Exercise 24. Looking at grammar. (Chart 11-7)
What units of measure are usually used with the given nouns? More than one unit of measure
can be used with some of the nouns.

Part I. At the store

bag	bottle	box	can	jar

1. a __*can/jar*__ of olives

2. a __*box*__ of crackers

3. a _____ of mineral water

4. a _____ of jam or jelly

5. a _____ of tuna

6. a _____ of soup

7. a _____ of sugar

8. a _____ of wine

9. a _____ of soda

10. a _____ of flour

11. a _____ of paint

12. a _____ of breakfast cereal

Part II. In the kitchen

bowl	cup	glass	piece	slice

13. a __*cup/glass*__ of green tea

14. a __*bowl*__ of cereal

15. a _____ of candy

16. a _____ of bread

17. a _____ of cake

18. a _____ of orange juice

19. a _____ of soup

20. a _____ of pizza

Part II. (*continued*)

bowl	cup	glass	piece	slice

21. a _____ of soda

22. a _____ of noodles

23. a _____ of mineral water

24. a _____ of popcorn

25. a _____ of cheese

26. a _____ of rice

27. a _____ of strawberries

28. a _____ of watermelon

watermelon

☐ **Exercise 25. Let's talk.** (Chart 11-7)

You and your partner are planning a party for the class. You have already prepared most of the food, but you still need to buy a few things at the store. Decide what you'd like to get using the sentences below as your guide. You can be serious or silly. Perform your conversation for the class. Then your classsmates will tell you if they want to come to your party or not.

NOTE: You can look at your conversation before you speak. When you speak, look at your partner.

Shopping list

A: So what else do we need from the store?

B: Let's see. We need a few jars of _____. We should also get a box of

_____. Oh, and a couple of bags of _____.

A: Is that it? Anything else?

B: I guess a few cans of _____ would be good.

I almost forgot. What should we do about drinks?

A: How about some bottles (or cans) of _____?

B: Good idea.

A: By the way, I thought we could serve slices of _____. How does that

sound?

B: Sure.

Exercise 26. Warm-up. (Chart 11-8)

Read the conversations. Why does Speaker A use *a* or *the*? Discuss what both Speaker A and Speaker B are thinking about.

Conversation 1

A: *A dog* makes a good pet.   B: I agree.

Conversation 2

A: I saw *a dog* in my yard

B: Oh?

continue...

Conversation 3

A: Did you feed *the dog?*   B: Yes.

11-8 Guidelines for Article Usage

	TO MAKE A GENERALIZATION

Singular Count Nouns: *A/An*

(a) *A dog* makes a good pet. (b) *An apple* is red. (c) *A pencil* contains lead.	In (a): The speaker is talking about any dog, all dogs, dogs in general.

Plural Count Nouns: Ø

(d) Ø *Dogs* make good pets. (e) Ø *Apples* are red. (f) Ø *Pencils* contain lead.	In (d): The speaker is talking about any dog, all dogs, dogs in general. NOTE: Examples (a) and (d) have the same meaning.

Noncount Nouns: Ø

(g) Ø *Fruit* is good for you. (h) Ø *Coffee* contains caffeine. (i) I like Ø *music*.	In (g): The speaker is talking about any fruit, all fruit, fruit in general.

	TO TALK ABOUT NON-SPECIFIC PERSON(S) OR THING(S)

Singular Count Nouns: *A/An*

(j) I saw *a dog* in my yard. (k) Mary ate *an apple*. (l) I need *a pencil*.	In (j): The speaker is saying, "I saw one dog (not two dogs, some dogs, many dogs). It wasn't a specific dog (e.g., your dog, the neighbor's dog, that dog). It was only one dog out of the whole group of animals called dogs."

Plural Count Nouns: *Some*

(m) I saw *some dogs* in my yard. (n) Mary bought *some apples*. (o) Bob has *some pencils* in his pocket.	In (m): The speaker is saying, "I saw more than one dog. They weren't specific dogs (e.g., your dogs, the neighbor's dogs, those dogs). The exact number of dogs isn't important (two dogs, five dogs); I'm simply saying that I saw an indefinite number of dogs." See Chart 11-5 for other words that can be used with plural count nouns, such as *several, a few*, and *a lot of*.

Noncount Nouns: *Some*

(p) I bought *some fruit*. (q) Bob drank *some coffee*. (r) Would you like to listen to *some music*?	In (p): The speaker is saying, "I bought an indefinite amount of fruit. The exact amount (e.g., two pounds of fruit, four bananas, and two apples) isn't important. And I'm not talking about specific fruit (e.g., that fruit, the fruit in that bowl.)" See Chart 11-5 for other words that can be used with noncount nouns, such as *a little* and *a lot of*.

THE SPEAKER AND THE LISTENER ARE THINKING ABOUT THE SAME SPECIFIC PERSON(S) OR THINGS.

Singular Count Nouns: *The*

(s) Did you feed *the* dog? (t) Kay is in *the* kitchen. (u) *The* sun is shining. (v) Please close *the* door. (w) *The* president is speaking on TV tonight.	In (s): The speaker and the listener are thinking about the same specific dog. The listener knows which dog the speaker is talking about: the dog that they own, the dog that they feed every day. There is only one dog that the speaker could possibly be talking about.

(x) I had a banana and an apple. I gave *the* banana to Mary.	In (x): A speaker uses *the* when she/he mentions a noun the second time.
	     First mention: *I had **a banana** . . .*
	     Second mention: *I gave **the banana** . . .*
	
	 In the second mention, the listener now knows which banana the speaker is talking about: the banana the speaker had (not the banana John had, not the banana in that bowl).

Plural Count Nouns: *The*

(y) Did you feed *the* dogs? (z) *The* pencils on that desk are Jim's. (aa) Please turn off *the* lights.	In (y): The speaker and the listener are thinking about more than one dog, and they are thinking about the same specific dogs.
(bb) I had some bananas and apples. I gave *the* bananas to Mary.	In (bb) *the* is used for second mention.

Noncount Nouns: *The*

(cc) *The* fruit in this bowl is ripe. (dd) I can't hear you. *The* music is too loud. (ee) *The* air smells fresh today. (ff) I drank some coffee and some milk. *The* coffee was hot.	When *the* is used with noncount nouns, the speaker knows or can assume the listener is familiar with and thinking about the same specific thing. In (ff): *the* is used for second mention. NOTE: *a*, *an*, and Ø are not possible for the situations described in (s) through (ff).

□ **Exercise 27. Looking at grammar.** (Chart 11-8)
Read the following conversations and answer the questions that follow.

Conversation 1

A: *Dogs* make good pets.   B: I agree.

Conversation 2

A: I saw *some dogs* in my yard.   B: Oh?

Conversation 3

A: Did you feed *the dogs?*   B: Yes.

1. In which conversation are the speakers thinking about all dogs?
2. In which conversation are the speakers talking about the same dogs?
3. In which conversation are the speakers talking about an indefinite number of dogs?

Conversation 4

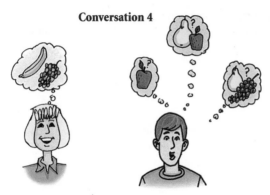

A: I ate *some fruit*.   B: Oh?

Conversation 5

A: *Fruit* is good for you.   B: I agree.

Conversation 6

A: *The fruit* in this bowl is ripe.   B: Good.

4. In which conversation are the speakers talking about all fruit? *5*
5. In which conversation are the speakers talking about an indefinite amount of fruit? *4*
6. In which conversation are the speakers thinking about the same fruit? *6*

□ **Exercise 28. Looking at grammar.** (Chart 11-8)
Read the conversations and decide whether the speakers would probably use **the** or **a/an**.

1. A: What did you do last night?
   B: I went to ___a___ party.
   A: Oh? Where was it?

2. A: Did you have a good time at ___the___ party last night?
   B: Yes.
   A: So did I. I'm glad that you decided to go with me.

3. A: Do you have ___a___ car?
   B: No. But I have ___a___ motorcycle.

4. A: Do you need ___the___ car today, honey?
   B: Yes. I have a lot of errands to do. Why don't I drive you to work today?
   A: Okay. But be sure to fill ___the___ car up with gas sometime today.

5. A: Have you seen my keys?
   B: Yes. They're on ___the___ table next to ___the___ front door.

6. A: Where's ___a the___ professor?
   B: She's absent today.

7. A: Is Mr. Jones ___a___ graduate student?
   B: No. He's ___a___ professor.

8. A: Would you like to go to ___the___ zoo this afternoon?
   B: Sure. Why not?

9. A: Does San Diego have ___a___ zoo?
   B: Yes. It's world famous.

10. A: Where's Dennis?
    B: He's in ___the___ kitchen.

11. A: Do you like your new apartment?
    B: Yes. It has ___a___ big kitchen.

12. A: Did you lock ___the___ door?
    B: Yes.
    A: Did you check ___the___ stove?
    B: Yes.
    A: Did you close all ___the___ windows downstairs?

B: Yes.

A: Did you set __the__ alarm clock?

B: Yes.

A: Then let's turn out __the__ lights.

B: Goodnight, dear.

A: Oh, don't forget your appointment with __the__ doctor tomorrow.

B: Yes, dear. Goodnight.

☐ **Exercise 29. Looking at grammar.** (Chart 11-8)

Decide if the **boldface** noun is singular, plural, or noncount. Then decide if it has a general or specific meaning.

	Singular	Plural	Noncount	General	Specific
1. **Birds** have feathers.		X		X	
2. A **bird** has feathers.					
3. A bird eats **worms**.					
4. A **worm** lives under the ground.					
5. Birds and worms need **water**.					
6. The **bird** is drinking water.					
7. The **birds** are drinking water.					
8. The **water** is on the ground.					

☐ **Exercise 30. Looking at grammar.** (Chart 11-8)

Complete the sentences with the given nouns. Use *the* for specific statements. Do not use *the* for general statements.

1. flowers   a. __The flowers__ in that vase are beautiful.

               b. __Flowers__ are beautiful.

2. mountains   a. _____ are beautiful.

               b. _____ in Switzerland are beautiful.

3. water   a. I don't want to go swimming today. _____ is too cold.

               b. _____ consists of hydrogen and oxygen.

4. information   a. _____ in this magazine article is upsetting.

               b. The Internet is a widely used source of _____.

5. health   a. _____ is more important than money.

               b. Doctors are concerned with _____ of their patients.

6. men   a. _____ generally have stronger muscles than

women   _____ .

b. At the party last night, _____ sat on one side of the

room, and _____ sat on the other.

7. problems   a. Everyone has _____ .

b. Irene told me about _____ she had with her car

yesterday.

8. vegetables   a. _____ we had for dinner last night

were overcooked.

b. _____ are good for you.

□ **Exercise 31. Reading.** (Chart 11-8)
Read the passage. Then cover it with a piece of paper and complete the sentences.

Money

In ancient times, people did not use coins for money. Instead, shells, beads, or salt were used. Around 2,600 years ago, the first metal coins were made. Today most money is made from paper. Of course, many people use plastic credit or debit cards to pay for goods. In the future, maybe we'll use only cards, and paper money won't exist.

1. In ancient times, two forms of money were _____ .

2. People first made _____ 2,600 years ago.

3. Nowadays, paper is used for _____ .

4. Today people can pay for goods with _____ or _____ .

5. In the future, _____ may replace _____ .

□ **Exercise 32. Looking at grammar.** (Chart 11-8)
Complete the sentences with *the* or Ø. Capitalize the beginning of sentences as necessary.

        B
1. __Ø__ ~~B~~utter is a dairy product.

2. Please pass me _____ butter.

3. _____ air is humid today.

4. When I was in Memorial Hospital, _____ nurses were wonderful.

5. I'm studying _____ grammar. I'm also studying _____ vocabulary.

6. _____ trees reduce _____ pollution by cleaning the air.

7. _____ trees in my yard are 200 years old.

□ **Exercise 33. Looking at grammar.** (Chart 11-8)
Complete the sentences with *a/an*, *the*, or *some*.

1. I had __*a*__ banana and __*an*__ apple. I gave __*the*__ banana to Mary. I ate __*the*__ apple.

2. I had _____ bananas and _____ apples. I gave _____ bananas to Mary. I ate _____ apples.

3. I forgot to bring my things with me to class yesterday, so I borrowed _____ pen and _____ paper from Joe. I returned _____ pen, but I used _____ paper for my homework.

4. A: What did you do last weekend?
   B: I went on _____ picnic Saturday and saw _____ movie Sunday.
   A: Did you have fun?
   B: _____ picnic was fun, but _____ movie was boring.

5. I bought _____ bag of flour and _____ sugar to make _____ cookies. _____ sugar was okay, but I had to return _____ flour. When I opened it, I found _____ little bugs in it. I took it back to the people at the store and showed them _____ little bugs. They gave me _____ new bag of flour. _____ new bag didn't have any bugs in it.

□ **Exercise 34. Listening.** (Chart 11-8)
Listen to the passage. Then listen again and write *a/an*, *the*, or *Ø*. Before you begin, you may want to check your understanding of these words: *roof (of your mouth)*, *nerves*, *blood vessels*, *avoid*.

CD 2
Track 43

Ice-Cream Headaches

Have you ever eaten something really cold like ice cream and suddenly gotten __*a*__
                                                                                      1
headache? This is known as _____ "ice-cream headache." About 30 percent of the
                              2
population gets this type of _____ headache. Here is one theory about why _____
                            3   4

ice-cream headaches occur. _____ roof of your mouth has a lot of nerves. When
                              5

something cold touches these nerves, they want to warm up _____ your brain. They
                                                           6

make _____ your blood vessels swell up (get bigger), and this causes _____ lot of pain.
      7   8

_____ ice-cream headaches generally go away after about 30–60 seconds. _____ best
 9   10

way to avoid these headaches is to keep cold food off _____ roof of your mouth.
                                                        11

❑ **Exercise 35. Looking at grammar.** (Chapter 11-8)
Write *a/an*, *the*, or Ø in the blanks.

1. I have ___*a*___ window in my bedroom. I keep it open at night because I like fresh air.
   ___*The*___ window is above my bed.

2. Kathy likes to listen to _____ music when she studies.

3. Would you please turn _____ radio down? _____ music is too loud.

4. Last week I read _____ book about _____ life of Indira Gandhi, India's only
   female prime minister, who was assassinated in 1984.

5. Let's go swimming in _____ lake today.

6. _____ water is essential to human life, but don't drink _____ water in the Flat
   River. It'll kill you! _____ pollution in that river is terrible.

7. People can drink _____ fresh water. They can't drink _____ seawater because it
   contains _____ salt.

8. Ted, pass _____ salt, please. And _____ pepper. Thanks.

9. A: How did you get here? Did you walk?
   B: No, I took _____ taxi.

10. A: Wow! What a great meal!
    B: I agree. _____ food was excellent — especially _____ fish. And _____
    service was exceptionally good. Let's leave _____ waitress a good tip.

11. A: Kids, get in _____ car, please.
    B: We can't. _____ doors are locked.

□ **Exercise 36. Warm-up.** (Chart 11-9)
Complete the questions with **the** or Ø.

Would you like to see . . .

1. ___the___ Amazon River?

2. ___Ø___ Korea?

3. ___✓___ Mexico City?

4. ___the___ Indian Ocean?

5. ___the___ Ural Mountains?

6. ___✓___ Australia?

7. ___the___ Mississippi River?

8. ___the___ Red Sea?

9. ___✓___ Lake Michigan?

10. ___✓___ Mount Fuji?

11-9 Using *The* or Ø with Names

(a) We met Ø *Mr. Wang.* I know Ø *Doctor Smith.* Ø *President Rice* has been in the news.	**The** is NOT used with titled names. INCORRECT: *We met the Mr. Wang.*
(b) He lives in Ø *Europe.* Ø *Asia* is the largest continent. Have you ever been to Ø *Africa?*	**The** is NOT used with the names of continents. INCORRECT: *He lives in the Europe.*
(c) He lives in Ø *France.* Ø *Brazil* is a large country. Have you ever been to Ø *Thailand?* (d) He lives in **the** *United States.* **The** *Netherlands* is in Europe. Have you ever been to **the** *Philippines?*	**The** is NOT used with the names of most countries. INCORRECT: *He lives in the France.* **The** is used in the names of only a few countries, as in (d). Others: *the Czech Republic, the United Arab Emirates, the Dominican Republic.*
(e) He lives in Ø *Paris.* Ø *New York* is the largest city in the United States. Have you ever been to Ø *Istanbul?*	**The** is NOT used with the names of cities. INCORRECT: *He lives in the Paris.*
(f) **The** *Nile River* is long. They crossed **the** *Pacific Ocean.* **The** *Yellow Sea* is in Asia. (g) Chicago is on Ø *Lake Michigan.* Ø *Lake Titicaca* lies on the border between Peru and Bolivia.	**The** is used with the names of rivers, oceans, and seas. **The** is NOT used with the names of lakes.
(h) We hiked in **the** *Alps.* **The** *Andes* are in South America. (i) He climbed Ø *Mount Everest.* Ø *Mount Fuji* is in Japan.	**The** is used with the names of mountain ranges. **The** is NOT used with the names of individual mountains.

□ **Exercise 37. Game: trivia.** (Chart 11-9)

Work in teams. Complete the sentences with *the* or **Ø**. Then decide if the statements are true or false. Circle "T" for true and "F" for false. The team with the most correct answers wins.*

1. _____ Moscow is the biggest city _____ Russia.   T   F

2. _____ Rhine River flows through _____ Germany.   T   F

3. _____ Vienna is in _____ Australia.   T   F

4. _____ Yangtze is the longest river in _____ Asia.   T   F

5. _____ Atlantic Ocean is bigger than _____ Pacific.   T   F

6. _____ Rocky Mountains are located in _____ Canada

    and _____ United States.   T   F

7. _____ Dr. Sigmund Freud is famous for his studies of astronomy.   T   F

8. _____ Lake Victoria is located in _____ Tanzania.   T   F

9. Another name for _____ Holland is _____ Netherlands.   T   F

10. _____ Swiss Alps are the tallest mountains in the world.   T   F

□ **Exercise 38. Game.** (Chart 11-9)

Work in groups. Choose a place in the world. It can be a continent, country, city, sea, river, mountain, etc. Your classmates will try to guess where it is by asking *yes/no* questions. Limit the number of questions to ten for each place.

Example:
SPEAKER A: (*thinking of the Mediterranean Sea*)
SPEAKER B: Is it a continent?
SPEAKER A: No.
SPEAKER C: Is it hot?
SPEAKER A: No.
SPEAKER D: Is it big?
SPEAKER A: Yes.
Etc.

□ **Exercise 39. Warm-up.** (Chart 11-10)

Complete the sentences with information about yourself.

1. I was born in _____.
   (continent)

2. I have lived most of my life in _____.
   (country)

3. This term I am studying _____.

4. Two of my favorite movies are _____ and

   _____.

---

*See *Trivia Answers*, p. 421.

11-10 Capitalization

Capitalize

1. The first word of a sentence	We saw a movie last night. It was very good.	*Capitalize* = use a big letter, not a small letter
2. The names of people	I met George Adams yesterday.	
3. Titles used with the names of people	I saw Doctor (Dr.) Smith. There's Professor (Prof.) Lee.	I saw a doctor. BUT I saw Doctor Wilson.
4. Months, days, holidays	I was born in April. Bob arrived last Monday. It snowed on New Year's Day.	NOTE: Seasons are not capitalized: *spring, summer, fall/autumn, winter.*

5. The names of places:
   city
   state/province
   country
   continent
 	
   ocean
   lake
   river
   desert
   mountain
 	
   school
   business
 	
   street
   building
   park, zoo
	He lives in Chicago.
	She was born in California.
	They are from Mexico.
	Tibet is in Asia.
	
	They crossed the Atlantic Ocean.
	Chicago is on Lake Michigan.
	The Nile River flows north.
	The Sahara Desert is in Africa.
	We visited the Rocky Mountains.
	
	I go to the University of Florida.
	I work for the Boeing Company.
	
	He lives on Grand Avenue.
	We have class in Ritter Hall.
	I went jogging in Forest Park.
		She lives in a city. BUT
		She lives in New York City.
		
		They crossed a river.
		They crossed the Yellow River.
		
		I go to a university. BUT
		I go to the University of Texas.
		
		We went to a park. BUT
		We went to Central Park.

6. The names of courses	I'm taking Chemistry 101.	Here's your history book. BUT I'm taking History 101.
7. The titles of books, articles, movies	*Gone with the Wind* *The Sound of the Mountain*	Capitalize the first word of a title. Capitalize all other words except articles (*the, a/an*), coordinating conjunctions (*and, but, or*), and short prepositions (*with, in, at, etc.*).
8. The names of languages and nationalities	She speaks Spanish. We discussed Japanese customs.	Words that refer to the names of languages and nationalities are always capitalized.
9. The names of religions	Buddhism, Christianity, Hinduism, Islam, and Judaism are major religions in the world. Talal is a Muslem.	Words that refer to the names of religions are always capitalized.

Add capital letters where necessary. Some sentences need no changes.

1. We're going to have a test next $\overset{T}{\text{tuesday}}$.

2. Do you know richard smith? he is a professor at this university.

3. I know that professor smith teaches at the university of arizona.

4. Where was your mother born?

5. John is a catholic. ali is a muslem.

6. Anita speaks french. she studied in france for two years.

7. I'm taking a history course this semester.

8. I'm taking modern european history 101 this semester.

9. We went to vancouver, british columbia, for our vacation last summer.

10. Venezuela is a spanish-speaking country.

11. Canada is in north america.*

12. Canada is north of the united states.

13. The sun rises in the east.

14. The mississippi river flows south.

15. The amazon is a river in south america.

16. We went to a zoo. We went to brookfield zoo in chicago.

17. The title of this book is *fundamentals of english grammar.*

18. I enjoy studying english grammar.

19. On valentine's day (february 14th), sweethearts give each other presents.

20. I read a book called *the cat and the mouse in my aunt's house.*

---

*When **north, south, east,** and **west** refer to the direction on a compass, they are not capitalized: *Japan is **east** of China.*
When they are part of a geographical name, they are capitalized: *Japan is in the Far **East**.*

Exercise 41. Grammar, reading, and writing. (Chapter 11)

Part I. Read the passage. Add capital letters as necessary.

Jane Goodall

(1) Do you recognize the name ʲane goodall? Perhaps you know her for her studies of chimpanzees. She became very famous from her work in tanzania.

(2) Jane goodall was born in england, and as a child, was fascinated by animals. Her favorite books were *the jungle book*, by rudyard kipling, and books about tarzan, a fictional character who was raised by apes.

(3) Her childhood dream was to go to africa. After high school, she worked as a secretary and a waitress to earn enough money to go there. During that time, she took evening courses in journalism and english literature. She saved every penny until she had enough money for a trip to africa.

(4) In the spring of 1957, she sailed through the red sea and southward down the african coast to mombasa in kenya. Her uncle had arranged a job for her in nairobi with a british company. When she was there, she met dr. louis leakey, a famous anthropologist. Under his guidance, she began her lifelong study of chimpanzees on the eastern shore of lake tanganyika.

(5) Jane goodall lived alone in a tent near the lake. Through months and years of patience, she won the trust of the chimps and was able to watch them closely. Her observations changed forever how we view chimpanzees — and all other animals we share the world with.

Part II. Read the passage again and then read these statements. Circle "T" for true and "F" for false.

1. Jane Goodall was interested in animals from an early age. T F

2. Her parents paid for her trip to Africa. T F

3. She studied animals in zoos as well as chimpanzees in the wild. T F

4. Dr. Leakey was helpful to Jane Goodall. T F

5. Jane studied chimpanzees with many other people. T F

6. Goodall's work changed how chimpanzees look at the world. T F

Part III. Read the sample paragraph about the organization called Roots and Shoots. Then write your own paragraph about an organization that is doing something to help people or animals. Focus on correct article usage and capitalization. Note the articles in green in the passage. Follow these steps:

(1) Choose an organization you are interested in.

(2) Research the organization. Find the organization's website if possible. Take notes on the information you find. Include information about its history, why it was formed, the person or people who formed it, and its goals.

(3) Review Chart 11-10 and check your paragraph for proper capitalization.

(4) Edit your paragraph for article use. You may also want to ask another student to read it.

Example:

Roots and Shoots

Jane Goodall went to Africa to study animals. She spent 40 years observing and studying chimpanzees in Tanzania. As a result of Dr. Goodall's work, an organization called Roots and Shoots was formed. This organization focuses on work children and teenagers can do to help the local and global community. The idea began in 1991. A group of 16 teenagers met with Dr. Goodall at her home in Dar Es Salaam, Tanzania. They wanted to discuss how to help with a variety of problems, such as pollution, deforestation, the treatment of animals, and the future of wildlife, like Dr. Goodall's chimpanzees. Dr. Goodall was involved in the meetings, but the teenagers chose the service projects and did the work themselves. The first Roots and Shoots community project was a local one. The group educated villagers about better treatment of chickens at home and in the marketplace. Today, there are tens of thousands of members in almost 100 countries. They work to make their environment and the world a better place through community-service projects.

Chapter 12
Adjective Clauses

☐ **Exercise 1. Warm-up.** (Chart 12-1)
Check (✓) the completions that are true for you.

I have a friend who . . .

1. ____ lives near me.
2. ____ is interested in soccer.
3. ____ likes to do exciting things.
4. ____ is studying to be an astronaut.

12-1 Adjective Clauses: Introduction

Adjectives	Adjective Clauses
An **adjective** modifies a noun. *Modify* means to change a little. An adjective describes or gives information about the noun. (See Chart 6-8, p. 160.)	An **adjective clause*** modifies a noun. It describes or gives information about a noun.
An adjective usually comes in front of a noun.	An adjective clause follows a noun.
adjective + noun (a) I met a ⌐kind⌐ ⌐man⌐. adjective + noun (b) I met a ⌐famous⌐ ⌐man⌐.	noun + adjective clause (c) I met a ⌐man⌐ ⌐who is kind to everybody⌐. noun + adjective clause (d) I met a ⌐man⌐ ⌐who is a famous poet⌐. noun + adjective clause (e) I met a ⌐man⌐ ⌐who lives in Chicago⌐.

*GRAMMAR TERMINOLOGY	
(1) *I met a man* = an independent clause; it is a complete sentence. (2) *He lives in Chicago* = an independent clause; it is a complete sentence. (3) *who lives in Chicago* = a dependent clause; it is NOT a complete sentence. (4) *I met a man who lives in Chicago* = an independent clause + a dependent clause; a complete sentence.	A **clause** is a structure that has a subject and a verb. There are two kinds of clauses: **independent** and **dependent**. • An **independent clause** is a main clause and can stand alone as a sentence, as in (1) and (2). • A **dependent clause**, as in (3), cannot stand alone as a sentence. It must be connected to an independent clause, as in (4).

❑ **Exercise 2. Looking at grammar.** (Chart 12-1)
Check (✓) the items that have complete sentences.

1. ____ I know a teenager. She flies airplanes.
2. ____ I know a teenager who flies airplanes.
3. ____ A teenager who flies airplanes.
4. ____ Who flies airplanes.
5. ____ Who flies airplanes?
6. ____ I know a teenager flies airplanes.

❑ **Exercise 3. Warm-up.** (Chart 12-2)
Complete the sentences with the correct words from the list. <u>Underline</u> the word that follows **doctor** in each sentence.

A dermatologist	An orthopedist	A pediatrician	A surgeon

1. _____ is a doctor who performs operations.
2. _____ is a doctor that treats skin problems.
3. _____ is a doctor who treats bone injuries.
4. _____ is a doctor that treats children.

12-2 Using *Who* and *That* in Adjective Clauses to Describe People

(a) The man is friendly.	S V *He* lives next to me. ↓ *who* ↓ S V *who* lives next to me	In adjective clauses, **who** and **that** are used as subject pronouns to describe people. In (a): **He** is a subject pronoun. **He** refers to "the man." To make an adjective clause, change **he** to **who**. **Who** is a subject pronoun. **Who** refers to "the man."
(b) The man **who** *lives next to me* is friendly.		
(c) The woman is talkative.	S V *She* lives next to me. ↓ *that* ↓ S V *that* lives next to me	**That** is also a subject pronoun and can replace **who**, as in (d). The subject pronouns **who** and **that** cannot be omitted from an adjective clause. *INCORRECT: The woman lives next to me is talkative.* As subject pronouns, both **who** and **that** are common in conversation, but **who** is more common in writing.
(d) The woman **that** *lives next to me* is talkative.		In (b) and (d): The adjective clause immediately follows the noun it modifies. *INCORRECT: The woman is talkative that lives next to me.*

❑ **Exercise 4. Looking at grammar.** (Chart 12-2)

Circle the two sentences that express the ideas in the given sentence.

1. The librarian who helped me with my research lives near my parents.
    a. The librarian lives near my parents.
    b. I live near my parents.
    c. The librarian helped my parents.
    d. The librarian helped me.

2. The veterinarian that took care of my daughter's goat was very gentle.
    a. The veterinarian took care of my goat.
    b. The goat was gentle.
    c. The veterinarian treated my daughter's goat.
    d. The veterinarian was gentle.

❑ **Exercise 5. Looking at grammar.** (Charts 12-1 and 12-2)

Underline each adjective clause. Draw an arrow to the noun it modifies.

1. The hotel clerk who gave us our room keys speaks several languages.

2. The manager that hired me has less experience than I do.

3. I like the manager that works in the office next to mine.

4. My mother is a person who wakes up every morning with a positive attitude.

5. A person who wakes up with a positive attitude every day is lucky.

❑ **Exercise 6. Looking at grammar.** (Charts 12-1 and 12-2)

Change the b. sentences to adjective clauses. Combine each pair of sentences with **who** or **that**.

Example: a. Do you know the people?   b. They live in the house on the corner.
        → *Do you know the people **who** (or **that**) live in the white house?*

1. a. The police officer was friendly.   b. She gave me directions.

2. a. The waiter was slow.   b. He served us dinner.

3. a. I talked to the women.   b. They walked into my office.

4. a. The man talked a lot.   b. He sat next to me on the plane.

5. a. The people have three cars.   b. They live next to me.

❑ **Exercise 7. Looking at grammar.** (Charts 12-1 and 12-2)

Add **who** or **that** as necessary.

1. I liked the people ^who sat next to us at the soccer game.

2. The man answered the phone was polite.

3. People paint houses for a living are called house painters.

4. I'm uncomfortable around married couples argue all the time.

5. While I was waiting at the bus stop, I stood next to an elderly man started a conversation with me about my school.

□ **Exercise 8. Let's talk.** (Charts 12-1 and 12-2)
Work in pairs or small groups. Complete the sentences. Make true statements. Share some of your sentences with the class.

1. I know a man/woman who . . . .
2. I have a friend who . . . .
3. I like athletes who . . . .
4. Workers who . . . are brave.
5. People who . . . make me laugh.
6. Doctors who . . . are admirable.

□ **Exercise 9. Warm-up.** (Chart 12-3)
Complete the sentences with your own words.

1. The teacher that I had for first grade was _____.

2. The first English teacher I had was _____.

3. The first English teacher who I had wasn't _____.

12-3 Using Object Pronouns in Adjective Clauses to Describe People

(a) The man was friendly. | S V O | I met *him.* ↓ *that*	In adjective clauses, pronouns are used as the object of a verb to describe people. In (a): *him* is an object pronoun. *Him* refers to "the man." One way to make an adjective clause is to change *him* to *that*. *That* is the object pronoun. *That* refers to "the man." *That* comes at the beginning of an adjective clause.
O S V (b) The man *that I met* was friendly. (c) The man Ø *I met* was friendly.	An object pronoun can be omitted from an adjective clause, as in (c).
S V | O | (d) The man was friendly. I met | *him.* ↓ *who* *whom*	*Him* can also be changed to *who* or *whom*, as in (e) and (f). As an object pronoun, *that* is more common than *who* in speaking. Ø is the most common choice for both speaking and writing.
O S V (e) The man *who I met* was friendly. (f) The man *whom I met* was friendly.	*Whom* is generally used only in very formal writing.

❑ **Exercise 10. Looking at grammar.** (Charts 12-2 and 12-3)
Check (✓) the sentences that have object pronouns.

1. _✓_ The children who we invited to the party are from the neighborhood.
2. _____ The children that we invited to the party were excited to come.
3. _____ The children whom we invited to the party had a good time.
4. _____ The children who live next door are a lot of fun.
5. _____ Marie and Luis Escobar still keep in touch with many of the students that they met in their English class five years ago.
6. _____ People who listen to loud music on earphones can suffer gradual hearing loss.
7. _____ I know a couple who sailed around the world.
8. _____ The couple whom we had over for dinner sailed around the world.

❑ **Exercise 11. Looking at grammar.** (Charts 12-2 and 12-3)
Circle all the correct completions.

1. The woman _____ was interesting.
   a. that I met last night
   b. I met last night
   c. who I met last night
   d. whom I met last night

2. The man _____ was fast.
   a. that painted our house
   b. painted our house
   c. who painted our house
   d. whom painted

3. The people _____ live on Elm Street.
   a. that Nadia is visiting
   b. Nadia is visiting
   c. who Nadia is visiting
   d. whom Nadia is visiting

4. The students _____ missed the quiz.
   a. that came to class late
   b. came to class late
   c. who came to class late
   d. whom came to class late

❑ **Exercise 12. Looking at grammar.** (Chart 12-3)
Combine each pair of sentences with *that, who,* or *whom*. Underline the object pronouns in the b. sentences and change the sentences to adjective clauses.

Example: a. A woman asked me for my phone number   b. I didn't know her.
   → *A woman that/whom I didn't know asked me for my phone number.*

1. a. The couple was two hours late.   b. I invited them for dinner.

2. a. The man snored the entire flight.   b. I sat next to him on the plane.

3. a. The man tried to shoplift some groceries.   b. The police arrested him.

4. a. The chef is very experienced.   b. The company hired her.

Adjective Clauses **325**

❑ **Exercise 13. Let's talk: pairwork.** (Charts 12-2 and 12-3)
Work with a partner. Take turns making adjective clauses by combining the given sentences with the main sentence.

Main sentence: The man was helpful.

1. He gave me directions. → *The man who/that gave me directions was helpful.*
2. He answered my question.
3. I called him.
4. You recommended him.
5. He is the owner.
6. You invited him to the party.
7. He was walking with his kids.
8. I saw him in the waiting room.
9. He sold us our museum tickets.
10. He gave us a discount.

❑ **Exercise 14. Looking at grammar.** (Charts 12-2 and 12-3)
Complete the sentences with *that*, *Ø*, *who*, or *whom*. Write all the possible completions.

1. The man _____ married my mother is now my stepfather.

2. The man _____ my mother married is now my stepfather.

3. Do you know the boy _____ is talking to Anita?

4. I've become good friends with several of the people _____ I met in my English class last year.

5. A woman _____ I saw in the park was holding several balloons.

6. The woman _____ was holding several balloons was entertaining some children.

❑ **Exercise 15. Warm-up.** (Chart 12-4)
Read the paragraph about James and then check (✓) the sentences that you agree with. What do you notice about the adjective clauses in green?

James is looking for a pet. He is single and a little lonely. He isn't sure what kind of pet would be best for him. He lives on a large piece of property in the country. He is gone during the day from 8:00 A.M. to 5:00 P.M. but is home on weekends. He travels about two months a year but has neighbors that can take care of a pet, as long as it isn't too big. What kind of pet should he get?

1. _____ He should get a pet that likes to run and be outside, like a dog.
2. _____ He needs to get a pet which is easy to take care of, like a fish or turtle.
3. _____ He should get an animal that he can leave alone for a few days, like a horse.
4. _____ He needs to get an animal his neighbors will like.

12-4 Using Pronouns in Adjective Clauses to Describe Things

(a) The river is polluted.	**S** **V** *It* flows through the town. ↓ *that* *which*	**Who** and **whom** refer to people. **Which** refers to things. **That** can refer to either people or things.
S **V** (b) The river **that** *flows through the town* is polluted. (c) The river **which** *flows through the town* is polluted.		In (a): To make an adjective clause, change **it** to **that** or **which**. **It**, **that**, and **which** all refer to a thing (the river). (b) and (c) have the same meaning, but (b) is more common than (c) in speaking and writing.
		When **that** and **which** are used as the subject of an adjective clause, they CANNOT be omitted. *INCORRECT: The river flows through the town is polluted.*
S **V** **O** (d) The books were expensive. I bought *them.* ↓ *that* *which*		**That** or **which** can be used as an object in an adjective clause, as in (e) and (f). An object pronoun can be omitted from an adjective clause, as in (g).
O **S** **V** (e) The books **that** *I bought* were expensive. (f) The books **which** *I bought* were expensive. (g) The books Ø *I bought* were expensive.		(e), (f), and (g) have the same meaning. In speaking, **that** and Ø are more common than **which**. In writing, **that** is the most common, and Ø is rare.

❑ **Exercise 16. Looking at grammar.** (Chart 12-4)
Underline each adjective clause. Draw an arrow to the noun it modifies.

1. I lost the scarf that I borrowed from my roommate.

2. The food we ate at the sidewalk café was delicious.

3. The bus that I take to school every morning is usually very crowded.

4. Pizza which is sold by the slice is a popular lunch in many cities throughout the world.

5. Piranhas are dangerous fish that can tear the flesh off an animal as large as a horse in a few minutes.

Exercise 17. Looking at grammar. (Chart 12-4)
Combine each pair of sentences into one sentence. Give all possible forms.

1. a. The pill made me sleepy. b. I took it.
   → *The pill that I took made me sleepy.*
   → *The pill Ø I took made me sleepy.*
   → *The pill which I took made me sleepy.*

2. a. The soup was too salty. b. I had it for lunch.

3. a. I have a class. b. It begins at 8:00 A.M.

4. a. The information helped me a lot. b. I found it on the Internet.

5. a. My daughter asked me a question. b. I couldn't answer it.

6. a. Where can I catch the bus? b. It goes downtown.

❑ **Exercise 18. Looking at grammar.** (Charts 12-3 and 12-4)
Cross out the incorrect pronouns in the adjective clauses.

1. The books I bought ~~them~~ at the bookstore were expensive.

2. I like the shirt you wore it to class yesterday.

3. Amanda Jones is a person I would like you to meet her.

4. The apartment we wanted to rent it had two bedrooms.

5. My wife and I are really enjoying the TV set that we bought it for our anniversary.

6. The woman you met her at Aunt Barbara's house is an Olympic athlete.

7. Ayako has a cat that it likes to catch mice.

8. The mice that Ayako's cat catches them live in the basement.

❑ **Exercise 19. Looking at grammar.** (Charts 12-2 → 12-4)
Write all the pronouns that can be used to connect the adjective clauses to the main clauses:
that, who, which, or *whom.* If the pronoun can be omitted, use **Ø**.

Example: The manager | *who* *that* | fired Tom is a difficult person to work for.

1. The box | | I mailed to my sister was heavy.

2. The people | | sat in the stadium cheered for the home team.

3. The calendar [ ] hangs in Paul's office has pictures of his kids.

4. The teenagers returned the wallet [ ] they found on the sidewalk.

5. The people [ ] my brother called didn't answer their phone.

6. The tree branch [ ] was lying in the street caused problems for drivers.

□ **Exercise 20. Listening.** (Charts 12-2 → 12-4)

Listen to the sentences. They all have adjective clauses. Circle the words you hear. If there is no subject or object pronoun, choose Ø. NOTE: In spoken English, *that* often sounds like "thut."

CD 2
Track 44

My mother's hospital stay

Example: You will hear: The doctor who treated my mother was very knowledgeable.
You will choose: (who) that which whom Ø

1. who	that	which	whom	Ø
2. who	that	which	whom	Ø
3. who	that	which	whom	Ø
4. who	that	which	whom	Ø
5. who	that	which	whom	Ø
6. who	that	which	whom	Ø
7. who	that	which	whom	Ø
8. who	that	which	whom	Ø

□ **Exercise 21. Let's talk.** (Charts 12-1 → 12-4)

Answer the questions in complete sentences. Use any appropriate pattern of adjective clause. Use *the* with the noun that is modified by the adjective clause.

1. • One phone wasn't ringing.
   • The other phone was ringing.
   QUESTIONS: Which phone did Hasan answer? Which phone didn't he answer?
   → *Hasan answered* **the** *phone that was ringing.*
   → *He didn't answer* **the** *phone that wasn't ringing.*

2. • One student raised her hand in class.
   • Another student sat quietly in his seat.
   QUESTIONS: Which student asked the teacher a question? Which one didn't?

3. • One girl won the bike race.
   • The other girl lost the bike race.
   QUESTIONS: Which girl is happy? Which girl isn't happy?

4. • We ate some food from our garden.
   • We ate some food at a restaurant.
   QUESTIONS: Which food was expensive? Which food wasn't expensive?

5. • One man was sleeping.
   • Another man was listening to the radio.
   QUESTIONS: Which man heard the special report about the earthquake in China? Which one didn't?

6. • One person bought a small car.
   • Another person bought a large car.
   QUESTIONS: Which person probably spent more money than the other?

❑ **Exercise 22. Game.** (Charts 12-3 and 12-4)
Work in teams. Complete each phrase in Column A with the correct phrase in Column B by using *that* or *who*. Check your dictionary if necessary. The team that finishes first and has the most grammatically correct sentences wins.

Column A

1. A hammer is a tool .... *that is used to pound nails.*
2. A comedian is someone ....
3. An obstetrician is a doctor ....
4. Plastic is a chemical material ....
5. An architect is someone ....
6. A puzzle is a problem ....
7. A carnivore is an animal ....
8. Steam is a gas ....
9. A turtle is an animal ....
10. A hermit is a person ....
11. A pyramid is a structure ....

Column B

a. She/He leaves society and lives completely alone.
b. He/She tells jokes.
c. It forms when water boils.
d. It is square at the bottom and has four sides that come together in a point at the top.
e. She/He designs buildings.
f. He/She delivers babies.
✓g. It is used to pound nails.
h. It can be shaped and hardened to form many useful things.
i. It can be difficult to solve.
j. It eats meat.
k. It has a hard shell and can live in water or on land.

❑ **Exercise 23. Warm-up.** (Chart 12-5)
Read the sentences. What do you notice about the verbs in green and the nouns that precede them?

1. I have a friend who is vegetarian. He doesn't eat any meat.
2. I have friends who are vegetarian. They don't eat any meat.

12-5 Singular and Plural Verbs in Adjective Clauses

(a) I know the **man** who **is** sitting over there.	In (a): The verb in the adjective clause (**is**) is singular because **who** refers to a singular noun, **man**.
(b) I know the **people** who **are** sitting over there.	In (b): The verb in the adjective clause (**are**) is plural because **who** refers to a plural noun, **people**.

❑ **Exercise 24. Looking at grammar.** (Chart 12-5)
Circle the correct word in parentheses. <u>Underline</u> the noun that determines whether the verb should be singular or plural.

1. A saw is a <u>tool</u> that ((*is*,) *are*) used to cut wood.

2. Shovels are tools that (*is*, *are*) used to dig holes.

3. I recently met a woman that (*live*, *lives*) in Montreal.

4. Most people that (*live*, *lives*) in Montreal speak French as their first language.

5. I have a cousin who (*works*, *work*) as a coal miner.

6. Some coal miners that (*works*, *work*) underground suffer from lung disease.

7. A professional athlete who (*play*, *plays*) tennis is called a tennis pro.

8. Professional athletes who (*play*, *plays*) tennis for a living can make a lot of money.

9. Biographies are books which (*tells*, *tell*) the stories of people's lives.

10. A book that (*tells*, *tell*) the story of a person's life is called a biography.

11. I talked to the men who (*was*, *were*) sitting near me.

12. The woman that (*was*, *were*) sitting next to me at the movie was texting on her cell phone.

□ **Exercise 25. Warm-up.** (Chart 12-6)
Complete the sentences with your own words.

1. A person that I recently spoke to was _____ .

2. A person whom I recently spoke to wasn't _____ .

3. The room which we are sitting in is _____ .

4. The room we are sitting in has _____ .

5. The room in which we are sitting doesn't have _____ .

12-6 Using Prepositions in Adjective Clauses

PREP OBJ (a) The man was nice. I talked *to him.*	*That, whom,* and *which* can be used as the object (OBJ) of a preposition (PREP) in an adjective clause.
OBJ PREP (b) The man *that* I talked *to* was nice. (c) The man Ø I talked *to* was nice. (d) The man *whom* I talked *to* was nice. **PREP OBJ** (e) The man *to whom* I talked was nice.	REMINDER: An object pronoun can be omitted from an adjective clause, as in (c) and (h). In very formal English, a preposition comes at the beginning of an adjective clause, followed by either *whom* or *which*, as in (e) and (j). This is not common in spoken English.
PREP OBJ (f) The chair is hard. I am sitting *in it.*	NOTE: In (e) and (j), *that* or *who* cannot be used, and the pronoun CANNOT be omitted.
OBJ PREP (g) The chair *that* I am sitting *in* is hard. (h) The chair Ø I am sitting *in* is hard. (i) The chair *which* I am sitting *in* is hard. **PREP OBJ** (j) The chair *in which* I am sitting is hard.	(b), (c), (d), and (e) have the same meaning. (g), (h), (i), and (j) have the same meaning.

□ **Exercise 26. Looking at grammar.** (Chart 12-6)
Change the b. sentences to adjective clauses. Combine each pair of sentences. Give all the possible forms of these clauses and underline them.

1. a. The movie was funny.   b. We went **to** it.
   → The movie *that we went **to** was funny.*
   → The movie *Ø we went **to** was funny.*
   → The movie *which we went **to** was funny.*
   → The movie *__to which__ we went was funny.*

2. a. The man is over there.   b. I told you **about** him.

332 CHAPTER 12

3. a. The woman pays me a fair salary.   b. I work **for** her.

4. a. Alicia likes the family.   b. She is living **with** them.

5. a. The picture is beautiful.   b. Tom is looking **at** it.

6. a. I enjoyed the music.   b. We listened **to** it after dinner.

❑ **Exercise 27. Looking at grammar.** (Chart 12-6)
Complete the sentences with appropriate prepositions.* Draw brackets around the adjective clauses.

1. I spoke __to__ a person. The person [I spoke __to__] was friendly.

2. We went _____ a movie. The movie we went _____ was very good.

3. We stayed _____ a motel. The motel we stayed _____ was clean and comfortable.

4. We listened _____ a new CD. I enjoyed the new CD we listened _____ .

5. Sally was waiting _____ a person. The person Sally was waiting _____ never came.

6. I talked _____ a man. The man _____ whom I talked was helpful.

7. I never found the book that I was looking _____ .

8. The interviewer wanted to know the name of the college I had graduated _____ .

9. Oscar likes the Canadian family _____ whom he is staying.

10. The man who is staring _____ us looks unfriendly.

11. My sister and I have the same ideas about almost everything. She is the one person _____ whom I almost always agree.

12. What's the name of the person you introduced me _____ at the restaurant last night? I've already forgotten.

13. My father is someone I've always been able to depend _____ when I need advice or help.

14. The person you waved _____ is waving back at you.

15. Your building supervisor is the person _____ whom you should complain if you have any problems with your apartment.

---

*See Appendix 2 for a list of preposition combinations.

□ **Exercise 28. Listening.** (Charts 12-1 → 12-6)

Listen to the sentences and choose all the true statements.

Example: You will hear: The university I want to attend is in New York.
You will choose: (a.) I want to go to a university.
b. I live in New York.
(c.) The university is in New York.

1. a. The plane is leaving Denver.
   b. I'm taking a plane.
   c. The plane leaves at 7:00 A.M.

2. a. Stores are expensive.
   b. Good vegetables are always expensive.
   c. The best vegetables are at an expensive store.

3. a. My husband made eggs.
   b. My husband made breakfast.
   c. The eggs were cold.

4. a. I sent an email.
   b. Someone wanted my bank account number.
   c. An email had my bank account number.

5. a. The hotel clerk called my wife.
   b. The speaker spoke with the hotel clerk.
   c. The hotel room is going to have a view.

□ **Exercise 29. Reading and grammar.** (Charts 12-1 → 12-6)

Part I. Answer the questions and then read the passage. Write the nouns that the pronouns refer to.

Have you ever visited or lived in another country?
What differences did you notice?
What customs did you like? What customs seemed strange to you?

An Exchange Student in Ecuador

Hiroki is from Japan. When he was sixteen, he spent four months in South America. He

stayed with a family who lived near Quito, Ecuador. Their way of life was very different from
                              1

his. At first, many things that they did and said seemed strange to Hiroki: their eating customs,
                            2

political views, ways of showing feelings, work habits, sense of humor, and more. He felt

homesick for people who were more similar to him in their customs and habits.
                        3

As time went on, Hiroki began to appreciate* the way of life that his host family had.
                                                                         4

Many activities which he did with them began to feel natural, and he developed a strong
                    5

---

appreciate = to understand a situation more completely

friendship with them. At the beginning of his stay in Ecuador, he had noticed only the customs

and habits that were different between his host family and himself. At the end, he appreciated
                6

the many things which they also had in common.
                7

1. who _____

2. that _____

3. who _____

4. that _____

5. which _____

6. that _____

7. which _____

Part II. Complete the sentences with information from the passage.

1. One thing that Hiroki found strange _____

    _____.

2. At first, he wanted to be with people _____

    _____.

3. After a while, he began to better understand _____

    _____.

4. At the end of his stay, he saw many things _____

    _____.

❑ **Exercise 30. Warm-up.** (Chart 12-7)
Check (✓) all the sentences that are true about the given statement.

We spoke with someone whose house burned down.

1. _____ Our house burned down.
2. _____ Another person's house burned down.
3. _____ Someone told us our house burned down.
4. _____ Someone told us their house burned down.
5. _____ Someone burned down their house.

12-7 Using *Whose* in Adjective Clauses

(a) The man called the police.	*His car* → *whose car* was stolen.	***Whose*** * shows possession. In (a): *His car* can be changed to *whose car* to make an adjective clause. In (b): *whose car was stolen* = an adjective clause.
(b) The man ***whose car*** *was stolen* called the police.		
(c) I know a girl.	*Her brother* → *whose brother* is a movie star.	In (c): *Her brother* can be changed to *whose brother* to make an adjective clause.
(d) I know a girl ***whose brother*** *is a movie star.*		
(e) The people were friendly. We bought	*their house.* → *whose house*	In (e): *Their house* can be changed to *whose house* to make an adjective clause.
(f) The people ***whose house*** *we bought* were friendly.		

*Whose and *who's* have the same pronunciation but NOT the same meaning.*
Who's = *who is:* ***Who's*** (*Who is*) *your teacher?*

❑ **Exercise 31. Looking at grammar.** (Chart 12-7)
Combine each pair of sentences. Follow these steps:
 (1) Underline the possessive adjective in sentence b.
 (2) Draw an arrow to the noun it refers to in sentence a.
 (3) Replace the possessive adjective with ***whose***.
 (4) Place ***whose*** + the noun (that follows) after the noun you drew an arrow to (in Step 2).
 (5) Complete the ***whose*** phrase by using the rest of the words from sentence b., and make one sentence.

whose

Examples: a. The woman is taking some time off from work.   b. Her baby is sick.
 → *The woman whose baby is sick is taking some time off from work.*

whose

 a. The man said there isn't a lot of damage.   b. You hit his car.
 → *The man whose car you hit said there isn't a lot of damage.*

1. a. The C.E.O.* is resigning.	b. His company lost money.
2. a. Let me introduce you to the woman.	b. Her company is hiring right now.
3. a. I talked to the couple.	b. Their house was burglarized.
4. a. The child is fine.	b. You stepped on her foot.
5. a. The man is on the phone.	b. You found his cell phone.

---

*C.E.O. = chief executive officer or head of a company

□ **Exercise 32. Let's talk: pairwork.** (Chart 12-7)

Work with a partner. Take turns changing the b. sentences to adjective clauses by combining each pair of sentences with **whose**.

SITUATION: You and your friend are at a party. You are telling your friend about the people at the party.

1. a. There is the man.   b. His car was stolen.
   → *There is the man whose car was stolen.*

2. a. There is the woman.   b. Her husband writes movie scripts.

3. a. Over there is the man.   b. His daughter is in my English class.

4. a. Over there is the woman.   b. You met her sister yesterday.

5. a. There is the professor.   b. I'm taking her course.

6. a. That is the man.   b. His daughter is a newscaster.

7. a. That is the girl.   b. I taught her brother.

8. a. There is the boy.   b. His mother is a famous musician.

□ **Exercise 33. Listening.** (Chart 12-7)

Listen to the sentences and choose the words you hear: **who's** or **whose**.

CD 2
Track 46

Example: You will hear: The neighbor who's selling her house is moving overseas.
           You will choose: (who's)   whose

1. who's   whose   4. who's   whose

2. who's   whose   5. who's   whose

3. who's   whose   6. who's   whose

Adjective Clauses **337**

Exercise 34. Looking at grammar. (Chapter 12)

Work in small groups. Change a. through f. to adjective clauses. Take turns completing each sentence.

1. The man _____ is an undercover police officer.
   a. His car was stolen.
      → *The man whose car was stolen*
         is an undercover police officer.
   b. He invited us to his party.
   c. His son broke our car window.
   d. His dog barks all night.
   e. He is standing out in the rain.
   f. His wife is an actress.

2. The nurse _____ is leaving for a trip across the Sahara Desert.
   a. Her picture was in the paper.
   b. Her father climbed Mount Everest.
   c. She helped me when I cut myself.
   d. She works for Dr. Lang.
   e. I found her purse.
   f. I worked with her father.

3. The book _____ is very valuable.
   a. Its pages are torn.
   b. It's on the table.
   c. Sam lost it.
   d. Its cover is missing.
   e. I gave it to you.
   f. I found.

□ **Exercise 35. Looking at grammar.** (Chapter 12)

Complete the sentences with all the correct answers. Use *who, that, Ø, which, whose,* or *whom*.

1. The people __*who / that*__ moved into town are Italian.

2. The lamp __*that / Ø / which*__ I bought downtown is beautiful but quite expensive.

3. Everyone _____ came to the audition got a part in the play.

4. Ms. Rice is the teacher _____ class I enjoy most.

5. The man _____ I found in the doorway had collapsed from heat exhaustion.

6. I like the people with _____ I work.

7. I have a friend _____ father is a famous artist.

8. The camera _____ I bought takes very sharp pictures.

9. Students _____ have part-time jobs have to budget their time very carefully.

10. Flying squirrels _____ live in tropical rain forests stay in the trees their entire lives without ever touching the ground.

11. The people _____ car I dented were a little upset.

12. The person to _____ you should send your application is the Director of Admissions.

13. Monkeys will eat almost anything _____ they can find.

Listen to the conversation. Complete the sentences with *that, which, whose,* or Ø.

CD 2
Track 47
Friendly advice

A: A magazine _____ I saw at the doctor's office had an article
                                       1

   _____ you ought to read. It's about the importance of exercise in
               2

   dealing with stress.

B: Why do you think I should read an article _____ deals with exercise
                                                 3

   and stress?

A: If you stop and think for a minute, you can answer that question yourself. You're under a

   lot of stress, and you don't get any exercise.

B: The stress _____ I have at work doesn't bother me. It's just a normal
                            4

   part of my job. And I don't have time to exercise.

A: Well, you should make time. Anyone _____ job is as stressful as
                                            5

   yours should make physical exercise part of their daily routine.

❏ **Exercise 37. Looking at grammar.** (Chapter 12)
Complete the sentences by making adjective clauses from the statements in the list. Omit the
object pronoun from the adjective clauses if possible.

> Their specialty is heart surgery.
> ✓James chose the color of paint for his bedroom walls.
> Its mouth was big enough to swallow a whole cow in one gulp.
> It erupted in Indonesia.
> His son was in an accident.
> They lived in the jungles of Southeast Asia.
> I slept on it in a hotel last night.

1. The color of paint __*James chose for his bedroom walls*__ was an unusual shade of blue.

2. The man _____

   called an ambulance.

3. My back hurts today. The mattress _____

   was too soft.

4. A volcano _____ killed six people

   and damaged large areas of crops.

5. Doctors and nurses _____

   are some of the best-trained medical personnel in the world.

6. Originally, chickens were wild birds _____.

At some point in time, humans learned how to raise them for food.

7. In prehistoric times, there was a dinosaur _____

_____.

☐ **Exercise 38. Let's talk: interview.** (Chapter 12)
Interview your classmates. Ask two classmates each question. Share their responses with the class and see which answers are the most popular.

1. What is a dessert that you like? → *A dessert that I like is ice cream.*
2. What are some of the cities in the world you would like to visit?
3. What is one of the programs which you like to watch on TV?
4. What is one subject that you would like to know more about?
5. What are some sports you enjoy playing? watching on TV?
6. What is one of the best movies that you've ever seen?
7. What is one of the hardest classes you've ever taken?
8. Who is one of the people that you admire most in the world?

☐ **Exercise 39. Game.** (Chapter 12)
Work in teams. Answer each question with sentences that have adjective clauses. The team that has the most grammatically correct answers wins.

Example: What are the qualities of a good friend?
→ *A good friend is someone who you can depend on in times of trouble.*
→ *A good friend is a person who accepts you as you are.*
→ *A good friend is someone you can trust with secrets.*
→ *Etc.*

1. What is your idea of the ideal roommate?
2. What are the qualities of a good neighbor?
3. What kind of people make good parents?
4. What are the qualities of a good boss and a bad boss?
5. What is your idea of the ideal school?

☐ **Exercise 40. Check your knowledge.** (Chapter 12)
Edit the sentences. Correct the mistakes in adjective clauses.

1. The book that I bought ~~it~~ at the bookstore was very expensive.

2. The woman was nice that I met yesterday.

3. I met a woman who her husband is a famous lawyer.

4. Do you know the people who lives in that house?

5. The professor teaches Chemistry 101 is very good.

6. The people who I painted their house want me to do other work for them.

7. The people who I met them at the party last night were interesting.

8. I enjoyed the music that we listened to it.

9. The apple tree is producing fruit that we planted it last year.

10. Before I came here, I didn't have the opportunity to speak to people who their native language is English.

11. One thing I need to get a new alarm clock.

12. The people who was waiting to buy tickets for the game they were happy because their team had made it to the championship.

☐ **Exercise 41. Reading and writing.** (Chapter 12)

Part I. Read the passage and <u>underline</u> the adjective clauses.

My Friend's Vegan Diet

    I have a friend <u>who is a vegan</u>. As you may know, a vegan is a person who eats no animal products. When I first met him, I didn't understand the vegan diet. I thought *vegan* was another name for *vegetarian*, except that vegans didn't eat eggs. I soon found out I was wrong. The first time I cooked dinner for him, I made a vegetable dish which had a lot of cheese. Since cheese comes from cows, it's not vegan, so he had to scrape it off. I also served him bread that had milk in it and a dessert that was made with ice cream. Unfortunately, there wasn't much that he could eat that night. In the beginning, I had trouble thinking of meals which we could both enjoy. But he is a wonderful cook and showed me how to create delicious vegan meals. I don't know if I'll ever become a complete vegan, but I've learned a lot about the vegan diet and the delicious possibilities it has.

Part II. Write a paragraph about someone you know and something interesting or unusual about his/her life. Try to use a few adjective clauses in your paragraph.

Sample beginnings:
    I have a friend who . . . .
    I know a person who . . . .
    I've heard of a movie star who . . . .

Chapter 13
Gerunds and Infinitives

☐ **Exercise 1. Warm-up.** (Chart 13-1)
Check (✓) all the completions that are true for you.

I enjoy . . .

1. _____ traveling.
2. _____ shopping for clothes.
3. _____ playing sports.
4. _____ watching TV commercials.
5. _____ surfing the Internet.
6. _____ learning about ancient history.

13-1 Verb + Gerund

VERB GERUND (a) I *enjoy walking* in the park.	A gerund is the *-ing* form of a verb. It is used as a noun. In (a): *walking* is a gerund. It is used as the object of the verb *enjoy*.

Common Verbs Followed by Gerunds
enjoy   (b) I *enjoy working* in my garden.
finish   (c) Ann *finished studying* at midnight.
quit   (d) David *quit smoking*.
mind   (e) Would you *mind opening* the window?
postpone (f) I *postponed doing* my homework.
put off   (g) I *put off doing* my homework.
keep (on) (h) *Keep* (on) *working*. Don't stop.
consider (i) I'*m considering going* to Hawaii.
think about (j) I'*m thinking about going* to Hawaii.
discuss   (k) They *discussed getting* a new car.
talk about (l) They *talked about getting* a new car.
	The verbs in the list are followed by gerunds. The list also contains phrasal verbs (e.g., *put off*) that are followed by gerunds.
	
	The verbs in the list are NOT followed by *to* + the simple form of a verb (an infinitive).
	   INCORRECT: *I enjoy to walk in the park.*
	   INCORRECT: *Bob finished to study.*
	   INCORRECT: *I'm thinking to go to Hawaii.*
	
	See Chart 2-2, p. 29, for the spelling of *-ing* verb forms.

(m) I *considered not going* to class.	Negative form: *not* + *gerund*

☐ **Exercise 2. Looking at grammar.** (Chart 13-1)
Complete each sentence with the correct form of a verb from the list.

clean	hand in	sleep
close	hire	smoke
eat	pay	work

1. The Boyds own a bakery. They work seven days a week and they are very tired. They are thinking about . . .
   a. _____ fewer hours a day.
   b. _____ their shop for a few weeks and going on vacation.
   c. _____ more workers for their shop.

2. Joseph wants to live a healthier life. He made several New Year's resolutions. For example, he has quit . . .
   a. _____ cigars
   b. _____ high-fat foods.
   c. _____ until noon on weekends.

3. Martina is a procrastinator.* She puts off . . .
   a. _____ her bills.
   b. _____ her assignments to her teacher.
   c. _____ her apartment.

❑ **Exercise 3. Looking at grammar.** (Chart 13-1)
Complete each sentence with a gerund.

1. We discussed __*going / driving*__ to the ocean for our vacation.

2. The Porters' car is too small for their growing family. They're considering

   _____ a bigger one.

3. When Martha finished _____ the floor, she dusted the furniture.

4. Beth doesn't like her job. She's talking about _____ a different job.

5. A: Are you listening to me?
   B: Yes. Keep _____. I'm listening.

6. A: Do you want to take a break?
   B: No. I'm not tired yet. Let's keep on _____ for another hour or so.

7. A: Would you mind _____ the window?
   B: No problem. I'm too hot too.

❑ **Exercise 4. Listening.** (Chart 13-1)
CD 2
Track 48
Complete each conversation with the words you hear. NOTE: There is a gerund in each completion.

Example: You will hear: A: I enjoy watching sports on TV, especially soccer.
                                        B: Me too.

           You will write: __*enjoy watching*__

1. A: When you _____ your homework, could you help me in the kitchen?
   B: Sure.

*procrastinator = someone who postpones or delays doing things

2. A: Do you have any plans for this weekend?

   B: Henry and I _____ the dinosaur exhibit at the museum.

3. A: I didn't understand the answer. _____ it?

   B: I'd be happy to.

4. A: I'm _____ the meeting tomorrow.

   B: Really? Why? I hope you go. We need your input.

5. A: I've been working on this math problem for the last half hour, and I still don't
      understand it.

   B: Well, don't give up. _____.

☐ **Exercise 5. Warm-up.** (Chart 13-2)
Complete the sentence using the activities in the pictures. Share your answers with a
classmate. Your classmate will report a few of your answers to the class.

When I'm on vacation, I like/don't like to go _____ing.

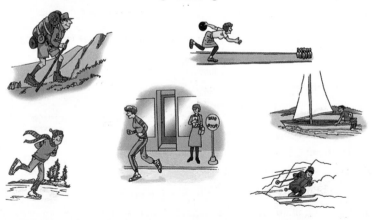

13-2 Go + -ing

(a) *Did* you *go shopping* yesterday?	*Go* is followed by a gerund in certain idiomatic expressions about activities.
(b) I *went swimming* last week.	
(c) Bob *hasn't gone fishing* in years.	NOTE: There is no *to* between *go* and the gerund.
	INCORRECT: *Did you go to shopping?*

Common Expressions with go + -ing

go boating	go dancing	go jogging	go (window) shopping	go (water) skiing
go bowling	go fishing	go running	go sightseeing	go skydiving
go camping	go hiking	go sailing	go (ice) skating	go swimming

Work with a partner. Take turns asking and answering questions. Use the expressions with
go + *-ing* listed in Chart 13-2.

1. Patricia often goes to the beach. She spends hours in the water. What does she like to do?
   → *She likes to go swimming.*
2. Nancy and Frank like to spend the whole day on a lake with poles in their hands. What do they like to do?
3. Last summer Adam went to a national park. He slept in a tent and cooked his food over a fire. What did Adam do last summer?
4. Tim likes to go to stores and buy things. What does he like to do?
5. Laura takes good care of her health. She runs a couple of miles every day. What does Laura do every day? (*There are two possible responses.*)
6. On weekends in the winter, Fred and Jean sometimes drive to a resort in the mountains. They like to race down the side of a mountain in the snow. What do they like to do?
7. Ivan likes to take long walks in the woods. What does Ivan like to do?
8. Sonia prefers indoor sports. She goes to a place where she rolls a 13-pound ball at some wooden pins. What does Sonia often do?
9. Liz and Greg know all the latest dances. What do they probably do a lot?
10. The Taylors are going to go to a little lake near their house tomorrow. The lake is completely frozen now that it's winter. The ice is smooth. What are the Taylors going to do tomorrow?
11. Mariko and Taka live near the ocean. When there's a strong wind, they like to spend the whole day in their sailboat. What do they like to do?
12. Tourists often get on tour buses that take them to see interesting places in an area. What do tourists do on these buses?
13. Colette and Ben like to jump out of airplanes. They don't open their parachutes until the last minute. What do they like to do?
14. What do you like to do for exercise and fun?

❑ **Exercise 7. Let's talk: interview.** (Chart 13-2)
Interview your classmates. Try to find someone who has done each activity. Make a question for each item before you begin the interview. Share some of your answers with the class.

Find someone who . . .
1. has gone skydiving before. → *Have you gone skydiving before?*
2. likes to go waterskiing. → *Do you like to go waterskiing?*
3. likes to go bowling.
4. goes dancing on weekends.
5. goes jogging for exercise.
6. goes fishing in the winter.
7. goes camping in the summer.
8. likes to go snow skiing.

□ **Exercise 8. Warm-up.** (Chart 13-3)

Check (✓) the sentences that are true for you.

1. ____ I hope to move to another town soon.

2. ____ I would like to get married in a few years.

3. ____ I intend to visit another country next year.

4. ____ I'm planning to become an English teacher.

13-3 Verb + Infinitive

(a) Tom *offered to lend* me some money.	Some verbs are followed by an infinitive.
(b) I've *decided to buy* a new car.	Infinitive = *to* + *the simple form of a verb*
(c) I've *decided not to keep* my old car.	Negative form: *not* + *infinitive*

Common Verbs Followed by Infinitives

want	hope	decide	seem	learn (how)
need	expect	promise	appear	try
would like	plan	offer	pretend	
would love	intend	agree		(can't) afford
	mean	refuse		(can't) wait

□ **Exercise 9. Looking at grammar.** (Chart 13-3)

Complete each sentence with the correct form of a word from the list.

be	fly to	hear	lend	visit
buy	get to	hurt	see	watch
eat	go to	leave	tell	

1. I'm planning ___to fly to / to go to___ Chicago next week.

2. Hasan promised not _____ late for the wedding.

3. My husband and I would love _____ Fiji.

4. What time do you expect _____ Chicago?

5. You seem _____ in a good mood today.

6. Nadia appeared _____ asleep, but she wasn't. She was only pretending.

7. Nadia pretended _____ asleep. She pretended not

   _____ me when I spoke to her.

8. The Millers can't afford _____ a house.

9. My friend offered _____ me some money.

10. Tommy doesn't like broccoli. He refuses _____ it.

11. My wife and I wanted to do different things this weekend. Finally, I agreed

     _____ a movie with her Saturday, and she agreed

     _____ the football game with me on Sunday.

broccoli

12. I try _____ class on time every day.

13. I can't wait _____ my family again! It's been a long time.

14. I'm sorry. I didn't mean _____ you.

15. I learned how _____ time when I was six.

□ **Exercise 10. Warm-up.** (Chart 13-4)
Check (✓) the completions that are grammatically correct.

Many children love . . .

1. _____ to eat ice cream.

2. _____ eating ice cream.

3. _____ eat ice cream.

13-4 Verb + Gerund or Infinitive

(a) It *began raining*.	Some verbs are followed by either a gerund, as in (a), or an infinitive, as in (b). Usually there is no difference in meaning.
(b) It *began to rain*.	Examples (a) and (b) have the same meaning.

Common Verbs Followed by Either a Gerund or an Infinitive		
begin	like*	hate
start	love*	can't stand
continue		

*COMPARE: *Like* and *love* can be followed by either a gerund or an infinitive:
   I like going / to go to movies. I love playing / to play chess.
Would like and *would love* are followed by infinitives:
   *I would like **to go** to a movie tonight. I'd love **to play** a game of chess right now.*

□ **Exercise 11. Looking at grammar.** (Chart 13-4)
Choose the correct verbs.

1. It started _____ around midnight.
   a. snow   (b.) snowing   (c.) to snow

2. I continued _____ even though everyone else stopped.
   a. work   b. working   c. to work

3. I like _____ emails from my friends.
   a. get   b. getting   c. to get

4. I would like _____ an email from my son who's away at college.
   a. get   b. getting   c. to get

5. I love _____ to baseball games.
   a. go   b. going   c. to go

6. I would love _____ to the baseball game tomorrow.
   a. go   b. going   c. to go

7. I hate _____ to pushy salespeople.
   a. talk   b. talking   c. to talk

8. I can't stand _____ in long lines.
   a. wait   b. waiting   c. to wait

☐ **Exercise 12. Let's talk: pairwork.** (Charts 13-1 → 13-4)
Work with a partner. Take turns combining the words in the list with the given ideas to make sentences about what you like and don't like to do.

I like	I enjoy	I hate	I don't mind
I love	I don't like	I can't stand	

1. cook
   → *I like to cook. / I like cooking. / I hate to cook. / I hate cooking. / I don't mind cooking. /
   I don't enjoy cooking. / Etc.*
2. live in this city
3. wash dishes
4. wait in airports
5. fly
6. eat food slowly
7. speak in front of a large group
8. drive in the city during rush hour
9. go to parties where I don't know anyone
10. listen to music while I'm trying to fall asleep
11. get in between two friends who are having an argument
12. travel to unusual places

☐ **Exercise 13. Grammar and speaking.** (Charts 13-1 → 13-4)
Complete each sentence with the infinitive or gerund form of the verb in parentheses. Then agree or disagree with the statement. Discuss your answers.

What do you do when you can't understand a native English speaker?

1. I pretend (*understand*) _____.   yes   no

2. I keep on (*listen*) _____ politely.   yes   no

3. I think, "I can't wait (get) _____ out of here!" OR   yes   no

   "I can't wait for this person (stop) _____ talking."   yes   no

4. I say, "Would you mind (repeat) _____ that?"   yes   no

5. I begin (nod) _____ my head so I look like I understand.   yes   no

6. I start (look) _____ at my watch, so it appears I'm in a hurry. yes   no

7. As soon as the person finishes (speak) _____,   yes   no
   I say I have to leave.

☐ **Exercise 14. Looking at grammar.** (Charts 13-1 → 13-4)
Complete the sentences with the infinitive or gerund form of the verbs in parentheses.

1. We finished (eat) _____ around seven.

2. My roommate offered (help) _____ me with my English.

3. I'm considering (move) _____ to a new apartment.

4. Some children hate (go) _____ to school.

5. What seems (be) _____ the problem?

6. I don't mind (live) _____ with four roommates.

7. My boss refused (give) _____ me a raise, so I quit.

8. That's not what I meant! I meant (say) _____ just the opposite.

9. Julia can't stand (sleep) _____ in a room with all of the windows
   closed.

10. Max seemed (want) _____ (leave) _____ the
    party, but he kept (talk) _____ anyway.

11. Sam's tomato crop always failed. Finally he quit (try) _____ to grow
    tomatoes in his garden.

☐ **Exercise 15. Let's talk: pairwork.** (Charts 13-1 → 13-4)
Work with a partner. Take turns completing the sentences with **to go/going** + *a place*.

Example: I would like . . . .
PARTNER A: I **would like to go** to the Beach Café for dinner tonight.
PARTNER B: I **would like to go** to the movies later today.

1. I like . . . .
2. I love . . . .
3. I'd love . . . .
4. I refuse . . . .
5. I expect . . . .
6. I promised . . . .
7. I can't stand . . . .
8. I waited . . . .
9. I am thinking about . . . .
10. Are you considering . . . ?
11. I can't afford . . . .
12. Would you mind . . . ?
13. My friend and I agreed . . . .
14. I hate . . . .
15. I don't enjoy . . . .
16. My friend and I discussed . . . .
17. I've decided . . . .
18. I don't mind . . . .
19. Sometimes I put off . . . .
20. I can't wait . . . .

☐ **Exercise 16. Looking at grammar.** (Charts 13-1 → 13-4)
Complete the sentences with the infinitive or gerund form of the verbs in parentheses.

1. I want (*relax*) _____ tonight.

2. I want (*stay*) _____ home and (*relax*)★ _____
   tonight.

3. I want (*stay*) _____ home, (*relax*) _____, and
   (*go*) _____ to bed early tonight.

4. I enjoy (*get*) _____ up early in the morning and (*watch*)
   _____ the sunrise.

5. I enjoy (*get*) _____ up early in the morning, (*watch*)
   _____ the sunrise, and (*listen*) _____ to the birds.

6. Mr. and Mrs. Bashir are thinking about (*sell*) _____ their old house
   and (*buy*) _____ a new one.

7. Kathy plans (*move*) _____ to New York City, (*find*)
   _____ a job, and (*start*) _____ a new life.

★When infinitives are connected by **and**, it is not necessary to repeat **to**.
   Example: *I need to **stay** home and (to) **study** tonight.*

8. Do you like (*go*) _____ out to eat and (*let*) _____

   someone else do the cooking?

9. Kevin is thinking about (*quit*) _____ his job and (*go*)

   _____ back to school.

10. Before you leave the office tonight, would you mind (*unplug*) _____

    the coffee pot, (*turn off*) _____ all the lights, and (*lock*)

    _____ the door?

❑ **Exercise 17. Game.** (Charts 13-1 → 13-4)
Work in teams. Your teacher will call out an item number. Make a sentence using the given words and any verb tense. Begin with *I*. The first team to come up with a grammatically correct sentence wins a point. The team with the most points wins the game.

Example: want \ go
> ▸ *I want to go to New York City next week.*

1. plan \ go	11. postpone \ go
2. consider \ go	12. finish \ study
3. offer \ help	13. would mind \ help
4. like \ visit	14. begin \ study
5. enjoy \ read	15. think about \ go
6. intend \ get	16. quit \ try
7. can't afford \ buy	17. continue \ walk
8. seem \ be	18. learn \ speak
9. put off \ write	19. talk about \ go
10. would like \ go \ swim	20. keep \ try

❑ **Exercise 18. Warm-up.** (Chart 13-5)
Agree or disagree with the statements. Notice the use of the prepositions and gerunds in green that follow the verbs.

I know someone who . . .

1. never *apologizes* for being late.	yes	no
2. is *interested* in coming to this country.	yes	no
3. is *worried* about losing his/her job.	yes	no
4. is *excited* about becoming a parent.	yes	no

13-5 Preposition + Gerund

(a) Kate *insisted **on coming*** with us. (b) We're *excited **about going*** to Tahiti. (c) I *apologized **for being*** late.	A preposition is followed by a gerund, not an infinitive. In (a): The preposition (*on*) is followed by a gerund (*coming*).

Common Expressions with Prepositions Followed by Gerunds

be afraid **of** (doing something) apologize **for** believe **in** dream **about/of** be excited **about** feel **like** forgive (someone) **for**	be good **at** insist **on** instead **of** be interested **in** look forward **to** be nervous **about** plan **on**	be responsible **for** stop (someone) **from** thank (someone) **for** be tired **of** worry **about**/be worried **about**

❑ **Exercise 19. Looking at grammar.** (Charts 13-5 and C-2)
Complete the sentences with a *preposition + gerund* and the given words.

1. I'm looking forward   +   go away for the weekend
    → I'*m looking forward **to** going away for the weekend.*

2. Thank you	+	hold the door open
3. I'm worried	+	be late for my appointment
4. Are you interested	+	go to the beach with us
5. I apologized	+	be late
6. Are you afraid	+	fly in small planes
7. Are you nervous	+	take your driver's test
8. We're excited	+	see the soccer game
9. Tariq insisted	+	pay the restaurant bill
10. Eva dreams	+	become a veterinarian someday
11. I don't feel	+	eat right now
12. Please forgive me	+	not write sooner
13. I'm tired	+	live with five roommates
14. I believe	+	be honest at all times
15. Let's plan	+	meet at the restaurant at six
16. Who's responsible	+	clean the classroom
17. The police stopped us	+	enter the building
18. Jake's not very good	+	cut his own hair

❑ **Exercise 20. Let's talk: pairwork.** (Charts 13-5 and C-2)
Work with a partner. Take turns asking and answering questions using the following pattern:
***What** + the given words + preposition + **doing**.*

Example: be looking forward
PARTNER A: What are you looking forward **to doing**?
PARTNER B: I'm looking forward **to going to a movie tonight**.

1. be interested
2. be worried
3. thank your friend
4. apologize
5. be afraid

6. be nervous
7. be excited
8. feel
9. plan
10. be tired

❑ **Exercise 21. Looking at grammar.** (Charts 13-5 and C-2)
Complete each sentence with the correct preposition and the gerund form of the verb in parentheses.

1. Carlos is nervous ___about___ (*meet*) ___meeting___ his girlfriend's parents for the first time.

2. I believe _____ (*tell*) _____ the truth no matter what.

3. I don't go swimming in deep water because I'm afraid _____ (*drown*)
   _____.

4. Every summer, I look forward _____ (*take*) _____ a vacation with my family.

5. Do you feel _____ (*tell*) _____ me why you're so sad?

6. My father-in-law always insists _____ (*pay*) _____ for everything when we go out for dinner.

7. I want you to know that I'm sorry. I don't know if you can ever forgive me _____
   (*cause*) _____ you so much trouble.

8. I'm not very good _____ (*remember*) _____ people's names.

9. How do you stop someone _____ (*do*) _____ something you know is wrong?

10. The kids are responsible _____ (*take*) _____ out the garbage.

11. Monique lost her job. That's why she is afraid _____ (*have, not*) _____
    _____ enough money to pay her rent.

12. Sheila is pregnant. She's looking forward _____ (*have*) _____ another child.

13. A: I'm not happy in my work. I often dream _____ (*quit*) _____ my job.

    B: Instead _____ (*quit*) _____ your job, why don't you see if you can transfer to another department?

Exercise 22. Listening. (Charts 13-1 → 13-5)

Listen to the conversation. Then listen again and complete the sentences with the words you hear.

CD 2
Track 49

A: Have you made any vacation plans?

B: Well, I _____ home because I don't like _____.
$\qquad$ 1 $\qquad$ 2

I hate _____ and _____ suitcases. But my wife
$\qquad$ 3 $\qquad$ 4

loves _____ and _____ a boat trip somewhere.
$\qquad$ 5 $\qquad$ 6

A: So, what are you going to do?

B: Well, we couldn't agree, so we _____ home and
$\qquad$ 7

_____ tourists in our own town.
8

A: Interesting. What are you planning _____?
9

B: Well, we haven't seen the new Museum of Space yet. There's also a new art exhibit

downtown. And my wife _____ a boat trip in
10

the harbor. Actually, when we _____ about it, we
11

discovered there were lots of things to do.

A: Sounds like a great solution!

B: Yeah, we're both really _____ more of our
12

own town.

❏ **Exercise 23. Warm-up.** (Chart 13-6)

Circle the completions that are true for you.

1. I sometimes pay for things _____ .
   a. by credit card   b. by check   c. in cash

2. I usually come to school _____ .
   a. by bus   b. by car   c. on foot

3. My favorite way to travel long distances is _____ .
   a. by plane   b. by boat   c. by train

4. I like to communicate with my family _____ .
   a. by email   b. by phone   c. in person

13-6 Using *By* and *With* to Express How Something Is Done

(a) Pat turned off the TV *by pushing* the "off" button.	*By* + *a gerund* is used to express how something is done.
(b) Mary goes to work *by bus*. (c) Andrea stirred her coffee *with a spoon*.	*By* or *with* followed by a noun is also used to express how something is done.

BY IS USED FOR MEANS OF TRANSPORTATION AND COMMUNICATION

by (air)plane	by subway*	by mail/email	by air
by boat	by taxi	by (tele)phone	by land
by bus	by train	by fax	by sea
by car	by foot (*or:* on foot)	(*but:* in person)	

OTHER USES OF BY

by chance	by mistake	by check (*but:* in cash)
by choice	by hand**	by credit card

WITH IS USED FOR INSTRUMENTS OR PARTS OF THE BODY
I cut down the tree *with an ax* (by using an ax).
I swept the floor *with a broom*.
She pointed to a spot on the map *with her finger*.

* *by subway* = American English; *by underground, by tube* = British English.

**The expression *by hand* is usually used to mean that something was made by a person, not by a machine: *This rug was made by hand.* (A person, not a machine, made this rug.)
COMPARE: *I touched his shoulder with my hand.*

❑ **Exercise 24. Looking at grammar.** (Chart 13-6)
Complete the sentences by using *by* + *a gerund*. Use the words in the list or your own words.

eat	smile	wag	wave
drink	stay	wash	✓write
guess	take	watch	

1. Students practice written English __*by writing*__ compositions.

2. We clean our clothes _____ them in soap and water.

3. Khalid improved his English _____ a lot of TV.

4. We show other people we are happy _____.

5. We satisfy our hunger _____ something.

6. We quench our thirst _____ something.

7. I figured out what *quench* means _____.

8. Alex caught my attention _____ his arms in the air.

9. My dog shows me she is happy _____ her tail.

10. Carmen recovered from her cold _____ in bed and

_____ care of herself.

□ **Exercise 25. Looking at grammar.** (Chart 13-6)
Complete the sentences. Use **with** and words in the list.

✓a broom	a pair of scissors	a spoon
a hammer	a saw	a thermometer
a needle and thread	a shovel	

1. I swept the floor ___with a broom___.

2. I sewed a button on my shirt _____.

3. I cut the wood _____.

4. I took my temperature _____.

5. I stirred cream in my coffee _____.

6. I dug a hole in the garden _____.

7. I nailed two pieces of wood together _____.

8. I cut the paper _____.

□ **Exercise 26. Looking at grammar.** (Chart 13-6)
Complete the sentences with **by** or **with**.

1. I opened the door ___with___ a key.

2. I went downtown ___by___ bus.

3. I dried the dishes _____ a dishtowel.

4. I went from Frankfurt to Vienna _____ train.

5. Ted drew a straight line _____ a ruler.

6. Rebecca tightened the screw in the corner of her eyeglasses _____ her fingernail.

7. I called Bill "Paul" _____ mistake.

8. I sent a copy of the contract _____ fax.

9. Talya protected her eyes from the sun _____ her hand.

10. My grandmother makes tablecloths _____ hand.

Exercise 27. Warm-up. (Chart 13-7)
Read the passage and then agree or disagree with the statements.

A White Lie

Jane gave her friend Lisa a book for her birthday. When Lisa opened it, she tried to look excited, but her husband had already given her the same book. Lisa had just finished reading it, but she thanked Jane and said she was looking forward to reading it. Lisa told a "white lie." White lies are minor or unimportant lies that a person often tells to avoid hurting someone else's feelings.

1. Telling white lies is common.	yes	no
2. It is sometimes acceptable to tell a white lie.	yes	no
3. I sometimes tell white lies.	yes	no

13-7 Using Gerunds as Subjects; Using *It* + Infinitive

(a) **Riding** horses is fun.	Examples (a) and (b) have the same meaning.
(b) **It** is fun **to ride** horses.	In (a): A gerund (**riding**) is the subject of the sentence.
	Notice: The verb (*is*) is singular because a gerund is singular.*
(c) **Coming** to class on time is important.	In (b): **It** is used as the subject of the sentence. **It** has the same
(d) **It** is important **to come** to class on time.	meaning as the infinitive phrase at the end of the sentence: **it** means **to ride horses.**

*It is also correct (but less common) to use an infinitive as the subject of a sentence: *To ride horses is fun.*

❑ **Exercise 28. Grammar and speaking: pairwork.** (Chart 13-7)
Make sentences with the same meaning as the given sentences, and then decide if you agree with them. Circle *yes* or *no*. Share your answers with a partner.

Living in this town

Part I. Use a gerund as the subject.

1. It's hard to meet people here. → *Meeting people here is hard.*	yes	no
2. It takes time to make friends here.	yes	no
3. It is easy to get around the town.	yes	no
4. Is it expensive to live here?	yes	no

Part II. Use **it** + an infinitive.

5. Finding things to do on weekends is hard. → *It's hard to find things to do on weekends.*	yes	no
6. Walking alone at night is dangerous.	yes	no
7. Exploring this town is fun.	yes	no
8. Is finding affordable housing difficult?	yes	no

❑ **Exercise 29. Let's talk: interview.** (Chart 13-7)
Interview your classmates. Ask a question and then agree or disagree with your classmate's answer. Practice using both gerunds and infinitives in your answers.

Example:
SPEAKER A (*book open*): Which is easier: to make money or to spend money?
SPEAKER B (*book closed*): It's easier to spend money than (it is) to make money.
SPEAKER A (*book open*): I agree. Spending money is easier than making money. OR
I don't agree. I think that making money is easier than spending money.

1. Which is more fun: to visit a big city or to spend time in the countryside?
2. Which is more difficult: to write English or to read English?
3. Which is easier: to understand spoken English or to speak it?
4. Which is more expensive: to go to a movie or to go to a concert?
5. Which is more comfortable: to wear shoes or to go barefoot?
6. Which is more satisfying: to give gifts or to receive them?
7. Which is more dangerous: to ride in a car or to ride in an airplane?
8. Which is more important: to come to class on time or to get an extra hour of sleep in the morning?

❑ **Exercise 30. Warm-up.** (Chart 13-8)
Agree or disagree with these statements.

In my culture . . .

1. it is common for people to shake hands when they meet.   yes   no

2. it is important for people to look one another in the eye when
   they are introduced.   yes   no

3. it is strange for people to kiss one another on the cheek when they meet. yes   no

13-8 *It* + Infinitive: Using *For* (*Someone*)

(a) *You* should study hard. (b) It is important *for you* to study hard. (c) *Mary* should study hard. (d) It is important *for Mary* to study hard. (e) *We* don't have to go to the meeting. (f) It isn't necessary *for us* to go to the meeting. (g) *A dog* can't talk. (h) It is impossible *for a dog* to talk.	Examples (a) and (b) have a similar meaning. Notice the pattern in (b): ***It is*** *+ adjective +* ***for*** *(someone) + infinitive phrase*

□ **Exercise 31. Looking at grammar.** (Chart 13-8)
Complete the sentences with the given information. Use *for* (*someone*) and an infinitive phrase in each completion.

1. Students should do their homework.

   It's really important ___*for students to do their homework*___.

2. Teachers should speak clearly.

   It's very important _____.

3. We don't have to hurry. There's plenty of time.

   It isn't necessary _____.

4. A fish can't live out of water for more than a few minutes.

   It's impossible _____.

5. Working parents have to budget their time carefully.

   It's necessary _____.

6. A young child usually can't sit still for a long time.

   It's difficult _____.

7. My family spends birthdays together.

   It's traditional _____.

8. My brother would love to travel to Mars someday.

   Will it be possible _____ to Mars someday?

9. I usually can't understand Mr. Alvarez. He talks too fast. How about you?

   Is it easy _____?

□ **Exercise 32. Let's talk.** (Charts 13-7 and 13-8)
Work in small groups. Make sentences by combining the given ideas with the words in the list. Use gerunds as subjects or *it* + *an infinitive*. Share some of your sentences for other groups to agree or disagree with.

boring	embarrassing ·	hard	impossible	scary
dangerous	exciting	illegal	interesting	waste of time
educational	fun	important	relaxing	

Example: ride a bicycle
→ *Riding a bicycle is fun.* OR *It's fun to ride a bicycle.*

1. ride a roller coaster
2. read newspapers
3. study economics
4. drive five miles over the speed limit
5. walk in a cemetery at night
6. know the meaning of every word in a dictionary
7. never tell a lie
8. visit museums

Gerunds and Infinitives **359**

□ **Exercise 33. Reading and grammar.** (Charts 13-7 and 13-8)
Part I. Read the passage.

Body Language

Different cultures use different body language. In some countries, when people meet one another, they offer a strong handshake and look the other person straight in the eye. In other countries, however, it is impolite to shake hands firmly, and it is equally rude to look a person in the eye.

How close do people stand to another person when they are speaking to each other? This varies from country to country. In the United States and Canada, people prefer standing just a little less than an arm's length from someone. But many people in the Middle East and Latin America like moving in closer during a conversation.

Smiling at another person is a universal, cross-cultural gesture. Although people may smile more frequently in some countries than in others, people around the world understand the meaning of a smile.

Part II. Complete the sentences with information about body language.

1. In some countries, it is important _____.

2. In some countries, _____ is impolite.

3. In my country, _____ is important.

4. In my country, it is impolite _____.

□ **Exercise 34. Warm-up.** (Chart 13-9)
Check (✓) all the sentences that are grammatically correct.

1. ____ I went to the store because I wanted to buy groceries.
2. ____ I went to the store in order to buy groceries.
3. ____ I went to the store to buy groceries.
4. ____ I went to the store for groceries.
5. ____ I went to the store for to buy groceries.

13-9 Expressing Purpose with *In Order To* and *For*

—Why did you go to the post office? (a) I went to the post office *because I wanted to mail a letter.* (b) I went to the post office *in order to* mail a letter. (c) I went to the post office *to mail* a letter.	*In order to* expresses purpose. It answers the question "Why?"
	In (c): *in order* is frequently omitted. Examples (a), (b), and (c) have the same meaning.
(d) I went to the post office *for* some stamps. (e) I went to the post office *to buy* some stamps. INCORRECT: *I went to the post office for to buy some stamps.* INCORRECT: *I went to the post office for buying some stamps.*	*For* is also used to express purpose, but it is a preposition and is followed by a noun phrase, as in (d).

❏ **Exercise 35. Looking at grammar.** (Chart 13-9)
Make sentences by combining the phrases in Column A with those in Column B. Connect the ideas with (*in order*) *to*.

Example: I called the hotel desk . . .
→ *I called the hotel desk (in order) to ask for an extra pillow.*

Column A

1. I called the hotel desk __e__.
2. I turned on the radio _____.
3. Andy went to Egypt _____.
4. People wear boots _____.
5. I looked on the Internet _____.
6. Ms. Lane stood on her tiptoes _____.
7. The dentist moved the light closer to my face _____.
8. I clapped my hands and yelled _____.
9. Maria took a walk in the park _____.
10. I offered my cousin some money _____.

Column B

a. keep their feet warm and dry
b. reach the top shelf
c. listen to a ball game
d. find the population of Malaysia
✓e. ask for an extra pillow
f. chase a mean dog away
g. help her pay the rent
h. get some fresh air and exercise
i. see the ancient pyramids
j. look into my mouth

❏ **Exercise 36. Looking at grammar.** (Chart 13-9)
Add *in order* to the sentences whenever possible.

1. I went to the bank to cash a check. → *I went to the bank in order to cash a check.*
2. I'd like to see that movie. → (*No change. The infinitive does not express purpose.*)
3. Steve went to the hospital to visit a friend.
4. I need to go to the bank today.
5. I need to go to the bank today to deposit my paycheck.
6. On my way home, I stopped at the store to buy some shampoo.
7. Masako went to the cafeteria to eat lunch.
8. Jack and Katya have decided to get married.
9. Pedro watches TV to improve his English.
10. I didn't forget to pay my rent.
11. Donna expects to graduate next spring.
12. Jerry needs to go to the bookstore to buy school supplies.

□ **Exercise 37. Looking at grammar.** (Chart 13-9)
Complete the sentences with *to* or *for*.

1. I went to Chicago ___*for*___ a visit.

2. I went to Chicago ___*to*___ visit my aunt and uncle.

3. I take long walks _____ relax.

4. I take long walks _____ relaxation.

5. I'm going to school _____ a good education.

6. I'm going to school _____ get a good education.

7. I sent a card to Carol _____ wish her a happy birthday.

8. Two police officers came to my apartment _____ ask me about a neighbor.

9. I looked on the Internet _____ information about Ecuador.

10. My three brothers, two sisters, and parents all came to town _____ my graduation.

□ **Exercise 38. Reading and grammar.** (Charts 13-1 → 13-9)
Part I. Read the passage.

Car Sharing

In hundreds of cities around the world, people can use a car without actually owning one. It's known as car sharing.

Car sharing works like this: people pay a fee to join a car-share organization. These organizations have cars available in different parts of a city 24 hours a day. Members make reservations for a car, and then go to one of several parking lots in the city to pick up the car. They pay an hourly or daily rate for driving it. They may also pay a charge for every mile/kilometer they drive. When they are finished, they return the car to a parking area for someone else to use.

Car sharing works well for several reasons. Some people only need to drive occasionally. Oftentimes, people only need a car for special occasions like moving items or taking long trips. Many people don't want the costs or responsibilities of owning a car. The car-share organization pays for gas, insurance, cleaning, and maintenance costs. Members also don't have to wait in line or fill out forms in order to get a car. They know a variety of cars will be available when they need one.

Car sharing also benefits the environment. People drive only when they need to, and fewer cars on the road means less traffic and air pollution. As more and more cities become interested in reducing traffic, car-share programs are becoming an effective alternative.

Part II. Complete the sentences with information from Part I. Use gerunds or infinitives.

1. _____ is helpful to people who don't own a car.

2. People pay a fee in order _____ a car-sharing organization.

3. Car-sharing members pay an hourly or daily rate for _____ a car.

4. Sometimes people need a car _____ furniture or to _____ a trip.

5. Many people don't want the costs of _____ a car.

Part III. Answer the questions.

1. What are three reasons that people car share?
2. What are two benefits of car sharing?
3. Does the city you live in have a form of car sharing? If yes, has it been successful? If not, why do you think there is no car-sharing program?

☐ **Exercise 39. Warm-up: pairwork.** (Chart 13-10)
Work with a partner. Read the conversation aloud and complete the sentences with the correct words in the list.

strong	heavy	strength

PARTNER A: Can you pick up a piano?

PARTNER B: No. It's too _____ for me to pick up. How about you?
                                    1
Can you pick up a piano?

PARTNER A: No, I'm not _____ enough to pick one up. What about the
                                    2
class? Can we pick up a piano together?

PARTNER B: Maybe. We might have enough _____ to do that as a class.
                                                              3

13-10 Using Infinitives with *Too* and *Enough*

too + adjective + (*for someone*) + infinitive					Infinitives often follow expressions with **too**. **Too** comes in front of an adjective. In the speaker's mind, the use of **too** implies a negative result.
(a)	That box is	**too** *heavy*		*to lift.*	
(b)	A piano is	**too** *heavy*	*for me*	*to lift.*	
(c)	That box is	**too** *heavy*	*for Bob*	*to lift.*	

enough + noun + infinitive				COMPARE: *The box is too heavy. I can't lift it.* *The box is very heavy, but I can lift it.*
(d)	I don't have	**enough** *money*	*to buy* that car.	
(e)	Did you have	**enough** *time*	*to finish* the test?	

adjective + enough + infinitive				Infinitives often follow expressions with **enough**. **Enough** comes in front of a noun.* **Enough** follows an adjective.
(f)	Jimmy isn't	*old* **enough**	*to go* to school.	
(g)	Are you	*hungry* **enough**	*to eat* three sandwiches?	

*__*Enough__ can also follow a noun: *I don't have **money enough** to buy that car.* In everyday English, however, **enough** usually comes in front of a noun.*

❏ **Exercise 40. Looking at grammar.** (Chart 13-10)
Complete the sentences with the given words. Use *too* or *enough* + *an infinitive.*

1. strong/lift   I'm not <u> *strong enough to lift* </u> a refrigerator.

2. weak/lift   Most people are <u> *too weak to lift* </u> a refrigerator without help.

3. busy/answer   I was _____ the phone. I let the call go to voice mail.

4. early/get   I got to the concert _____ good seats.

5. full/hold   My suitcase is _____

          _____ any more clothes.

6. large/hold   My suitcase isn't _____

all the clothes I want to take on my trip.

7. big/get   Rex is _____

into the doghouse.

8. big/hold   Julie's purse is _____

          _____ her dog Pepper.

Exercise 41. Looking at grammar. (Chart 13-10)
Combine each pair of sentences.

Part I. Use *too*.

1. We can't go swimming today. It's very cold.
   → *It's **too** cold (for us) **to go** swimming today.*
2. I couldn't finish my homework last night. I was very sleepy.
3. Mike couldn't go to his aunt's housewarming party. He was very busy.
4. This jacket is very small. I can't wear it.
5. I live far from school. I can't walk there.

Part II. Use *enough*.

6. I can't reach the top shelf. I'm not that tall.
   → *I'm not tall **enough to reach** the top shelf.*
7. I can't move this furniture. I'm not that strong.
8. It's not warm today. You can't go outside without a coat.
9. I didn't stay home and miss work. I wasn't really sick, but I didn't feel good all day.

□ **Exercise 42. Let's talk: pairwork.** (Chart 13-10)
Work with a partner. Take turns completing the sentences with infinitives.

1. I'm too short . . . .
2. I'm not tall enough . . . .
3. I'm not strong enough . . . .
4. Last night I was too tired . . . .
5. Yesterday I was too busy . . . .
6. A Mercedes-Benz is too expensive . . . .
7. I don't have enough money . . . .
8. Yesterday I didn't have enough time . . . .
9. A teenager is old enough . . . but too young . . . .
10. I know enough English . . . but not enough . . . .

□ **Exercise 43. Looking at grammar.** (Chapter 13)
Complete each sentence with the gerund or infinitive form of the word in parentheses.

1. It's difficult for me (*remember*) __*to remember*__ phone numbers.

2. My cat is good at (*catch*) __*catching*__ mice.

3. I called my friend (*invite*) _____ her for dinner.

4. Fatima talked about (*go*) _____ to graduate school.

5. Sarosh found out what was happening by (*listen*) _____ carefully to everything that was said.

6. Michelle works 16 hours a day in order (*earn*) _____ enough money (*take*) _____ care of her elderly parents and her three children.

7. No matter how wonderful a trip is, it's always good (*get*) _____ back home and (*sleep*) _____ in your own bed.

8. I keep (*forget*) _____ to call my friend Jae. I'd better write myself a note.

9. Exercise is good for you. Why don't you walk up the stairs instead of (*use*) _____ the elevator?

☐ **Exercise 44. Listening.** (Chapter 13)
Listen to each item. Then listen again and complete the sentences with the words you hear.

CD 2
Track 50

1. My professor goes through the lecture material too quickly. It is difficult for us _____ him. He needs _____ down and _____ us time to understand the key points.

2. _____ others about themselves and their lives is one of the secrets of _____ along with other people. If you want to make and _____ friends, it is important _____ sincerely interested in other people's lives.

3. Large bee colonies have 80,000 workers. These worker bees must visit 50 million flowers _____ one kilogram, or 2.2 pounds, of honey. It's easy _____ why "busy as a bee" is a common expression.

☐ **Exercise 45. Reading and grammar.** (Chapter 13)
Part I. Read the passage.

Uncle Ernesto

Have you ever had an embarrassing experience? My Uncle Ernesto did a few years ago while on a business trip in Norway.

Uncle Ernesto is a businessman from Buenos Aires, Argentina. He manufactures equipment for ships and needs to travel around the world to sell his products. Last year, he went to Norway to meet with a shipping company. While he was there, he found himself in an uncomfortable situation.

Uncle Ernesto was staying at a small hotel in Oslo. One morning, as he was getting ready to take a shower, he heard a knock at the door. He opened it, but no one was there. He stepped into the hallway. He still didn't see anyone, so he turned to go back to his room. Unfortunately, the door was locked. This was a big problem because he didn't have his key and he was wearing only a towel.

Instead of standing in the hallway like this, he decided to get help at the front desk and started walking toward the elevator. He hoped it would be empty, but it wasn't. He took a deep breath and got in. The other people in the elevator were surprised when they saw a man who was wrapped in a towel.

Uncle Ernesto thought about trying to explain his problem, but unfortunately he didn't know Norwegian. He knew a little English, so he said, "Door. Locked. No key." A businessman in the elevator nodded, but he wasn't smiling. Another man looked at Uncle Ernesto and smiled broadly.

The elevator seemed to move very slowly for Uncle Ernesto, but it finally reached the ground floor. He walked straight to the front desk and looked at the hotel manager helplessly. The hotel manager didn't have to understand any language to figure out the problem. He grabbed a key and led my uncle to the nearest elevator.

My uncle is still embarrassed about this incident. But he laughs a lot when he tells the story.

Part II. Check (✓) all the sentences that are grammatically correct.

1. a. _____ Uncle Ernesto went to Norway for a business meeting.
    b. _____ Uncle Ernesto went to Norway to have a business meeting.
    c. _____ Uncle Ernesto went to Norway for having a business meeting.

2. a. _____ Is necessary for him to travel in order to sell his products.
    b. _____ To sell his products, he needs to travel.
    c. _____ In order to sell his products, he needs to travel.

3. a. _____ Instead staying in the hall, he decided to get help.
    b. _____ Instead of staying in the hall, he decided to get help.
    c. _____ Instead to stay in the hall, he decided to get help.

4. a. _____ Uncle Ernesto thought about trying to explain his problem.
    b. _____ Uncle Ernesto considered about trying to explain his problem.
    c. _____ Uncle Ernesto decided not to explain his problem.

5. a. _____ It wasn't difficult for the hotel manager figuring out the problem.
    b. _____ It wasn't difficult for the hotel manager figure out the problem.
    c. _____ It wasn't difficult for the hotel manager to figure out the problem.

□ **Exercise 46. Let's write.** (Chapter 13)

Read the sample paragraph. Then write a paragraph about one of the most embarrassing experiences you have had in your life. Include some gerunds and infinitives in your writing.

Example:

My Most Embarrassing Experience

My most embarrassing experience happened at work. One morning, I was in a hurry to get to my office, so I quickly said good-bye to my wife. She knew I was planning to give an important presentation at my firm, so she wished me good luck and kissed me on the cheek. Because traffic was heavy, I got to work a few minutes after the meeting had begun. I quietly walked in and sat down. A few people looked at me strangely, but I thought it was because I was late. During my presentation, I got more stares. I began to think my presentation wasn't very good, but I continued speaking. As soon as my talk was over, I went to the restroom. When I looked in the mirror, it wasn't hard to see the problem. There was smudge of red lipstick on my cheek. I felt pretty embarrassed, but later in the day I started laughing about it and tried not to take myself so seriously.

□ **Exercise 47. Check your knowledge.** (Chapter 13)

Edit the sentences. Correct the errors in the use of infinitives, gerunds, prepositions, and word order.

             to get
1. It is important ~~getting~~ an education.

2. I went to the bank for cashing a check.

3. Did you go to shopping yesterday?

4. I cut the rope by a knife.

5. I thanked my friend for drive me to the airport.

6. Is difficult to learn another language.

7. Timmy isn't enough old to get married.

8. Is easy this exercise to do.

9. Last night too tired no do my homework.

10. I've never gone to sailing, but I would like to.

11. Reading it is one of my hobbies.

12. The teenagers began to built a campfire to keep themselves warm.

13. Instead of settle down in one place, I'd like to travel around the world.

14. I enjoy to travel because you learn so much about other countries and cultures.

15. My grandmother likes to fishing.

16. Martina would like to has a big family.

Chapter 14
Noun Clauses

(Chart 14-1)

❑ **Exercise 1. Warm-up.** (Chart 14-1)

Check (✓) all the sentences that are grammatically correct.

1. _____ How much does this book cost?

2. _____ I don't know.

3. _____ How much this books costs?

4. _____ I don't know how much this book costs.

14-1 Noun Clauses: Introduction

S V O
(a) I know ⌐his address.⌐
(noun phrase)
S V O
(b) I know ⌐where he lives.⌐
(noun clause)
	Verbs are often followed by objects. The object is usually a noun phrase.*
	In (a): **his address** is a noun phrase;
	    his address is the object of the verb *know*.
	
	Some verbs can be followed by noun clauses.*
	In (b): **where he lives** is a noun clause;
	    where he lives is the object of the verb *know*.

O S V ⌐S V⌐ (c) I know *where he lives.*	A noun clause has its own subject and verb. In (c): **he** is the subject of the noun clause; **lives** is the verb of the noun clause.
(d) I know **where my book is**. (noun clause)	A noun clause can begin with a question word. (See Chart 14-2.)
(e) I don't know **if Ed is married**. (noun clause)	A noun clause can begin with **if** or **whether**. (See Chart 14-3.)
(f) I know **that the world is round**. (noun clause)	A noun clause can begin with **that**. (See Chart 14-4.)

*A *phrase* is a group of related words. It does NOT contain a subject and a verb.

A *clause* is a group of related words. It contains a subject and a verb.

❑ **Exercise 2. Looking at grammar.** (Chart 14-1)

<u>Underline</u> the noun clauses. Some sentences have no noun clauses.

1. Where are the Smiths living?

2. I don't know where the Smiths are living.

3. We don't know what city they moved to.

4. We know that they moved a month ago.

5. Are they coming back?

6. I don't know if they are coming back.

Exercise 3. Warm-up: pairwork. (Chart 14-2)

Work with a partner. Ask and answer the questions. Make true statements.

1. PARTNER A: Where do I live?
   PARTNER B: I *know / don't know* where you live.

2. PARTNER B: Where does our teacher live?
   PARTNER A: I *know / don't know* where our teacher lives.

3. PARTNER B: In your last sentence, why is "does" missing?
   PARTNER A: I *know / don't know* why "does" is missing.

4. PARTNER A: In the same sentence, why does "lives" have an "s"?
   PARTNER B: I *know / don't know* why "lives" has an "s."

14-2 Noun Clauses That Begin with a Question Word

These question words can be used to introduce a noun clause: **when**, **where**, **why**, **how**, **who**, (**whom**), **what**, **which**, **whose**.

Information Question	Noun Clause	Notice in the examples: Usual question word order is NOT used in a noun clause.
Where *does he live?*	(a) I don't know *where he lives*. S V	INCORRECT: *I know where does he live.* CORRECT: *I know where he lives.*
When *did they leave?*	(b) Do you know *when they left*?* S V	
What *did she say?*	(c) Please tell me *what she said*. S V	
Why *is Tom absent?*	(d) I wonder *why Tom is absent*. S V	
Who *is* *that boy?* V S	(e) Tell me *who that boy is*. S V	A noun or pronoun that follows main verb *be* in a question comes in front of *be* in a noun clause, as in (e) and (f).
Whose pen *is* *this?* V S	(f) Do you know *whose pen this is*? S V	
Who is in the office? S V	(g) I don't know *who is* in the office. S V	A prepositional phrase (e.g., *in the office*) does not come in front of *be* in a noun clause, as in (g) and (h).
Whose keys are on the counter? S V	(h) I wonder *whose keys are* on the counter. S V	
Who came to class?	(i) I don't know *who came* to class. S V	In (i) and (j): Question word order and noun clause word order are the same when the question word is used as a subject.
What happened?	(j) Tell me *what happened*. S V	

*A question mark is used at the end of this sentence because *Do you know* asks a question.

   Example: *Do you know when they left?*

Do you know asks a question; *when they left* is a noun clause.

□ **Exercise 4. Looking at grammar.** (Charts 5-2 and 14-2)
Decide if the given words are a noun clause or an information question. If a noun clause, add *I don't know*. If an information question, add a capital letter and a question mark.

		NOUN CLAUSE	INFORMATION QUESTION
1. a. ___I don't know___ why he left.		x	☐
b. _____ W why did he leave?		☐	x
2. a. _____ where she is living		☐	☐
b. _____ where is she living		☐	☐
3. a. _____ where did Nick go		☐	☐
b. _____ where Nick went		☐	☐
4. a. _____ what time the movie begins		☐	☐
b _____ what time does the movie begin		☐	☐
5. a. _____ why is Yoko angry		☐	☐
b. _____ why Yoko is angry		☐	☐

□ **Exercise 5. Looking at grammar.** (Charts 5-2 and 14-2)
Underline and identify the subject (S) and verb (V) of Speaker A's question. Complete Speaker B's response with a noun clause.

1. A: Why is fire hot?
   B: I don't know _why fire is_ hot.

2. A: Where does Frank go to school?
   B: I don't know _____ to school.

3. A: Where did Natasha go yesterday?
   B: I don't know. Do you know _____ yesterday?

4. A: Why is Maria laughing?
   B: I don't know. Does anybody know _____?

5. A: How much does an electric car cost?
   B: Peter can tell you _____.

6. A: How long do elephants live?
   B: I don't know _____.

7. A: When was the first wheel invented?

   B: I don't know. Do you know _____?

8. A: How many hours does a light bulb burn?

   B: I don't know exactly _____.

9. A: Where did Emily buy her computer?

   B: I don't know _____.

10. A: Who lives next door to Kate?

    B: I don't know _____ next door to Kate.

11. A: Who did Julie talk to?

    B: I don't know _____ to.

12. A: Why is Mike always late?

    B: You tell me! I don't understand _____ late.

□ **Exercise 6. Let's talk: pairwork.** (Charts 14-1 and 14-2)
   Work with a partner. Take turns asking questions. Begin with *Can you tell me*.

   Questions to a teacher

   1. How do I pronounce this word? → *Can you tell me how I pronounce this word?*
   2. What does this mean?
   3. When will I get my grades?
   4. What is our next assignment?
   5. How soon is the next assignment due?
   6. Why is this incorrect?
   7. When is a good time to meet?
   8. What day does the term end?
   9. Why did I fail?
   10. Who will teach this class next time?

□ **Exercise 7. Looking at grammar.** (Chart 14-2)
Complete the responses with noun clauses.

1. A: Who is that woman?
   B: I don't know ___who that woman is___.

2. A: Who is on the phone?
   B: I don't know ___who is on the phone___.

3. A: What is a lizard?
   B: I don't know _____.

4. A: What is in that bag?
   B: I don't know _____.

5. A: Whose car is that?
   B: I don't know _____.

6. A: Whose car is in the driveway?
   B: I don't know _____.

7. A: Who is Bob's doctor?
   B: I'm not sure _____.

8. A: Whose ladder is this?
   B: I don't know _____. Hey, Hank, do you know

   _____?

   C: It's Hiro's.

9. A: What's at the end of a rainbow?
   B: What did you say, Susie?
   A: I want to know _____.

□ **Exercise 8. Let's talk: pairwork.** (Charts 14-1 and 14-2)
Work with a partner. Take turns asking questions. Begin with **Do you know**.

Questions at home

1. Where is the phone?
2. Why is the front door open?
3. Who just called?
4. Whose socks are on the floor?

5. Why are all the lights on?
6. There's water all over the floor. What happened?
7. What did the plumber say about the broken pipe?
8. What is the repair going to cost?

☐ **Exercise 9. Looking at grammar.** (Charts 5-2 and 14-2)
Complete the sentences with the correct form of the words in parentheses.

1. A: Where (*Sophia, eat*) ___did Sophia eat___ lunch yesterday?

   B: I don't know where (*she, eat*) ___she ate___ lunch yesterday.

2. A: Do you know where (*Jason, work*) _____?

   B: Who?

   A: Jason. Where (*he, work*) _____?

   B: I don't know.

3. A: Where (*you, see*) _____ the ad for the computer sale

   last week?

   B: I don't remember where (*I, see*) _____ it. In one of the local papers,

   I think.

4. A: How can I help you?

   B: How much (*that camera, cost*) _____?

   A: You want to know how much (*this camera, cost*) _____, is that right?

   B: No, not that one. The one next to it.

5. A: How far (*you, can run*) _____ without stopping?

   B: I have no idea. I don't know how far (*I, can run*) _____

   without stopping. I've never tried.

6. A: Ann was out late last night, wasn't she? When (*she, get*) _____ in?

   B: Why do you want to know when (*she, get*) _____ home?

   A: Just curious.

7. A: What time (*it, is*) _____?

   B: I don't know. I'll ask Sara. Sara, do you know what time (*it, is*) _____?

   C: Almost four-thirty.

8. A: Mom, why (*some people, be*) _____ mean to other

   people?

   B: Honey, I don't really understand why (*some people, be*) _____

   mean to others. It's difficult to explain.

□ **Exercise 10. Warm-up.** (Chart 14-3)
Check (✓) all the sentences that are grammatically correct.

Is Sam at work?

1. _____ I don't know if Sam is at work.

2. _____ I don't know Sam is at work.

3. _____ I don't know if Sam is at work or not.

4. _____ I don't know whether Sam is at work.

14-3 Noun Clauses That Begin with *If* or *Whether*

Yes/No Question	Noun Clause	When a yes/no question is changed to a noun clause, *if* is usually used to introduce the clause.*
Is Eric at home?	(a) I don't know *if Eric is at home.*	
Does the bus stop here?	(b) Do you know *if the bus stops here?*	
Did Alice go to Chicago?	(c) I wonder *if Alice went to Chicago.*	
(d) I don't know *if Eric is at home **or not**.*		When *if* introduces a noun clause, the expression ***or not*** sometimes comes at the end of the clause, as in (d).
(e) I don't know ***whether*** Eric is at home (or not).	In (e): ***whether*** has the same meaning as *if*.	

*See Chart 14-10 for the use of *if* with *ask* in reported speech.

□ **Exercise 11. Looking at grammar.** (Chart 14-3)
Change the yes/no questions to noun clauses.

1. YES/NO QUESTION: Is Carl here today?

   NOUN CLAUSE: Can you tell me ___*if / whether Carl is here today*___ ?

2. YES/NO QUESTION: Will Mr. Piper be at the meeting?

   NOUN CLAUSE: Do you know _____ ?

3. YES/NO QUESTION: Did Niko go to work yesterday?

   NOUN CLAUSE: I wonder _____ .

4. YES/NO QUESTION: Is there going to be a windstorm tonight?

   NOUN CLAUSE: I'm not sure _____ .

5. YES/NO QUESTION: Do you have Yung Soo's email address?

   NOUN CLAUSE: I don't know _____ .

Exercise 12. Looking at grammar. (Chart 14-3)

Complete the noun clause in each conversation. Use *if* to introduce the noun clause.

1. A: Are you tired?

   B: Why do you want to know ___*if I am*___ tired?

   A: You look tired. I'm worried about you.

2. A: Are you going to be in your office later today?

   B: What? Sorry. I didn't hear you.

   A: I need to know _____ in your office later today.

3. A: Did Tim borrow my cell phone?

   B: Who?

   A: Tim. I want to know _____ my cell phone.

4. A: Can Pete watch the kids tonight?

   B: Sorry. I wasn't listening. I was thinking about something else.

   A: Have you talked to your brother Pete? We need to know _____

   _____ the kids tonight.

5. A: Are my car keys in here?

   B: Why are you asking me? How am I supposed to know _____

   _____ in here?

   A: You're sure in a bad mood, aren't you?

6. A: Does your car have a CD player?

   B: What was that?

   A: I want to know _____.

❑ **Exercise 13. Let's talk: interview.** (Charts 14-2 and 14-3)
Interview your classmates. Begin your questions with **Do you know**. Try to find people who can answer your questions.

1. What does it cost to fly from London to Paris?
2. When was this building built?
3. How far is it from Vancouver, Canada, to Riyadh, Saudi Arabia?
4. Is Australia the smallest continent?
5. How many eyes does a bat have?
6. What is one of the longest words in English?
7. Does a chimpanzee have a good memory?
8. How old is the Great Wall of China?
9. Do all birds fly?
10. Did birds come from dinosaurs?

❑ **Exercise 14. Let's talk.** (Charts 14-2 and 14-3)
Work in small groups. Choose a famous movie star or celebrity. Make complete statements using noun clauses and the given words. Share some of your sentences with the class. See if anyone knows the information.

1. What do you wonder about him/her?
   a. where → *I wonder where she lives.*
   b. what
   c. if
   d. who
   e. how
   f. why

2. What do you want to ask him/her?
   a. who → *I want to ask him who his friends are.*
   b. when
   c. what
   d. whether
   e. why
   f. where

❑ **Exercise 15. Warm-up.** (Chart 14-4)
Check (✓) the sentences that are grammatically correct. Which checked sentences do you agree with?

1. _____ I think that noun clauses are hard.
2. _____ I suppose that this chapter is useful.
3. _____ I think that some of the exercises are easy.
4. _____ Is interesting this chapter I think.

14-4 Noun Clauses That Begin with *That*

(a) I think *that Mr. Jones is a good teacher.* (b) I hope *that you can come to the game.* (c) Mary realizes *that she should study harder.* (d) I dreamed *that I was on the top of a mountain.*	A noun clause can be introduced by the word ***that.*** In (a): *that Mr. Jones is a good teacher* is a noun clause. It is the object of the verb *think.* *That*-clauses are frequently used as the objects of verbs that express mental activity.
(e) I think *that Mr. Jones is a good teacher.* (f) I think Ø *Mr. Jones is a good teacher.*	The word ***that*** is often omitted, especially in speaking. Examples (e) and (f) have the same meaning.

In (a): S V O above "I think that Mr. Jones is a good teacher."

Common Verbs Followed by *That*-clauses*

agree that	dream that	know that	realize that
assume that	feel that	learn that	remember that
believe that	forget that	notice that	say that
decide that	guess that	predict that	suppose that
discover that	hear that	prove that	think that
doubt that	hope that	read that	understand that

*See Appendix Chart A-4 for more verbs that can be followed by *that*-clauses.

❑ **Exercise 16. Looking at grammar.** (Chart 14-4)
Add the word ***that*** to mark the beginning of a noun clause.

      that
1. I think ∧ most people have kind hearts.

2. Last night I dreamed a monster was chasing me.

3. I believe we need to protect the rain forests.

4. Did you notice Yusef wasn't in class yesterday? I hope he's okay.

5. I trust Linda. I believe what she said. I believe she told the truth.

❑ **Exercise 17. Let's talk: pairwork.** (Chart 14-4)
Work with a partner. Take turns asking and answering questions. Use *that*-clauses. Share some of your partner's answers with the class.

1. What have you noticed about English grammar?
2. What have you heard in the news recently?
3. What did you dream recently?
4. What do you believe about people?
5. What can scientists prove?
6. What can't scientists prove?

□ **Exercise 18. Warm-up.** (Chart 14-5)

Check (✓) the sentences that you agree with.

1. ____ I'm sure that vitamins give people more energy.

2. ____ It's true that vitamins help people live longer.

3. ____ It's a fact that vitamins help people look younger.

14-5 Other Uses of *That*-Clauses

(a) I'm *sure that* the bus stops here. (b) I'm *glad that* you're feeling better today. (c) I'm *sorry that* I missed class yesterday. (d) I *was disappointed that* you couldn't come.	*That*-clauses can follow certain expressions with **be** + *adjective* or **be** + *past participle.* The word **that** can be omitted with no change in meaning: *I'm sure Ø the bus stops here.*

(e) *It is true that* the world is round.
(f) *It is a fact that* the world is round.
	Two common expressions followed by *that*-clauses are:
	   It is true (that) . . . .
	   It is a fact (that) . . . .

Common Expressions Followed by *That*-clauses*

be afraid that	be disappointed that	be sad that	be upset that
be angry that	be glad that	be shocked that	be worried that
be aware that	be happy that	be sorry that	
be certain that	be lucky that	be sure that	It is a fact that
be convinced that	be pleased that	be surprised that	It is true that

*See Appendix Chart A-5 for more expressions that can be followed by *that*-clauses.

□ **Exercise 19. Looking at grammar.** (Charts 14-4 and 14-5)

Add *that* wherever possible.

           that

1. A: Welcome. We're glad ∧ you could come.

   B: Thank you. I'm happy to be here.

2. A: Thank you so much for your gift.

   B: I'm pleased you like it.

3. A: I wonder why Paulo was promoted to general manager instead of Andrea.

   B: So do I. I'm surprised Andrea didn't get the job. I think she is more qualified.

4. A: Are you aware you have to pass the English test to get into the university?

   B: Yes, but I'm certain I'll do well on it.

5. Are you surprised dinosaurs lived on earth for one hundred and twenty-five million (125,000,000) years?

6. Is it true human beings have lived on earth for only four million (4,000,000) years?

❑ Exercise 20. Let's talk. (Charts 14-4 and 14-5)

Part I. Work in small groups. Look at the health treatments below. Which ones do you know about? Which ones do you think are helpful? You may need to check your dictionary.

acupuncture	massage	naturopathy
hypnosis	meditation	yoga

Part II. Complete the sentences with words from the list. Use noun clauses. Discuss your sentences with other students.

1. I believe/think _____ is useful for _____.

2. I am certain _____.

3. I am not convinced _____.

❑ Exercise 21. Listening and grammar. (Charts 14-4 and 14-5)

Listen to each conversation and then complete the sentences.

CD 2
Track 51

Example: You will hear: MAN: I heard Jack is in jail. I can't believe it!
WOMAN: Neither can I! The police said he robbed a house. They must have the wrong person.
You will say: a. The man is shocked that <u>Jack is in jail</u>.
b. The woman is sure that <u>the police have the wrong person</u>.

1. a. The woman thinks that . . . .
   b. The man is glad that . . . .

2. a. The mother is worried that . . . .
   b. Her son is sure that . . . .

3. a. The man is surprised that . . . .
   b. The woman is disappointed that . . . .

4. a. The man is happy that . . . .
   b. The woman is pleased that . . . .

5. a. The woman is afraid* that . . . .
   b. The man is sure that . . . .

---

*Sometimes *be afraid* expresses fear:
    I don't want to go near that dog. I'm afraid that it will bite me.
Sometimes *be afraid* expresses polite regret:
    I'm afraid you have the wrong number. = I'm sorry, but I think you have the wrong number.
    I'm afraid I can't come to your party. = I'm sorry, but I can't come to your party.

□ **Exercise 22. Warm-up.** (Chart 14-6)
Circle all the statements that are true for each conversation.

1. A: Did Taka remember to get food for dinner tonight?
   B: I think so.
   a. Speaker B thinks Taka got food for dinner.
   b. Speaker B is sure that Taka got food for dinner.
   c. Speaker B doesn't know for sure if Taka got food for dinner.

2. A: Is Ben marrying Tara?
   B: I hope not.
   a. Speaker B says Ben is not going to marry Tara.
   b. Speaker B doesn't know if Ben is going to marry Tara.
   c. Speaker B doesn't want Ben to marry Tara.

14-6 Substituting *So* for a *That*-Clause in Conversational Responses

(a) A: Is Ana from Peru? B: I think so. (*so = that Ana is from Peru*) (b) A: Does Judy live in Dallas? B: I believe so. (*so = that Judy lives in Dallas*) (c) A: Did you pass the test? B: I hope so. (*so = that I passed the test*)	***Think, believe***, and ***hope*** are frequently followed by ***so*** in conversational English in response to a yes/no question. They are alternatives to *yes, no,* or *I don't know.* ***So*** replaces a *that*-clause. *INCORRECT:* I think so that Ana is from Peru.
(d) A: Is Jack married? B: I *don't* think so. / I *don't* believe so.	Negative usage of ***think so*** and ***believe so:*** *do not think so / do not believe so*
(e) A: Did you fail the test? B: I hope *not.*	Negative usage of ***hope*** in conversational responses: *hope not.* In (e): ***I hope not*** = I hope I didn't fail the test. *INCORRECT:* I don't hope so.

(f) A: Do you want to come with us?
B: Oh, I don't know. I guess *so.*
	Other common conversational responses:
	  I guess so. I guess not.
	  I suppose so. I suppose not.
	
	NOTE: In spoken English, ***suppose*** often sounds like "spoze."

□ **Exercise 23. Looking at grammar.** (Chart 14-6)
Restate Speaker B's answers by using a *that*-clause.

1. A: Is Karen going to be home tonight?
   B: I think so.
   → *I think that Karen is going to be home tonight.*

2. A: Are we going to have a grammar test tomorrow?
   B: I don't believe so.

3. A: Will Margo be at the conference in March?
   B: I hope so.

4. A: Can horses swim?
   B: I believe so.

5. A: Do gorillas have tails?
   B: I don't think so.

6. A: Will Janet be at Omar's wedding?
   B: I suppose so.

7. A: Will your flight be canceled because of the storms?
   B: I hope not.

□ **Exercise 24. Let's talk: pairwork.** (Chart 14-6)
Work with a partner. Take turns answering the questions. If you are not sure, use *think so*.
If you are sure, use *Yes* or *No*.

Example:
SPEAKER A (*book open*):   Does this book have more than 500 pages?
SPEAKER B (*book closed*): I think so. / I don't think so.
                           Yes, it does. / No, it doesn't.

1. Are we going to have a grammar quiz tomorrow?
2. Do spiders have noses?
3. Do spiders have eyes?
4. Is there a fire extinguisher in this room?
5. Does the word *patient* have more than one meaning?
6. Does the word *dozen* have more than one meaning?
7. Is your left foot bigger than your right foot?
8. Is there just one sun in our universe?
9. Do any English words begin with the letter "x"?
10. Do you know what a noun clause is?

□ **Exercise 25. Warm-up.** (Chart 14-7)
Circle the quotation marks and underline the punctuation inside each quotation. What are the
differences in punctuation?

1. "Help!" Marcos yelled.

2. "Can someone help me?" he asked.

3. "I'm going to drop this box of jars," he said.

14-7 Quoted Speech

Sometimes we want to quote a speaker's words — to write a speaker's exact words. Exact quotations are used in many kinds of writing, such as newspaper articles, stories, novels, and academic papers. When we quote a speaker's words, we use quotation marks.

(a) **SPEAKERS' EXACT WORDS** Jane: Cats are fun to watch. Mike: Yes, I agree. They're graceful and playful. Do you have a cat?	(b) **QUOTING THE SPEAKERS' WORDS** Jane said, "Cats are fun to watch." Mike said, "Yes, I agree. They're graceful and playful. Do you have a cat?"

(c) **HOW TO WRITE QUOTATIONS**
1. Add a comma after *said*.* ————————————————→ Jane said,
2. Add quotation marks.** ——————————————————→ Jane said, "
3. Capitalize the first word of the quotation. ——————→ Jane said, "Cats
4. Write the quotation. Add a final period. —————————→ Jane said, "Cats are fun to watch.
5. Add quotation marks **after** the period. ——————————→ Jane said, "Cats are fun to watch."

(d) Mike said, "Yes, I agree. They're graceful and playful. Do you have a cat?" (e) INCORRECT: *Mike said, "Yes, I agree." "They're graceful and playful." "Do you have a cat?"*	When there are two (or more) sentences in a quotation, put the quotation marks at the beginning and end of the whole quote, as in (d). Do NOT put quotation marks around each sentence. As with a period, put the quotation marks after a question mark at the end of a quote.
(f) "Cats are fun to watch," Jane said. (g) "Do you have a cat?" Mike asked.	In (f): Notice that a comma (not a period) is used at the end of the QUOTED SENTENCE because ***Jane said*** comes after the quote. In (g): Notice that a question mark (not a comma) is used at the end of the QUOTED QUESTION.

*Other common verbs besides *say* that introduce questions: *admit, announce, answer, ask, complain, explain, inquire, report, reply, shout, state, write.*

**Quotation marks are called "inverted commas" in British English.

☐ **Exercise 26. Looking at grammar.** (Chart 14-7)
Make sentences in which you quote the speaker's exact words. Use ***said*** or ***asked***. Punctuate carefully.

1. ANN: My sister is a student.
    → Ann said, "My sister is a student." OR "My sister is a student," Ann said.

2. ANN: Is your brother a student?

3. RITA: We're hungry.

4. RITA: Are you hungry too?

5. RITA: Let's eat. The food is ready.

6. JOHN F. KENNEDY: Ask not what your country can do for you. Ask what you can do for your country.

□ **Exercise 27. Looking at grammar.** (Chart 14-7)
A teacher recently had a conversation with Roberto. Practice punctuating their quoted speech.

(TEACHER) You know sign language, don't you I asked Roberto.

(ROBERTO) Yes, I do he replied both my grandparents are deaf.

(TEACHER) I'm looking for someone who knows sign language. A deaf student is going to visit our class next Monday I said. Could you interpret for her I asked.

(ROBERTO) I'd be happy to he answered. Is she going to be a new student?

(TEACHER) Possibly I said. She's interested in seeing what we do in our English classes.

□ **Exercise 28. Reading and writing.** (Chart 14-7)
Part I. Read the story. <u>Underline</u> the quoted speech.

The Ugly Duckling

Once upon a time, there was a mother duck. She lived on a farm and spent her days sitting on her nest of eggs. One morning, the eggs began to move and out came six little ducklings. But there was one egg that was bigger than the rest, and it didn't hatch. The mother didn't remember this egg. "I thought I had only six," she said. "But maybe I counted incorrectly."

A short time later, the seventh egg hatched. But this duckling had gray feathers, not brown like his brothers, and was quite ugly. His mother thought, "Maybe this duck isn't one of mine." He grew faster than his brothers and ate more food. He was very clumsy, and none of the other animals wanted to play with him. Much of the time he was alone.

He felt unloved by everyone, and he decided to run away from the farm. He asked other animals on the way, "Do you know of any ducklings that look like me?" But they just laughed and said, "You are the ugliest duck we have ever seen." One day, the duckling looked up and saw a group of beautiful birds overhead. They were white, with long slender necks and large wings. The duckling thought, "I want to look just like them."

He wandered alone most of the winter and finally found a comfortable bed of reeds in a pond. He thought to himself, "No one wants me. I'll just hide here for the rest of my life." There was plenty of food there, and although he was lonely, he felt a little happier.

By springtime, the duck was quite large. One morning, he saw his reflection in the water. He didn't even recognize himself. A group of swans coming back from the south saw him and flew down to the pond. "Where have you been?" they asked. "You're a swan like us." As they began to swim across the pond, a child saw them and said, "Look at the youngest swan. He's the most beautiful of all." The swan beamed with happiness, and he lived happily ever after.

Part II. Work in small groups and answer this question: What lessons does this story teach?

Part III. Write a story that includes quoted speech. Choose one of these topics:

1. Write a fable★ from your country in which animals speak.
2. Write a story that you learned when you were young.

□ **Exercise 29. Warm-up.** (Chart 14-8)
Circle the correct words in *italics*.

Kathy and Mark said that *we / they* didn't like *our / their* new apartment.

★*a fable* = a traditional story that teaches a lesson about life

14-8 Quoted Speech vs. Reported Speech

QUOTED SPEECH	QUOTED SPEECH = giving a speaker's exact words. Quotation marks are used.*
(a) Ann said, "*I'm* hungry."	
(b) Tom said, "*I need my* pen."	
REPORTED SPEECH	REPORTED SPEECH = giving the idea of a speaker's words. Not all of the exact words are used; pronouns and verb forms may change. Quotation marks are NOT used.*
(c) Ann said (that) *she was* hungry.	
(d) Tom said (that) *he needed his* pen.	***That*** is optional; it is more common in writing than in speaking.

*Quoted speech is also called *direct speech*. Reported speech is also called *indirect speech*.

☐ **Exercise 30. Looking at grammar.** (Chart 14-8)
Change the pronouns from quoted speech to reported speech.

1. Mr. Smith said, "I need help with my luggage."

   → Mr. Smith said that ___*he*___ needed help with ___*his*___ luggage.

2. Mrs. Hart said, "I am going to visit my brother."

   → Mrs. Hart said that _____ was going to visit _____ brother.

3. Sergey said to me, "I will call you."

   → Sergey said _____ would call _____ .

4. Rick said to us, "I'll meet you at your house after I finish my work at my house."

   → Rick said that _____ would meet _____ at _____ house

   after _____ finished _____ work at _____ house.

☐ **Exercise 31. Warm-up.** (Chart 14-9)
Read the conversation and look at the sentences that describe it. All are correct. What difference do you notice?

JENNY: What are you doing tomorrow?
ELLA: I'm going to take my parents out to dinner.

   a. Ella said she was going to take her parents out to dinner.
   b. Ella just said she is going to take her parents out to dinner.
   c. Last week Ella said she was going to take her parents out to dinner.
   d. Ella says she is going to take her parents out to dinner.

14-9 Verb Forms in Reported Speech

(a) QUOTED: Joe said, "I *feel* good." (b) REPORTED: Joe said (that) he *felt* good. (c) QUOTED: Ken said, "I *am* happy." (d) REPORTED: Ken said (that) he *was* happy.	In formal English, if the reporting verb (e.g., *said*) is in the past, the verb in the noun clause is often also in a past form, as in (b) and (d).
— Ann said, "I am hungry." (e) — What did Ann just say? I didn't hear her. — She said (that) she *is* hungry. (f) — What did Ann say when she got home last night? — She said (that) she *was* hungry.	In informal English, often the verb in the noun clause is not changed to a past form, especially when words are reported *soon after* they are said, as in (e). In *later reporting*, however, or in formal English, a past verb is commonly used, as in (f).
(g) Ann *says* (that) she *is* hungry.	If the reporting verb is present tense (e.g., *says*), no change is made in the noun clause verb.

QUOTED SPEECH	REPORTED SPEECH (formal or later reporting)	REPORTED SPEECH (informal or immediate reporting)
He said, "I *work* hard."	He said he *worked* hard.	He said he *works* hard.
He said, "I *am working* hard."	He said he *was working* hard.	He said he *is working* hard.
He said, "I *worked* hard."	He said he *had worked* hard.	He said he *worked* hard.
He said, "I *have worked* hard."	He said he *had worked* hard.	He said he *has worked* hard.
He said, "I *am going to work* hard."	He said he *was going to work* hard.	He said he *is going to work* hard.
He said, "I *will work* hard."	He said he *would work* hard.	He said he *will work* hard.
He said, "I *can work* hard."	He said he *could work* hard.	He said he *can work* hard.

☐ **Exercise 32. Looking at grammar.** (Chart 14-9)
Complete the reported speech sentences. Use formal verb forms.

1. Sonia said, "I need some help."

   → Sonia said (that) she ___*needed*___ some help.

2. Linda said, "I'm meeting David for dinner."

   → Linda said (that) she _____ David for dinner.

3. Ms. Chavez said, "I have studied in Cairo."

   → Ms. Chavez said (that) she _____ in Cairo.

4. Kazu said, "I forgot to pay my electric bill."

   → Kazu said (that) he _____ to pay his electric bill.

5. Barbara said, "I am going to fly to Hawaii for my vacation."

   → Barbara said (that) she _____ to Hawaii for her vacation.

6. I said, "I'll carry the box up the stairs."

   → I said (that) I _____ the box up the stairs.

7. Tarik said to me, "I can teach you to drive."

   → Tarik said (that) he _____ me to drive.

□ **Exercise 33. Looking at grammar.** (Charts 14-8 and 14-9)
Change the quoted speech to reported speech. Change the verb in quoted speech to a past form in reported speech if possible.

1. Jim said, "I'm sleepy."
   → *Jim said (that) he was sleepy.*
2. Kristina said, "I don't like chocolate."
3. Carla said, "I'm planning to take a trip with my family."
4. Ahmed said, "I have already eaten lunch."
5. Kate said, "I called my doctor."
6. Mr. Rice said, "I'm going to go to Chicago."
7. Pedro said, "I will be at your house at ten."
8. Emma said, "I can't afford to buy a new car."
9. Olivia says, "I can't afford to buy a new car."
10. Ms. Acosta said, "I want to see you in my office after your meeting with your supervisor."

Will you marry me?   I'm not sure.

□ **Exercise 34. Warm-up.** (Chart 14-10)
Circle all the sentences that are grammatically correct.

1. a. David asked Elena if she would marry him.
   b. David asked Elena would she marry him.
   c. David wanted to know if Elena would marry him.

2. a. Elena said she wasn't sure.
   b. Elena told she wasn't sure.
   c. Elena told David she wasn't sure.

14-10 Common Reporting Verbs: *Tell, Ask, Answer/Reply*

(a) Kay *said* that* she was hungry. (b) Kay *told me* that she was hungry. (c) Kay *told Tom* that she was hungry. INCORRECT: *Kay told that she was hungry.* INCORRECT: *Kay told to me that she was hungry.* INCORRECT: *Kay said me that she was hungry.*	A main verb that introduces reported speech is called a "reporting verb." *Say* is the most common reporting verb** and is usually followed immediately by a noun clause, as in (a). *Tell* is also commonly used. Note that *told* is followed by *me* in (b) and by *Tom* in (c). *Tell* needs to be followed immediately by a (pro)noun object and then by a noun clause.
(d) QUOTED: Ken asked me, "Are you tired?" REPORTED: Ken *asked* (*me*) *if* I was tired.	*Asked* is used to report questions.
(e) Ken *wanted to know if* I was tired. Ken *wondered if* I was tired. Ken *inquired whether or not* I was tired.	Questions are also reported by using *want to know*, *wonder*, and *inquire*.
(f) QUOTED: I said (to Kay), "I am not tired." REPORTED: I *answered / replied* that I wasn't tired.	The verbs *answer* and *reply* are often used to report replies.

*___*That* is optional. See Chapter 14–8.

**Other common reporting verbs: *Kay announced / commented / complained / explained / remarked / stated that she was hungry.*

□ **Exercise 35. Looking at grammar.** (Chart 14-10)
Complete the sentences with *said*, *told*, or *asked*.

1. Karen ___*told*___ me that she would be here at one o'clock.

2. Jamal ___*said*___ that he was going to get here around two.

3. Sophia ___*asked*___ me what time I would arrive.

4. William _____ that I had a message.

5. William _____ me that someone had called me around ten-thirty.

6. I _____ William if he knew the caller's name.

7. I had a short conversation with Alice yesterday. I _____ her that I would help

   her move into her new apartment next week. She _____ that she would welcome

   the help. She _____ me if I had a truck or knew anyone who had a truck. I

   _____ her Dan had a truck. She _____ she would call him.

8. My uncle in Toronto called and _____ that he was organizing a surprise party for

   my aunt's 60th birthday. He _____ me if I could come to Toronto for the party.

   I _____ him that I would be happy to come. I _____ when it was. He

   _____ it was the last weekend in August.

□ **Exercise 36. Let's talk: pairwork.** (Charts 5-2, 14-2, 14-3, and 14-10)
Work with a partner. Write down five questions to ask your partner about his/her life or
opinions. Interview your partner and write down the answers. Then report to the class some
of the information you found out about your partner. Include both the question and the
response. Use either formal or informal verb forms.*

Examples:
STUDENT A's question: Where were you born?
STUDENT B's response: In Nepal.
STUDENT A's report: I asked him where he was born. He said he was born in Nepal.

STUDENT B's question: Who do you admire most in the world?
STUDENT A's response: I admire my parents.
STUDENT B's report: I asked him who he admires most in the world. He said he admires his
parents the most.

---

*In everyday spoken English, native speakers sometimes change formal/later noun clause verbs to past forms, and sometimes
they don't. In an informal reporting situation such as in this exercise, either informal/immediate reporting or reporting tenses
are appropriate.

❑ **Exercise 37. Looking at grammar.** (Charts 14-8 → 14-10)
Complete the paragraph based on what the people in the picture are saying. Use the formal
sequence of tenses.

One day Katya and Pavel were at a restaurant. Katya picked up her menu and looked at it.

Pavel left his menu on the table. Katya asked Pavel ___*what he was going to have*___. He said

1

_____ anything because he

2

_____. He _____ already. Katya was

3   4

surprised. She asked him why _____. He told her

5

_____.

6

❑ **Exercise 38. Looking at grammar.** (Charts 14-8 → 14-10)
Change the reported speech to quoted speech. Begin a new paragraph each time the speaker
changes. Pay special attention to pronouns, verb forms, and word order.

Example:
REPORTED SPEECH: This morning my mother asked me if I had gotten enough sleep last night.
I told her that I was fine. I explained that I didn't need a lot of sleep. She
told me that I needed to take better care of myself.

QUOTED SPEECH: *This morning my mother said, "Did you get enough sleep last night?"*
"I'm fine," I replied. "I don't need a lot of sleep."
She said, "You need to take better care of yourself."

1. In the middle of class yesterday, my friend tapped me on the shoulder and asked me what I
was doing after class. I told her that I would tell her later.

2. When I was putting on my coat, Robert asked me where I was going. I told him that I had
a date with Anna. He wanted to know what we were going to do. I told him that we were
going to a movie.

□ **Exercise 39. Listening.** (Charts 14-8 → 14-10)
🎧 Listen to Roger's report of his phone conversation with Angela. Then listen again and write
the missing words.

CD 2
Track 52

Angela called and _____ me where Bill _____.
                       1   2

I _____ her he _____ in the lunchroom. She
        3   4

_____ when he _____ back. I _____
        5   6   7

he _____ back around 2:00. I _____ her if I
        8   9

_____ something for her.
        10

She _____ that Bill had the information she _____,
            11   12

and only he _____ her. I _____ her that I
                13   14

_____ him a message. She thanked me and hung up.
        15

□ **Exercise 40. Reading.** (Chapter 14)

Part I. Read the passage.

The Last Lecture

In 2007, a 47-year-old computer science professor from Carnegie Mellon
University was invited to give a lecture at his university. His name was Randy
Pausch, and the lecture series was called "The Last Lecture." Pausch was
asked to think about what wisdom he would give to people if he knew it was
his last opportunity to do so. In Pausch's case, it really was his last lecture
because he had cancer and wasn't expected to survive. Pausch gave an
uplifting lecture called "Really Achieving Your Childhood Dreams." The
lecture was recorded and put on the Internet. A reporter for the *Wall Street
Journal* was also there and wrote about it. Soon millions of people around the
world heard about Pausch's inspiring talk.

Here are some quotes from Randy Pausch:

To the general public:

"Proper apologies have three parts: (1) What I did was wrong. (2) I'm sorry that I
hurt you. (3) How do I make it better? It's the third part that people tend to forget."

"If I could only give three words of advice, they would be 'tell the truth.' If I got
three more words, I'd add 'all the time'."

"The key question to keep asking is, 'Are you spending your time on the right
things?' Because time is all you have."

"We cannot change the cards we are dealt, just how we play the hand."

To his students: "Whether you think you can or can't, you're right."

To his children: "Don't try to figure out what I wanted you to become. I want you to
become what you want to become."

Sadly, in 2008, Randy Pausch died. Before his death he was able to put down his thoughts in a book, appropriately called *The Last Lecture*.

Part II. Work in small groups. Make sure the members of your group understand each quotation in Part I. Then, individually, choose one of the quotes to agree or disagree with. Use some of these phrases and support your statement with reasons.

I agree / disagree that   I think / don't think that
I believe / don't believe that   It's true that

❑ **Exercise 41. Check your knowledge.** (Chapter 14)
Edit the sentences. Correct the errors in noun clauses.

1. My friend knows where ~~do~~ I live.

2. I don't know what is your email address?

3. I think so that Mr. Lee is out of town.

4. Can you tell me that where Victor is living now?

5. I asked my uncle what kind of movies does he like.

6. I think, that my English has improved a lot.

7. Is true that people are basically the same everywhere in the world.

8. A man came to my door last week. I didn't know who is he.

9. I want to know does Pedro have a laptop computer.

10. Sam and I talked about his classes. He told that he don't like his algebra class.

11. A woman came into the room and ask me Where is your brother?

12. I felt very relieved when the doctor said, you will be fine. It's nothing serious.

13. My mother asked me that: "When you will be home?

Appendix

Supplementary Grammar Charts

UNIT A

A-1	The Present Perfect vs. The Past Perfect	
Present Perfect before now / now	(a) I am not hungry now. I *have* already *eaten*.	The PRESENT PERFECT expresses an activity that *occurred before now, at an unspecified time in the past,* as in (a).
Past Perfect before 1:00 / 1:00 P.M.	(b) I was not hungry at 1:00 P.M. I *had* already *eaten*.	The PAST PERFECT expresses an activity that *occurred before **another** time in the past.* In (b): I ate at noon. I was not hungry at 1:00 P.M. because I had already eaten before 1:00 P.M.

I laughed when I saw my son.
He *had poured* a bowl of noodles on top of his head.

A-2 The Past Progressive vs. The Past Perfect

Past Progressive	(a) I *was eating* when Bob came.	The PAST PROGRESSIVE expresses an activity that was *in progress at a particular time in the past.*
began eating / Bob came / eating in progress		In (a): I began to eat at noon. Bob came at 12:10. My meal was in progress when Bob came.
Past Perfect	(b) I *had eaten* when Bob came.	The PAST PERFECT expresses an activity that was *completed before a particular time in the past.*
finished eating / Bob came		In (b): I finished eating at noon. Bob came at 1:00 P.M. My meal was completed before Bob came.

A-3 *Still* vs. *Anymore*

Still

(a) It was cold yesterday. It is *still* cold today. We *still* need to wear coats.	***Still*** = A situation continues to exist from past to present without change. ***Still*** is used in either affirmative or negative sentences.
(b) The mail didn't come an hour ago. The mail *still* hasn't come.	Position: midsentence*

Anymore

(c) I lived in Chicago two years ago, but then I moved to another city. I don't live in Chicago *anymore.*	***Anymore*** = A past situation does not continue to exist at present; a past situation has changed. ***Anymore*** has the same meaning as *any longer*. ***Anymore*** is used in negative sentences.
	Position: end of sentence

*See Chart 1-3, p. 10. A midsentence adverb
  (1) precedes a simple present verb: *We **still need** to wear coats.*
  (2) follows *am, is, are, was, were*: *It **is still** cold.*
  (3) comes between a helping verb and a main verb: *Bob **has already arrived.***
  (4) precedes a negative helping verb: *Ann **still hasn't** come.*
  (5) follows the subject in a question: *Have **you already** seen that movie?*

A-4 Additional Verbs Followed by *That*-Clauses*

conclude that	guess that	pretend that	show that
demonstrate that	imagine that	recall that	suspect that
fear that	indicate that	recognize that	teach that
figure out that	observe that	regret that	
find out that	presume that	reveal that	

*See Chart 14-4, p. 379, for more information.

Scientists *have **concluded that*** dolphins can communicate with each other.

A-5 Additional Expressions with *Be* + *That*-Clauses*

be ashamed that	be furious that	be proud that
be amazed that	be horrified that	be terrified that
be astounded that	be impressed that	be thrilled that
be delighted that	be lucky that	
be fortunate that	be positive that	

*See Chart 14-5, p. 380, for more information.

UNIT B: Phrasal Verbs

NOTE: See the *Fundamentals of English Grammar Workbook* appendix for more practice exercises for phrasal verbs.

B-1 Phrasal Verbs

(a) We *put off* our trip. We'll go next month instead of this month. (*put off = postpone*)	In (a): *put off* = a phrasal verb A PHRASAL VERB = a verb and a particle that together have a special meaning. For example, *put off* means "postpone."
(b) Jimmy, *put on* your coat before you go outdoors. (*put on = place clothes on one's body*)	A PARTICLE = a "small word" (e.g., *off, on, away, back*) that is used in a phrasal verb.
(c) Someone left the scissors on the table. They didn't belong there. I *put* them *away*. (*put away = put something in its usual or proper place*)	Notice that the phrasal verbs with *put* in (a), (b), (c), and (d) all have different meanings.
(d) After I used the dictionary, I *put* it *back* on the shelf. (*put back = return something to its original place*)	
Separable	Some phrasal verbs are **separable**: a NOUN OBJECT can either

(e) We *put off our trip*. = (vb + **particle** + NOUN)
(f) We *put our trip off*. = (vb + NOUN + **particle**)
(g) We *put it off*. = (vb + PRONOUN + **particle**)
	(1) follow the particle, as in (e), OR
	   (2) come between (separate) the verb and the particle, as in (f).
	If a phrasal verb is separable, a PRONOUN OBJECT comes between the verb and the particle, as in (g).
	   INCORRECT: We put off it.

Nonseparable	If a phrasal verb is **nonseparable**, a NOUN or PRONOUN always follows (never precedes) the particle, as in (h) and (i).
(h) I *ran into Bob*. = (vb + **particle** + NOUN) (i) I *ran into him*. = (vb + **particle** + PRONOUN)	*INCORRECT: I ran Bob into.* *INCORRECT: I ran him into.*
Phrasal Verbs: Intransitive	Some phrasal verbs are intransitive; i.e., they are not followed by an object.
(j) The machine *broke down*. (k) Please *come in*. (l) I *fell down*.	
Three-Word Phrasal Verbs	Some two-word verbs (e.g., *drop in*) can become three-word verbs (e.g., *drop in on*).
(m) Last night some friends *dropped in*.	In (m): *drop in* is not followed by an object. It is an intransitive phrasal verb (i.e., it is not followed by an object).
(n) Let's *drop in on* Alice this afternoon.	In (n): *drop in on* is a three-word phrasal verb. Three-word phrasal verbs are transitive (they are followed by objects).
(o) We *dropped in on* her last week.	In (o): Three-word phrasal verbs are nonseparable (the noun or pronoun follows the phrasal verb).

B-2 Phrasal Verbs: A Reference List

A **ask out** = ask (someone) to go on a date

B **blow out** = extinguish (a match, a candle)

break down = stop functioning properly

break out = happen suddenly

break up = separate, end a relationship

bring back = return

bring up = (1) raise (children)
   (2) mention, start to talk about

C **call back** = return a telephone call

call off = cancel

call on = ask (someone) to speak in class

call up = make a telephone call

cheer up = make happier

clean up = make neat and clean

come along (with) = accompany

come from = originate

come in = enter a room or building

come over (to) = visit the speaker's place

cross out = draw a line through

cut out (of) = remove with scissors or knife

D **dress up** = put on nice clothes

drop in (on) = visit without calling first or
   without an invitation

drop out (of) = stop attending (school)

E **eat out** = eat outside of one's home

F **fall down** = fall to the ground

figure out = find the solution to a problem

fill in = complete by writing in a blank space

fill out = write information on a form

fill up = fill completely with gas, water, coffee,
   etc.

find out (about) = discover information

fool around (with) = have fun while wasting
   time

G **get on** = enter a bus/an airplane/a train/a
   subway

get out of = leave a car, a taxi

get over = recover from an illness or a shock

get together (with) = join, meet

get through (with) = finish

get up = get out of bed in the morning

give away = donate, get rid of by giving

give back = return (something) to (someone)

give up = quit doing (something) or quit trying

go on = continue

go back (to) = return to a place

go out = not stay home

go over (to) = (1) approach
   (2) visit another's home

grow up (in) = become an adult

H **hand in** = give homework, test papers, etc., to
   a teacher

hand out = give (something) to this person,
   then to that person, then to
   another person, etc.

hang around/out (with) = spend time relaxing

hang up = (1) hang on a hanger or a hook
   (2) end a telephone conversation

have on = wear

help out = assist (someone)

K **keep away (from)** = not give to

keep on = continue

L **lay off** = stop employment

leave on = (1) not turn off (a light, a machine)
   (2) not take off (clothing)

look into = investigate

look over = examine carefully

look out (for) = be careful

look up = look for information in a dictionary,
   a telephone directory, an
   encyclopedia, etc.

P **pay back** = return borrowed money to
   (someone)

pick up = lift

point out = call attention to

(continued)

print out = create a paper copy from a computer

put away = put (something) in its usual or proper place

put back = return (something) to its original place

put down = stop holding or carrying

put off = postpone

put on = put clothes on one's body

put out = extinguish (stop) a fire, a cigarette

R **run into** = meet by chance

run out (of) = finish the supply of (something)

S **set out (for)** = begin a trip

shut off = stop a machine or a light, turn off

sign up (for) = put one's name on a list

show up = come, appear

sit around (with) = sit and do nothing

sit back = put one's back against a chair back

sit down = go from standing to sitting

speak up = speak louder

stand up = go from sitting to standing

start over = begin again

stay up = not go to bed

T **take back** = return

take off = (1) remove clothes from one's body (2) ascend in an airplane

take out = invite out and pay

talk over = discuss

tear down = destroy a building

tear out (of) = remove (paper) by tearing

tear up = tear into small pieces

think over = consider

throw away/out = put in the trash, discard

try on = put on clothing to see if it fits

turn around }
turn back } change to the opposite direction

turn down = decrease the volume

turn off = stop a machine or a light

turn on = start a machine or a light

turn over = turn the top side to the bottom

turn up = increase the volume

W **wake up** = stop sleeping

watch out (for) = be careful

work out = solve

write down = write a note on a piece of paper

☐ **EXERCISE 1. Looking at grammar.** (Charts B-1 and B-2)
Underline the second part of the phrasal verb in each sentence.

1. I picked up a book and started to read.

2. The teacher called on me in class.

3. I get up early every day.

4. I feel okay now. I got over my cold last week.

5. I woke my roommate up when I got home.

6. I turned the radio on to listen to some music.

7. When I don't know how to spell a word, I look it up.

□ **EXERCISE 2. Looking at grammar.** (Charts B-1 and B-2)
Check (✓) the correct sentences. In some cases, both are correct.

1. _____ I turned the light on.
   _____ I turned on the light.

2. _____ I ran into Mary.
   _____ I ran Mary into.

3. _____ Joe looked up the definition.
   _____ Joe looked the definition up.

4. _____ I took off my coat.
   _____ I took my coat off.

5. _____ I got in the car and left.
   _____ I got the car in and left.

6. _____ I figured out the answer.
   _____ I figured the answer out.

□ **EXERCISE 3. Looking at grammar.** (Charts B-1 and B-2)
Complete the sentences with particles and the pronouns *it* or *them*. If the phrasal verb is separable, circle SEP. If it is nonseparable, circle NONSEP.

1. I got over my cold. → I got _over it_____.	SEP	(NONSEP)
2. I made up the story. → I made _____.	SEP	NONSEP
3. I put off my homework. → I put _____.	SEP	NONSEP
4. I wrote down the numbers. → I wrote _____.	SEP	NONSEP
5. I looked up the answer. → I looked _____.	SEP	NONSEP
6. I got on the bus. → I got _____.	SEP	NONSEP
7. I looked into the problem. → I looked _____.	SEP	NONSEP
8. I shut off the engine. → I shut _____.	SEP	NONSEP
9. I turned off the lights. → I turned _____.	SEP	NONSEP
10. I got off the subway. → I got _____.	SEP	NONSEP

NOTE: See the *Fundamentals of English Grammar Workbook* appendix for more practice exercises for phrasal verbs.

UNIT C: Prepositions

NOTE: See the *Fundamentals of English Grammar Workbook* appendix for practice exercises for preposition combinations.

C-1 Preposition Combinations: Introduction

ADJ + PREP (a) Ali is *absent from* class today. V + PREP (b) This book *belongs to* me.	*At, from, of, on,* and *to* are examples of prepositions. Prepositions are often combined with adjectives, as in (a), and verbs, as in (b).

C-2 Preposition Combinations: A Reference List

A
be absent from
be accustomed to
   add (*this*) to (*that*)
be acquainted with
   admire (*someone*) for (*something*)
be afraid of
   agree with (*someone*) about (*something*)
be angry at / with (*someone*) about / over (*something*)
   apologize to (*someone*) for (*something*)
   apply for (*something*)
   approve of
   argue with (*someone*) about / over (*something*)
   arrive at (*a building / a room*)
   arrive in (*a city / a country*)
   ask (*someone*) about (*something*)
   ask (*someone*) for (*something*)
be aware of

B
be bad for
   believe in
   belong to
be bored with / by
   borrow (*something*) from (*someone*)

C
be clear to
   combine with
   compare (*this*) to / with (*that*)
   complain to (*someone*) about (*something*)
be composed of
   concentrate on
   consist of
be crazy about
be crowded with
be curious about

D
   depend on (*someone*) for (*something*)
be dependent on (*someone*) for (*something*)

be devoted to
   die of / from
be different from
   disagree with (*someone*) about (*something*)
be disappointed in
   discuss (*something*) with (*someone*)
   divide (*this*) into (*that*)
be divored from
be done with
   dream about / of
   dream of

E
be engaged to
be equal to
   escape from (*a place*)
be excited about
   excuse (*someone*) for (*something*)
   excuse from
be exhausted from

F
be familiar with
be famous for
   feel about
   feel like
   fill (*something*) with
be finished with
   forgive (*someone*) for (*something*)
be friendly to / with
be frightened of / by
be full of

G
   get rid of
be gone from
be good for
   graduate from

H
happen to
be happy about (*something*)
be happy for (*someone*)
   hear about / of (*something*) from (*someone*)
   help (*someone*) with (*something*)
   hide (*something*) from (*someone*)
   hope for
be hungry for

I
   insist on
be interested in
   introduce (*someone*) to (*someone*)
   invite (*someone*) to (*something*)
be involved in

K
be kind to
   know about

L
   laugh at
   leave for (*a place*)
   listen to
   look at
   look for
   look forward to
   look like

M
be made of
be married to
   matter to
be the matter with
   multiply (*this*) by (*that*)

N
be nervous about
be nice to

O
be opposed to

P
   pay for
be patient with
be pleased with / about
   play with
   point at
be polite to
   prefer (*this*) to (*that*)

be prepared for
   protect (*this*) from (*that*)
be proud of
   provide (*someone*) with

Q
be qualified for

R
   read about
be ready for
be related to
   rely on
be resonsible for

S
be sad about
be satisfied with
be scared of / by
   search for
   separate (*this*) from (*that*)
be similar to
   speak to / with (*someone*) about (*something*)
   stare at
   subtact (*this*) from (*that*)
be sure of / about

T
   take care of
   talk about (*something*)
   talk to / with (*someone*) about (*something*)
   tell (*someone*) about (*something*)
be terrified of / by
   thank (*someone*) for (*something*)
   think about / of
be thirsty for
be tired from
be tired of
   translate from (*one language*) to (*another*)

U
be used to

W
   wait for
   wait on
   warn about / of
   wonder about
be worried about

Listening Script

NOTE: You may want to pause the audio after each item or in longer passages so that there is enough time to complete each task.

Chapter 1: Present Time

Exercise 1, p. 1.

SAM: Hi. My name is Sam.

LISA: Hi. I'm Lisa. It's nice to meet you.

SAM: Nice to meet you too. Where are you from?

LISA: I'm from Boston. How about you?

SAM: I'm from Quebec. So, how long have you been here?

LISA: Just one day. I still have a little jet lag.

SAM: Me too. I got in yesterday morning. So we need to ask each other about a hobby. What do you like to do in your free time?

LISA: I spend a lot of time outdoors. I love to hike. When I'm indoors, I like to surf the Internet.

SAM: Me too. I'm studying Italian right now. There are a lot of good websites for learning languages on the Internet.

LISA: I know. I found a good one for Japanese. I'm trying to learn a little. Now, when I introduce you to the group, I have to write your full name on the board. What's your last name and how do you spell it?

SAM: It's Sanchez. S-A-N-C-H-E-Z.

LISA: My last name is Paterson — with one "t": P-A-T-E-R-S-O-N.

SAM: It looks like our time is up. Thanks. It's been nice talking to you.

LISA: I enjoyed it too.

Exercise 5, p. 4.

Lunch at the Fire Station

It's 12:30, and the firefighters are waiting for their next call. They are taking their lunch break. Ben, Rita, and Jada are sitting at a table in the fire station. Their co-worker Bruno is making lunch for them. He is an excellent cook. He often makes lunch. He is fixing spicy chicken and rice. Their captain isn't eating. He is doing paperwork. He skips lunch on busy days. He works in his office and finishes his paperwork.

Exercise 6, p. 5.

1. Irene designs video games.
2. She is working on a new project.
3. She is sitting in front of her computer.
4. She spends her weekends at the office.
5. She's finishing plans for a new game.

Exercise 9, p. 6.

A problem with the printer

1. Does it need more paper?
2. Does it have enough ink?
3. Are you fixing it yourself?
4. Do you know how to fix it?
5. Do we have another printer in the office?
6. Hmmm. Is it my imagination or is it making a strange noise?

Exercise 21, p. 14.

Natural disasters: a flood

1. The weather causes some natural disasters.
2. Heavy rains sometimes create floods.
3. A big flood causes a lot of damage.
4. In towns, floods can damage buildings, homes, and roads.
5. After a flood, a town needs a lot of financial help for repairs.

Exercise 24, p. 15.

1. talks	9.	mixes
2. fishes	10.	bows
3. hopes	11.	studies
4. teaches	12.	buys
5. moves	13.	enjoys
6. kisses	14.	tries
7. pushes	15.	carries
8. waits		

Exercise 33, p. 21.
Part I.

At the doctor's office

1. Do you	becomes	Dyou	Do you have an appointment?
2. Does he	becomes	Dze	Does he have an appointment?
3. Does she	becomes	Duh-she	Does she have an appointment?
4. Do we	becomes	Duh-we	Do we have an appointment?
5. Do they	becomes	Duh-they	Do they have an appointment?
6. Am I	becomes	Mi	Am I late for my appointment?
7. Is it	becomes	Zit	Is it time for my appointment?
8. Does it	becomes	Zit	Does it hurt?

Part II.

1. Do you have pain anywhere?
2. Does it hurt anywhere else?
3. Does she have a cough or sore throat?
4. Does he have a fever?
5. Does she need lab tests?
6. Am I very sick?
7. Is it serious?
8. Does he need to make another appointment?
9. Do they want to wait in the waiting room?
10. Do we pay now or later?

Exercise 35, p. 22.

1. We have a few minutes before we need to leave. Do you want a cup of coffee?
2. We need to leave. Are you ready?
3. Look outside. Is it raining hard?
4. Do we need to take an umbrella?
5. Mr. Smith has his coat on. Is he leaving now?
6. I'm looking for the office supplies. Are they in here?

Exercise 37, p. 24.

Aerobic Exercise

Jeremy and Nancy believe exercise is important. They go to an exercise class three times a week. They like aerobic exercise.

Aerobic exercise is a special type of exercise. It increases a person's heart rate. Fast walking, running, and dancing are examples of aerobic exercise. During aerobic exercise, a person's heart beats fast. This brings more oxygen to the muscles. Muscles work longer when they have more oxygen.

Right now Jeremy and Nancy are listening to some lively music. They are doing special dance steps. They are exercising different parts of their body.

How about you? Do you like to exercise? Do your muscles get exercise every week? Do you do some type of aerobic exercise?

Chapter 2: Past Time

Exercise 4, p. 27.

1. We studied . . .
2. Mr. Green wrote a magazine article . . .
3. The sun sets . . .
4. A substitute teacher taught . . .
5. Mr. Watson drove a sports car . . .

Exercise 5, p. 28.

Part I.

1. I was in a hurry. I wasn't in a hurry.
2. They were on time. They weren't on time.
3. He was at the doctor's. He wasn't at the doctor's.
4. We were early. We weren't early.

Part II.

At a wedding

1. The bride wasn't nervous before the ceremony.
2. The groom was nervous before the ceremony.
3. His parents weren't nervous about the wedding.
4. The bride and groom were excited about their wedding.
5. The ceremony was in the evening.
6. The wedding reception wasn't after the wedding.
7. It was the next day.
8. It was at a popular hotel.
9. A lot of guests were there.
10. Some relatives from out of town weren't there.

Exercise 8, p. 30.

1. Shhh. The movie is beginning.
2. Oh, no. The elevator door is stuck. It isn't opening.
3. Here's a letter for you. I opened it accidentally.
4. I'm listening to the phone message that you aready listened to.
5. Are you lying to me or telling me the truth?
6. We enjoyed the party.
7. I'm enjoying the nice weather today.
8. You look upset. What happened?

Exercise 16, p. 37.

Part I.

1. Did you	becomes	Did-ja	Did you forget something? OR
Did you	becomes	Did-ya	Did you forget something?
2. Did I	becomes	Dih-di	Did I forget something? OR
Did I	becomes	Di	Did I forget something?
3. Did he	becomes	Dih-de	Did he forget something? OR
Did he	becomes	De	Did he forget something?

4. Did she   becomes   Dih-she   Did she forget something?
5. Did we   becomes   Dih-we   Did we forget something?
6. Did they   becomes   Dih-they   Did they forget something?

Part II.

1. Alex hurt his finger. Did he cut it with a knife?
2. Ms. Jones doesn't have any money in her wallet. Did she spend it all yesterday?
3. Karen's parents visited. Did you meet them yesterday?
4. The Browns don't have a car anymore. Did they sell it?
5. I dropped the glass. Did I break it?
6. Ann didn't throw away her old clothes. Did she keep them?
7. John gave a book to his son. Did he read it to him?
8. You don't have your glasses. Did you lose them?
9. Mr. Jones looked for his passport in his desk drawer. Did he find it?
10. The baby is crying. Did I upset her?

Exercise 17, p. 37.

Luka wasn't home last night.

1. Did he go to a party last night?
2. Did he have a good time?
3. Did he eat a lot of food?
4. Did he drink a lot of soda?
5. Did he meet some new people?
6. Did he shake hands with them when he met them?
7. Did he dance with friends?
8. Did he sit with his friends and talk?

Exercise 19, p. 38.

A Deadly Flu

Every year, the flu kills 200,000 to 300,000 people around the world. But in 1918, a very strong flu virus killed millions of people. This flu began in 1918 and lasted until 1920. It spread around the world, and between 20 million and 100 million people died. Unlike other flu viruses that usually kill the very young and the very old, many of the victims were healthy young adults. This was unusual and made people especially afraid.

Exercise 20, p. 39.

Part I.

1. watch, watched
2. studied, studied
3. works, worked
4. decided, decided

Part II.

1. We watched a movie.
2. They studied in the morning.
3. She worked at the library.
4. They decided to leave.

Exercise 21, p. 39.

1. We agree with you.
2. We agreed with you.
3. I arrived on time.
4. The teacher explains the answers well.
5. My doctor's appointment ended late.
6. The train stopped suddenly.
7. You touched a spider!

Exercise 22, p. 40.

1. It rains in the spring . . .
2. It rained a lot . . .
3. The mail carrier walks to our house . . .
4. My friend surprised me with a birthday present . . .
5. The taxi picks up passengers at the airport . . .
6. I passed my final exam in math . . .

Exercise 23, p. 40.

1. cooked	5. started	9. added
2. served	6. dropped	10. passed
3. wanted	7. pulled	11. returned
4. asked	8. pushed	12. pointed

Exercise 24, p. 40.

A: Did you have a good weekend?
B: Yeah, I went to a waterslide park.
A: Really? That sounds like fun!
B: It was great! I loved the fast slides. How about you? How was your weekend?
A: I visited my aunt.
B: Did you have a good time?
A: Not really. She didn't like my clothes or my haircut.

Exercise 31, p. 46.

At a checkout stand in a grocery store

1. A: Hi. Did you find what you needed?
   B: Almost everything. I was looking for sticky rice, but I didn't see it.
   A: It's on aisle 10, in the Asian food section.

2. A: This is the express lane. Ten items only. It looks like you have more than ten. Did you count them?
   B: I thought I had ten. Oh, I guess I have more. Sorry.
   A: The checkout stand next to me is open.

3. A: Do you have any coupons you wanted to use?
   B: I had a couple in my purse, but I can't find them now.
   A: What were they for? I might have some extras here.
   B: One was for eggs, and the other was for ice cream.
   A: I think I have those.

Exercise 39, p. 51.

Jennifer's Problem

Jennifer works for an insurance company. When people need help with their car insurance, they call her. Right now it is 9:05 A.M., and Jennifer is sitting at her desk.

She came to work on time this morning. Yesterday Jennifer was late to work because she had a minor auto accident. While she was driving to work, her cell phone rang. She reached for it.

While she was reaching for her phone, Jennifer lost control of the car. Her car ran into a row of mailboxes beside the road and stopped. Fortunately, no one was hurt in the accident.

Jennifer is okay, but her car isn't. It needs repairs. Jennifer feels very embarrassed now. She made a bad decision, especially since it is illegal to talk on a cell phone and drive at the same time where she lives.

Exercise 43, p. 53.

1. I used to stay up past midnight, but now I often go to bed at 10:00 because I have an 8:00 class.
2. What time did you used to go to bed when you were a child?
3. Tom used to play tennis after work every day, but now he doesn't.
4. I used to skip breakfast, but now I always have something to eat in the morning because I read that students who eat breakfast do better in school.
5. I didn't used to like grammar, but now I do.

Chapter 3: Future Time

Exercise 2, p. 56.

At the airport

1. The security line will take about a half hour.
2. The plane is going to arrive at Gate 10.
3. Your flight is already an hour late.
4. Your flight will be here soon.
5. Did you print your boarding pass?
6. Are you printing my boarding pass too?
7. Are we going to have a snack on our flight?
8. We will need to buy snacks on the flight.

Exercise 6, p. 58.

Part I.

Looking for an apartment

A: We're going to look for an apartment to rent this weekend.
B: Are you going to look in this area?
A: No, we're going to search in an area closer to our jobs.
B: Is the rent going to be cheaper in that area?
A: Yes, apartment rents are definitely going to be cheaper.

B: Are you going to need to pay a deposit?
A: I'm sure we're going to need to pay the first and last month's rent.

Part II.

A: Where are you going to move to?
B: We're going to look for something outside the city. We're going to spend the weekend apartment hunting.
A: What fees are you going to need to pay?
B: I think we are going to need to pay the first and last month's rent.
A: Are there going to be other fees?
B: There is probably going to be an application fee and a cleaning fee. Also, the landlord is probably going to run a credit check, so we are going to need to pay for that.

Exercise 10, p. 60.

Part I.

1. I'll be ready to leave soon.
2. You'll need to come.
3. He'll drive us.
4. She'll come later.
5. We'll get there a little late.
6. They'll wait for us.

Part II.

1. Don't wait up for me tonight. I'll be home late.
2. I paid the bill this morning. You'll get my check in the next day or two.
3. We have the better team. We'll probably win the game.
4. Henry twisted his ankle while running down a hill. He'll probably take a break from running this week.
5. We can go to the beach tomorrow, but it'll probably be too cold to go swimming.
6. I invited some guests for dinner. They'll probably get here around seven.
7. Karen is doing volunteer work for a community health-care clinic this week. She'll be gone a lot in the evenings.

Exercise 11, p. 61.

Part I.

At the doctor's office

1. The doctor'll be with you in a few minutes.
2. Your appointment'll take about an hour.
3. Your fever'll be gone in a few days.
4. Your stitches'll disappear over the next two weeks.
5. The nurse'll schedule your tests.
6. The lab'll have the results next week.
7. The receptionist at the front desk'll set up your next appointment.

Part II.

At the pharmacy

1. Your prescription'll be ready in ten minutes.
2. The medicine'll make you feel a little tired.
3. The pharmacist'll call your doctor's office.

4. This cough syrup'll help your cough.
5. Two aspirin'll be enough.
6. The generic drug'll cost less.
7. This information'll explain all the side effects for this medicine.

Exercise 13, p. 62.

My day tomorrow

1. I'm going to go to the bank tomorrow.
2. I'll probably do other errands too.
3. I may stop at the post office.
4. I will probably pick up groceries at the store.
5. It is going to be hot.
6. Maybe I'll do my errands early.

Exercise 17, p. 64.

Predictions about the future

1. People'll have flying cars.
2. Cars'll use solar power or energy from the sun instead of gas.
3. Some people'll live underwater.
4. Some people may live in outer space.
5. Maybe creatures from outer space'll live here.
6. Children'll learn on computers in their homes, not at school.
7. Robots may clean our homes.
8. Maybe computers'll have feelings.
9. People won't die.
10. The earth'll be too crowded.

Exercise 23, p. 67.

1. Could someone please open the window?
2. Do you have plans for the weekend?
3. Do you have a car?
4. I feel sick. I need to leave.

Exercise 33, p. 73.

Going on vacation

A: I'm going on vacation tomorrow.
B: Where are you going?
A: To San Francisco.
B: How are you getting there? Are you flying or driving your car?
A: I'm flying. I have to be at the airport by seven tomorrow morning.
B: Do you need a ride to the airport?
A: No, thanks. I'm taking a taxi. What about you? Are you planning to go somewhere over vacation?
B: No. I'm staying here.

Exercise 44, p. 79.

At a Chinese restaurant

A: Okay, let's all open our fortune cookies.
B: What does yours say?
A: Mine says, "You will receive an unexpected gift." Great! Are you planning to give me a gift soon?

B: Not that I know of. Mine says, "Your life will be long and happy."
Good. I want a long life.
C: Mine says, "A smile solves all communication problems." Well, that's good! After this, when I don't understand someone, I'll just smile at them.
D: My fortune is this: "If you work hard, you will be successful."
A: Well, it looks like all of us will have good luck in the future!

Chapter 4: Present Perfect and Past Perfect

Exercise 2, p. 82.

1. call, called, called	6. come, came, come
2. speak, spoke, spoken	7. eat, ate, eaten
3. do, did, done	8. cut, cut, cut
4. know, knew, known	9. read, read, read
5. meet, met, met	10. be, was/were, been

Exercise 12, p. 88.

1. I saw a two-headed snake once. Have you ever . . . ?
2. I flew in a small plane last year. Have you ever . . . ?
3. I rode in a limousine once. Have you ever . . . ?
4. I did volunteer work last month. Have you ever . . . ?
5. I accidentally tore my shirt yesterday. Have you ever . . . ?
6. I had a scary experience on an airplane last year. Have you ever . . . ?
7. I fell out of a boat last week. Have you ever . . . ?
8. I felt very, very embarrassed once, and my face got hot. Have you ever . . . ?
9. I spoke to a famous person yesterday. Have you ever . . . ?
10. I wanted to be famous once. Have you ever . . . ?

Exercise 17, p. 91.

1. Lori holds the baby a lot.
2. Richard gives the baby a bath at the end of the day.
3. Lori changes the baby's diapers.
4. Richard has taken lots of pictures of the baby.
5. Lori wakes up when the baby cries.
6. Richard does some of the household chores.
7. Lori is tired during the day.

Exercise 19, p. 92.

At a restaurant

1. My coffee's a little cold.
2. My coffee's gotten a little cold.
3. Your order's not ready yet.
4. Wow! Our order's here already.
5. Excuse me, I think our waiter's forgotten our order.
6. Actually, your waiter's just gone home sick. I'll take care of you.

Exercise 20, p. 93.

A job interview

Mika is a nurse. She is interviewing for a job with the manager of a hospital emergency room. He is looking at her resume and asking her some general questions.

INTERVIEWER: It looks like you've done a lot of things since you became a nurse.

MIKA: Yes, I've worked for a medical clinic. I've worked in a prison. I've worked in several area hospitals. And I've done volunteer work at a community health center for low-income patients.

INTERVIEWER: Very good. But, let me ask you, why have you changed jobs so often?

MIKA: Well, I like having new challenges and different experiences.

INTERVIEWER: Why have you applied for this job?

MIKA: Well, I'm looking for something more fast-paced, and I've been interested in working in an E.R. for a long time. I've heard that this hospital provides great training for its staff, and it offers excellent patient care.

INTERVIEWER: Thank you for coming in. I'll call you next week with our decision.

MIKA: It was good to meet you. Thank you for your time.

Exercise 26, p. 97.

1. Every day, I spend some money. Yesterday, I spent some money. Since Friday, I have . . .
2. I usually make a big breakfast. Yesterday, I made a big breakfast. All week, I have . . .
3. Every day, I send emails. Yesterday I sent an email. Today I have already . . .
4. Every time I go to a restaurant, I leave a nice tip. Last night I left a nice tip. I just finished dinner, and I have . . .
5. Every weekend, I sleep in late. Last weekend, I slept in late. Since I was a teenager, I have . . .
6. I drive very carefully. On my last trip across the country, I drove very carefully. All my life, I have . . .
7. Every morning, I sing in the shower. Earlier today, I sang in the shower. Since I was little, I have . . .

Exercise 31, p. 100.

Part 1.

1. Jane's been out of town for two days.
2. My parents've been active in politics for 40 years.
3. My friends've moved into a new apartment.
4. I'm sorry. Your credit card's expired.
5. Bob's been traveling in Montreal since last Tuesday.
6. You're the first one here. No one else's come yet.

Part II.

1. The weather's been warm since the beginning of April.

2. This month's been unusually warm.
3. My parents've been living in the same house for 25 years.
4. My cousins've lived in the same town all their lives.
5. You slept late. Your friend's already gotten up and made breakfast.
6. My friends've planned a going-away party for me. I'm moving back to my hometown.
7. I'm afraid your work's been getting a little sloppy.
8. My roommate's traveled a lot. She's visited many different countries.

Exercise 34, p. 103.

Today's Weather

The weather has certainly been changing today. Boy, what a day! We've already had rain, wind, hail, and sun. So, what's in store for tonight? As you have probably seen, dark clouds have been building. We have a weather system moving in that is going to bring colder temperatures and high winds. We've been saying all week that this system is coming, and it looks like tonight is it! We've even seen snow down south of us, and we could get some snow here too. So hang onto your hats! We may have a rough night ahead of us.

Exercise 36, p. 104.

1. A: What song is playing on the radio?
   B: I don't know, but it's good, isn't it?
2. A: How long have you lived in Dubai?
   B: About a year.
3. A: Where are the kids?
   B: I don't know. I've been calling them for ten minutes.
4. A: Who have you met tonight?
   B: Actually, I've met a few people from your office. How about you? Who have you met?
   A: I've met some interesting artists and musicians.

Exercise 37, p. 104.

A common illness

LARA: Hi, Mom. I was just calling to tell you that I can't come to your birthday party this weekend. I'm afraid I'm sick.

MOM: Oh, I'm sorry to hear that.

LARA: Yeah, I got sick Wednesday night, and it's just been getting worse.

MOM: Are you going to see a doctor?

LARA: I don't know. I don't want to go to a doctor if it's not serious.

MOM: Well, what symptoms have you been having?

LARA: I've had a cough, and now I have a fever.

MOM: Have you been taking any medicine?

LARA: Just over-the-counter stuff.

MOM: If your fever doesn't go away, I think you need to call a doctor.

LARA: Yeah, I probably will.

MOM: Well, call me tomorrow and let me know how you're doing.

LARA: Okay. I'll call you in the morning.

Exercise 43, p. 110.

1. A: Oh, no! We're too late. The train has already left.
    B: That's okay. We'll catch the next one.

2. A: Last Thursday we went to the station to catch the train, but we were too late.
    B: Yeah, the train had already left.

3. A: You sure woke up early this morning!
    B: Well, I wasn't sleepy. I had already slept for eight hours.

4. A: Go back to sleep. It's only six o'clock in the morning.
    B: I'm not sleepy. I'm going to get up. I have already slept for eight hours.

Chapter 5: Asking Questions

Exercise 4, p. 113.

Leaving for the airport

1. Do you have your passport?
2. Did you remember to pack a snack for the plane?
3. Will your carry-on bag fit under the seat?
4. Is your taxi coming soon?
5. Will you call me when you get there?

Exercise 6, p. 113.

Part I.

1. Is he absent?	becomes	*Ih-ze* absent? OR *Ze* absent?
2. Is she absent?	becomes	*Ih-she* absent?
3. Does it work?	becomes	*Zit* work?
4. Did it break?	becomes	*Dih-dit* break? OR *Dit* break?
5. Has he been sick?	becomes	*Ze* been sick? OR *A-ze* been sick?
6. Is there enough?	becomes	*Zere* enough?
7. Is that okay?	becomes	*Zat* okay?

Part II.

At the grocery store

1. I need to see the manager. Is she available?
2. I need to see the manager. Is he in the store today?
3. Here is one bag of apples. Is that enough?
4. I need a drink of water. Is there a drinking fountain?
5. My credit card isn't working. Hmmm. Did it expire?
6. Where's Simon? Has he left?
7. The price seems high. Does it include the tax?

Exercise 9, p. 116.

Where are Roberto and Isabel?

A: Do you know Roberto and Isabel?

B: Yes, I do. They live around the corner from me.

A: Have you seen them lately?

B: No, I haven't. They're out of town.

A: Did they go to their parents? I heard Roberto's parents are ill.

B: Yes, they did. They went to help them.

A: Are you going to see them soon?

B: Yes, I am. In fact, I'm going to pick them up at the airport.

A: Will they be back this weekend? I'm having a party, and I'd like to invite them.

B: No, they won't. They won't be back until Monday.

Exercise 14, p. 118.

1. Do you want to go to the mall?
2. When are the Waltons coming?
3. Where will I meet you?
4. Why were you late?
5. What did you buy?

Exercise 19, p. 120.

A secret

A: John told me something.

B: What did he tell you?

A: It's confidential. I can't tell you.

B: Did he tell anyone else?

A: He told a few other people.

B: Who did he tell?

A: Some friends.

B: Then it's not a secret. What did he say?

A: I can't tell you.

B: Why can't you tell me?

A: Because it's about you. But don't worry. It's nothing bad.

B: Gee. Thanks a lot. That sure makes me feel better.

Exercise 29, p. 126.

1. Who's ringing the doorbell?
2. Whose coat is on the floor?
3. Whose glasses are those?
4. Who's sitting next to you?
5. Whose seat is next to yours?
6. Who's out in the hallway?

Exercise 30, p. 126.

An old vacation photo

1. Whose picture is this?
2. Who's in the picture?
3. Who's standing in back?
4. You don't wear glasses. Whose glasses are you wearing?
5. Who's the woman in the purple jacket?
6. Whose cabin are you at?

Exercise 34, p. 128.

1. A: How fresh are these eggs?
   B: I just bought them at the Farmers' Market, so they should be fine.

2. A: How cheap were the tickets?
   B: They were 50% off.

3. A: How hard was the driver's test?
   B: Well, I didn't pass, so that gives you an idea.

4. A: How clean is the car?
   B: There's dirt on the floor. We need to vacuum it inside.

5. A: How hot is the frying pan?
   B: Don't touch it! You'll burn yourself.

6. A: How noisy is the street you live on?
   B: There is a lot of traffic, so we keep the windows closed a lot.

7. A: How serious are you about interviewing for the job?
   B: Very. I already scheduled an interview with the company.

Exercise 37, p. 130.

Questions:

1. How old are you?
2. How tall are you?
3. How much do you weigh?
4. In general, how well do you sleep at night?
5. How quickly do you fall asleep?
6. How often do you wake up during the night?
7. How tired are you in the mornings?
8. How many times a week do you exercise?
9. How are you feeling right now?
10. How soon can you come in for an overnight appointment?

Exercise 44, p. 134.

A birthday

1. When's your birthday?
2. When'll your party be?
3. Where'd you decide to have it?
4. Who're you inviting?

Exercise 45, p. 135.

1. Where's my key?
2. Where're my keys?
3. Who're those people?
4. What's in that box?
5. What're you doing?
6. Where'd Bob go last night?
7. Who'll be at the party?
8. Why's the teacher absent?
9. Who's that?
10. Why'd you say that?
11. Who'd you talk to at the party?

12. How're we going to get to work?
13. What'd you say?
14. How'll you do that?

Exercise 46, p. 135.

On an airplane

1. Who're you going to sit with?
2. How're you going to get your suitcase under the seat?
3. What'd the flight attendant just say?
4. Why'd we need to put our seat belts back on?
5. Why's the plane descending?
6. Why're we going down?
7. When'll the pilot tell us what's going on?
8. Who'll meet you when you land?
9. When's our connecting flight?
10. How'll we get from the airport to our hotel?

Exercise 47, p. 135.

A mother talking to her teenage daughter

1. Where're you going?
2. Who're you going with?
3. Who's that?
4. How long've you known him?
5. Where'd you meet him?
6. Where's he go to school?
7. Is he a good student?
8. What time'll you be back?
9. Why're you wearing that outfit?
10. Why're you giving me that look?
11. Why am I asking so many questions? Because I love you!

Exercise 48, p. 136.

1. What do you want to do?
2. What are you doing?
3. What are you having for dinner?
4. What are you doing that for?
5. What do you think about that?
6. What are you laughing for?
7. What do you need?
8. What do you have in your pocket?

Exercise 53, p. 138.

1. A: Did you like the movie?
   B: It was okay, I guess. How about you?

2. A: Are you going to the company party?
   B: I haven't decided yet. What about you?

3. A: Do you like living in this city?
   B: Sort of. How about you?

4. A: What are you going to have?
   B: Well, I'm not really hungry. I think I might order just a salad. How about you?

Exercise 56, p. 140.

1. a. You're Mrs. Rose, aren't you?
   b. Are you Mrs. Rose?
2. a. Do you take cream with your coffee?
   b. You take cream with your coffee, don't you?
3. a. You don't want to leave, do you?
   b. Do you want to leave?

Exercise 57, p. 141.

1. Simple Present
   a. You like strong coffee, don't you?
   b. David goes to Ames High School, doesn't he?
   c. Leila and Sara live on Tree Road, don't they?
   d. Jane has the keys to the storeroom, doesn't she?
   e. Jane's in her office, isn't she?
   f. You're a member of this class, aren't you?
   g. Oleg doesn't have a car, does he?
   h. Lisa isn't from around here, is she?
   i. I'm in trouble, aren't I?

2. Simple Past
   a. Paul went to Indonesia, didn't he?
   b. You didn't talk to the boss, did you?
   c. Ted's parents weren't at home, were they?
   d. That was Pat's idea, wasn't it?

3. Present Progressive, *Be Going To,* and Past Progressive
   a. You're studying hard, aren't you?
   b. Greg isn't working at the bank, is he?
   c. It isn't going to rain today, is it?
   d. Michelle and Yoko were helping, weren't they?
   e. He wasn't listening, was he?

4. Present Perfect
   a. It has been warmer than usual, hasn't it?
   b. You've had a lot of homework, haven't you?
   c. We haven't spent much time together, have we?
   d. Fatima has started her new job, hasn't she?
   e. Bruno hasn't finished his sales report yet, has he?
   f. Steve's had to leave early, hasn't he?

Exercise 59, p. 142.

Checking in at a hotel

1. You have our reservation, don't you?
2. We have a non-smoking room, don't we?
3. There's a view of the city, isn't there?
4. I didn't give you my credit card yet, did I?
5. The room rate doesn't include tax, does it?
6. Breakfast is included in the price, right?
7. Check-out time's noon, isn't it?
8. You don't have a pool, do you?
9. There are hair dryers in the rooms, aren't there?
10. Kids aren't allowed in the hot tub, are they?

Exercise 61, p. 143.

Part I.

1. What kind of music do you enjoy listening to?
2. I just saw you for a few minutes last night. What did you leave so early for?
3. How are you feeling?
4. How long does the bus ride take?
5. Whose children are those?
6. When did the Browns move into their new apartment?

Part II.

7. A: We only have a few minutes before the movie starts.
   B: I'm hurrying.
   A: Do you have enough money for the tickets?

8. A: Is the mail here yet?
   B: No, I just checked.
   A: I'm expecting a package. How soon will it be here?

9. A: I start my new job next week.
   B: Wow, that's soon.
   A: Yeah, I wanted to start as soon as possible.
   B: Now, how come you're changing jobs?

10. A: Are you new to the area?
    B: Yes, I moved here last month. My company transferred me here.
    A: Oh, so what do you do?

Exercise 62, p. 143.

Ordering at a fast-food restaurant

Cashier: So, what'll it be?
Customer: I'll have a burger.
Cashier: Would you like fries or a salad with your burger?
Customer: I'll have fries.
Cashier: What size?
Customer: Medium.
Cashier: Anything to drink?
Customer: I'll have a vanilla shake.
Cashier: Size?
Customer: Medium.
Cashier: Okay. So that's a burger, fries, vanilla shake.
Customer: About how long'll it take?
Cashier: We're pretty crowded right now. Probably 10 minutes or so. That'll be $6.50. Your number's on the receipt. I'll call the number when your order's ready.
Customer: Thanks.

Chapter 6: Nouns and Pronouns

Exercise 6, p. 149.

1. hat	3. pages	5. keys
2. toys	4. bridge	6. dish

Exercise 7, p. 150.

1. pants	3. boxes	5. wishes
2. cars	4. pens	6. lakes

Exercise 8, p. 150.

1. prizes	ways
2. lips	pants
3. glasses	matches
4. taxes	shirts
5. pills	stars
6. toes	fingers
7. laws	maps
8. lights	places

Exercise 9, p. 150.

1. names	4. boats	7. lips
2. clocks	5. eyelashes	8. bridges
3. eyes	6. ways	9. cars

Exercise 10, p. 150.

1. This shirt comes in three sizes: small, medium, and large.
2. I found this fax on my desk. It's for you.
3. I found these faxes on my desk. They're for you.
4. I'm not going to buy this car. The price is too high.
5. I can't find my glasses anywhere. Have you seen them?
6. The prize for the contest is a new bike.

Exercise 28, p. 159.

How Some Animals Stay Cool

How do animals stay cool in hot weather? Many animals don't sweat like humans, so they have other ways to cool themselves.

Dogs, for example, have a lot of fur and can become very hot. They stay cool mainly by panting. By the way, if you don't know what panting means, this is the sound of panting.

Cats lick their paws and chests. When their fur is wet, they become cooler.

Elephants have very large ears. When they are hot, they can flap their huge ears. The flapping ear acts like a fan and it cools them. Elephants also like to roll in the mud to stay cool.

Exercise 36, p. 163.

A: I'm looking for a new place to live.
B: How come?
A: My two roommates are moving out. I can't afford my apartment. I need a one-bedroom.
B: I just helped a friend find one. I can help you. What else do you want?
A: I want to be near the subway . . . within walking distance. But I want a quiet location. I don't want to be on a busy street.
B: Anything else?
A: A small balcony would be nice.
B: That's expensive.
A: Yeah. I guess I'm dreaming.

Exercise 49, p. 170.

1. Be careful with that knife! It's very sharp. If you're not careful, you'll cut . . .
2. My wife and I have our own business. We don't have a boss. In other words, we work for . .
3. Rebecca is home in bed because she has the flu. She's resting and drinking plenty of fluids. She's being careful about her health. In other words, she is taking care of . . .
4. In a cafeteria, people walk through a section of the restaurant and pick up their food. They are not served by waiters. In other words, in a cafeteria people serve. . .
5. When Joe walked into the room, he didn't know anyone. He smiled confidently and began introducing . . .
6. When I didn't get the new job, I felt sad and depressed. I sat in my apartment and felt sorry for . . .

Exercise 58, p. 176.

1. A: Did you buy the black jacket?
   B: No. I bought the other one.

2. A: One of my favorite colors is dark blue. Another one is red.
   B: Me too.

3. A: This looks like the wrong street. Let's go back and take the other road.
   B: Okay.

4. A: What's the best way to get downtown from here?
   B: It's pretty far to walk. Some people take the bus. Others prefer the subway.

5. A: When I was a kid, I had lots of pets. One was a black dog. Another was an orange cat. Some others were a goldfish and a turtle.
   B: Pets are great for kids.

Exercise 59, p. 177.

A: What do you do when you're feeling lonely?
B: I go someplace where I can be around other people. Even if they are strangers, I feel better when there are others around me. How about you?
A: That doesn't work for me. For example, if I'm feeling lonely and I go to a movie by myself, I look at all the other people who are there with their friends and family, and I start to feel even lonelier. So I try to find other things to do to keep myself busy. When I'm busy, I don't feel lonely.

Chapter 7: Modal Auxiliaries

Exercise 3, p. 179.

1. I have to go downtown tomorrow.
2. You must fasten your seat belt.
3. Could you please open the window?

4. May I borrow your eraser?
5. I'm not able to sign the contract today.
6. Today is the deadline. You must sign it!
7. I have got to go to the post office this afternoon.
8. Shouldn't you save some of your money for emergencies?
9. I feel bad for Elena. She has to have more surgery.
10. Alexa! Stop! You must not run into the street!

Exercise 7, p. 181.

In the classroom

A: I can't understand this math assignment.
B: I can help you with that.
A: Really? Can you explain this problem to me?
B: Well, we can't figure out the answer unless we do this part first.
A: Okay! But it's so hard.
B: Yeah, but I know you can do it. Just go slowly.
A: Class is almost over. Can you meet me after school today to finish this?
B: Well, I can't meet you right after school, but how about at 5:00?
A: Great!

Exercise 13, p. 184.

1. A: Mom, are these oranges sweet?
   B: I don't know. I can't tell if an orange is sweet just by looking at it.

2. A: What are you going to order?
   B: I'm not sure. I might have pasta, or I might have pizza.

3. A: Mom, can I have some candy?
   B: No, but you can have an apple.

4. A: What are you doing this weekend?
   B: I don't know yet. I may go snowboarding with friends, or I may try to fix my motorcycle.

5. May I have everyone's attention? The test is about to begin. If you need to leave the room during the examination, please raise your hand. You may not leave the room without asking. Are there any questions? No? Then you may open your test booklets and begin.

Exercise 17, p. 186.

In a home office

A: Look at this cord. Do you know what it's for?
B: I don't know. We have so many cords around here with all our electronic equipment. It could be for the printer, I guess.
A: No, I checked. The printer isn't missing a cord.
B: It might be for one of the kid's toys.
A: Yeah, I could ask. But they don't have many electronic toys.
B: I have an idea. It may be for the cell phone. You know—the one I had before this one.
A: I bet that's it. We can probably throw this out.
B: Well, let's be sure before we do that.

Exercise 32, p. 194.

Filling out a job application

1. The application has to be complete. You shouldn't skip any parts. If a section doesn't fit your situation, you can write N/A (not applicable).
2. You don't have to type it, but your writing has to be easy to read.
3. You've got to use your full legal name, not your nickname.
4. You've got to list the names and places of your previous employers.
5. You have to list your education, beginning with either high school or college.
6. You don't always have to apply in person. Sometimes you can do it online.
7. You don't have to write some things, like the same telephone number, twice. You can write "same as above."
8. All spelling has to be correct.

Exercise 45, p. 201.

Puzzle steps

1. Write down the number of the month you were born. For example, write the number 2 if you were born in February. Write 3 if you were born in March, etc.
2. Double the number.
3. Add 5 to it.
4. Multiply it by 50.
5. Add your age.
6. Subtract 250.

Exercise 50, p. 204.

A: Why don't we go dancing tonight?
B: I don't know how to dance.
A: Oh. Then why don't we go to a movie?
B: I don't like movies.
A: You don't like movies?!
B: No.
A: Well then, let's go to a restaurant for dinner.
B: That's a waste of money.
A: Well, you do what you want tonight, but I'm going to go out and have a good time.

Chapter 8: Connecting Ideas

Exercise 11, p. 213.

Paying It Forward

A few days ago, a friend and I were driving from Benton Harbor to Chicago. We didn't have any delays for the first hour, but we ran into some highway construction near Chicago. The traffic wasn't moving. My friend and I sat and waited. We talked about our jobs, our families, and the terrible traffic. Slowly it started to move.

We noticed a black sports car on the shoulder. Its blinker was on. The driver obviously wanted to get back into traffic. Car after car passed without letting him in. I decided to do a good deed, so I motioned for him to get in line ahead of me. He waved thanks, and I waved back at him.

All the cars had to stop at a toll booth a short way down the road. I held out my money to pay my toll, but the toll-taker just smiled and waved me on. She told me that the man in the black sports car had already paid my toll. Wasn't that a nice way of saying thank you?

Exercise 15, p. 215.

A strong storm

1. The noise lasted only a short time, but the wind and rain . . .
2. Some roads were under water, but ours . . .
3. Our neighbors didn't lose any trees, but we . . .
4. My son got scared, but my daughter . . .
5. My son couldn't sleep, but my daughter . . .
6. My daughter can sleep through anything, but my son . . .
7. We still need help cleaning up from the storm, but our neighbors . . .
8. We will be okay, but some people . . .

Exercise 21, p. 219.

Part I.

To get more information:

1. A: I'm going to drop this class.
   B: You are? Why? What's the matter?
2. A: My laptop doesn't have enough memory for this application.
   B: Really? Are you sure?
3. A: I can read Braille.
   B: You can? How did you learn to do that?

Part II.

To disagree:

4. A: I love this weather.
   B: I don't.
5. A: I didn't like the movie.
   B: I did!
6. A: I'm excited about graduation.
   B: I'm not.

Exercise 28, p. 223.

Understanding the Scientific Term "Matter"

The word *matter* is a chemical term. Matter is anything that has weight. This book, your finger, water, a rock, air, and the moon are all examples of matter. Heat and radio waves are not matter because they do not have weight. Happiness, dreams, and fears have no weight and are not matter.

Exercise 33, p. 225.

1. Even though I looked all over the house for my keys, . . .
2. Although it was a hot summer night, we went inside and shut the windows because . . .
3. My brother came to my graduation ceremony although . . .
4. Because the package cost so much to send, . . .
5. Even though the soccer team won the game, . . .

Chapter 9: Comparisons

Exercise 4, p. 231.

1. Lara is as old as Tanya.
2. Sylvia isn't as old as Lara.
3. Sylvia and Brigita aren't as old as Tanya.
4. Brigita isn't quite as old as Sylvia.
5. Brigita is almost as old as Sylvia.

Exercise 8, p. 234.

1. Old shoes are more comfortable for me than new shoes.
2. I like food from other countries better than food from my country.
3. Winter is more enjoyable than summer for me.
4. I am the most talkative person in my family.
5. I am the friendliest person in my family.
6. Cooked vegetables are tastier than raw vegetables.
7. Taking a bath is more relaxing than taking a shower.
8. Speaking English is the easiest of all the English skills for me.

Exercise 12, p. 237.

My family

1. My father is younger than my mother.
2. My mother is the tallest person in our family.
3. My father is a fun person to be around. He seems happy all the time.
4. My mother was happier when she was younger.
5. I have twin sisters. They are older than me.
6. I have one brother. He is the funniest person in our family.
7. He is a doctor. He works hard every day.
8. My sisters just like to have fun. I don't think they work hard at all.

Exercise 15, p. 238.

1. Frank owns a coffee shop. Business is busier this year for him than last year.
2. I've know Steven for years. He's the friendliest person I know.
3. Sam expected a hard test, but it wasn't as hard as he expected.

4. The road ends here. This is as far as we can go.
5. Jon's decision to leave his job was the worst decision he has ever made.
6. I don't know if we'll get to the theater on time, but I'm driving as fast as I can.
7. When you do the next assignment, please be more careful.
8. The dessert looks delicious, but I've eaten as much as I can.
9. It takes about an hour to drive to the airport and my flight takes an hour. So the drive takes as long as my flight.

Exercise 23, p. 242.

1. a sidewalk, a road
   a. A sidewalk is as wide as a road.
   b. A road is wider than a sidewalk.
2. a hill, a mountain
   a. A hill isn't as high as a mountain.
   b. A hill is higher than a mountain.
3. a mountain path, a mountain peak
   a. In general, hiking along a mountain path is more dangerous than climbing a mountain peak.
   b. In general, hiking along a mountain path is less dangerous than climbing a mountain peak.
4. toes, fingers
   a. Toes are longer than fingers.
   b. Fingers aren't as long as toes.
   c. Toes are shorter than fingers.
5. basic math, algebra
   a. Basic math isn't as hard as algebra.
   b. Algebra is harder than basic math.
   c. Basic math is as confusing as algebra.
   d. Basic math is less confusing than algebra.

Exercise 36, p. 249.

5. Tom has never told a funny joke.
6. Food has never tasted better.
7. I've never slept on a hard mattress.
8. I've never seen a scarier movie.

Exercise 42, p. 253.

Gold vs. Silver

Gold is similar to silver. They are both valuable metals that people use for jewelry, but they aren't the same. Gold is not the same color as silver. Gold is also different from silver in cost: gold is more expensive than silver.

Two Zebras

Look at the two zebras in the picture. Their names are Zee and Bee. Zee looks like Bee. Is Zee exactly the same as Bee? The pattern of the stripes on each zebra in the world is unique. No two zebras are exactly alike. Even though Zee and Bee are similar to each other, they are different from each other in the exact pattern of their stripes.

Chapter 10: The Passive

Exercise 3, p. 260.

An office building at night

1. The janitors clean the building at night.
   The building is cleaned by the janitors at night.
2. Window washers wash the windows.
   The windows are washed by window washers.
3. A window washer is washing a window right now.
   A window is being washed by a window washer right now.
4. The security guard has checked the offices.
   The offices have been checked by the security guard.
5. The security guard discovered an open window.
   An open window was discovered by the security guard.
6. The security guard found an unlocked door.
   An unlocked door was found by the security guard.
7. The owner will visit the building tomorrow.
   The building will be visited by the owner tomorrow.
8. The owner is going to announce new parking fees.
   New parking fees are going to be announced by the owner.

Exercise 15, p. 267.

A bike accident

A: Did you hear about the accident outside the dorm entrance?
B: No. What happened?
A: A guy on a bike was hit by a taxi.
B: Was he injured?
A: Yeah. Someone called an ambulance. He was taken to City Hospital and treated in the emergency room for cuts and bruises.
B: What happened to the taxi driver?
A: He was arrested for reckless driving.
B: He's lucky that the bicyclist wasn't killed.

Exercise 17, p. 268.

Swimming Pools

Swimming pools are very popular nowadays, but can you guess when swimming pools were first built? Was it 100 years ago? Five hundred years ago? A thousand years ago? Actually, ancient Romans and Greeks built the first swimming pools. Male athletes and soldiers swam in them for training. Believe it or not, as early as 1 B.C., a heated swimming pool was designed for a wealthy Roman. But swimming pools did not become popular until the middle of the 1800s. The city of London built six indoor swimming pools. Soon after, the modern Olympic games began, and swimming races were included in the events. After this, swimming pools became even more popular, and now they are found all over the world.

Exercise 26, p. 274.

1. When will you be done with your work?
2. I hope it's sunny tomorrow. I'm tired of this rainy weather.
3. Jason is excited about going to Hollywood.
4. Are you prepared for the driver's license test?
5. The students are involved in many school activities.
6. The kids want some new toys. They're bored with their old ones.
7. Sam is engaged to his childhood sweetheart.
8. Some animals are terrified of thunderstorms.

Exercise 28, p. 275.

1. This fruit is spoiled. I think I'd better throw it out.
2. When we got to the post office, it was closed.
3. Oxford University is located in Oxford, England.
4. Haley doesn't like to ride in elevators. She's scared of small spaces.
5. What's the matter? Are you hurt?
6. Excuse me. Could you please tell me how to get to the bus station from here? I am lost.
7. Your name is Tom Hood? Are you related to Mary Hood?
8. Where's my wallet? It's gone! Did someone take it?
9. Oh, no! Look at my sunglasses. I sat on them and now they are broken.
10. It's starting to rain. Are all of the windows shut?

Exercise 31, p. 276.

1. Jane doesn't like school because of the boring classes and assignments.
2. The store manager stole money from the cash register. His shocked employees couldn't believe it.
3. I bought a new camera. I read the directions twice, but I didn't understand them. They were too confusing for me.
4. I was out to dinner with a friend and spilled a glass of water on his pants. I felt very embarrassed, but he was very nice about it.
5. Every year for their anniversary, I surprise my parents with dinner at a different restaurant.
6. We didn't enjoy the movie. It was too scary for the kids.

Exercise 33, p. 277.

Situation: Julie was walking along the edge of the fountain outside her office building. She was with her co-worker and friend Paul. Suddenly she lost her balance and accidentally fell into the water.

1. Julie was really embarrassed.
2. Falling into the fountain was really embarrassing.
3. Her friend Paul was shocked by the sight.
4. It was a shocking sight.
5. The people around the office building were very surprised when they saw Julie in the fountain.

6. And Julie had a surprised look on her face.
7. When she fell into the fountain, some people laughed at her. It was an upsetting experience.
8. The next day Julie was a little depressed because she thought she had made a fool of herself.
9. Her friend Paul told her not to lose her sense of humor. He told her it was just another interesting experience in life.
10. He said that people were probably interested in hearing about how she fell into the fountain.

Exercise 37, p. 280.

1. In winter, the weather gets ...
2. In summer, the weather gets ...
3. I think I'll stop working. I'm getting ...
4. My brother is losing some of his hair. He's getting ...
5. Could I have a glass of water? I'm getting really ...
6. You don't look well. Are you getting ...

Exercise 42, p. 282.

1. What are you accustomed to doing in the evenings?
2. What time are you used to going to bed?
3. What are you accustomed to having for breakfast?
4. Are you accustomed to living in this area?
5. Do you live with someone, or do you live alone? Are you used to that?
6. Are you used to speaking English every day?
7. What are you accustomed to doing on weekends?
8. What do you think about the weather here? Are you used to it?

Exercise 51, p. 286.

1. Doctors are supposed to take good care of their patients.
2. Passengers in a car are not supposed to buckle their seat belts.
3. Teachers are supposed to help their students.
4. Airline pilots are supposed to sleep during short flights.
5. People who live in apartments are supposed to pay the rent on time.
6. A dog is not supposed to obey its master.
7. People in a movie theater are supposed to turn off their cell phones.
8. People in libraries are supposed to speak quietly.

Exercise 52, p. 286.

Zoos

Zoos are common around the world. The first zoo was established around 3,500 years ago by an Egyptian queen for her enjoyment. Five hundred years later, a Chinese emperor established a huge zoo to show his power and wealth. Later, zoos were established for the purpose of studying animals.

Zoos were supposed to take good care of animals, but some of the early ones were dark holes or dirty cages. At that time, people became disgusted with the poor care the animals were given. Later, these early zoos were replaced by scientific institutions. Animals were studied and kept in better conditions there. These research centers became the first modern zoos.

Because zoos want to treat animals well and encourage breeding, animals today are put in large, natural settings instead of small cages. They are fed a healthy diet and are watched carefully for any signs of disease. Most zoos have specially trained veterinarians and a hospital for their animals. Today, animals in these zoos are treated well, and zoo breeding programs have saved many different types of animals.

Chapter 11: Count/Noncount Nouns and Articles

Exercise 3, p. 291.

1. We have a holiday next week.
2. What are you going to do?
3. Thomas told an unusual story.
4. Thomas often tells unusual stories.
5. I have an idea!
6. Let's go shopping.
7. There's a sale on shirts and jeans.
8. Let's leave in an hour.
9. Here's a message for you.
10. You need to call your boss.

Exercise 11, p. 296.

1. At our school, teachers don't use chalk anymore.
2. Where is the soap? Did you use all of it?
3. The manager's suggestions were very helpful.
4. Which suggestion sounded best to you?
5. Is this ring made of real gold?
6. We have a lot of storms with thunder and lightning.
7. During the last storm, I found my daughter under her bed.
8. Please put the cap back on the toothpaste.
9. What do you want to do with all this stuff in the hall closet?
10. We have too much soccer and hockey equipment.

Exercise 34, p. 313.

Ice-Cream Headaches

Have you ever eaten something really cold like ice cream and suddenly gotten a headache? This is known as an "ice-cream headache." About 30 percent of the population gets this type of headache. Here is one theory about why ice-cream headaches occur. The roof of your mouth has a lot of nerves. When something cold touches these nerves, they want to warm up your brain. They make your blood vessels swell up (get bigger), and this causes a lot of pain. Ice-cream headaches generally go away after about 30–60 seconds. The best way to avoid these headaches is to keep cold food off the roof of your mouth.

Chapter 12: Adjective Clauses

Exercise 20, p. 329.

My mother's hospital stay

1. The doctor who my mother saw first spent a lot of time with her.
2. The doctor I called for a second opinion was very patient and understanding.
3. The room that my mother had was private.
4. The medicine which she took worked better than she expected.
5. The hospital that my mom chose specializes in women's care.
6. The day my mom came home happened to be her birthday.
7. I thanked the people that helped my mom.
8. The staff whom I met were all excellent.

Exercise 28, p. 334.

1. The plane which I'm taking to Denver leaves at 7:00 A.M.
2. The store that has the best vegetables is also the most expensive.
3. The eggs which my husband made for our breakfast were cold.
4. The person who sent me an email was trying to get my bank account number.
5. The hotel clerk my wife spoke with on the phone is going to give us a room with a view.

Exercise 33, p. 337.

1. I like the people whose house we went to.
2. The man whose daughter is a doctor is very proud.
3. The man who's standing by the window has a daughter at Oxford University.
4. I know a girl whose parents are both airline pilots.
5. I know a girl who's lonely because her parents travel a lot.
6. I met a 70-year-old woman who's planning to go to college.

Exercise 36, p. 339.

Friendly advice

A: A magazine that I saw at the doctor's office had an article you ought to read. It's about the importance of exercise in dealing with stress.
B: Why do you think I should read an article which deals with exercise and stress?
A: If you stop and think for a minute, you can answer that question yourself. You're under a lot of stress, and you don't get any exercise.
B: The stress that I have at work doesn't bother me. It's just a normal part of my job. And I don't have time to exercise.
A: Well, you should make time. Anyone whose job is as stressful as yours should make physical exercise part of their daily routine.

Chapter 13: Gerunds and Infinitives

Exercise 4, p. 343.

1. A: When you finish doing your homework, could you help me in the kitchen?
   B: Sure.

2. A: Do you have any plans for this weekend?
   B: Henry and I talked about seeing the dinosaur exhibit at the museum.

3. A: I didn't understand the answer. Would you mind explaining it?
   B: I'd be happy to.

4. A: I'm thinking about not attending the meeting tomorrow.
   B: Really? Why? I hope you go. We need your input.

5. A: I've been working on this math problem for the last half hour, and I still don't understand it.
   B: Well, don't give up. Keep trying.

Exercise 22, p. 354.

A: Have you made any vacation plans?
B: Well, I wanted to stay home because I don't like traveling. I hate packing and unpacking suitcases. But my wife loves to travel and wanted to take a boat trip somewhere.
A: So, what are you going to do?
B: Well, we couldn't agree, so we decided to stay home and be tourists in our own town.
A: Interesting. What are you planning to do?
B: Well, we haven't seen the new Museum of Space yet. There's also a new art exhibit downtown. And my wife would like to take a boat trip in the harbor. Actually, when we began talking about it, we discovered there were lots of things to do.
A: Sounds like a great solution!
B: Yeah, we're both really excited about seeing more of our own town.

Exercise 44, p. 366.

1. My professor goes through the lecture material too quickly. It is difficult for us to follow him. He needs to slow down and give us time to understand the key points.

2. Asking others about themselves and their lives is one of the secrets of getting along with other people. If you want to make and keep friends, it is important to be sincerely interested in other people's lives.

3. Large bee colonies have 80,000 workers. These worker bees must visit 50 million flowers to make one kilogram, or 2.2 pounds, of honey. It's easy to see why "busy as a bee" is a common expression.

Chapter 14: Noun Clauses

Exercise 21, p. 381.

1. WOMAN: My English teacher is really good. I like her a lot.
   MAN: That's great! I'm glad you're enjoying your class.

2. MOM: How do you feel, honey? You might have the flu.
   SON: I'm okay, Mom. Honest. I don't have the flu.

3. MAN: Did you really fail your chemistry course? How is that possible?
   WOMAN: I didn't study hard enough. Now I won't be able to graduate on time.

4. MAN: Rachel! Hello! It's nice to see you.
   WOMAN: Hi, it's nice to be here. Thank you for inviting me.

5. WOMAN: Carol has left. Look. Her closet is empty. Her suitcases are gone. She won't be back. I just know it!
   MAN: She'll be back.

Exercise 39, p. 392.

Angela called and asked me where Bill was. I told her he was in the lunchroom. She asked when he would be back. I said he would be back around 2:00. I asked her if I could do something for her.

She said that Bill had the information she needed, and only he could help her. I told her that I would leave him a message. She thanked me and hung up.

Trivia Answers

Chapter 1, Exercise 10, p. 7.

1. T
2. T
3. F [According to a 1993 study: the death rate for right-handed people = 32.2%; for left-handed people = 33.8%, so the death rate is about the same.]
4. T
5. F [The official Eiffel Tower Web site says 1,665.]
6. F [Honey never spoils.]
7. T
8. T
9. T
10. T

Chapter 5, Exercise 35, p. 129.

1. c   4. a
2. d   5. e
3. b

Chapter 6, Exercise 18, p. 154.

1. Georgia, Azerbaijan, Kazakhstan, China, Mongolia
2. Denmark
3. The Thames
4. The Dominican Republic, Cuba, Puerto Rico, Jamaica
5. Laos, Thailand, Cambodia, China
6. (*Answers will vary.*)
7. Liechtenstein
8. Vatican City
9. (*Answers will vary.*)
10. Egypt, Sudan, Eritrea, Iran

Chapter 6, Exercise 44, p. 167.

1. T
2. F [gray and wrinkled]
3. T
4. T
5. T
6. T [about 11% to 12% bigger]
7. T
8. F [Men's voices have a higher pitch.]

Chapter 9, Exercise 7, p. 233.

1. T
2. T

3. T
4. F [The Arctic Ocean is the coldest.]
5. F [The South China Sea is the biggest.]
6. T
7. F [Asia is the largest continent in the world.]
8. T
9. F [It's South America.]
10. T

Chapter 9, Exercise 24, p. 242.

Seattle and Singapore have more rain than Manila in December.

[Manila: 58 mm. or 2.3 in.]
[Seattle: 161 mm. or 6.3 in.]
[Singapore: 306 mm. or 12 in.]

Chapter 9, Exercise 25, p. 243.

2. Indonesia has more volcanoes than Japan.
3. Saturn has more moons than Venus.
4. Sao Paulo, Brazil, has more people than New York City.
5. Finland has more islands than Greece.
6. Nepal has more mountains than Switzerland.
7. A banana has more sugar than an apple.
8. The dark meat of a chicken has more fat than the white meat of a chicken.

Chapter 9, Exercise 40, p. 251.

A: 4   D: 5
B: 50   E: 381
C: 381

Chapter 10, Exercise 10, p. 264.

3. Princess Diana was killed in a car crash in 1997.
4. Marie and Pierre Curie discovered radium.
5. Oil was discovered in Saudi Arabia in 1938.
6. Mahatma Gandhi and Martin Luther King Jr. were arrested several times for peaceful protests.
7. Michael Jackson died in 2009.
8. Leonardo da Vinci painted the Mona Lisa.
9. John F. Kennedy was elected president of the United States in 1960.

Chapter 10, Exercise 21, p. 271.

1. sand
2. whales
3. China and Mongolia
4. small spaces

Chapter 11, Exercise 37, p. 316.

1. T
2. T
3. F [Austria]
4. T
5. F
6. T
7. F [psychology/psychiatry]
8. T
9. T
10. F [The Himalayas]

Answer Key

Exercise 5, p. 4.
1. happening right now
2. happening right now
3. happening right now
4. happening right now
5. usual activity
6. happening right now
7. happening right now
8. happening right now
9. usual activity
10. usual activity
11. usual activity

Exercise 6, p. 5.
1. usual activity
2. happening right now
3. happening right now
4. usual activity
5. happening right now

Exercise 7, p. 5.
2. am sitting . . . sit
3. speaks . . . is speaking
4. A: Does it rain
   B: is
5. A: Is it raining?
   B: is starting
6. is walking
7. A: walks . . . Do you walk
   B: Does Oscar walk

Exercise 9, p. 6.
1. Does it
2. Does it
3. Are you
4. Do you
5. Do we
6. is it

Exercise 10, p. 7.
1. runs   T
2. run   T
3. live F [According to a 1993 study: the death rate for right-handed people = 32.2 percent; for left-handed people = 33.8 percent, so the death rate is about the same.]
4. cover T
5. has   F [The official Eiffel Tower Web site says 1665.]

6. spoils F [Honey never spoils.]
7. is   T
8. takes T
9. beats T
10. die   T

Exercise 12, p. 9.
1. It grows one-half inch per month or 15 centimeters a year.
2. They don't hurt because the hair on our scalp is dead.
3. About 100,000.
4. (*Any country near the equator.*)

Exercise 16, p. 11.
1. c. Kazu frequently doesn't shave . . .
   d. Kazu occasionally doesn't shave . . .
   e. Kazu sometimes doesn't shave . . .
   f. Kazu always shaves . . .
   g. Kazu doesn't ever shave . . .
   h. Kazu never shaves . . .
   i. Kazu hardly ever shaves . . .
   j. Kazu rarely shaves . . .
   k. Kazu seldom shaves . . .
2. a. I usually don't eat breakfast.
   b. I don't always eat breakfast.
   c. I seldom eat breakfast.
   d. I don't ever eat breakfast.
3. a. My roommate generally isn't home . . .
   b. My roommate sometimes isn't home . . .
   c. My roommate isn't always home . . .
   d. My roommate is hardly ever home . . .

Exercise 17, p. 12.
2. sometimes makes
3. frequently / often goes
4. is frequently / often late
5. always cooks
6. almost always reads
7. seldom does
8. never goes

Exercise 19, p. 13.
1. A dolphin swims.
2. Dolphins swim.

Exercise 20, p. 13.
3. verb, singular
4. noun, plural
5. verb, singular
6. noun, plural
7. noun, plural
8. verb, singular

Exercise 21, p. 14.
2. create Ø, floods
3. flood Ø, causes
4. towns, floods, buildings, homes, roads
5. flood Ø, town Ø, needs, repairs

Exercise 22, p. 14.

add -s only	add -es	add -ies
stays	wishes	studies
takes	mixes	tries
speaks		

Exercise 23, p. 15.
3. A boat <u>floats</u> on water. (*no change*)
4. Rivers <u>flow</u> toward the sea. (*no change*)
5. My mother <u>worries</u> about me.
6. A student <u>buys</u> a lot of books at the beginning of each term.
7. Airplanes <u>fly</u> all around the world. (*no change*)
8. The teacher <u>asks</u> us a lot of questions in class every day.
9. Mr. Cook <u>watches</u> game shows on TV every evening.
10. Water <u>freezes</u> at 32°F (0°C) and <u>boils</u> at 212°F (100°C).
11. Mrs. Taylor never <u>crosses</u> the street in the middle of a block. She always <u>walks</u> to the corner and <u>uses</u> the crosswalk.

Exercise 24, p. 15.
3. hopes
4. teaches
5. moves
6. kisses
7. pushes
8. waits
9. mixes
10. bows
11. studies
12. buys
13. enjoys
14. tries
15. carries

Exercise 26, p. 16.
(*Order of sentences may vary.*)
1. A car causes air pollution.
2. A rubber band stretches when you pull on it.
3. A hotel supplies its guests with clean towels.
4. Oceans support a huge variety of marine life.
5. A bee collects nectar from flowers.
6. Does exercise improve your health?
7. A hurricane causes great destruction when it reaches land.
8. A river flows downhill.
9. An elephant uses its long trunk like a hand to pick things up.
10. Brazil produces one-fourth of the world's coffee.

Exercise 27, p. 16.
Charlie: a, a
Dad: a, a

Exercise 28, p. 17.
2. a
3. a
4. A: a
   B: a
5. B: b
   A: b

Exercise 29, p. 18.
2. think
3. am thinking
4. are having
5. have

Exercise 30, p. 18.
2. Do you need . . . Do you want
3. A: think . . . know . . . forget
   B: remember
4. A: Do you believe
   B: exist
5. are . . . are having . . . have . . . are building . . . like . . . are lying . . . (are) listening . . . aren't listening . . . hear

Exercise 31, p. 19.
1. a
2. a
3. b

Exercise 32, p. 20.
2. A: Is it raining
   B: it isn't . . . don't think
3. A: Do your friends write
   B: they do . . . get
4. A: Does the weather affect
   B: it does . . . get
5. A: Is Jean studying
   B: she isn't . . . is . . . is playing
   A: Does Jean play
   B: No, she doesn't . . . studies
   A: Is she
   B: she is . . . plays
   A: Do you play
   B: I do . . . am not

Exercise 33, p. 21.
1. Do you
2. Does it
3. Does she
4. Does he
5. Does she
6. Am I
7. Is it
8. Does he
9. Do they
10. Do we

Exercise 34, p. 22.
1. Is the earth revolving around the sun right now? [Yes.]
2. Does the moon revolve around the earth every 28 days? [Yes.]

3. Are the sun and moon planets? [No.]
4. Is Toronto in western Canada? [No.]
5. Do whales lay eggs? [No.]
6. Does your country have gorillas in the wild?
7. Are gorillas intelligent? [Yes.]
8. Do mosquitoes carry malaria? [Yes, some do.]
9. Do you like vegetarian food?
10. Is our teacher from Australia?
11. Is it raining outside now?
12. Are you tired of this interview?

Exercise 35, p. 22.

1. b   3. a   5. b
2. a   4. a   6. a

Exercise 36, p. 22.

2. A: Are they watching
   B: aren't . . . are playing

3. A: Are you listening
   B: want

4. A: are
   B: am
   A: are you doing
   B: am trying

5. A: do you think
   B: think . . . don't think . . . do you think
   A: don't think . . . count

6. A: are you thinking
   B: am thinking . . . am not thinking
   A: don't believe . . . are thinking

7. A: Do you know
   B: do
   A: is
   B: doesn't make
   A: know

Exercise 37, p. 24.

Part I.

2. prefer   6. are doing
3. makes   7. Do you exercise
4. need   8. Are you exercising
5. work

Part II.

1. believe   11. are listening
2. go   12. are doing
3. like   13. are exercising
4. is   14. Do
5. increases   15. like
6. are   16. Do
7. beats   17. get
8. brings   18. Do
9. work   19. do
10. have

Exercise 38, p. 25.

Omar's Visit

(1) My friend Omar **owns** his own car now. It's brand new. Today he **is** driving to a small town north of the city to visit his aunt. He **loves** to listen to music, so the CD player is **playing** one of his favorite CDs — loudly. Omar is very happy: he is **driving** his own car and **listening** to loud music. He's **looking** forward to his visit with his aunt.

(2) Omar **visits** his aunt once a week. She's elderly and **lives** alone. She **thinks** Omar **is** a wonderful nephew. She **loves** his visits. He **tries** to be helpful and considerate in every way. His aunt **doesn't hear** well, so Omar **speaks** loudly and clearly when he's with her.

(3) When he's there, he **fixes** things for her around her apartment and **helps** her with her shopping. He **doesn't stay** with her overnight. He usually **stays** for a few hours and then **heads** back to the city. He **kisses** his aunt good-bye and **gives** her a hug before he **leaves**. Omar is a very good nephew.

Chapter 2: Past Time

Exercise 2, p. 27.

2. She didn't drink . . . Did she drink
3. They didn't play . . . Did they play
4. I didn't leave . . . Did I / you leave
5. They didn't wear . . . Did they wear
6. We didn't have . . . Did we / you have
7. It wasn't . . . Was it
8. You weren't . . . Were you / Was I

Exercise 3, p. 27.

(*Answers may vary.*)

2. I didn't come . . . I came . . . .
3. The students in this class didn't swim . . . They walked . . . .
4. (_____) isn't . . . He/She is a teacher.
5. I didn't sleep . . . I slept in a bed.
6. The Internet didn't become . . . It became popular in the 1990s

Exercise 4, p. 27.

1. French, together, last week
2. yesterday, last summer
3. in the evening, behind the mountains
4. our class, yesterday
5. two weeks ago

Exercise 5, p. 28.

1. wasn't   6. wasn't
2. was   7. was
3. weren't   8. was
4. were   9. were
5. was   10. weren't

Exercise 6, p. 28.
Part I.
giving   hitting   dying   trying

Part II.
stopped   studied   enjoyed   tied

Exercise 7, p. 29.
1. waiting . . . waited
2. cleaning . . . cleaned
3. planting . . . planted
4. planning . . . planned
5. hoping . . . hoped
6. hopping . . . hopped
7. playing . . . played
8. studying . . . studied
9. trying . . . tried
10. dying . . . died
11. sleeping
12. running

Exercise 8, p. 30.
2. opening
3. opened
4. listening . . . listened
5. lying
6. enjoyed
7. enjoying
8. happened

Exercise 9, p. 30.
2. stayed . . . stayed . . . staying
4. gave . . . given . . . giving
5. was / were . . . been . . . being

Exercise 10, p. 33.
Sample answers:
1. rode . . . took
2. froze
3. chose
4. hung
5. rang . . . woke
6. rose . . . set
7. sent
8. taught
9. stole
10. caught
11. shook
12. flew
13. dug
14. spent
15. wore

Exercise 11, p. 34.
2. We left . . . We didn't leave . . . Did we leave
3. She does . . . She didn't do . . . Did she do
4. He was . . . He wasn't . . . Was he
5. We drove . . . We didn't drive . . . Did we (you) drive
6. You were . . . You weren't . . . Were you (Was I)
7. I planned . . . I didn't plan . . . Did I (you) plan

Exercise 12, p. 34.
2. Yes, I fell down.
3. Yes, I hurt myself when I fell down.
4. Yes, I broke my arm.
5. Yes, I went to the emergency room.
6. Yes, I saw a doctor.
7. Yes, I sat in the waiting room for a long time.
8. Yes, the doctor put a cast on my arm.
9. Yes, I paid a lot of money.
10. Yes, I came home exhausted.

Exercise 13, p. 34.
2. A: Did Ella's plane arrive
   B: it did . . . got
3. A: Did you go
   B: I didn't . . . stayed . . . didn't feel
4. A: Did you eat
   B: I didn't . . . didn't have . . . didn't ring
5. A: Did da Vinci paint
   B: he did . . . painted

Exercise 14, p. 35.
Part I.
3. didn't ride
4. got
5. didn't watch
6. made
7. brought
8. didn't read
9. didn't fix

Part II.
3. took
4. didn't go
5. fell
6. came
7. didn't lie
8. thought
9. didn't begin
10. finished

Exercise 16, p. 37.
2. did . . . spent
3. did . . . met
4. did . . . sold
5. did . . . broke
6. did . . . kept
7. did . . . read
8. did . . . lost
9. did . . . found
10. did . . . upset

Exercise 17, p. 37.
2. had
3. ate
4. drank
5. met
6. shook
7. danced
8. sat . . . talked

Exercise 18, p. 38.
The Daily News

    Yesterday morning, Jake read the newspaper online. He wanted to know the latest news. He enjoyed the business section most. His wife, Eva, didn't read any newspapers on her computer. She downloaded them on her ebook reader. She looked at the front pages first. She didn't have a lot of time. She finished the articles later in the day. Both Jake and Eva were very knowledgeable about the day's events.

Exercise 19, p. 38.
Part II.
1. T
2. F
3. F

Part III.
1. kills
2. killed
3. began
4. lasted
5. spread
6. died
7. kill
8. were
9. was
10. made

Exercise 20, p. 39.

Part I.
1. different
2. same
3. different
4. same

Part II.
1. /t/
2. /d/
3. /t/
4. /əd/

Exercise 21, p. 39.
1. agree
2. agreed
3. arrived
4. explains
5. ended
6. stopped
7. touched

Exercise 22, p. 40.
1. every day.
2. last week.
3. six days a week.
4. last weekend.
5. every day.
6. yesterday.

Exercise 23, p. 40.
2. /d/
3. /əd/
4. /t/
5. /əd/
6. /t/
7. /d/
8. /t/
9. /əd/
10. /t/
11. /d/
12. /əd/

Exercise 24, p. 40.
Sample answers:
1. He went to a water-slide park and loved the fast slides.
2. She visited her aunt.

Exercise 25, p. 41.
1. b
2. a

Exercise 26, p. 43.
2. was eating . . . came
3. came . . . was eating
4. was sleeping
5. was sleeping . . . rang
6. rang . . . was sleeping
7. began
8. was walking . . . saw
9. saw . . . was standing . . . was holding
10. waved . . . saw

Exercise 27, p. 44.
3. spilled . . . was sitting
4. was standing . . . sent
5. ran into . . . was standing
6. dropped . . . was standing
7. avoided . . . was swimming
8. was swimming . . . saw
9. was swimming . . . found

Exercise 29, p. 45.
1. Julia
2. James
3. Paul

Exercise 30, p. 46.
1. F
2. T
3. F
4. F
5. F

Exercise 31, p. 46.
1. B: Did you find . . . was looking . . . didn't see
   A: It's
2. A: looks . . . Did you
   B: thought . . . had . . . guess
3. A: Did you have
   B: had
   A: were
   B: was . . . was

Exercise 32, p. 47.
Underlined verbs:
2. were traveling
3. A: was . . . talking
   B: were describing
4. A: 's (is) . . . talking
   B: 's (is) describing

Exercise 33, p. 47.
2. is doing
3. isn't studying
4. is staring
5. wants
6. is looking
7. are you looking
8. am watching
9. is turning
10. is
11. looks
13. was doing
14. wasn't studying
15. was staring
16. wanted
17. was looking
18. pointed
19. said
20. offered

Exercise 34, p. 48.
Checked sentences: 1, 2, 3

Exercise 35, p. 49.
Clauses: 2, 3, 4, 5, 6, 7

Exercise 36, p. 49.

1. b. <u>I remembered my coat in the backseat</u>[2] <u>after the taxi dropped me off</u>[1].

2. a. <u>Before I got out of the taxi,</u>[2] <u>I double-checked the address</u>[1].

   b. <u>Before I double-checked the address,</u>[2] <u>I got out of the taxi</u>[1].

3. a. <u>As soon as I tipped the driver</u>, <u>he helped me with</u>
   <u>my luggage.</u>
      ₁
   b. <u>As soon as the driver helped me with my luggage,</u>
         ₂
   <u>I tipped him.</u>

Exercise 37, p. 49.
2. Before I left my apartment this morning, I
   unplugged the coffee pot.
   I unplugged the coffee pot before I left my
   apartment this morning.
3. Until I was seven years old, I lived on a farm.
   I lived on a farm until I was seven years old.
4. As soon as I heard the doorbell, I opened the door.
   I opened the door as soon as I heard the doorbell.
5. When it began to rain, I stood under my umbrella.
   I stood under my umbrella when it began to rain.
6. While I was lying in bed with the flu, my friends
   were swimming at the beach.
   My friends were swimming at the beach while I was
   lying in bed with the flu.
   While my friends were swimming at the beach, I was
   lying in bed with the flu.
   I was lying in bed with the flu while my friends were
   swimming at the beach.

Exercise 38, p. 50.
2. bought . . . went
   [before I went to the hospital to visit my friend]
3. went . . . got . . . was . . . was planting . . . was . . .
   was changing . . . were playing . . . was changing . . .
   were throwing
   [When I got there]
   [while Mr. Lopez was changing the oil in the car]
4. hit . . . was using . . . hurt
   [while I was using the hammer]
5. heard . . . began
   [As soon as we heard about the hurricane]
6. got . . . stopped . . . rested . . . felt
   [until he felt strong enough to continue]

Exercise 39, p. 51.
2. need	11. was reaching
3. call	12. lost
4. is sitting	13. ran
5. came	14. stopped
6. was	15. is
7. had	16. isn't
8. was driving	17. needs
9. rang	18. feels
10. reached	19. made

Exercise 41, p. 52.
2. used to think
3. did you use/used to live
4. Did you use/used to work

5. didn't use to wake up / didn't used to wake up . . .
   used to sleep
6. used to watch . . . didn't use to watch / didn't used
   to watch . . . did you use to watch / did you used to
   watch

Exercise 43, p. 53.
2. did you used to go/did you use to go
3. used to play
4. used to skip
5. didn't used to like/didn't use to like

Exercise 44, p. 53.
2. Junko used to **work** for an investment company.
3. **Margo used** to teach English, but now she works at
   a publishing company.
4. Where **did** you used to live?
5. I **didn't used/use** to get up early, but now I do.
6. **Did** you used to live in Singapore?
7. My family used to **go** to the beach every weekend,
   but now we don't.

Exercise 45, p. 54.
1. F		4. T	
2. T		5. F	
3. F			

Chapter 3: Future Time

Exercise 1, p. 55.
Sentences: 1, 3

Exercise 2, p. 56.
1. yes	5. no
2. yes	6. no
3. no	7. yes
4. yes	8. yes

Exercise 4, p. 57.
1. am going to pick
2. A: is Alex going to go
   B: is going to stop
3. A: Are you going to finish
   B: I am going to finish
4. A: is Dr. Ahmad going to talk
   B: is going to discuss
5. A: are you going to call
   B: am not going to call . . . am going to text

Exercise 5, p. 57.
Questions:
1. Where are you going to go . . .
2. What time are you going to wake up . . .
3. What are you going to have . . .
4. Are you going to be . . .

5. Where are you going to be . . .
6. Are you going to become . . .
7. Are you going to take . . .
8. Are you going to do . . .

Exercise 6, p. 58.

2. are going to	8. is
3. are going to	9. going to
4. are you going to	10. is
5. are going to	11. going to
6. Are	12. are going to
7. going to	

Exercise 7, p. 58.

1. What did you do yesterday? (*also possible:* were you doing)
2. What are you going to do tomorrow? [*Note:* The present progressive (*are you doing*) can replace *going to.*]
3. What are you doing right now?
4. What do you do every day?
5. What are you going to do a week from now?
6. What did you do the day before yesterday? (were you doing)
   What were you doing the day before yesterday?
7. What are you going to do the day after tomorrow?
8. What did you do last week? (were you doing)
9. What do you do every week?
10. What are you going to do this weekend?

Exercise 10, p. 60.

2. You'll	5. it'll
3. We'll	6. They'll
4. He'll	7. She'll

Exercise 11, p. 61.

2. will make	5. will be
3. will call	6. will cost
4. will help	7. will explain

Exercise 12, p. 61.

1. 50%	3. 100%	5. 100%
2. 50%	4. 90%	6. 100%

Exercise 13, p. 62.

1. 100%	3. 50%	5. 100%
2. 90%	4. 90%	6. 50%

Exercise 14, p. 63.

2. She probably won't go / She probably isn't going to go to work tomorrow.
   She'll probably stay / She is probably going to stay home and rest.
3. He'll probably go / He is probably going to go to bed early tonight.
   He probably won't stay / He probably isn't going to stay up all night again tonight.

4. She probably won't run / isn't going to run in the marathon race this week.
   She'll probably skip / She is probably going to skip the race.

Exercise 15, p. 63.

2. Maybe Lisa won't get here.
3. You may win the contest.
4. Maybe the plane will land early.
5. Sergio may not pass the class.

Exercise 18, p. 64.

2. will	5. won't	8. won't
3. will	6. will	9. will
4. will	7. will	

Exercise 19, p. 65.
Conversation 1

Exercise 20, p. 66.

1. no	5. no
2. yes	6. yes
3. no	7. A: yes
4. yes	B: no

Exercise 21, p. 66.

1. I'm going to be away for three weeks.
2. My husband and I are going to stay in small towns and camp on the beach.
3. We're going to bring a tent.
4. We're going to celebrate our wedding anniversary there.
5. My father, who was born in Thailand, is going to join us, but he's going to stay in a hotel.

Exercise 22, p. 66.

3. am going to	7. are going to
4. will (I'll)	8. will (I'll)
5. am going to	9. will (I'll)
6. will (I'll)	

Exercise 23, p. 67.

1. a	3. b
2. b	4. a

Exercise 25, p. 68.

2. returns	5. are
3. lands	6. find out
4. find	7. isn't . . . is

Exercise 26, p. 69.

2. is going to call . . . returns
3. go . . . am going to make
4. are going to take . . . visits
5. am going to keep . . . calls
6. misses . . . isn't going to understand
7. gets . . . are going to eat

Exercise 28, p. 70.

2. Before Sue picks up groceries, she is going to go to the dentist.
3. Before Sue has lunch with Hiro, she is going to pick up groceries.
4. After Sue picks up groceries, she is going to have lunch with Hiro.
5. Before Sue takes her father to his doctor's appointment, she is going to have lunch with Hiro.

Exercise 29, p. 70.

Sample answers:
1. will see changing scenery
2. will turn on the lights
3. the lights will be on
4. will remember the temperature a person likes
5. he/she can lock the doors with a remote control
6. will move
7. will deliver warm clothes
8. will be inexpensive

Exercise 30, p. 71.

2. goes . . . will email / is going to email
3. went . . . took
4. was taking . . . rang
5. rang . . . jumped
6. gets . . . will brush
7. brushes . . . gets

Exercise 31, p. 71.

All three sentences express future time.

Exercise 32, p. 72.

1. B: are you doing
   A: am going . . . are going
   B: am meeting
2. A: are you majoring
   B: am majoring
   A: are you taking
   B: am taking
3. A: are you doing
   B: am cutting

Exercise 33, p. 73.

A: am going
B: are . . . going
B: Are . . . flying . . . driving
A: 'm flying
A: 'm taking
B: 'm staying

Exercise 36, p. 74.

1. a, b
2. a, b, c
3. b, c
4. a, c

Exercise 37, p. 74.

1. a, b, c   6. a, b, c
2. b, c   7. a, b, c
3. b, c   8. b, c
4. a, b, c   9. b, c
5. b, c   10. a, b, c

Exercise 38, p. 75.

Picture B

Exercise 39, p. 76.

(*Answers may vary.*)
1. The chimpanzee is about to eat a banana.
2. The man is about to pour coffee.
3. The plane is about to land.
4. The man is about to answer/pick up the phone.
5. The dog is about to go to sleep.
6. The man is about to start a fire.
7. The woman is about to hit a fly.
8. The man is about to leave.
9. The astronauts are about to meet creatures from outer space.

Exercise 41, p. 77.

1. a, b
2. f

Exercise 42, p. 77.

1. was reading . . . listening
2. will move . . . look . . . graduates
3. calls . . . complains
4. is crying . . . laughing
5. get . . . am going to take . . . go
6. was carrying . . . climbing . . . landed . . . stung . . . dropped . . . spilled

Exercise 43, p. 78.

1. was raining . . . took . . . got . . . found
2. opens . . . leave
3. A: cut . . . is bleeding
   B: 'll / will get
4. A: is ringing
   B: know
   A: Do you want
   B: don't answer
5. A: is . . . are flashing
   B: know . . . know . . . see
   A: is going . . . Are you speeding
   B: am driving
   A: is passing (*also possible:* is going to pass)

Exercise 44, p. 79.

B: does . . . say
A: will receive
B: will be . . . want
C: solves . . . don't understand . . . I'll . . . smile
D: work . . . will be
A: looks . . . will have

My Cousin Pablo

I want to tell you about Pablo. He **is** my cousin. He **came** here four years ago. Before he came here, he **studied** statistics in Chile. He **left** Chile and **moved** here. Then he went to New York and **stayed** there for three years. He graduated from New York University. Now he **is studying** at this school. After he **finishes** his master's degree, he **will/is going to** return to Chile.

Chapter 4: Present Perfect and Past Perfect

Exercise 1, p. 81.
3. helped	7. written
4. visited	8. seen

Exercise 2, p. 82.
1. called	6. come
2. spoken	7. eaten
3. done	8. cut
4. known	9. read
5. met	10. been

Exercise 3, p. 82.
2. had	5. lived	8. died
3. thought	6. heard	9. bought
4. taught	7. studied	10. started

Exercise 4, p. 82.
1. a
2. b

Exercise 5, p. 84.
3. since	12. since
4. since	13. since
5. for	14. for
6. for	15. since
7. for	16. for
8. since	17. for
9. for	18. since
10. for	19. since
11. since	20. since

Exercise 7, p. 85.
2. has interviewed	7. has signed
3. has met	8. has shaken
4. has found	9. has written
5. has made	10. has thought
6. has become	

Exercise 9, p. 86.
2. has changed . . . started
3. was . . . have been
4. haven't slept . . . left

5. met . . . has not thought
6. has had . . . bought
7. A: have you eaten . . . got
   B: have eaten

Exercise 11, p. 87.
2. A: Have you ever stayed
   B: have . . . have stayed
3. A: Have you ever met
   B: haven't . . . have never met
4. A: Has Ted ever traveled
   B: has . . . has traveled
5. A: Has Lara ever been
   B: hasn't . . . has never been

Exercise 12, p. 88.
1. seen	6. had
2. flown	7. fallen
3. ridden	8. felt
4. done	9. spoken
5. torn	10. wanted

Exercise 13, p. 88.
Questions: Have you ever . . .
1. cut your own hair?
2. caught a big fish?
3. taken care of an injured animal?
4. lost something very important?
5. sat on a bee?
6. flown in a private plane?
7. broken your arm or your leg?
8. found something very valuable?
9. swum near a shark?
10. thrown a ball and broken a window?

Exercise 14, p. 89.
Questions: How long have you . . .
1. lived in (_____)?
2. studied English?
3. been in this class/at this school?
4. had long hair/short hair?
5. had a beard/a mustache?
6. worn glasses/contact lenses?
7. had a roommate/a pet?
8. been interested in (_____)?
9. been married?

Exercise 15, p. 89.
1. b	3. b
2. a	4. a

Exercise 16, p. 91.
1. a, b
2. b, d
3. a, b, c

Exercise 17, p. 91.

2. given
3. changed
4. taken
5. woken
6. done
7. been

Exercise 18, p. 92.

2. No, he hasn't picked up his kids at school yet.
3. Yes, he has already taken his car for an oil change.
4. No, he hasn't finished his errands yet.
5. Yes, he has already shopped for groceries.
6. No, he hasn't had lunch with Michael yet.

Exercise 19, p. 92.

1. is
2. has
3. is
4. is
5. has
6. has

Exercise 20, p. 93.

1. you've done
2. I've worked
3. I've worked
4. I've worked
5. I've done
6. have you changed
7. have you applied
8. I've been
9. I've heard

Exercise 21, p. 94.

Pamela

Exercise 23, p. 95.

3. present perfect . . . unspecified
4. simple past . . . specified
5. simple past . . . specified
6. present perfect . . . unspecified
7. present perfect . . . unspecified
8. simple past . . . specified
9. present perfect . . . unspecified
10. simple past . . . specified

Exercise 24, p. 95.

3. nave . . . nave eaten . . . ate
4. have already seen . . . saw
5. have already written . . . wrote
6. A: Has Antonio ever had
   B: has . . . has had . . . had
7. have already read . . . read
8. A: have you visited
   B: have visited . . . visited . . . was

Exercise 26, p. 97.

1. spent
2. made
3. sent
4. left
5. slept
6. driven
7. sung

Exercise 29, p. 99.

2. is waiting . . . has been waiting
3. are talking . . . have been talking
4. are doing . . . have been doing

5. A: are you doing
   B: am working
   A: have you been working
   B: have been working

Exercise 31, p. 100.

2. month has
3. parents have
4. cousins have
5. friend has
6. friends have
7. work has
8. roommate has

Exercise 32, p. 100

a. 1
b. 3
c. 1

Exercise 33, p. 102.

4. have been reading
5. have read
6. have stayed
7. has been crying
8. has been teaching / has taught
9. A: has been playing / has played
   B: have been playing / have played
10. B: has been working / has worked
    B: has worked

Exercise 34, p. 103.

1. has
2. been changing
3. We've
4. had
5. have
6. seen
7. have been building
8. We've been saying
9. We've
10. seen

Exercise 35, p. 103.

Checked sentences:

1. a, b
2. a
3. b
4. a, c
5. d, e

Exercise 36, p. 104.

1. b
2. b
3. a
4. a

Exercise 38, p. 105.

1. b
2. c
3. b, c
4. b
5. b, c

Exercise 39, p. 106.

1. F
2. T
3. T
4. F
5. F

Exercise 40, p. 107.

2. am
3. am studying
4. have been
5. arrived
6. began
7. came
8. have done
9. have met
10. went
11. met
12. spoke
13. didn't practice
14. were
15. came
16. have met
17. know
18. have become

Exercise 41, p. 108.

Answer b.

Exercise 42, p. 109.

3. a. 1st
   b. 2nd
4. a. 2nd
   b. 1st
5. a. 1st
   b. 2nd
6. a. 2nd
   b. 1st
7. a. 1st
   b. 2nd

Exercise 43, p. 110.

1. has
2. had
3. had
4. have

Exercise 44, p. 110.

2. I started English classes at this school four weeks ago and I **have been learning / have learned** a lot of English since then.
3. I **have wanted** to learn English since I **was** a child.
4. I have been thinking about how to improve my English skills quickly since I came here, but I **haven't** found a good way.
5. Our teacher likes to give tests. We **have had** six tests since the beginning of the term.
6. I like learning English. When I was young, my father found an Australian girl to teach my brothers and me English, but when I **moved** to another city, my father didn't find anyone to teach us.
7. I **have met** many friends in this class. I **met** Abdul in the cafeteria on the first day. He was friendly and kind. We **have been** friends since that day.
8. Abdul **has** been **studying** English **for** three months. His English is better than mine.

Chapter 5: Asking Questions

Exercise 1, p. 111.

1. b
2. d

Exercise 2, p. 111.

1. Is . . . is
2. Do . . . do
3. Did . . . did
4. Was . . . wasn't
5. Is . . . is
6. Are . . . am
7. Was . . . was
8. Have . . . haven't
9. Will . . . will

Exercise 3, p. 112.

2. A: Do snakes have legs?
   B: they don't
3. A: Is Mexico in North America
   B: it is
4. A: Will you be at home tonight?
   B: I won't.
5. A: Do you have a bike?
   B: I do
6. A: Has Simon left?
   B: Yes, he has.
7. A: Did Simon leave with Kate?
   B: Yes, he did.
8. A: Does acupuncture relieve pain?
   B: Yes, it does.

Exercise 4, p. 113.

1. b
2. a
3. b
4. c
5. b

Exercise 5, p. 113.

Questions:
1. Do you like animals?
2. Have you ever had a pet snake?
3. Is it cold in this room?
4. Is it raining right now?
5. Did you sleep well last night?
6. Are you tired right now?
7. Will you be here next year?

Exercise 6, p. 113.

1. Is she
2. Is he
3. Is that
4. Is there
5. Did it
6. Has it
7. Does it

Exercise 7, p. 114.

1. a, c
2. a, d
3. b, c

Exercise 8, p. 115.

2. Do they live a simple life?   b
3. What do they pick from the trees?   a
4. Do they have electricity?   a
5. Do they enjoy their life?   a
7. Are they happy?   b

Exercise 9, p. 116.

1. Do you know
2. I do
3. Have you seen
4. I haven't.
5. Did they go
6. they did
7. Are you going to see
8. I am
9. Will they be
10. they won't

Exercise 10, p. 116.
1. Where . . . b
2. Why . . . c
3. When . . . a

Exercise 11, p. 117.
2. are your kids transferring to
   are your kids transferring to Lakeview Elementary
   School
3. will you meet Taka at the mall
   will you meet Taka at 10:00
4. does class begin
   does class begin
5. did you stay home from work
   did you stay home from work

Exercise 12, p. 118.
1. How come you are going?
   What are you going for?
2. How come they came?
   What did they come for?
3. How come he needs more money?
   What does he need more money for?
4. How come they are going to leave?
   What are they going to leave for?

Exercise 13, p. 118.
1. When did Tom get home?
2. Where was his wife?
3. What did Tom buy?
4. Why was Tom late?
5. What present did Nina get?

Exercise 14, p. 118.
1. c   4. b
2. b   5. a
3. a

Exercise 15, p. 118.
1. b   3. c
2. d   4. a

Exercise 16, p. 119.
3. Who knocked on the door?
4. Who(m) did Talya meet?
5. What did Mike learn?
6. What changed Gina's mind?
7. Who(m) is Gina talking about?
8. What is Gina talking about?

Exercise 17, p. 120.
1. Who   4. What
2. What   5. Who
3. Who   6. Who

Exercise 18, p. 120.
Questions:
1. What   5. What
2. What   6. What
3. Who   7. Who
4. What

Exercise 19, p. 120.
1. What did he   4. What did he
2. Did he tell   5. Why . . . you tell
3. Who did he

Exercise 22, p. 121.
2. What did you do
3. What are you going to do
4. What do you want to do
5. What would you like to do
6. What are you doing
7. What do you do
8. A: What do you do . . . A: What does . . . do

Exercise 25, p. 123.
3. Which pen / Which one / Which would you like?
4. What did Hassan borrow from you?
5. What do you have in your hand?
   Which piece / Which one / Which would you like?
6. What did Tony buy?
7. What / Which countries did you visit?
   Which country did you enjoy the most?

Exercise 27, p. 125.
1. b
2. a

Exercise 29, p. 126.
1. Who's   4. Who's
2. Whose   5. Whose
3. Whose   6. Who's

Exercise 30, p. 126.
1. Whose   4. Whose
2. Who's   5. Who's
3. Who's   6. Whose

Exercise 31, p. 126.
1. e   4. b
2. d   5. c
3. a

Exercise 32, p. 127.
(*Answers may vary.*)
1. He's very tall. He's six foot, six inches (2 meters).
2. He's fourteen years old.
3. He doesn't sleep well.
4. He's very uncomfortable.
5. He likes / prefers to travel by train.

Exercise 33, p. 128.

2. How important is education?
3. How did you get to school?
4. How deep is the ocean?
5. How are you going to get to Buenos Aires?
6. How difficult was the test?
7. How high is Mt. Everest?
8. How did you get here?

Exercise 34, p. 128.

1. How fresh
2. How cheap
3. How hard
4. How clean
5. How hot
6. How noisy
7. How serious

Exercise 35, p. 129.

1. c
2. d
3. b
4. a
5. e

Exercise 37, p. 130.

1. How old are
2. How tall are
3. How much do
4. how well do
5. How quickly do
6. How often do
7. How tired are
8. How many times a week do
9. How are
10. How soon can

Exercise 38, p. 131.

1. 774 miles / 1,250 kilometers
2. 227 miles
3. 1,030 kilometers

Exercise 39, p. 131.

2. How far is it from Montreal to Quebec?
3. How far is it from here to the post office?
4. How far do you live from work?

Exercise 43, p. 133.

2. How long will Mr. McNally be in the hospital?
3. How long does it take to learn a second language?
4. How long have you been living here?
5. How long did you live in Oman?
6. How long have you known Mr. Pham?
7. How long has he been living in Canada?

Exercise 44, p. 134.

1. is
2. will
3. did
4. are

Exercise 46, p. 135.

1. Who are
2. How are
3. What did
4. Why did
5. Why is
6. Why are
7. When will
8. Who will
9. When is
10. How will

Exercise 47, p. 135.

1. Where are you
2. Who are you
3. Who is
4. How long have you
5. Where did you
6. Where does he
7. Is he
8. What time will you
9. Why are you
10. Why are you
11. Why am I

Exercise 48, p. 136.

1. What do you
2. What are you
3. What are you
4. What are you
5. What do you
6. What are you
7. What do you
8. What do you

Exercise 49, p. 136.

1. a
2. a
3. 1, 2

Exercise 52, p. 138.

A: Let's invite the Thompsons over for dinner.
B: Good idea! How about next Sunday?
A: Let's do it sooner. What about this Saturday?

Exercise 53, p. 138.

1. a
2. c
3. b
4. a

Exercise 55, p. 139.

1. yes
2. no

Exercise 56, p. 140.

1. a
2. a
3. a

Exercise 57, p. 141.

1. b. doesn't
   c. don't
   d. doesn't
   e. isn't
   f. aren't
   g. does
   h. is
   i. aren't

2. a. didn't   c. were
    b. did   d. wasn't

3. a. aren't   d. weren't
    b. is   e. was
    c. is

4. a. hasn't   d. hasn't
    b. haven't   e. has
    c. have   f. hasn't

Exercise 59, p. 142.
Expected answers:
1. Yes.   6. Yes.
2. Yes.   7. Yes.
3. Yes.   8. No.
4. No.   9. Yes.
5. No.   10. No.

Exercise 60, p. 142.
2. Where **do** I buy subway tickets?
3. Whose **backpack is that**?
4. What kind of tea **do** you like best?
5. It's freezing out and you're not wearing gloves, **are** you?
6. Who **did you study** with at school?
7. She is going to work this weekend, **isn't** she?
8. How long **does it** take to get to the airport from here?
9. How **tall is your father**?
10. It's midnight. Why **are** you so late? Why **did** you forget to call?

Exercise 61, p. 143.
1. b   6. b
2. a   7. c
3. a   8. a
4. c   9. b
5. b   10. b

Exercise 63, p. 144.
(Answers may vary.)
1. He wanted husbands for them.
2. A frog claimed Trina because he found the diamond.
3. She ran away from the castle and went to live in the woods.
4. She met him in a lake.
5. She felt great affection for him.
6. The evil wizard changed a man from a prince into a frog.
7. They had unhappy lives.
8. They lived happily ever after.

Exercise 1, p. 146.
5. pronoun   9. adjective
6. noun   10. pronoun
7. adjective   11. noun
8. preposition   12. preposition

Exercise 2, p. 146.
1. two   3. two   5. two
2. one   4. one   6. two

Exercise 3, p. 147.
1. chairs   8. leaves
2. window   9. half
3. wishes   10. beliefs
4. dish   11. wolves
5. taxes   12. radios
6. boys   13. sheep
7. hobbies   14. foot

Exercise 4, p. 148.
People

babies	heroes
boys	thieves
children	women
girls	

Food

fish	sandwiches
potatoes	tomatoes

Things people catch

fish	mosquitoes
mice	thieves

Places people visit

cities	zoos
libraries	

Exercise 5, p. 149.

supplies	dresses
shirts	outfits
jeans	shoes
pants	babies

Exercise 6, p. 149.
1. no   4. no
2. yes   5. yes
3. yes   6. no

Exercise 7, p. 150.
1. /s/   4. /z/
2. /z/   5. /əz/
3. /əz/   6. /s/

Exercise 8, p. 150.

1. different
2. same
3. same
4. different
5. same
6. same
7. different
8. different

Exercise 9, p. 150.

3. /z/
4. /s/
5. /əz/
6. /z/
7. /s/
8. /əz/
9. /z/

Exercise 10, p. 150.

1. sizes
2. fax
3. faxes
4. price
5. glasses
6. prize

Exercise 12, p. 151.

3. | Cows | eat | grass |
   subject — verb — object of verb

4. | The actor | sang | *(none)* |
   subject — verb — object of verb

5. | The actor | sang | a song |
   subject — verb — object of verb

6. | Accidents | happen | *(none)* |
   subject — verb — object of verb

7. | The accident | injured | a woman |
   subject — verb — object

Exercise 13, p. 152.

3. noun
4. verb
5. verb
6. noun
7. verb
8. noun
9. noun
10. verb

Exercise 15, p. 153.

Checked sentences:

2. in a <u>minute</u>
4. down the <u>hill</u>
5. next to the <u>phone</u>
7. in a few <u>hours</u>
8. from my <u>parents</u>

Exercise 16, p. 153.

2. a.   P   Obj. of P
   Kimiko saw a picture on the wall.

   c.   P   Obj. of P
   Kimiko looked at the picture closely.

3. b.   P   Obj. of P
   Annika lost her ring in the sand.

   c.   P   Obj. of P   P   Obj. of P
   Annika lost her ring in the sand   at the beach.

4. a.   P   Obj. of P
   A talkative woman sat with her husband.

   b.   P   Obj. of P
   We were at a meeting.

   c.   P   Obj. of P
   She talked to her husband the entire time.

Exercise 19, p. 155.

1. Birds and insects.
2. The understory is above the ground and under leaves.
3. In the understory.
4. The emergent layer is the top layer. It gets sun. The understory is lower. It is dark and cool, etc.

Exercise 21, p. 156.

1. in
2. in
3. in
4. at
5. on
6. on
7. on
8. at
9. at
10. on
11. on
12. in
13. in
14. in
15. in
16. at
17. at
18. in

Exercise 22, p. 157.

Completed questions:

1. in
2. at
3. on
4. on
5. on
6. in
7. in

Exercise 23, p. 157.

1. a, c
2. a, b

Exercise 24, p. 157.

1. to Paris next month
2. through Turkey last week
3. Alexi works at his uncle's bakery on Saturday mornings
4. My plane arrived at the airport in the early morning

Exercise 25, p. 158.

1. Ø
2. s
3. Ø
4. s
5. Ø
6. Ø

Exercise 26, p. 159.

1. barks
2. bark
3. roar
4. roar
5. hisses
6. chirps
7. meow
8. bark
9. hisses
10. chirp

Exercise 27, p. 159.

3.   S   V
   <u>Every student</u> in my class speaks English well.

          S   V
   <u>All students</u> in my class speak . . .

4.   V   S
   (There) are <u>five students</u> from Korea in Mr. Ahmad's class.

5.   V   S
   (There)'s <u>a vacant apartment</u> in my building.
   (no changes)

S   V
6. Do (aux verb) <u>people</u> in your neighborhood know each other?

S   V
7. <u>The neighbors</u> in the apartment next to mine are very friendly and helpful.

Exercise 28, p. 159.
1. s	8. s	15. s
2. s	9. Ø	16. Ø
3. s	10. s	17. s
4. s	11. s	18. s
5. s	12. Ø	19. s
6. Ø	13. s	20. Ø
7. Ø	14. s	

Exercise 30, p. 160.
Checked phrases:
3. <u>famous</u>
4. <u>small</u>, <u>dark</u>, <u>smelly</u>
6. <u>long</u>, <u>short</u>

Exercise 31, p. 160.
1. Red roses are beautiful flowers.
2. The waiter poured hot coffee into my empty cup.
3. Mrs. Fields gave the hungry children a fresh snack.
4. After our delicious dinner, Frank helped me with the dirty dishes.

Exercise 33, p. 161.
3. hot chicken
4. chicken recipe
5. chicken soup

Exercise 34, p. 162.
2. vegetable garden	6. mountain villages
3. bean soup	7. art lesson
4. magazine articles	8. flag poles
5. toy factory	

Exercise 35, p. 162.
1. (*no change*)	5. Bicycles
2. computers	6. (*no change*)
3. (*no change*)	7. (*no change*)
4. Airplanes	8. vegetables

Exercise 37, p. 163.
1. subject	4. object
2. subject	5. object
3. object	

Exercise 38, p. 164.
1. a. apples
   b. children
2. a. bees
   b. bees
   c. bees
3. a. table tennis
   b. table tennis
   c. my brother
   d. my brother

Exercise 39, p. 165.
1. me	4. me . . . us
2. me	5. them . . . They are
3. I	

Exercise 40, p. 165.
2. He . . . them   4. it
3. They . . . her   5. They . . . them

Exercise 41, p. 166.
1. B
2. A

Exercise 42, p. 166.
2. more than one	5. more than one
3. more than one	6. one
4. one	

Exercise 43, p. 167.
2. Lisa's	6. William's
3. Lisa's	7. Ned's
4. Monica's	8. William's
5. William's	

Exercise 44, p. 167.
1. earth's   T
2. elephant's   F [gray and wrinkled]
3. man's   T
4. woman's   T
5. women's   T
6. Men's   T [about 11% to 12% bigger]
7. person's   T
8. People's   F [Men's voices have a higher pitch.]

Exercise 45, p. 167.
Checked responses: 1, 2, 4, 5, 7, 8

Exercise 46, p. 168.
2. his
3. It's . . . its
4. its . . . its
5. Hers
6. her
7. mine
8. yours
9. A: my . . . yours
   B: mine . . . Yours . . . your
10. a. They
    b. Their
    c. Our . . . theirs
    d. They're . . . there . . . they're . . . their

Exercise 48, p. 170.
2. himself	5. ourselves
3. yourself . . . themselves	6. herself
4. itself	7. yourself
(*also possible:* himself, herself)	8. myself

Exercise 49, p. 170.

1. yourself
2. ourselves
3. herself
4. themselves
5. himself
6. myself

Exercise 51, p. 171.

Picture B

Exercise 52, p. 172.

2. a. another
   b. The other
3. a. Another
   b. Another
   c. Another
   d. Another
4. another
5. The other
6. another

Exercise 53, p. 172.

1. Picture A
2. Picture B

Exercise 55, p. 174.

2. other
3. The others
4. The other
5. Others
6. Other . . . others
7. The other
8. The others

Exercise 56, p. 175.

(*Answers may vary.*)
1. One is by imagining a peaceful place. Another is deep breathing. Another is exercise.
2. It makes them tired.

Exercise 57, p. 176.

2. the other
3. Others
4. Other
5. Others . . . other
6. another
7. The other
8. another
9. The others
10. Other

Exercise 58, p. 176.

1. a
2. b
3. b
4. b
5. a

Exercise 59, p. 177.

B: other . . . others
A: the other . . . other

Exercise 60, p. 177.

2. I had some black **bean** soup for lunch.
3. The windows in our classroom **are** dirty.
4. People in Brazil **speak** Portuguese.
5. **There** are around 8,600 types of birds in the world.

6. My mother and father work in Milan. **They're teachers**.
7. Today many **women** are carpenters, pilots, and doctors.
8. **There** is a new student in our class. Have you met her?
9. There are two pools at the park. The smaller one is for **children**. The **other** (**one**) is for adults.
10. The highways in my country are **excellent**.
11. I don't like my apartment. **It's** in a bad neighborhood. **There is** a lot of crime. I'm going to move to **another** neighborhood.

Chapter 7: Modal Auxiliaries

Exercise 1, p. 178.

Correct sentences: 1, 4

Exercise 2, p. 179.

1. may come
2. should come
3. ought to come
4. will not (won't) come
5. could not (couldn't) come
6. might come
7. had better come
8. has to come
9. has got to come
10. is not (isn't) able to come

Exercise 3, p. 179.

3. Ø
4. Ø
5. to
6. Ø
7. to
8. Ø
9. to
10. Ø

Exercise 4, p. 179.

(*Answers will vary.*)

Exercise 5, p. 180.

1. can . . . can't
2. can . . . can't
3. can't . . . can
4. can . . . can't
1. A dog is able to swim, but it isn't able to fly.
2. A frog is able to live on land and in water, but a cat isn't (able to).
3. A bilingual person isn't able to speak three languages, but a trilingual person is (able to).
4. People with a Ph.D. degree are able to use "Dr." in front of their name, but people with a master's degree aren't (able to).

Exercise 7, p. 181.

1. can't understand
2. can help
3. Can you explain
4. can't figure
5. can do
6. Can you meet
7. can't meet

Exercise 9, p. 182.
Checked sentences:
Group A: 1, 2, 3
Group B: 4, 5
Group C: The sentences have different meanings; no
checkmarks.

Exercise 10, p. 183.
2. may/might . . . may/might . . . possibility
3. may/can . . . permission
4. may/might . . . may/might . . . possibility

Exercise 11, p. 183.
1. It might snow tonight.
   Maybe it will snow tonight.
2. You may need to wear your boots.
   Maybe you will need to wear your boots.
3. There may be a blizzard.
   There might be a blizzard.

Exercise 13, p. 184.
1. ability   4. possibility
2. possibility   5. permission
3. permission

Exercise 14, p. 184.
1. a future possibility
2. a present possibility
3. a past ability

Exercise 15, p. 185.
2. Past, Ability
3. Present, Possibility
4. Past, Ability
5. Future, Possibility
6. Present, Possibility

Exercise 17, p. 186.
1. could be   4. may be
2. might be   5. can
3. could ask

Exercise 18, p. 186.
Checked sentences: 1, 2, 3

Exercise 19, p. 187.
1. B: Can / May I / Could I speak/talk
2. B: May I / Could I speak / talk
   (*possibly too informal:* Can I)
   A: May I / Could I ask
3. B: Can I talk (*more formal:* Could I)
4. B: May / Could / Can I help
5. B: Could / Can I speak / talk
   Can / Could I take
6. B: May / Could / Can I speak / talk
   B: May / Could / Can I leave

Exercise 21, p. 188.
Checked sentences: 1, 2, 4, 5
More polite sentences: 2, 5

Exercise 22, p. 189.
(Answers may vary.)
2. Formal: Could you please talk in another room?
   Informal: Can you be quiet?
3. Formal: Could you please check the bill? I think
             there's a mistake.
   Informal: Will you fix the bill? It has a mistake.

Exercise 26, p. 191.
(Answers may vary.)
More serious or urgent sentences: 1, 3

Exercise 28, p. 192.
2. Anna shouldn't **wear** shorts to work.
3. I **should go** to the post office today.
4. I ought **to pay** my bills today.
5. **You'd better call** the doctor today.
6. You **shouldn't** stay up too late tonight.
7. **You'd better** not **leave** your key in the door.
8. Mr. Lim is having a surprise party for his wife. He
   ought **to tell** people soon.

Exercise 30, p. 193.
Sentence 1 is more common in writing.
Sentences 2 and 3 are more common in speaking.

Exercise 32, p. 194.
1. has to
2. You don't have to . . . has to
3. You've got to
4. You've got to
5. You have to
6. You don't . . . have to
7. You don't have to
8. has to

Exercise 34, p. 195.
Sentence b.

Exercise 35, p. 196.
3. doesn't have to
4. doesn't have to
5. must not
6. don't have to
7. must not

Exercise 37, p. 197.
3. must
4. must not
5. must not
6. must
7. must
8. must

Exercise 38, p. 198.
(Answers may vary.)
2. She must be happy.
3. She must be cold.
4. She must love movies.
5. He must be hot.
6. He must be strong.

Exercise 40, p. 198.
1. must be
2. had to stay
3. have to work
4. must be

Exercise 41, p. 199.
3. can't
2. will
3. wouldn't
4. do

Exercise 42, p. 199.
1. can't
2. will
3. wouldn't
4. do
5. should
6. can't
7. wouldn't
8. doesn't
9. shouldn't
10. won't
11. could
12. don't

Exercise 43, p. 200.
Group 1 speaker: a police officer
Possible situation: a person speeding
Group 2 speaker: a doctor
Possible situation: a doctor examining a patient's throat

Exercise 44, p. 201.
(Sentence order may vary.) 3, 1, 4, 5, 7, 2, 8, 9, 6

Exercise 45, p. 201.
1. Write . . . Write . . . Write
2. Double
3. Add
4. Multiply
5. Add
6. Subtract

Exercise 47, p. 203.
Checked items: 2, 3

Exercise 50, p. 204.
Correct order:
1. go dancing
2. go to a movie
3. go to a restaurant

Exercise 52, p. 204.
4. to
5. than
6. than
7. to
8. than
9. than
10. than
11. to
12. than

Exercise 55, p. 206.
1. c
2. a
3. a
4. b
5. c
6. b
7. c
8. b
9. a
10. c
11. b
12. b
13. a
14. b
15. b
16. a
17. c
18. a

Chapter 8: Connecting Ideas

Exercise 1, p. 208.
Checked sentences: 2, 3, 5

Exercise 2, p. 209.
adjective + adjective
3. wide and deep

adjective + adjective + adjective
4. wide, deep, and dangerous

verb + verb + verb
5. played music, ate pizza, and told ghost stories

verb + verb
6. played music and ate pizza

noun + noun + noun + noun + noun
7. My mom, dad, sister, and grandfather . . . my son

+ noun
and daughter

verb + verb + verb
8. mooed like a cow, roared like a lion, and barked like a dog

Exercise 4, p. 210.
3. I talked. He listened.
4. I talked to Ryan about his school grades, and he listened to me carefully.
5. The five most common words in English are *the*, *and*, *of*, *to*, and *a*.
6. The man asked a question. The woman answered it.
7. The man asked a question, and the woman answered it.
8. Rome is an Italian city. It has a mild climate and many interesting attractions.
9. You should visit Rome. Its climate is mild, and there are many interesting attractions.

Exercise 6, p. 211.
4. , but
5. but
6. , and
7. and
8. , but
9. or
10. , or

Exercise 7, p. 211.
1. Laptops are electronic devices. Cell phones are electronic devices.
2. Laptops and portable DVD players are electronic devices, but flashlights aren't.
3. Passengers can't use these electronic devices during takeoffs and landings. They can use them the rest of the flight.
4. During takeoffs and landings, airlines don't allow passengers to use laptops, DVD players, electronic readers, or PDAs.
5. The devices may cause problems with the navigation system, and they may cause problems with the communication system.

Exercise 8, p. 211.
1. b
2. a

Exercise 9, p. 212.
3. so
4. but
5. but
6. so
7. so
8. but
9. but
10. so

Exercise 10, p. 212.
1. Some tarantulas can go two and a half years without food. When they eat, they like grasshoppers, beetles, small spiders, and sometimes small lizards.
2. A female elephant is pregnant for approximately twenty months and almost always has only one baby. A young elephant stays close to its mother for the first ten years of its life.
3. Dolphins sleep with one eye open. They need to be conscious or awake in order to breathe. If they fall asleep when they are breathing, they will drown, so they sleep with half their brain awake and one eye open.

Exercise 11, p. 213.

Paying It Forward

A few days ago, a friend and I were driving from Benton Harbor to Chicago. We didn't have any delays for the first hour, but we ran into some highway construction near Chicago. The traffic wasn't moving. My friend and I sat and waited. We talked about our jobs, our families, and the terrible traffic. Slowly it started to move.

We noticed a black sports car on the shoulder. Its right blinker was blinking. The driver obviously wanted to get back into traffic. Car after car passed without letting him in. I decided to do a good deed, so I motioned for him to get in line ahead of me. He waved thanks, and I waved back at him.

All the cars had to stop at a toll booth a short way down the road. I held out my money to pay my toll, but the tolltaker just smiled and waved me on. She told me that the man in the black sports car had already paid my toll. Wasn't that a nice way of saying thank you?

Exercise 13, p. 214.

Part I.	Part II.
3. isn't	3. is
4. aren't	4. are
5. didn't	5. did
6. hasn't	6. has
7. haven't	7. have
8. isn't	8. is
9. aren't	9. are
10. won't	10. will

Exercise 15, p. 215.
1. didn't
2. wasn't
3. did
4. didn't
5. could
6. can't
7. don't
8. won't

Exercise 16, p. 216.
1. B
2. B
3. C
4. C

Exercise 17, p. 217.
1. b. so does James.
2. a. Ivan doesn't either.
   b. neither does Ivan.
3. a. Omar is too.
   b. so is Omar.
4. a. James isn't either.
   b. neither is James.

Exercise 18, p. 217.

Part I.	Part II.
2. do	2. don't
3. is	3. isn't
4. are	4. aren't
5. did	5. didn't
6. has	6. has
7. have	7. have
8. is	8. is
9. are	9. are
10. will	10. will

Exercise 20, p. 219.
1. So did I.
2. So do I.
3. So would I.
4. Neither am I.
5. Neither have I.
6. So is . . .
7. Neither do . . .
8. So does . . .
9. So did I.
10. Neither do I.
11. So is . . .
12. Neither does . . .
13. Neither have I.
14. So do . . .
15. So can . . .
16. So would I.

Exercise 23, p. 220.
Logical completions: a, c

Exercise 24, p. 221.
2. The children were hungry because there was no food in the house. OR
   Because there was no food in the house, the children were hungry.
3. We can't get across the river because the bridge is closed. OR
   Because the bridge is closed, we can't get across the river.
4. My car didn't start because the battery was dead. OR
   Because the battery was dead, my car didn't start.

5. Tayla and Patti laughed hard because the joke was very funny. OR
Because the joke was very funny, Tayla and Patti laughed hard.

Exercise 25, p. 221.
2. Mr. El-Sayed had a bad cold. **B**ecause he was not feeling well, he stayed home from the office.
3. Judy went to bed early because she was tired. **S**he likes to get at least eight hours of sleep a night.
4. Frank put his head in his hands. **H**e was angry and upset because he had lost a lot of work on his computer.

Exercise 26, p. 222.
2. The room was hot, so I opened the window.
3. It was raining, so I stayed indoors.
5. Because the water in the river is polluted, we shouldn't go swimming there.
6. Because my alarm clock didn't go off, I was late for my job interview.

Exercise 27, p. 222.
2. Jim was hot and tired, so he sat in the shade.
3. Jim was hot, tired, and thirsty.
4. Because he was hot, Jim sat in the shade.
5. Because they were hot and thirsty, Jim and Susan sat in the shade and drank iced-tea.
6. (no change)
7. Jim sat in the shade, drank iced-tea, and fanned himself with his cap because he was hot, tired, and thirsty.
8. Because Jim was hot, he stayed under the shade of the tree, but Susan went back to work.

Exercise 28, p. 223.
Understanding the Scientific Term "Matter"

The word *matter* is a chemical term. **M**atter is anything that has weight. This book, your finger, water, a rock, air, and the moon are all examples of matter. **H**eat and radio waves are not matter because they do not have weight. **H**appiness, dreams, and fears have no weight and are not matter.

Exercise 29, p. 223.
Sentences: 1, 3

Exercise 30, p. 223.
1. a. isn't
   b. is
   c. is
2. a. didn't go
   b. didn't go
   c. went

Exercise 31, p. 224.
3. Even though
4. Because
5. Even though
6. Because
7. because
8. Because . . . even though
9. even though

Exercise 32, p. 224.
2. b
3. c
4. a
5. c
6. b

Exercise 33, p. 225.
1. c
2. b
3. a
4. b
5. c

Exercise 35, p. 226.
1. Because
2. Even though / Although
3. Even though / Although
4. so
5. Because
6. so

Exercise 36, p. 227.
2. Gold, silver, and **copper are** metals.
3. The children crowded around the **teacher because** he was doing a magic trick.
4. I had a cup of coffee, and so **did** my friend.
5. My roommate didn't go **and neither did I**. OR My roommate didn't go **and I didn't either**.
6. Even **though** I was exhausted, I didn't stop working until after midnight.
7. Although I like **chocolate, I** can't eat it because I'm allergic to it.
8. I like to eat raw eggs for breakfast, and everybody else in my family **does** too. OR . . . , and **so does** everybody else in my family.
9. A hardware store sells **tools, nails, plumbing supplies,** and **paint**.
10. Most insects have wings. **S**piders do not. OR Most insects have wings, but spiders do not.

Chapter 9: Comparisons

Exercise 1, p. 229.
1. E
2. B
3. C

Exercise 2, p. 230.
2. not nearly as
3. just as
4. almost as / not quite as
5. not nearly as
6. just as
7. almost as / not quite as

Exercise 3, p. 230.
(*Answers will vary.*)

Exercise 4, p. 231.
1. is as old as
2. isn't as old as
3. aren't as old as
4. isn't quite as old as
5. is almost as old as

Exercise 5, p. 232.

2. an ox
3. a bird
4. a mule
5. a rock
6. the hills
7. a cat
8. a feather
9. a kite
10. a hornet

Exercise 6, p. 233.

1. David
2. David/Paolo
3. Matt

Exercise 7, p. 233.

1. T
2. T
3. T
4. F [The Arctic Ocean is the coldest.]
5. F [The South China Sea is the biggest.]
6. T
7. F [Asia is the largest continent in the world.]
8. T
9. F [It's South America.]
10. T

Exercise 9, p. 234.

Sample answers:

2. A . . . C
3. B . . . A
4. C . . . A
5. C
6. A
7. C . . . A

Exercise 10, p. 236.

2. better, the best
3. lazier, the laziest
4. hotter, the hottest
5. neater, the neatest
6. later, the latest
7. happier, the happiest
8. more dangerous, the most dangerous
9. more slowly, the most slowly
10. more common, the most common
11. friendlier, the friendliest
12. more careful, the most careful
13. worse, the worst
14. farther / further, the farthest / the furthest

Exercise 11, p. 236.

2. funnier
3. more dangerous
4. more confusing
5. darker
6. cleaner
7. prettier
8. wetter

Exercise 12, p. 237.

1. younger
2. tallest
3. happy
4. happier
5. older
6. funniest
7. hard
8. hard

Exercise 13, p. 237.

2. b
3. b
4. a, b
5. a, b
6. b
7. a, b

Exercise 15, p. 238.

1. a
2. a
3. b
4. b
5. b
6. b
7. b
8. a
9. a

Exercise 17, p. 239.

2. she is / her
3. they are / them
4. he can / him
5. he did / him
6. she can / her
7. mine . . . hers
8. theirs . . . ours

Exercise 19, p. 240.

3. An airplane is **very** fast.
4. Taking an airplane is **much / a lot / far** faster than driving.
5. Learning a second language is **very** difficult for many people.
6. Learning a second language is **much / a lot / far** more difficult than learning chemistry formulas.
7. You can live **much / a lot / far** more inexpensively in student housing than in a rented apartment.
8. You can live **very** inexpensively in student housing.

Exercise 21, p. 241.

1. b
2. a, b
3. b
4. a, b
5. a, b
6. b

Exercise 23, p. 242.

1. a. F
   b. T
2. a. T
   b. F
3. a. F
   b. T
4. a. F
   b. F
   c. T
5. a. T
   b. T
   c. F
   d. T

Exercise 24, p. 242.

Seattle and Singapore have more rain than Manila in December.
(Manila: 58 mm. or 2.3 in.; Seattle: 161 mm. or 6.3 in.; Singapore: 306 mm. or 12 in.)

Exercise 25, p. 243.

2. Indonesia has more volcanoes than Japan.
3. Saturn has more moons than Venus.
4. Sao Paulo, Brazil, has more people than New York City.
5. Finland has more islands than Greece.
6. Nepal has more mountains than Switzerland.
7. A banana has more sugar than an apple.
8. The dark meat of a chicken has more fat than the white meat of a chicken.

Exercise 26, p. 243.

Underlined nouns: doctors, happiness, information, mistakes, responsibilities
2. more information
3. happier
4. more happily
5. more happiness
6. more mistakes
7. more responsibly
8. more responsibilities
9. more responsible
10. more doctors

Exercise 28, p. 244.

2. bigger and bigger
3. better and better
4. louder and louder
5. longer and longer
6. warmer and warmer
7. more and more discouraged
8. harder and harder . . . wetter and wetter
9. more and more tired

Exercise 30, p. 245.

2. The closer . . . the warmer
3. The sharper . . . the easier
4. The noisier (The more noisy) . . . the angrier (the more angry)
5. more shrimp . . . the pinker
7. The more he thought about his family, the more homesick he became.
8. The darker the sky grew, the faster we ran to reach the house.

Exercise 32, p. 246.

3. the most beautiful . . . in
4. the worst . . . in
5. the farthest / furthest . . . in
6. the best . . . of
7. the oldest . . . in
8. the most comfortable . . . in
9. the most exhausted of

Exercise 33, p. 247.

2. The highest mountains on earth
3. the biggest bird
4. The two greatest natural dangers
5. the most popular forms of entertainment
6. The three most common street names
7. The longest river in South America

Exercise 34, p. 248.

1. the best experiences
2. the nicest times
3. the most difficult courses
4. the worst mistakes
5. the most beautiful buildings
6. the easiest exams

Exercise 36, p. 248.

1. a   5. b
2. b   6. a
3. a   7. b
4. a   8. a

Exercise 37, p. 249.

Questions:
2. What is the most interesting sport to watch on TV?
3. What is the most crowded city you have ever visited?
4. Where is the best restaurant to eat around here?
5. What is the most fun place to visit in this area?
6. Who is the kindest person you know?
7. What is the most important thing in life?
8. What is the most serious problem in the world?
9. Who is the most interesting person in the news right now?

Exercise 39, p. 250.

2. easier . . . than
3. two more wheels
4. longer . . . narrower (more narrow) . . . wider
5. more education
6. the longest
7. the friendliest . . . most delightful
8. the most famous . . . in
9. the loudest . . . in
10. The harder . . . the more impossible
11. the biggest . . . in . . . more people than
12. shorter
13. the highest . . . of
14. The longer . . . the more difficult
15. faster than / as fast as . . . the fastest
16. The greatest . . . in

Exercise 40, p. 251.

(Answers for items 3 and 6 may vary.)
1. C . . . E   6. A . . . B
2. A . . . D   7. C . . . E
3. A . . . B   8. A . . . D
4. C . . . E   9. A . . . D
5. A . . . D

Exercise 41, p. 252.

2. as   6. as
3. from   7. from
4. Ø . . . Ø   8. Ø . . . Ø
5. to

Exercise 42, p. 253.

1. to   8. like
2. the   9. the
3. the   10. as
4. as   11. alike
5. from   12. to
6. more   13. from
7. than

Exercise 43, p. 254.
(Answers may vary.)
2. similar to
3. similar
4. the same
5. different from
6. the same as
7. the same as

Exercise 44, p. 254.
(Answers may vary.)
3. different from / not the same as
4. the same
5. the same . . . as
6. like
7. the same
8. the same . . . as
9. alike . . . alike
10. like / the same as / similar to

Exercise 45, p. 255.
1. T   4. T
2. F   5. F
3. F

Exercise 47, p. 257.
2. Alaska is **the** largest state in the United States.
3. A pillow is **softer** than a rock.
4. Who is **the** most generous person in your family?
5. **The harder** you work, **the more successful** you will be.
6. One of **the** biggest disappointments in my life was when my soccer team lost the championship.
7. My sister is **much taller** than me.
8. A firm mattress is **more comfortable** for many people than a soft mattress.
9. One of the most talkative students in the class is Frederick.
10. Professor Bennett's lectures were the **most** confusing I have ever heard.

Chapter 10: The Passive

Exercise 1, p. 258.
1. b
2. a, b
3. a, b

Exercise 2, p. 259.
1. c. We are
2. a. He was
   b. They were
3. a. We are being
   b. She is being
4. a. I was being
   b. He was being

5. a. She has been
   b. He has been
6. a. I will be
   b. We are going to be

Exercise 3, p. 260.
2. are . . . ed
3. is being . . . ed
4. have been . . . ed
5. was . . . ed
6. was
7. will be . . . ed
8. are going to be . . . ed

Exercise 4, p. 261.
Checked sentences: 2, 4, 7

Exercise 5, p. 261.
2. are employed
3. has been hired
4. are going to be faxed
5. was bought
6. will be done
7. was being examined

Exercise 6, p. 262.
2. a. Erin is surprised
   b. Are you surprised
3. a. Greta will be shocked
   b. Will Pat be shocked
4. a. The birthday card is being signed
   b. Is it being signed
5. a. The card was signed
   b. Was it signed
6. a. It was being signed
   b. Was it being signed
7. a. It has been signed
   b. Has it been signed
8. a. It is going to be signed
   b. Is it going to be signed

Exercise 7, p. 262.
2. Are hair dryers provided by the hotel?
3. Were extra towels brought by housekeeping?
4. Has our meal been brought by room service?
5. Is our luggage being brought to our room by the bellhop?
6. Is the air-conditioning going to be fixed by maintenance?
7. Will our room be upgraded by the front desk?

Exercise 8, p. 263.
Checked sentences:
2. the truck
5. the driver

Exercise 9, p. 264.

Underlined verbs:

3. fell, v.i.
4. slept, v.i.
5. felt, v.t. *Passive:* An earthquake was felt by many people yesterday.
6. existed, v.i.
7. agree, v.i.
8. die, v.i.
9. discover, v.t. *Passive:* A cure for cancer will be discovered by scientists someday.
10. invent, v.t. *Passive:* Was spaghetti invented by the Italians?

Exercise 10, p. 264.

3. a. Princess Diana was killed in a car crash in 1997.
4. j. Marie and Pierre Curie discovered radium.
5. f. Oil was discovered in Saudi Arabia in 1938.
6. g. Mahatma Ghandhi and Martin Luther King Jr. were arrested several times for peaceful protests.
7. b. Michael Jackson died in 2009.
8. d. Leonardo da Vinci painted the Mona Lisa.
9. e. John F. Kennedy was elected president of the United States in 1960.
10. i. Nelson Mandela was released from prison in 1990.

Exercise 11, p. 265.

1. Pearson Longman
2. Betty Azar . . . Stacy Hagen
3. Don Martinetti . . . Chris Pavely

Exercise 12, p. 265.

2. This house was built in 1904.
3. Rice is grown in India.
4. Is Spanish spoken in Peru?
5. The telephone was invented by Alexander Graham Bell.
6. When was the first computer invented?
7. Hammers are sold at a hardware store.
8. Have you ever been hypnotized?
9. *The Origin of Species* was published in 1859.
10. *The Origin of Species* was written by Charles Darwin.

Exercise 13, p. 266.

2. b. = <u>was built</u>; no, b
3. a., b., c. = <u>was designed</u>; the *by*-phrases tells who designed the building. The important information is in c.
4. <u>was ruled</u>; It means that Thailand has never had a ruler.

Exercise 14, p. 266.

2. The driver was told to get out of the car by the police.
3. The driver took out his license.
4. The driver gave his license to the police officer.
5. The license was checked.

6. The driver was given a ticket.
7. The driver was told to drive more carefully.

Exercise 15, p. 267.

1. happened
2. was hit
3. Was
4. injured
5. called
6. was taken
7. treated
8. happened
9. was arrested
10. wasn't killed

Exercise 16, p. 267.

2. was interrupted
3. belongs
4. is delivered
5. is not pronounced
6. happened
7. arrived . . . was met
8. heard . . . was not surprised . . . was shocked
9. will be built / is going to be built
10. wrote . . . was written
11. was kicked . . . attended
12. agree . . . prefer
13. was your bike stolen
14. A: Have you paid
    B: will be shut off / is going to be shut off

Exercise 17, p. 268.

2. were
3. built
4. Was
5. built
6. swam
7. was designed
8. did not become
9. built
10. began
11. were
12. became
13. are found

Exercise 18, p. 269.

1. T
2. T
3. T
4. T
5. T

Exercise 19, p. 269.

2. should be planted
3. cannot be controlled
4. had to be fixed
5. can be reached
6. ought to be washed
7. may be cooked . . . (may be) eaten
8. could be destroyed
9. must be kept

Exercise 20, p. 270.

Possible answers:

1. He was an immigrant from Germany. He invented Levi jeans.
2. He went to California because his brother wanted him to open a store.
3. They were created for miners.
4. Denim is a cotton fabric.

5. Rivets were put in pants, and a red tab was added to the rear pocket.
6. Rivets made the pants stronger.
7. A red tab was added so the jeans could be more easily identified.
8. They are known as Levis.

Exercise 21, p. 271.
1. sand
2. whales
3. China . . . Mongolia
4. small spaces

Exercise 22, p. 272.
2. a, c
3. b, c
4. a, c
5. b
6. a, b, c
7. a, c

Exercise 23, p. 272.
1. about
2. of
3. of
4. of
5. from
6. about
7. with
8. in
9. in
10. with

Exercise 24, p. 273.
2. is interested
3. am . . . finished
4. am satisfied
5. is married to
6. are opposed
7. Are . . . prepared
8. is composed

Exercise 25, p. 273.
1. with
2. for
3. to
4. to
5. with
6. to
7. with
8. about

Exercise 26, p. 274.
1. with
2. of
3. about
4. for
5. in
6. with
7. to
8. of

Exercise 27, p. 274.
2. is made of
3. is crowded
4. is located in
5. am exhausted
6. are disappointed
7. is spoiled
8. is composed of
9. am . . . qualified for
10. am . . . acquainted with

Exercise 28, p. 275.
1. is spoiled
2. was closed
3. is located in

4. scared of
5. Are . . . hurt
6. am lost
7. Are . . . related to
8. gone
9. are broken
10. Are . . . shut

Exercise 29, p. 275.
1. A
2. B
3. No picture matches.
4. A

Exercise 30, p. 276.
1. man
2. roller coaster
3. girl
4. roller coaster
5. roller coaster
6. girl

Exercise 31, p. 276.
1. boring
2. shocked
3. confusing
4. embarrassed
5. surprise
6. scary

Exercise 32, p. 277.
2. a. excited
   b. exciting
3. a. fascinating
   b. fascinated
4. a. depressed
   b. depressing
5. a. interested
   b. interesting

Exercise 33, p. 277.
1. embarrassed
2. embarrassing
3. shocked
4. shocking
5. surprised
6. surprised
7. upsetting
8. depressed
9. interesting
10. interested

Exercise 35, p. 279.
2. busy
3. lost
4. dirty
5. nervous
6. late
7. rich
8. serious
9. bald
10. hurt

Exercise 37, p. 280.
Sample answers:
1. cold
2. hot
3. tired
4. bald
5. thirsty
6. sick

Exercise 38, p. 280.
2. get well
3. get married
4. gets hungry
5. gets dark
6. get dry
7. getting tired
8. getting worried
9. got killed
10. getting cold
11. got lost
12. get crowded
13. get . . . angry
14. get involved
15. got dressed

Exercise 39, p. 281.
1. T
2. F
3. T

Exercise 41, p. 282.
2. is used to
3. am not used . . . am used to
4. are used to
6. am accustomed to . . . am not accustomed to
7. are accustomed to
8. are not accustomed to

Exercise 42, p. 282.
1. are you accustomed to
2. are you used to
3. are you accustomed to
4. Are you accustomed to
5. Are you used to
6. Are you used to
7. are you accustomed to
8. Are you used to

Exercise 46, p. 284.
3. am	6. are
4. Ø	7. is
5. Ø	8. Ø

Exercise 47, p. 284.
3. used to eat
4. is used to growing
5. is used to eating
6. used to have
7. am used to taking
8. used to go

Exercise 49, p. 285.
2. The weather is supposed to be cold tomorrow.
3. The plane is supposed to arrive at 6:00.
4. I am supposed to work late tonight.
5. The mail was supposed to come an hour ago, but it didn't.

Exercise 50, p. 286.
2. Ann is supposed to call Lena at nine.
3. Johnny is supposed to make his bed before he goes to school.
4. The students are supposed to read the test directions carefully and raise their hands if they have any questions.
5. The patient is supposed to take one pill every eight hours and drink plenty of fluids.

Exercise 51, p. 286.
1. T	3. T	5. T	7. T
2. F	4. F	6. F	8. T

Exercise 52, p. 286.
Part I.
1. a, c	4. a, b, c
2. b	5. a, b
3. b, c	

Part II.
2. established
3. were established
4. were supposed to
5. became
6. were given
7. were
8. were studied
9. kept
10. are put
11. are fed
12. are watched
13. have
14. are treated
15. have saved

(*Answers to questions may vary.*)
1. It was established for an Egyptian queen for her enjoyment.
2. They were dark holes or dirty cages.
3. The purpose was to study animals.
4. They keep animals in large, natural settings, feed them a healthy diet, and watch them for signs of disease.
5. They want to encourage breeding to save different types of animals.

Exercise 53, p. 288.
2. Something **happened**.
3. This pen **belongs** to me.
4. I'm **interested** in that subject.
5. He is **married to** my cousin.
6. Mary's dog **died** last week.
7. Were you **surprised** when you heard the news?
8. When I went downtown, **I got** lost.
9. The **bus arrived** ten minutes late.
10. We're not suppose**d** to have pets in our apartment.

Exercise 54, p. 289.
My Favorite Holiday

   (1) New Year's is the most important holiday of the year in my country. New Year's <u>is celebrated</u> for fifteen days, but my favorite day is the first day.
   (2) The celebration actually begins at midnight. Fireworks <u>are set off</u>, and the streets <u>are filled</u> with people. Neighbors and friends greet each other and wish one another good luck for the year. The next morning, gifts <u>are exchanged</u>. Children <u>are given</u> money. It <u>is wrapped</u> in red envelopes because red is the color for good luck. When I was younger, this was always my favorite part of the holiday.

(3) On New Year's Day, everyone wears new clothes. These clothes <u>are bought</u> especially for the holiday. People are very polite to each other. It <u>is considered</u> wrong to yell, lie, or use bad language on the first day of the year. It is a custom for younger generations to visit their elders. They wish them good health and a long life.

Chapter 11: Count/Noncount Nouns and Articles

Exercise 2, p. 291.

2. an	8. an	14. a
3. a	9. an	15. a
4. an	10. an	16. a
5. an	11. a	17. an
6. a	12. an	18. an
7. a	13. an	

Exercise 3, p. 291.

1. a	6. Ø
2. Ø	7. a
3. an	8. an
4. Ø	9. a
5. an	10. Ø

Exercise 4, p. 291.

1. a	3. a, b
2. a	4. a, b

Exercise 5, p. 292.

3. Correct.
4. some furniture OR four chairs
5. Correct.
6. some furniture OR a chair
7. some chairs
8. some furniture

Exercise 6, p. 292.

advice: ideas, suggestions
mail: letters, postcards
jewelry: bracelets, rings

Exercise 7, p. 293.

3. a, count	7. some, noncount
4. some, noncount	8. an, count
5. a, count	9. some, noncount
6. some, noncount	10. a, count

Exercise 8, p. 294.

3. Ø	10. Ø
4. s . . . s	11. Ø
5. Ø	12. s
6. s	13. es
7. s	14. Ø
8. Ø	15. s
9. s	16. Ø

Exercise 10, p. 295.

3. Ø	8. s . . . s
4. es	9. Ø
5. Ø	10. s
6. Ø is . . . s are	11. Ø
7. Ø	12. Ø

Exercise 11, p. 296.

1. Ø	6. s
2. Ø	7. Ø
3. s	8. Ø
4. Ø	9. Ø
5. Ø	10. Ø

Exercise 15, p. 297.

1. apples	4. fruit
2. apples/fruit	5. apples
3. apples	6. fruit

Exercise 16, p. 297.

3. Correct.
4. Correct.
5. Correct.
6. too **many** new words
7. a few **words** / **a little** vocabulary
8. Correct.
9. several new **words**
10. **are a lot** of new words / **is a lot** of new **vocabulary**
12. are a lot of new **words** / **is** a lot of new vocabulary

Exercise 17, p. 298.

1. d. many cars
   e. much stuff
   f. much experience
2. a. much fruit
   b. many vegetables
   c. many bananas
   d. many tomatoes
   e. many oranges
   f. much food
3. a. much fun
   b. much help
   c. much time
   d. much information
   e. many facts
   f. much money

Exercise 18, p. 298.

6. [Canada has ten provinces.]
7. [There are 47 countries on the continent of Africa and six island nations.]

Exercise 19, p. 299.

3. a little help
4. a little pepper
5. a few things
6. a few apples
7. a little fruit

8. a little advice
9. a little . . . money
10. A few friends
11. a little rain
12. a little French
13. a few . . . hours

Exercise 20, p. 299.
1. C
2. A
3. B

Exercise 21, p. 300.
1. E   4. C
2. B   5. A
3. F   6. D

Exercise 22, p. 301.
3. papers
4. paper
5. a . . . paper
6. works
7. work
8. hair . . . hair
9. hairs
10. glasses
11. glasses
12. glass
13. Iron is
14. Irons are
15. experiences
16. experience
17. some . . . chicken
18. chickens
19. are . . . lights
20. A: light . . . isn't
    B: It

Exercise 24, p. 303.
(Other completions are possible.)

Part I.
3. bottle   8. bottle
4. jar   9. can/bottle
5. can   10. bag
6. can   11. can
7. bag/box   12. box

Part II.
15. piece   22. bowl/cup
16. slice/piece   23. glass
17. slice/piece   24. bowl
18. glass/cup   25. slice/piece
19. bowl/cup   26. bowl/cup
20. slice/piece   27. bowl/cup
21. glass   28. slice/piece

Exercise 27, p. 308.
1. 1   3. 2   5. 4
2. 3   4. 5   6. 6

Exercise 28, p. 310.
3. A: a
   B: a
4. A: the . . . the
5. B: the . . . the
6. the
7. A: a
   B: a
8. the
9. a
10. the
11. a
12. A: the . . . the . . . the . . . the . . . the . . . the

Exercise 29, p. 311.
2. singular, general   6. singular, specific
3. plural, general   7. plural, specific
4. singular, general   8. noncount, specific
5. noncount, general

Exercise 30, p. 311.
2. a. Mountains
   b. The mountains
3. a. The water
   b. Water
4. a. The information
   b. information
5. a. Health
   b. the health
6. a. Men . . . women
   b. the men . . . the women
7. a. problems
   b. the problems
8. a. The vegetables
   b. Vegetables

Exercise 31, p. 312.
Sample answers:
1. salt and shells (*also possible:* beads)
2. coins
3. money
4. credit . . . debit cards (*also possible:* paper money)
5. plastic (credit or debit cards) . . . paper money

Exercise 32, p. 312.
2. the   5. Ø . . . Ø
3. Ø The   6. Ø Trees . . . Ø
4. the   7. Ø The

Exercise 33, p. 313.
2. some . . . some . . . the . . . the
3. a . . . some . . . the . . . the
4. B: a . . . a . . . The . . . the
5. a . . . some . . . some . . . The . . . the . . . some
   . . . the . . . a . . . The

Exercise 34, p. 313.
2. an
3. Ø
4. Ø
5. The
6. Ø
7. Ø
8. a
9. Ø
10. The
11. the

Exercise 35, p. 314.
2. Ø
3. the . . . The
4. a . . . the
5. the
6. Ø . . . the . . . The
7. Ø . . . Ø . . . Ø
8. the . . . the
9. a
10. The . . . the . . . the . . . the
11. A: the
    B: the

Exercise 36, p. 315.
3. Ø
4. the
5. the
6. Ø
7. the
8. the
9. Ø
10. Ø

Exercise 37, p. 316.
1. Ø . . . Ø   T
2. The . . . Ø   T
3. Ø . . . Ø   F [Austria]
4. The . . . Ø   T
5. The . . . the   F
6. The . . . Ø . . . the T
7. Ø   F [psychology / psychiatry]
8. Ø . . . Ø   T
9. Ø . . . the   T
10. The   F [The Himalayas]

Exercise 40, p. 318.
2. Do you know **Richard Smith**? **He** is a professor at this university.
3. I know that **Professor Smith** teaches at the **University of Arizona**.
4. (*no change*)
5. John is a **Catholic**. Ali is a **Moslem**.
6. Anna speaks **French**. She studied in **France** for two years.
7. (*no change*)
8. I'm taking **Modern European History 101** this semester.
9. We went to **Vancouver, British Columbia**, for our vacation last summer.
10. **Venezuela** is a **Spanish**-speaking country.
11. **Canada** is in **North America**.
12. **Canada** is north of the **United States**.
13. (*no change*)

14. The **Mississippi River** flows south.
15. The **Amazon** is a river in **South America**.
16. We went to a zoo. We went to **Brookfield Zoo** in **Chicago**.
17. The title of this book is *Fundamentals of English Grammar.*
18. I enjoy studying **English** grammar.
19. On **Valentine's Day** (**February** 14th), sweethearts give each other presents.
20. I read a book called *The Cat and the Mouse in My Aunt's House.*

Exercise 41, p. 319.

Part I.

Jane Goodall

(1) Do you recognize the name **Jane Goodall**? Perhaps you know her for her studies of chimpanzees. She became very famous from her work in **Tanzania**.

(2) Jane Goodall was born in **England**, and as a child, was fascinated by animals. Her favorite books were *The Jungle Book,* by **Rudyard Kipling**, and books about **Tarzan**, a fictional character who was raised by apes.

(3) Her childhood dream was to go to **Africa**. After high school, she worked as a secretary and a waitress to earn enough money to go there. During that time, she took evening courses in journalism and **English** literature. She saved every penny until she had enough money for a trip to **Africa**.

(4) In the spring of 1957, she sailed through the **Red Sea** and southward down the African coast to **Mombasa** in **Kenya**. Her uncle had arranged a job for her in **Nairobi** with a British company. When she was there, she met **Dr. Louis Leakey**, a famous anthropologist. Under his guidance, she began her lifelong study of chimpanzees on the eastern shore of **Lake Tanganyika**.

(5) Jane Goodall lived alone in a tent near the lake. Through months and years of patience, she won the trust of the chimps and was able to watch them closely. Her observations changed forever how we view chimpanzees— and all other animals we share the world with.

Part II.
1. T
2. F
3. F
4. T
5. F
6. F

Chapter 12: Adjective Clauses

Exercise 2, p. 322.
Checked sentences: 1, 2, 5

Exercise 3, p. 322.
1. An orthopedist
2. A dermatologist
3. A surgeon
4. A pediatrician

Exercise 4, p. 323.
1. a, d
2. c, d

Exercise 5, p. 323.
2. The manager <u>that hired me</u> has less experience than I do.
3. I like the manager <u>that works in the office next to mine</u>.
4. My mother is a person <u>who wakes up every morning with a positive attitude</u>.
5. A person <u>who wakes up with a positive attitude every day</u> is lucky.

Exercise 6, p. 323.
1. The police officer who/that gave me directions was friendly.
2. The waiter who/that served us dinner was slow.
3. I talked to the women who/that walked into my office.
4. The man who/that sat next to me on the plane talked a lot.
5. The people who/that live next to me have three cars.

Exercise 7, p. 323.
2. The man who/that answered the phone was polite.
3. People who/that paint houses for a living are called house painters.
4. I'm uncomfortable around married couples who/that argue all the time.
5. While I was waiting at the bus stop, I stood next to an elderly man who/that started a conversation with me about my school.

Exercise 10, p. 325.
Checked sentences: 2, 3, 5, 8

Exercise 11, p. 325.
1. a, b, c, d   3. a, b, c, d
2. a, c   4. a, c

Exercise 12, p. 325.
2. b. them; The couple that/who/whom I invited for dinner was two hours late.
3. b. him; The man that/who/whom I sat next to on the plane snored the entire flight.
4. b. him; The man that/who/whom police arrested tried to shoplift some groceries.
5. b. her; The chef that/who/whom the company hired is very experienced.

Exercise 13, p. 326.
2. The man who/that answered my question . . .
3. The man who/that/Ø/whom I called . . .

4. The man who/that/Ø/whom you recommended . . .
5. The man who/that is the owner . . .
6. The man who/that you invited . . .
7. The man who/that was walking with his kids . . .
8. The man who/that/Ø/whom I saw in the waiting room . . .
9. The man who/that sold us our museum tickets . . .
10. The man who/that gave us a discount . . .

Exercise 14, p. 326.
1. who, that
2. that, Ø, who, whom
3. who, that
4. that, Ø, who, whom
5. that, Ø, who, whom
6. who, that

Exercise 16, p. 327.
2. The food <u>we ate at the sidewalk café</u> was delicious.
3. The bus <u>that I take to school every morning</u> is usually very crowded.
4. Pizza <u>which is sold by the slice</u> is a popular lunch in many cities throughout the world.
5. Piranhas are dangerous fish <u>that can tear the flesh off an animal as large as a horse in a few minutes</u>.

Exercise 17, p. 328.
2. The soup that/Ø/which I had for lunch was too salty.
3. I have a class that/which begins at 8:00 A.M.
4. The information that/Ø/which I found on the Internet helped me a lot.
5. My daughter asked me a question that/Ø/which I couldn't answer.
6. Where can I catch the bus that/which goes downtown?

Exercise 18, p. 328.
2. . . . you wore ~~it~~ to class yesterday
3. . . . you to meet ~~her~~
4. . . . to rent ~~it~~ had two bedrooms
5. . . . we bought ~~it~~ for our anniversary
6. . . . you met ~~her~~ at
7. . . . cat that ~~it~~ likes
8. . . . cat catches ~~them~~ live

Exercise 19, p. 328.
1. that, Ø, which
2. who, that
3. that, which
4. that, Ø, which
5. that, Ø, who, whom
6. that, which

Exercise 20, p. 329.
1. who
2. Ø
3. that
4. which
5. that
6. Ø
7. that
8. whom

Exercise 21, p. 329.
2. **The** student who/that raised her hand in class asked the teacher a question.
   The student who/that sat quietly in his seat didn't.
3. **The** girl who/that won the bike race is happy.
   The girl who/that lost the bike race isn't happy.
4. **The** food that/which/Ø we ate from our garden was inexpensive.
   The food that/which/Ø we ate at the restaurant was expensive.
5. **The** man who/that was listening to the radio heard the special report about the earthquake in China.
   The man who/that was sleeping didn't hear it.
6. **The** person who/that bought a large car probably spent more money (than the person who bought a small car).

Exercise 22, p. 330.
2. b. who/that tells jokes.
3. f. who/that delivers babies.
4. h. who/that can be shaped . . .
5. e. who designs buildings.
6. i. that can be difficult to solve.
7. j. that eats meat.
8. c. that forms when water boils.
9. k. that has a hard shell . . .
10. a. who leaves society . . .
11. d. that is square . . .

Exercise 23, p. 330.
The verb in the adjective clause agrees with the noun that precedes it.

Exercise 24, p. 331.
2. tools . . . are
3. woman . . . lives
4. people . . . live
5. cousin . . . works
6. miners . . . work
7. athlete . . . plays
8. athletes . . . play
9. books . . . tell
10. book . . . tells
11. men . . . were
12. woman . . . was

Exercise 26, p. 332.
2. The man that/Ø/who/whom I told you **about** is over there.
   The man **about** whom I told you is over there.

3. The woman that/Ø/who/whom I work **for** pays me a fair salary.
   The woman **for** whom I work pays me a fair salary.
4. Alicia likes the family that/Ø/who/whom she is living **with**.
   Alicia likes the family **with** whom she is living.
5. The picture that/Ø/which Tom is looking **at** is beautiful.
   The picture **at** which Tom is looking is beautiful.
6. I enjoyed the music that/Ø/which we listened **to** after dinner
   I enjoyed the music **to** which we listened after dinner.

Exercise 27, p. 333.
2. to . . . [we went **to**]
3. in/at . . . [we stayed **in/at**]
4. to . . . [we listened **to**]
5. for . . . [Sally was waiting **for**]
6. to . . . [**to** whom I talked]
7. [that I was looking **for**]
8. [I had graduated **from**]
9. [**with** whom he is living]
10. [who is staring **at** us]
11. [**with** whom I almost always agree]
12. [you introduced me **to** at the restaurant last night]
13. [I've always been able to depend **on**]
14. [you waved **at**]
15. [**to** whom you should complain]

Exercise 28, p. 334.
1. b, c
2. c
3. a, b, c
4. b
5. c

Exercise 29, p. 334.
Part II.
1. family
2. activities
3. people
4. way (of life)
5. things
6. customs and habits
7. things

Part III.
Sample answers:
1. was their eating customs
2. who were similar to him in their customs and habits
3. the way of life that his host family had
4. he had in common with them

Exercise 30, p. 335.
Checked sentences: 2, 4

Exercise 31, p. 336.
1. The C.E.O. whose company lost money is resigning.
2. Let me introduce you to the woman whose company is hiring right now.
3. I talked to the couple whose house was burglarized.
4. The child whose foot you stepped on is fine.
5. The man whose cell phone you found is on the phone.

Exercise 32, p. 337.

2. There is the woman whose husband writes movie scripts.
3. Over there is the man whose daughter is in my English class.
4. Over there is the woman whose sister you met yesterday.
5. There is the professor whose course I'm taking.
6. That is the man whose daughter is a newscaster.
7. That is the girl whose brother I taught.
8. There is the boy whose mother is a famous musician.

Exercise 33, p. 337.

1. whose	3. who's	5. who's
2. whose	4. whose	6. who's

Exercise 34, p. 338.

Sample answers:

1. b. who invited us to his party
   c. whose son broke our car window
   d. whose dog barks all night
   e. who is standing out in the rain
   f. whose wife is an actress

2. a. whose picture was in the paper
   b. whose father climbed Mt. Everest
   c. who helped me when I cut myself
   d. that works for Dr. Lang
   e. whose purse I found
   f. whose father I worked with

3. a. whose pages are torn
   b. that is on the table
   c. that Sam lost
   d. whose cover is missing
   e. that I gave to you
   f. which I found

Exercise 35, p. 338.

3. who, that	9. who, that
4. whose	10. whom
5. who, that, Ø, whom	11. whose
6. whom	12. that, which
7. whose	13. that, Ø, which
8. that, Ø, which	

Exercise 36, p. 339.

1. that	4. that
2. Ø	5. whose
3. which	

Exercise 37, p. 339.

2. whose son was in an accident
3. I slept on in a hotel last night
4. that/which erupted in Indonesia
5. whose specialty is heart surgery
6. that/which lived in the jungles of Southeast Asia
7. whose mouth was big enough to swallow a whole cow in one gulp

Exercise 40, p. 340.

2. The woman **that I met yesterday was nice**.
4. I met a woman **whose husband** is a famous lawyer.
5. Do you know the people who **live** in that house?
6. The professor **who/that** teaches Chemistry 101 is very good.
7. The people **whose house I painted** want me to do other work for them.
8. The people who I **met at** the party last night were interesting.
9. I enjoyed the music that we listened **to**.
10. The apple tree **that we planted last** year is producing fruit.
11. Before I came here, I didn't have the opportunity to speak to people **whose native** tongue is English.
12. One thing I need to get **is** a new alarm clock.
13. The people who **were** waiting to buy tickets for the **game were** happy because their team had made it to the championship.

Exercise 41, p. 341.

My Friend's Vegan Diet

I have a friend <u>who is a vegan</u>. As you may know, a vegan is a person <u>who eats no animal products</u>. When I first met him, I didn't understand the vegan diet. I thought *vegan* was another name for *vegetarian,* except that vegans didn't eat eggs. I soon found out I was wrong. The first time I cooked dinner for him, I made a vegetable dish <u>which had a lot of cheese</u>. Since cheese comes from cows, it's not vegan, so he had to scrape it off. I also served him bread <u>that had milk in it</u> and a dessert <u>that was made with ice cream</u>. Unfortunately, there wasn't much <u>that he could eat that night</u>. In the beginning, I had trouble thinking of meals <u>which we could both enjoy</u>. But he is a wonderful cook and showed me how to create delicious vegan meals. I don't know if I'll ever become a complete vegan, but I've learned a lot about the vegan diet and the delicious possibilities <u>it has</u>.

Chapter 13: Gerunds and Infinitives

Exercise 2, p. 342.

1. a. working
   b. closing
   c. hiring

2. a. smoking
   b. eating
   c. sleeping

3. a. paying
   b. handing in
   c. cleaning

Exercise 3, p. 343.
Sample answers:
2. buying
3. sweeping
4. getting
5. talking
6. working
7. opening

Exercise 4, p. 343.
1. finish doing
2. talked about seeing
3. Would you mind explaining
4. thinking about not attending
5. Keep trying

Exercise 6, p. 345.
2. Nancy and Frank like to go fishing.
3. Adam went camping.
4. Tim likes to go shopping.
5. Laura goes jogging/running.
6. Fred and Jean like to go skiing.
7. Joe likes to go hiking.
8. Sara often goes bowling.
9. Liz and Greg probably go dancing a lot.
10. The Taylors are going to go (ice) skating.
11. Alex and Barbara like to go sailing/boating.
12. Tourists go sightseeing on buses.
13. Colette and Ben like to go skydiving
14. (*Answers will vary.*)

Exercise 7, p. 345.
Questions:
2. Do you like to go water skiing?
3. Do you like to go bowling?
4. Do you go dancing on weekends?
5. Do you go jogging for exercise?
6. Do you go fishing in the winter?
7. Do you go camping in the summer?
8. Do you like to go snow skiing?

Exercise 9, p. 346.
Sample answers:
2. to be
3. to visit
4. to get to
5. to be
6. to be
7. to be . . . to hear
8. to buy
9. to lend
10. to eat
11. to watch . . . to go to
12. to get to
13. to see
14. to hurt
15. to tell

Exercise 10, p. 347.
Checked sentences: 1, 2

Exercise 11, p. 347.
1. b, c
2. b, c
3. b, c
4. c
5. b, c
6. c
7. b, c
8. b, c

Exercise 13, p. 348.
1. to understand
2. listening
3. to get . . . to stop
4. repeating
5. to nod / nodding
6. to look / looking
7. speaking

Exercise 14, p. 349.
1. eating
2. to help
3. moving
4. to go / going
5. to be
6. living
7. to give
8. to say
9. to sleep / sleeping
10. trying
11. to want to leave . . . talking

Exercise 15, p. 350.
1. to go / going
2. to go / going
3. to go
4. to go
5. to go
6. to go
7. to go / going
8. to go
9. going
10. going
11. to go
12. going
13. to go
14. to go / going
15. going
16. going
17. to go
18. going
19. going
20. to go

Exercise 16, p. 350.
1. to relax
2. to stay . . . relax
3. to stay . . . relax . . . go
4. getting . . . watching
5. getting . . . watching . . . listening
6. selling . . . buying
7. to move . . . find . . . start
8. going . . . letting
9. quitting . . . going
10. unplugging . . . turning off . . . locking

Exercise 17, p. 351.
Verbs:
1. plan to go
2. consider going
3. offer to help
4. like to visit / visiting
5. enjoy reading
6. intend to get
7. can't afford to buy
8. seems to be
9. put off writing
10. would like to go swimming

11. postpone going
12. finish studying
13. would mind helping
14. begin to study / studying
15. think about going
16. quit trying
17. continue to walk / walking
18. learn to speak
19. talk about going
20. keep trying

Exercise 19, p. 352.
2. for holding
3. about being
4. in going
5. for being
6. of flying
7. about taking
8. about seeing
9. on paying
10. about / of becoming
11. like eating
12. for not writing
13. of living
14. in being
15. on meeting
16. for cleaning
17. from entering
18. at cutting

Exercise 21, p. 353.
2. in telling
3. of drowning
4. to taking
5. like telling
6. on paying
7. for causing
8. at remembering
9. from doing
10. for taking
11. of not having
12. to having
13. A: about / of quitting
    B: of quitting

Exercise 22, p. 354.
1. wanted to stay
2. traveling
3. packing
4. unpacking
5. to travel
6. wanted to take
7. decided to stay
8. be
9. to do
10. would like to take
11. began talking
12. excited about seeing

Exercise 24, p. 355.
2. by washing
3. by watching
4. by smiling
5. by eating
6. by drinking
7. by guessing
8. by waving
9. by wagging
10. by staying . . . taking

Exercise 25, p. 356.
2. with a needle and thread
3. with a saw
4. with a thermometer
5. with a spoon
6. with a shovel
7. with a hammer
8. with a pair of scissors

Exercise 26, p. 356.
3. with
4. by
5. with
6. with
7. by
8. by
9. with
10. by

Exercise 28, p. 357.
2. Making friends here takes time.
3. Getting around town is easy.
4. Is living here expensive?
6. It's dangerous to walk alone at night.
7. It's fun to explore this town.
8. Is it difficult to find affordable housing?

Exercise 31, p. 359.
2. for teachers to speak clearly.
3. for us to hurry.
4. for a fish to live out of water for more than a few minutes.
5. for working parents to budget their time carefully.
6. for a young child to sit still for a long time.
7. for my family to spend birthdays together.
8. for my brother to travel.
9. for you to understand Mr. Alvarez.

Exercise 33, p. 360.
Sample answers:
1. to offer a strong handshake when people meet one another
2. shaking hands firmly
3 and 4. (*Answers will vary.*)

Exercise 34, p. 360.
Checked sentences: 1, 2, 3, 4

Exercise 35, p. 361.
2. c. (in order) to listen
3. i. (in order) to see
4. a. (in order) to keep
5. d. (in order) to find
6. b. (in order) to reach

7. j.   (in order) to look
8. f.   (in order) to chase
9. h.   (in order) to get
10. g. (in order) to help

Exercise 36, p. 361.

3. Sam went to the hospital **in order** to visit a friend.
4. (*no change*)
5. I need to go to the bank today **in order** to deposit my paycheck.
6. On my way home, I stopped at the store **in order** to buy some shampoo.
7. Masako went to the cafeteria **in order** to eat lunch.
8. (*no change*)
9. Pedro watches TV **in order** to improve his English.
10. (*no change*)
11. (*no change*)
12. Jerry needs to go to the bookstore **in order** to buy school supplies.

Exercise 37, p. 362.

3. to   7. to
4. for   8. to
5. for   9. for
6. to   10. for

Exercise 38, p. 362.

1. Car sharing   4. move . . . take
2. join   5. owning
3. driving

Exercise 39, p. 363.

1. heavy
2. strong
3. strength

Exercise 40, p. 364.

3. too busy to answer
4. early enough to get
5. too full to hold
6. large enough to hold
7. too big to get
8. big enough to hold

Exercise 41, p. 365.

2. I was too sleepy to finish my homework last night.
3. Mike was too busy to go to his aunt's housewarming party.
4. This jacket is too small for me to wear.
5. I live too far from school to walk there.
7. I'm not strong enough to move this furniture.
8. It's not warm enough for you to go outside without a coat.
9. I wasn't sick enough to stay home and miss work.

Exercise 43, p. 365.

3. to invite   7. to get . . .
4. going   sleep
5. listening   8. forgetting
6. to earn . . .   9. using
   to take

Exercise 44, p. 366.

1. to follow . . . to slow . . . give
2. Asking . . . getting . . . keep . . . to be
3. to make . . . to see

Exercise 45, p. 366.

1. a, b   4. a, c
2. b, c   5. c
3. b

Exercise 47, p. 368.

2. I went to the bank **to cash** a check.
3. Did you **go shopping** yesterday?
4. I cut the rope **with** a knife.
5. I thanked my friend for **driving** me to the airport.
6. **It is** difficult to learn another language.
7. Timmy isn't **old enough** to get married.
8. **This exercise is easy** to do. OR **It's easy to do this exercise.**
9. Last night **I was** too tired **to** do my homework.
10. I've never **gone sailing**, but I would like to.
11. **Reading is** one of my hobbies.
12. The teenagers began to **build** a campfire to keep themselves warm.
13. Instead of **settling** down in one place, I'd like to travel around the world.
14. I **enjoy traveling** because you learn so much about other countries and cultures.
15. My grandmother likes to **fish/go fishing/likes fishing**.
16. Martina would like to **have** a big family.

Chapter 14: Noun Clauses

Exercise 1, p. 370.
Checked sentences: 1, 2, 4

Exercise 2, p. 370.

1. Where are the Smiths living?
2. I don't know <u>where the Smiths are living</u>.
3. We don't know <u>what city they moved to</u>.
4. We know <u>that they moved a month ago</u>.
5. Are they coming back?
6. I don't know <u>if they are coming back</u>.

Exercise 4, p. 372.

2. a. I don't know where she is living.   NC
   b. Where is she living?   IQ
3. a. Where did Nick go?   IQ
   b. I don't know where Nick went.   NC
4. a. I don't know what time the movie begins.   NC
   b. What time does the movie begin?   IQ
5. a. Why is Yoko angry?   IQ
   b. I don't know why Yoko is angry.   NC

Exercise 5, p. 372.

2. where Frank goes
3. where Natasha went
4. why Maria is laughing
5. how much an electric car costs
6. how long elephants live
7. when the first wheel was invented
8. how many hours a light bulb burns
9. where Emily bought her first computer
10. who lives
11. who Julie talked
12. why Mike is always

Exercise 6, p. 373.

Can you tell me . . .
2. what this means?
3. when I will get my grades.
4. what our next assignment is.
5. how soon the next assignment is due.
6. why this is incorrect.
7. when a good time to meet is.
8. what day the term ends.
9. why I failed.
10. who will teach this class next time.

Exercise 7, p. 374.

3. what a lizard is
4. what is in the bag
5. whose car that is
6. whose car is in the driveway
7. whose Bob's doctor is
8. whose ladder this is . . . whose ladder this is
9. what is at the end of a rainbow

Exercise 8, p. 374.

Do you know . . .
1. where the phone is?
2. why the front door is open?
3. who just called?
4. whose socks are on the floor?
5. why all the lights are on?
6. what happened?
7. what the plumber said about the broken pipe?
8. what the repair is going to cost?

Exercise 9, p. 375.

2. Jason works
   does he work
3. did you see
   I saw
4. does that camera cost
   this camera costs
5. can you run
   I can run
6. did she get
   she got
7. is it
   it is
8. are some people
   some people are

Exercise 10, p. 376.
Checked sentences: 1, 3, 4

Exercise 11, p. 376.

2. if Mr. Piper will be at the meeting
3. if Niko went to work yesterday.
4. if there is going to be a windstorm tonight.
5. if I have Yung Soo's email address.

Exercise 12, p. 377.

2. if you are going to be
3. if Tim borrowed
4. if he can watch
5. if your car keys are
6. if your car has a CD player

Exercise 13, p. 378.
Questions:
2. when this building was built?
3. how far it is from Vancouver, Canada, to Riyadh, Saudi Arabia? [Around 7,774 mi. / 12,511 km.]
4. if Australia is the smallest continent? [Yes.]
5. how many eyes a bat has? [Two.]
6. what the longest word in English is? (*Answers will vary.*)
7. if a chimpanzee has a good memory? [Yes.]
8. how old the Great Wall of China is? [About 2,300 years old.]
9. if all birds fly? [No. For example, penguins don't fly.]
10. if birds **came** from dinosaurs? [Most dinosaur researchers think so.]

Exercise 15, p. 378.
Checked sentences: 1, 2, 3

Exercise 16, p. 379.

2. dreamed that
3. believe that
4. notice that . . . hope that
5. believe that she told the truth

Exercise 19, p. 380.
2. B: pleased that
3. B: surprised that . . . think that
4. A: aware that
   B: certain that
5. surprised that
6. true that

Exercise 21, p. 381.
Sample answers:
1. a. her English teacher is really good.
   b. she is enjoying her class.
2. a. her son has the flu.
   b. he doesn't have the flu.
3. a. the woman failed her chemistry course.
   b. she won't be able to graduate on time.
4. a. Rachel is there.
   b. she is there / she was invited.
5. a. Carol won't come back.
   b. she will be back.

Exercise 22, p. 382.
1. a, c
2. b, c

Exercise 23, p. 382.
Sample answers:
2. I don't believe that we are going to have a grammar test tomorrow.
3. I hope that Margo will be at the conference in March.
4. I believe that horses can swim.
5. I don't think that gorillas have tails
6. I don't think that Janet will be at Omar's wedding.
7. I hope my flight won't be cancelled because of the storms.

Exercise 26, p. 384.
2. Ann asked, "Is your brother a student?" OR
   "Is your brother a student?" Ann asked.
3. Rita **said**, "We're hungry." OR
   "We're hungry," Rita said.
4. Rita **asked**, "Are you hungry too?" OR
   "Are you hungry too?" Rita asked.
5. Rita **said**, "Let's eat. The food's ready." OR
   "Let's eat," Rita **said**. "The food is ready." OR
   "Let's eat. The food's ready," Rita **said**.
6. John F. Kennedy **said**, "Ask not . . . do for you. Ask what . . . for your country." OR
   "Ask not . . . do for you," John F. Kennedy **said**. "Ask what . . . for your country." OR
   "Ask not . . . do for you. Ask what . . . for your country," John F. Kennedy **said**.

Exercise 27, p. 385.
"You know sign language, don't you?" I asked Roberto.

"Yes, I do," he replied. "Both my grandparents are deaf."

"I'm looking for someone who knows sign language. A deaf student is going to visit our class next Monday," I said. "Could you interpret for her?" I asked.

"I'd be happy to," he answered. "Is she going to be a new student?"

"Possibly," I said. "She's interested in seeing what we do in our English classes."

Exercise 29, p. 386.
they . . . their

Exercise 30, p. 387.
1. she . . . her
2. he . . . me
3. he . . . us . . . our . . . he . . . his . . . his

Exercise 32, p. 388.
2. was meeting
3. had studied
4. had forgotten
5. was going
6. would carry
7. could teach

Exercise 33, p. 389.
2. Kristina said (that) she didn't like chocolate.
3. Carla said (that) she was planning . . . her family.
4. Tom said (that) he had already eaten lunch.
5. Kate said (that) she had called her doctor.
6. Mr. Rice said (that) he was going to go to Chicago.
7. Eric said (that) he would be at my house at ten.
8. Emma said (that) she couldn't afford to buy a new car.
9. Olivia said (that) she couldn't afford to buy a new car.
10. Ms. Todd said (that) she wanted to see me in her office after my meeting with my supervisor.

Exercise 34, p. 389.
1. a, c
2. a, c

Exercise 35, p. 390.
4. said
5. told
6. asked
7. told . . . said . . . asked . . . told . . . said
8. said . . . asked . . . told . . . asked . . . said

Exercise 37, p. 391.
(that) he wasn't going to have . . . wasn't hungry . . . had eaten . . . he had come . . . he needed to talk to her about a problem he was having at work.

Exercise 38, p. 391.

1. In the middle of class yesterday, my friend tapped me on the shoulder and asked me, **"W**hat are you doing after class**?"**

   "I will tell you later," I answered.

3. When I was putting on my hat and coat, Robert asked me, **"W**here are you going**?"**

   "I have a date with Anna," I told him.

   "What are you going to do?" he wanted to know.

   "We're going to a movie," I answered.

Exercise 39, p. 392.

1. asked	9. asked
2. was	10. could do
3. told	11. said
4. was	12. needed
5. asked	13. could help
6. would be	14. told
7. said	15. would leave
8. would be	

Exercise 41, p. 393.

2. I don't know **what your email address is.**

3. I **think that** Mr. Lee is out of town.

4. Can you tell **me where** Victor is living now?

5. I asked my uncle what kind of movies **he likes.**

6. I **think that** my English has improved a lot.

7. **It is** true that people are basically the same everywhere in the world.

8. A man came to my door last week. I **didn't** know who **he was**.

9. I want to know **if Pedro has** a laptop computer.

10. Sam and I talked about his classes. He told **me** that he **didn't** like his algebra class.
    (*also possible:* doesn't like)

11. A woman came into the room and **asked** me **where my brother was**. / **asked me, "Where is your brother?"**

12. I felt very relieved when the doctor said, **"You** will be fine. It's nothing serious.**"**

13. My mother asked **me, "When will you** be home?"

Index

A/an, 290, 292, 306–307
  (*Look on pages 290 and 292 and also on*
  pages 306 through 307.)
	The numbers following the words listed in the index
	refer to page numbers in the text.

Consonants, 14*fn.* (*Look at the footnote on page 14.*)	The letters *fn.* mean "footnote." Footnotes are at the bottom of a chart or the bottom of a page.

NOTES

NOTES

NOTES

AUDIO CD TRACKING LIST

CD 1

	TRACK	EXERCISE
Introduction	1	
Chapter 1	2	Exercise 1, p. 1
	3	Exercise 5, p. 4
	4	Exercise 6, p. 5
	5	Exercise 9, p. 6
	6	Exercise 21, p. 14
	7	Exercise 24, p. 15
	8	Exercise 33, p. 21
	9	Exercise 35, p. 22
	10	Exercise 37, p. 24
Chapter 2	11	Exercise 4, p. 27
	12	Exercise 5, p. 28
	13	Exercise 8, p. 30
	14	Exercise 16, p. 37
	15	Exercise 17, p. 37
	16	Exercise 19, p. 38
	17	Exercise 20, p. 39
	18	Exercise 21, p. 39
	19	Exercise 22, p. 40
	20	Exercise 23, p. 40
	21	Exercise 24, p. 40
	22	Exercise 31, p. 46
	23	Exercise 39, p. 51
	24	Exercise 43, p. 53
Chapter 3	25	Exercise 2, p. 56
	26	Exercise 6, p. 58
	27	Exercise 10, p. 60
	28	Exercise 11, p. 61
	29	Exercise 13, p. 62
	30	Exercise 17, p. 64
	31	Exercise 23, p. 67
	32	Exercise 33, p. 73
	33	Exercise 44, p. 79
Chapter 4	34	Exercise 2, p. 82
	35	Exercise 12, p. 88
	36	Exercise 17, p. 91
	37	Exercise 19, p. 92
	38	Exercise 20, p. 93
	39	Exercise 26, p. 97
	40	Exercise 31, p. 100
	41	Exercise 34, p. 103
	42	Exercise 36, p. 104
	43	Exercise 37, p. 104
	44	Exercise 43, p. 110
Chapter 5	45	Exercise 4, p. 113
	46	Exercise 6, p. 113
	47	Exercise 9, p. 116
	48	Exercise 14, p. 118
	49	Exercise 19, p. 120
	50	Exercise 29, p. 126
	51	Exercise 30, p. 126
	52	Exercise 34, p. 128
	53	Exercise 37, p. 130
	54	Exercise 44, p. 134
	55	Exercise 45, p. 135
	56	Exercise 46, p. 135
	57	Exercise 47, p. 135
	58	Exercise 48, p. 136
	59	Exercise 53, p. 138
	60	Exercise 56, p. 140
	61	Exercise 57, p. 141
	62	Exercise 59, p. 142
	63	Exercise 61, p. 143
	64	Exercise 62, p. 143

CD 2

	TRACK	EXERCISE
Chapter 6	1	Exercise 6, p. 149
	2	Exercise 7, p. 150
	3	Exercise 8, p. 150
	4	Exercise 9, p. 150
	5	Exercise 10, p. 150
	6	Exercise 28, p. 159
	7	Exercise 36, p. 163
	8	Exercise 49, p. 170
	9	Exercise 58, p. 176
	10	Exercise 59, p. 177
Chapter 7	11	Exercise 3, p. 179
	12	Exercise 7, p. 181
	13	Exercise 13, p. 184
	14	Exercise 17, p. 186
	15	Exercise 32, p. 194
	16	Exercise 45, p. 201
	17	Exercise 50, p. 204
Chapter 8	18	Exercise 11, p. 213
	19	Exercise 15, p. 215
	20	Exercise 21, p. 219
	21	Exercise 28, p. 223
	22	Exercise 33, p. 225
Chapter 9	23	Exercise 4, p. 231
	24	Exercise 8, p. 234
	25	Exercise 12, p. 237
	26	Exercise 15, p. 238
	27	Exercise 23, p. 242
	28	Exercise 36, p. 249
	29	Exercise 42, p. 253
Chapter 10	30	Exercise 3, p. 260
	31	Exercise 15, p. 267
	32	Exercise 17, p. 268
	33	Exercise 26, p. 274
	34	Exercise 28, p. 275
	35	Exercise 31, p. 276
	36	Exercise 33, p. 277
	37	Exercise 37, p. 280
	38	Exercise 42, p. 282
	39	Exercise 51, p. 286
	40	Exercise 52, p. 286
Chapter 11	41	Exercise 3, p. 291
	42	Exercise 11, p. 296
	43	Exercise 34, p. 313
Chapter 12	44	Exercise 20, p. 329
	45	Exercise 28, p. 334
	46	Exercise 33, p. 337
	47	Exercise 36, p. 339
Chapter 13	48	Exercise 4, p. 343
	49	Exercise 22, p. 354
	50	Exercise 44, p. 366
Chapter 14	51	Exercise 21, p. 381
	52	Exercise 39, p. 392

0 048572 020000